An Independent Study Guide to
Reading Greek

SECOND EDITION

First published in 1978 and now thoroughly revised, *Reading Greek* is a best-selling one-year introductory course in ancient Greek for students of any age. It combines the best of modern and traditional language-learning techniques and is used in schools, summer schools and universities across the world. This *Independent Study Guide* is intended to help students who are learning Greek on their own or with only limited access to a teacher. It contains notes on the texts that appear in the *Text and Vocabulary* volume, translations of all the texts, answers to the exercises in the *Grammar and Exercises* volume and cross-references to the relevant fifth-century background in *The World of Athens*. There are instructions on how to use the course and the *Study Guide*. The book will also be useful to students in schools, universities and summer schools who have to learn Greek rapidly.

THE JOINT ASSOCIATION OF CLASSICAL TEACHERS' GREEK COURSE

An Independent Study Guide to
Reading Greek

SECOND EDITION

CAMBRIDGE
UNIVERSITY PRESS

CAMBRIDGE
UNIVERSITY PRESS

University Printing House, Cambridge CB2 8BS, United Kingdom

Cambridge University Press is part of the University of Cambridge.

It furthers the University's mission by disseminating knowledge in the pursuit of education, learning and research at the highest international levels of excellence.

www.cambridge.org
Information on this title: www.cambridge.org/9780521698504

First published in 1995
Reprinted in 1996, 1997, 1999 (twice), 2001, 2002 (twice)
Second edition 2008
9th printing 2016

Printed in the United Kingdom by Clays, St Ives plc.

A catalogue record for this publication is available from the British Library

Library of Congress Cataloguing in Publication data
An independent study guide to reading Greek/Joint Association of
Classical Teachers, Greek Course.
    p.   cm.
ISBN 0 521 47863 4 (paperback)
1. Greek language – Readers.   2. Greek language – Self-instruction.
I. Joint Association of Classical Teachers. Greek Course.
II. Title: Reading Greek.
PA260.13   1995
489'.382421 – dc20   94-26432 CIP

ISBN 978-0-521-69850-4 Paperback

Contents

Preface

How to use this course
You have three books:

> *Reading Greek: Text and Vocabulary (RGT)*
> *Reading Greek: Grammar and Exercises (GE)*
> *Independent Study Guide to Reading Greek (ISG)*

In addition there is a CD *Speaking Greek* which illustrates pronunciation, and records readings from passages in *RGT*.

You may also like to have *The World of Athens* (second edition 2008), which gives you background information about Athenian history and life.

The first two books, *RGT* and *GE*, were designed to be used together so that

1. You read the passage in *RGT* with the aid of the running vocabulary for the section.
2. Then you look at the explanations of the grammar in *GE*.
3. Then you learn the grammar and the lists of 'vocabulary to be learnt' in *GE*.
4. Then you do the exercises for the section to make sure that you have understood the grammar. You may want to do each section of the exercises as you study the grammar in *GE*, so that you get immediate practice in a new feature of language. It is not essential to do all the exercises on morphology and syntax, but they will help you to practise the language and to make sure that you understand the grammar. However, you should always do the final 'Test Exercise' in each section, as it is an important check on your grasp of the section.

The Independent Study Guide (ISG) contains notes on translating the text of *RGT*, translations of the text, and a key to the exercises in *GE*.

The notes will give you some general advice at the start of a new section and some additional help as you read the text. They are designed to help you with the reading and to amplify the explanation of the grammar in *GE;* they will refer you to relevant pages and paragraphs in *GE* and in *RGT*.

The translations of the text and the exercises will help you if you get stuck, and will also allow you to check whether you have got everything right. Since the translations are there to help you to understand the Greek, they are literal rather than elegant in style.

Some people prefer to look at the explanations of the grammar in a new section before they embark on reading the text. It is a matter of personal choice whether you prefer to look out for new forms in reading, and then find out how they work, or whether you like to look at a new pattern of grammar and then see how it is used in the text.

In the first section, *ISG* assumes that you will be using the first procedure, but it will work just as well if you prefer the second.

It is always a good idea to re-read the text of a section after you have finished it. You will be surprised at how much more you remember if you do this. It will also help you to absorb more of the very varied vocabulary which is used in *Reading Greek* to provide a greater range of interest and a wider experience of the language from an early stage.

Abbreviations used in the text

ISG = *The Independent Study Guide*
RGT = *Reading Greek: Text and Vocabulary*
GE   = *Reading Greek: Grammar and Exercises*
WA = *The World of Athens*

References with no prefix are to the text of this *ISG*, giving chapter and paragraph numbers.

Grammatical Introduction

In the Introduction to *Grammar and Exercises* you will find the Greek alphabet and a guide to pronunciation (*GE* pp. 1–3), as well as a description of the basic terms used to describe the grammar (*GE* pp. 4–7 #1–7).

Reading and writing

Look at the alphabet and the pronunciation guide in *GE* pages 1–3. If you have the *Speaking Greek* CD it is very helpful to listen to the first section, 'The sounds of Greek', at the same time.

Exercise 1

Try the exercise on the alphabet on *GE* p. 3. In their English form the words will be:

Byzantium (Busdantion)	Parthenon
Dicaeopolis or Dikaiopolis	Chios (Khios)
Euboea or Euboia	acropolis (akropolis)
Zenothemis or Sdenothemis	emporium (emporion)
Hegestratus or Hegestratos	

As you see, this is not straightforward. For centuries it was common practice in English usage to turn all Greek spellings into their Latin equivalents. More recently it has been fashionable to keep to a spelling that is closer to the original Greek, but the difficulty with this practice is that some words and names, in particular, have become so much part of our English heritage that they look strange and unfamiliar in their 'Greek' form. E.g. we all recognise 'Achilles', but 'Akhilleus' comes as a shock.

Editors therefore have to make a decision whether to be consistently 'Latin' or consistently 'Greek', or whether to keep the familiar words in their 'Latin' form while treating the less familiar words in a 'Greek' way. The latter course has been followed in this book.

Exercise 2

The words in their Greek form (without accents) are:

drama	δραμα	comma	κομμα
panthēr	πανθηρ	cōlon	κωλον

1

crocus	κροκος	Sōcratēs	Σωκρατης
geranium	γερανιον	Zeus	Ζευς
hippopotamus	ἱπποποταμος	Artemis	Ἀρτεμις
ibis	ἰβις	*Hēraclēs	Ἡρακλης
asbestos	ἀσβεστος	asthma	ἀσθμα
charactēr	χαρακτηρ	dyspepsia	δυσπεψια
scēnē	σκηνη	cinēma	κινημα
Periclēs	Περικλης	orchēstra	ὀρχηστρα
Sophoclēs	Σοφοκλης	mēlon	μηλον
Euripidēs	Εὐριπιδης	iris	ἰρις
*Hippocratēs	Ἱπποκρατης		

Case: Subject and object (pp. 6–7, #7)

1. ὁ Ἡγέστρατος is the subject.
   τὸν Ζηνόθεμιν is the object.
2. ὁ Ζηνόθεμις is the subject.
   τοὺς ναύτας is the object.
3. ἡ γυνὴ is the subject.
   τὸν Ἡγέστρατον is the object.

Hegestratos as subject will be	ὁ Ἡγέστρατος
Hegestratos as object will be	τὸν Ἡγέστρατον
Zenothemis as subject will be	ὁ Ζηνόθεμις

When you have studied the Grammatical introduction you will be aware that in reading Greek it is necessary to learn not only to interpret the new script, but also to look closely at the endings of words. This is something which we do not need to do in English. You will have to train yourself consciously to notice the endings, or you will find that you are making avoidable mistakes in understanding Greek.

You will find more information about the Greek language in Part B of *GE* in the Reference Grammar (*GE* pp. 369–463, #340–406) and in Part C Language Surveys (*GE* pp. 465–495, #408–454). However, most of this will be of future interest, and you should certainly not try to absorb it all at this stage.

Section One: The insurance scam

Section 1A–G

Speaking Greek CD

First, read the English introduction at the beginning of Section 1A.

Now listen to the whole of Section 1A as read on the *Speaking Greek* CD.

Replay the first paragraph (lines 1–7), pausing at the end of every sentence and repeating the Greek aloud.

Then try working out the translation of that first paragraph, with the aid of the running vocabulary on p. 5. You will find that several complete phrases are listed (e.g. ἐν Βυζαντίῳ) and that all the nouns appear with their articles (e.g. ὁ κυβερνήτης).

If you are uncertain, check with the translation suggested below.

NB. This procedure is recommended for the whole of Section 1. It should help you to get used to the script and the sound of the language.

If you think you would prefer to find out about the grammar and how it works before you start reading, then look at *GE* pp. 8–12, #8–11. You will find the answers to the exercises in this volume after our grammar and notes on 1A and 1B (p. 6).

Translation for 1A (ll. 1–7)

The ship is in Byzantium. And in Byzantium, Hegestratos goes into the ship, then Sdenothemis goes into the ship, and finally the captain and the sailors go into the ship. The ship sails to Chios. In Chios, the rhapsode boards. Then the ship sails to Euboea. And in Euboea, Dikaiopolis gets on board. Finally, the ship sails to Athens and the Piraeus.

Grammar

1. Greek, as you see, does not always have the same word order as English. This is because in Greek (as in Latin) case-endings, not word order, determine the functions of words in the sentence – the subject and object. (If these terms are not familiar to you, please see the Grammatical introduction *GE* 1–7 pp. 4–7, and the Grammar for Section 1A–B #8–11.)

2. Notice the various different forms of the definite article. They can be tabulated as follows:

	Singular			*Plural*		
Nominative	ὁ	ἡ	τό	οἱ	αἱ	(τά)
Accusative	τόν	τήν	τό	(τούς)	τάς	(τά)

(You may be puzzled by the change in accent. An acute accent on the last syllable usually changes to a grave when it is followed by another word. It is a printing convention to change this grave back to an acute when the word is printed in isolation with no word following it. So you will see τὸ πλοῖον in the text, but τό in the above table.)

3. Note also the change in verb-ending between βαίνει (line 2) and εἰσβαίνουσιν (line 3):
   βαίνει is 3rd person singular ('he, she, it goes').
   βαίνουσι(ν) is 3rd person plural ('they go').
4. The preposition πρός ('towards') in line 6 is followed by the accusative case (τὰς Ἀθήνας, τὸν Πειραιᾶ).
5. The preposition ἐν ('in') is followed by the dative (ἐν Χίῳ, ἐν Εὐβοίᾳ).

Now move on to the second paragraph of 1A, using the same method.

Translation for 1A (ll. 8–14) (continued)

So the ship sails, and Sdenothemis looks towards the land. What does Sdenothemis see? Sdenothemis sees the acropolis and the Parthenon. Then both Dikaiopolis and the captain look towards the land. What do Dikaiopolis and the captain see? Dikaiopolis and the captain see the acropolis and the Parthenon. Suddenly, Dikaiopolis and the captain hear a noise.

Grammar

1. Notice again the flexibility of Greek word order: you will find that it is essential to concentrate upon word-endings and not word order to determine the structure.
2. Note slight variation in the verb-ending -ῶσι(ν) in ὁρῶσι(ν) (lines 11, 13). If the -ουσι or -ῶσι ending is followed by a word beginning with a vowel, or is the last word in a clause, then the (ν) is added.
3. Notice that Greek often includes a τε and καί to form a closely linked pair; it means (literally) 'both … and', though in English this often seems strained, and it may seem more natural, when translating, to omit the 'both'.

1B

Using the same method as that recommended for Section 1A, listen to Section 1B on the CD. Then read it to yourself, before trying to translate it.

Notice that in Greek a semicolon is used as a question mark.

Note that καί can mean 'and', 'also' or 'even'. Often here it is used in phrases like 'I too', or 'you too'.

Page 6

3 ἆρα καὶ σὺ τὴν ἀκρόπολιν ὁρᾷς;   'Can *you too* see the Acropolis?' καί means 'also' and σύ emphasises *you*. Cf. line 11 ὁρῶ καὶ ἐγώ.

12 There is no indefinite article ('a', 'an') in Greek, only the absence of the definite article. Thus ὁ ψόφος = 'the noise', but ψόφος = 'a noise'.

15 μὴ φρόντιζε   'Don't worry!' μή is the negative used with imperatives. οὐ is used with statements. Thus, 'He doesn't worry' would be οὐ φροντίζει.

Translation for 1B

SDENOTHEMIS   Come over here, Dikaiopolis, and look. For I see the acropolis. Can you also see the acropolis?

DIKAIOPOLIS   Where is the acropolis? For I cannot see the acropolis.

SDEN.   Come over here and look. Do you not see the Parthenon?

DIK.   Yes. Now I too can see the acropolis.

SDEN.   O Zeus! How beautiful is the Parthenon, and [how] beautiful [is] the acropolis.

CAPTAIN   You are right, Sdenothemis. (*Lit.* You speak the truth.)
Listen! A noise. Do you hear? What is the noise? Do you also hear the noise, Sdenothemis?

SDEN.   No, by Zeus, I hear nothing, captain. Don't worry. But come over here and look. For I see the dockyard and the Piraeus. Do you also see the dockyard?

CAPT.   Yes.

SDEN.   O Zeus, how beautiful is the dockyard, and [how] beautiful the Piraeus.

CAPT.   You are right, Sdenothemis. Hey! A noise. For again I hear the noise.

DIK.   I too hear the noise again, captain, clearly. So you and I hear the noise.

Grammar

Verbs. Here the other person-endings of the present tense are introduced. Note the pattern of endings (*GE* p. 14, #12):

the regular	-ω	-εις	-ει	-ομεν	-ετε	-ουσι(ν)
the variant	-ῶ	-ᾷς	-ᾷ	-ῶμεν	-ᾶτε	-ῶσι(ν)

Learn the regular ones first. The other endings, which are logical variants, are set out fully in *GE* pp. 19–20, #23–25 and are explained in 1E–F.

EXERCISES

Translate the following sentences: (p. 9)

The rhapsode goes.

The ship is at Byzantium.

The sailors see the land and the rhapsode.

Practice (p. 10)

feminine, accusative, singular	the city
masculine, accusative, singular	the king
masculine, nominative, plural	the old men
feminine, accusative, plural	the triremes
feminine, genitive, singular	of [the] democracy
masculine, dative, singular	for [the] Homer
m., f., or n., genitive, plural	of the atoms
feminine, dative, plural	by the skills

EXERCISES FOR SECTION 1A–B

1A–B: 1

1. fem. dat. sing.
   stage
2. fem. nom. sing.
   democracy
3. neut. nom. acc. sing.
   nerve, sinew
4. masc. gen. sing.
   skeleton
5. masc. acc. pl.
   eyes

6. neut. nom/acc. sing.
   breathing, gasping
7. masc. dat. pl.
   masters
8. fem. gen. pl.
   sponges
9. neut. nom. acc. pl.
   heads
10. fem. gen. sing.
    tragedy

ADJECTIVES

1A–B: 2

1. ὁ καλὸς κυβερνήτης
2. τὸ καλὸν πλοῖον
3. τοῦ καλοῦ ἔργου
4. τὰς καλὰς Ἀθήνας
5. τοῖς καλοῖς ἀνθρώποις

6. τὴν καλὴν ἀκρόπολιν
7. τὸν καλὸν Παρθενῶνα
8. ταῖς καλαῖς βοαῖς
9. τῷ καλῷ πλοίῳ
10. τῇ καλῇ ἀκροπόλει

Note that the accent on καλός has changed from acute in the table to grave καλὸς in the exercise. This is because an acute accent on the last syllable of a word changes to grave when it is followed by another word (unless that word is an enclitic *GE* p. 30, #42). Unless you are planning to learn to use all accents, you need not remember this.

1C

Now you will have more practice with the different persons of the verb. Go on reading and listening to the CD.

Notice the words for 'where from' πόθεν and 'where to' ποῖ.
The same suffix -θεν as in πόθεν appears in κάτωθεν 'from below'.

Translation for 1C

SDENOTHEMIS   I do not hear [it], friends. Don't worry. But come over here and look, over here. For I see the markets and the merchant ships. Do you also see the markets?

CAPTAIN AND DIKAIOPOLIS   We also see them. So what?

SDEN.   O Poseidon, how beautiful are the merchant ships, how beautiful are the markets. But look over here, friends.

CAPT.   Listen, Sdenothemis, and don't say 'How beautiful are the markets.' For we hear the noise clearly.

DIK.   But where is the noise [coming] from?

CAPT.   From below, Dikaiopolis. Why don't we go down? Come on, Dikaiopolis –

SDEN.   Where are you going? Where are you going? Why don't you stay, friends? Don't worry. For I see –

Grammar

In this section you met the remaining person-endings:
    2nd person plural: βαίνετε (14) and imperative plural: φροντίζετε (1).

1D

In this section you will meet another contracted verb, one with an -ε- rather than an -α-. You should have no difficulty in recognising the person from the ending (*GE* p. 20, #24).

Page 10

1 καταβαίνει μὲν ..., καταβαίνουσι δὲ ...   Notice the word order. The verb is particularly important here, so it is brought forward to the beginning of the phrase.

3 Similarly notice that τὸν Ἡγέστρατον is brought forward for emphasis. The only way we can express this emphasis in English is to say something like 'It is Hegestratos whom ...'

8 τί with an accent means 'what?', but τι without an accent (see line 13) means 'something'. διὰ τί, literally 'on account of what?', means 'why?'

Translation for 1D

So down goes the captain, and down go both Dikaiopolis and the sailors. For the noise [is] from below. And below, it is Hegestratos that the captain and the sailors see. Hegestratos is making the noise below.

CAPTAIN   Hey, you! What are you doing? But what are *you* doing, Hegestratos? What [is] the noise?

HEGESTRATOS   I am not doing anything, captain, nor do I hear any noise. Don't worry.

DIKAIOPOLIS   Come over here and look, captain. For Hegestratos has something in his right hand.

CAPT.   What have you in your right hand, Hegestratos?

HE.   I have nothing, friend, not me.

DIK.   O Zeus! For Hegestratos is not telling the truth. For Hegestratos has an axe in his right hand. The fellow is sinking the ship.

CAPT.   What are you saying, Dikaiopolis? Hegestratos is sinking the ship? But why don't you catch the man, sailors? Over here, over here.

HE.   O dear, I'm off, and I'm throwing myself out of the ship.

CAPT.   Help, sailors, help and pursue [him].

Grammar

Notice again the way in which the pronouns can be used to emphasise the person in the verb-ending, e.g.:

τί ποιεῖς <u>σύ</u>;
οὐδὲν ἔχω <u>ἔγωγε</u>.

EXERCISES FOR SECTION 1C–D

VERBS IN -ω

1C–D: 1

1. you (s.) don't hear
2. we are looking
3. they remain
4. he/she does not flee
5. you (s.) are pursuing
6. they go
7. you (pl.) are not looking
8. he/she hears
9. you (s.) are running away
10. he/she/it remains

1C–D: 2

1. ἀκούουσι(ν)
2. βλέπει
3. διώκετε
4. βαίνω
5. οὐ μένουσι(ν)
6. φεύγει
7. διώκουσι(ν)
8. βλέπεις
9. μένομεν
10. οὐκ ἀκούει

IMPERATIVES

1C–D: 3

1. go! (s.)
2. look! (s.)
3. Sailors, pursue! (pl.)
4. listen! (s.)
5. flee!(pl.)/ you (pl.) are fleeing
6. don't look! (pl.)
7. go down! (pl.)/ you (pl.)are going down
8. you (pl.) are going/ go! (pl.).
9. Hegestratos, don't wait! (s.)
10. don't go in! (pl.)

Page 12

1 ὁ μὲν 'Ηγέστρατος ... οἱ δὲ ναῦται ...   The particles μέν and δέ are frequently used to make a contrast. They can never be the first word in a phrase.

Notice the word order in this passage. The important words are often brought forward to the beginning of the sentence or phrase.

Translation for 1E

Hegestratos flees from below, and the sailors help, and chase Hegestratos. Sdenothemis remains above. Hegestratos looks towards Sdenothemis, Sdenothemis towards the sailors. For the sailors are coming up and are in pursuit.

SDENOTHEMIS   But what are you doing, Hegestratos?

HEGESTRATOS   Look, the sailors are chasing me, Sdenothemis. I'm running away. Don't wait, but run away yourself as well, and throw yourself out of the ship. For the men are coming up here now.

SDEN.   Oh dear! For now I see the sailors clearly. Where are *you* running away to?

HE.   I'm escaping into the sea, I am. For the lifeboat is in the sea. Come along, save yourself. Throw yourself into the sea, and don't wait around.

1F

Translation for 1F

Hegestratos and Sdenothemis do not wait around but run away. For the men throw themselves into the sea and look for the lifeboat. The sailors clearly see their flight from the ship, and the captain unties the lifeboat. The lifeboat drifts away from the ship.

SDENOTHEMIS   Oh dear! Where is the lifeboat? Where is it, Hegestratos?

HEGESTRATOS   I can't see the lifeboat, Sdenothemis – oh dear!

SDEN.   We are dying, Hegestratos. Help, sailors, help!

HE.   I'm dying –

DIKAIOPOLIS   Do you see those men, captain? The men are dying. For the lifeboat is clearly drifting away from the ship.

CAPTAIN   Don't worry about it. For the men are bad, Dikaiopolis, and they are dying badly.

The main new point of grammar here is the conjugation of 'contract' verbs, verbs ending in -εω, -αω and -οω. *GE* pp. 19–21, #23–25 sets this out and shows how the stem vowel contracts with the endings. You will find it easy to recognise the persons from the pattern of the endings.

EXERCISES FOR SECTION 1E–F

CONTRACT VERBS

1E–F: 1

1. you (s.) see
2. he/she sees
3. they see
4. we are doing/making
5. they show
6. you (s.) help
7. you (s.) show
8. you (s.) make/do
9. you (pl.) show
10. he/she helps

1E–F: 2

1. ὁρῶσι(ν)
2. ποιεῖ
3. ποιεῖτε
4. δηλῶ
5. βοηθοῦσι(ν)
6. ποιεῖ
7. ποιοῦσι(ν)
8. δηλοῖς
9. ὁρῶμεν
10. ποιεῖ

1E–F: 3

1. τιμῶ
2. γαμεῖς
3. οἰκοῦσι(ν)
4. σιγῶμεν
5. ἀσεβεῖτε
6. ἀσθενεῖ
7. ἐλευθεροῦμεν
8. ἐξαπατᾷ
9. νοσῶ
10. τιμᾶτε

CONTRACT IMPERATIVES

1E–F: 4

1. see!
2. do/make! (s.)
3. he/she is doing/making
4. he/she sees
5. don't show! (pl.)
6. stay (s.)
7. you (pl.) go, Go!
8. you (s.) are doing/making
9. don't show!
10. he/she is showing

1E–F: 5

1. μὴ μένετε
2. δίωκε
3. δηλοῦτε
4. μὴ ἄκουε
5. βοήθει
6. ποιεῖ
7. μὴ ποίει
8. ὁρᾷ
9. ὅρα
10. μὴ βαῖνε

Page 16

2 σῷοι δὲ καὶ ἡμεῖς   Notice that the verb 'to be' is often left out in Greek if the meaning is clear. You will meet this repeatedly in this section.
καί   Here means 'also'.

3 περι-σκοπῶ   Compound verb. It means 'to look (σκοπῶ) round' (περι).

5 ἡ ἡμετέρα σωτηρία   Notice that Greek normally uses only the definite article where we in English would often use the possessive adjective. Greek will say 'the father' or 'the safety' if it is clear from the context that it means 'his father' or 'our safety'. The possessive is normally only used to stress ownership, or if the context is ambiguous.

9 τοὺς ἀνθρώπους   Another of the differences in the way Greek uses the article. When English speaks of a class of people it does not use the article. We say 'Men are lazy' or 'Women are clever', but Greek will use the article in this situation. Thus the Greeks would say '*The* men are lazy', '*The* women are clever.'

16 σῶον μέν … σῷοι δέ …   Note the contrast pointed by μέν and δέ.

Translation for 1G

CAPTAIN   But is our ship safe, and are we safe as well? Why don't I go down below and look around carefully? For I [am] the captain: so it [is] my job, and our safety [depends] on me.
(The captain goes down and looks round. But Dikaiopolis remains above.)

DIKAIOPOLIS   Now, O Poseidon, save us [bring us safely] into the harbour. For we always make sacrifices to you, and you always save people from the sea. We are now dying badly: for our ship is clearly sinking into the sea, our lifeboat is clearly drifting away and our safety [is] not assured.
(The captain comes up.)

CAPT.   Be quiet, Dikaiopolis. Our ship is safe and we also are safe. So we are not in danger. And moreover the harbour is near by. So our safety [is] assured.

EXERCISES FOR SECTION 1G

THE DECLENSIONS

1G: 1

1. ἄνθρωπον
2. ἀνθρώπων, ἔργων
3. ἄνθρωποι
4. ἀνθρώποις, ἔργοις
5. ἀνθρώπῳ, ἔργῳ
6. ἀνθρώπους
7. ἀνθρώπῳ, ἔργῳ
8. ἔργον

1G: 2

1. ἐστι(ν)
2. διώκουσι(ν)
3. ποιεῖ
4. ὁρᾷ
5. ἐστι(ν)

MORE ADJECTIVES

1G: 3

1. τὴν καλὴν γῆν
2. τοῖς ἡμετέροις ἔργοις
3. τῶν κακῶν ἀνθρώπων
4. τοὺς ἡμετέρους ἀνθρώπους
5. τὰ καλὰ ἔργα
6. τῷ ἡμετέρῳ πλοίῳ
7. τῶν καλῶν ἐμπορίων
8. τοῖς κακοῖς ἀνθρώποις

1G: 4

1. ἄνθρωπον acc. s.
2. ἀνθρώπων gen. pl.
3. ἀνθρώπους acc. pl.
4. ἀνθρώποις dat. pl.
5. ἀνθρώπου gen. s.

PREPOSITIONS

1G: 5

1. in the markets
2. into the ships
3. in the work
4. from the men
5. from the market
6. from the ships
7. towards the markets
8. into the ship
9. in the lifeboats
10. towards the men

1G: 6

1. ἐκ τοῦ πλοίου
2. εἰς τὸν λέμβον
3. ἀπὸ τοῦ ἀνθρώπου
4. ἐν τοῖς πλοίοις
5. πρὸς τὸν λέμβον
6. εἰς τὸ πλοῖον
7. πρὸς τοὺς ἀνθρώπους
8. εἰς τὰ ἐμπόρια

REVISION EXERCISES

As you are advised in *GE*, you should do the revision exercises only after completing work on text, grammar and vocabulary.

How many of the exercises you do will depend upon your own choice and interest. The more you do, the more competent you will become.

The exercises on Word shape and Syntax are designed to help you absorb and retain particular features of the language; if you feel you have grasped these aspects, then you can omit these exercises or do them quickly.

The Test Exercises, however, you should regard as essential. They have been carefully designed so that, if you have mastered all elements of the language

required so far (vocabulary, morphology and syntax), you will be able to do the
Test Exercises without any looking up at all.

If you find you do have to look up a word or an ending, or if you make a mistake
in your translation, the error or omission should alert you to the area needing
further consolidation.

REVISION EXERCISES FOR SECTION 1A–G

Note the advice on tackling these exercises in *GE* pp. 33–35

A – VOCABULARY-BUILDING

I go	I go out
I chase	I chase out
sea	belonging to the sea, maritime, nautical
helmsman	I steer
sailor	nautical, to do with sailing
I see	I see/look into
I flee	I run away, run from

B – WORD SHAPE

1. you (s.) go   pl. βαίνετε
   I see   pl. βλέπομεν
   he/she makes, does   pl. ποιοῦσι(ν)
   he/she sees   pl. ὁρῶσι(ν)
   help! (s.)   pl. βοηθεῖτε

2. worry (pl.)   s. φρόντιζε
       or you (pl.) are worrying s. φροντίζεις
   they go down   s. καταβαίνει
   we come up   s. ἀναβαίνω
   you (pl.) see   s. ὁρᾷς
       or see! (pl.)   s. ὅρα
   you (pl.) are going away   s. ἀποχωρεῖς
       or go away! (pl.)   s. ἀποχώρει

3. οἱ ἄνθρωποι, τοῖς ψόφοις, τὰ πλοῖα, τῷ λέμβῳ, τὸ νεώριον, τῶν
   ἀνθρώπων

4. a. ὁ καλὸς ἄνθρωπος
   b. τὰ καλὰ νεώρια
   c. τῷ καλῷ ἐμπορίῳ
   d. τοῖς καλοῖς ἀνθρώποις
   e. τὸν καλὸν ἄνθρωπον

Notes on English into Greek

Don't worry about word order yet. But go on noticing how it works in Greek.

If you used ἀνήρ ἀνδρ- for 'man' in 3 and 5, you may have got it wrong. Don't worry. You have not yet learned the pattern for this noun, although it has occurred in the Text. It would be ὁ ανὴρ in 3, τοὺς ἄνδρας in 5.

C – SYNTAX

1. Hegestratos sees the acropolis.
   τὸν Ἡγέστρατον.
2. The sailors pursue Sdenothemis.
   ὁ Ζηνόθεμις
3. Dikaiopolis saves the men.
   ὁ ἄνθρωπος
4. The helmsman casts off the life-boats.
   ὁ λέμβος
5. The men don't see the life-boats.
   τοὺς ἀνθρώπους.

D – ENGLISH INTO GREEK

1. Sdenothemis goes into the ship.
   ὁ ἄνθρωπος/ὁ ανὴρ (ἀπο)φεύγει πρὸς τὸ πλοῖον.
2. The sailors don't see Hegestratos.
   ὁ Ἡγέστρατος οὐχ ὁρᾷ τοὺς ἀνθρώπους/τοὺς ἄνδρας
3. Can you not see the Acropolis?
   ἆρα ὁρᾷς τοὺς ἀνθρώπους/τοὺς ἄνδρας καὶ σύ;
4. Come over here and look.
   ἔλθετε καὶ βοηθεῖτε. διώκετε τὸν ἄνθρωπον/τὸν ἄνδρα. μὴ (ἀπο)φεύγετε.
5. The men are coming up.
   οἱ φίλοι οὐ μένουσιν.

E – TEST EXERCISE 1 A–G

The ship departs from Euboea and sails towards the Piraeus. Sdenothemis is looking towards the land. But Hegestratos remains below and is sinking the ship. For the fellow has an axe. The captain and Dikaiopolis are up above. They look towards the land and see both the dockyards and the Parthenon. But suddenly they hear the noise. Then they go down.

CAPTAIN Who is making the noise? Do you see, Dikaiopolis?

DIKAIOPOLIS Yes, I see. For Hegestratos is making the noise. For he has an axe in his right hand.

CAPT. Don't wait around, sailors, but help and chase the man.

Hegestratos flees from below, while Sdenothemis remains above. The sailors come up from below. The men see the sailors clearly and throw themselves into the sea. The men escape into the sea, and in the sea they die.

1H

Page 18

1 λιμένα   Check the English introduction above.

1–2 ναύτης δέ τις   This is the indefinite τις, without an accent, which follows the word it agrees with. τίς with an accent, coming first, would mean 'Who?' or 'What sailor?'

3 λέγει ὅτι   Remember ὅτι carefully: it is extremely common, and extensively used in this and subsequent sections.

4 ῥαψῳδός τις   'a rhapsode'. A rhapsode is a professional, itinerant reciter of Homer, rather like a medieval troubadour.

5 ὁμηρίζει   Transliterate first, then see if you can identify the person. Note also the English explanation in introduction. The -ιζω ending in Greek verbs is like our '-ize/-ise' ending. Thus this might be translated 'Homerise'.
παίζει πρός   It means 'makes fun of'.

8 ἐσμεν   New here, but the ἡμεῖς indicates which person of the verb this is.
οἶσθα   Also new, but pronoun σύ should help. See *GE* p. 36, #44.

9 οἶδα   Yet another new form, again reinforced by the inclusion of the pronoun.

13 οἴνοπα πόντον   A lovely phrase and frequent in Homer, but a problem for translators. Literally it means 'wine-faced' but it is usually rendered, more poetically, as 'wine-dark'.

17 ἐν νηὶ μελαίνη   This is another common Homeric phrase. νηί is irregular dative of ναῦς (line 28) meaning 'ship'.

18 τί τὸ ...   Literally, 'What (is) the ...?', i.e. 'What's that ...?'

19 μῶρος   English 'moron' suggests the answer, though note that μῶρος is an adjective.
εἶ   Another new person of the verb, also explained by its pronoun σύ. See *GE* p. 36, #44.

21 ἐν νηὶ θοῇ, and κοίλη ἐνὶ νηί   Two more common Homeric phrases.

Translation for 1H

So the captain steers the ship towards the harbour. A sailor asks the captain where they are. For the sailor does not clearly know where they are: for it is night. So the captain says that they are sailing into the harbour. There is on the ship a rhapsode. The rhapsode is always quoting Homer. Dikaiopolis makes fun of the rhapsode like Socrates with his students.

SAILOR   Where are we, captain? Do you know? For I do not clearly know. For I see nothing, because of the night, and I do not know where we are.

CAPTAIN   I know clearly. We are sailing towards the harbour, sailor.

RHAPSODE   'We are sailing on the wine-dark sea.'

SAIL.   What's the fellow saying?

DIKAIOPOLIS   It's clear that the fellow is quoting Homer. He's a rhapsode.

RHAP.   You are right, my friend. 'We are sailing in a black ship.'

DIK.   What are you saying, rhapsode? What's that 'in a black ship'? For our ship
            isn't black. It is clear that you are stupid, and don't know anything, but are
            joking at us.

RHAP.   Be quiet. 'In a swift ship' we are sailing, 'in a hollow ship.'

DIK.   Do you hear, sailors? Come here and listen. It is clear that our rhapsode is
            stupid. For the fellow does not know anything accurately, but is joking at us.

1I

Page 20

1   εἰμί   A new form, person indicated by pronoun.
    γιγνώσκω   A new word (Latin *cognosco*).

2   ἀπαίδευτος   The prefix α- is often a negative one in Greek (cf. English
    'amoral', 'asymmetrical'); παιδ- is the root of the English word 'p(a)
    edagogue', so the whole Greek word means 'uneducated'.

6   διότι   'because'.

7–12   The various -ικος adjectives here correspond to many -ic/ical adjectives in
       English: e.g. 'polemics', 'nautical' and 'strategic' should help to establish the
       meaning of three. στρατηγός was so called because he was an army (στρατός)
       leader (ἄγω – 'I lead'). Similarly a στρατιώτης was a member of the army, i.e.
       a soldier; hence στρατιωτικά refers to soldiering, the business of the soldier.

       Note the thrust of the rhapsode's argument: he knew much about Homer –
       Homer knew much about everything – therefore he (the rhapsode) knew much
       about everything. This form of argument reflects some forms of Socratic and
       Platonic dialectic where an attempt is made to use words in as defined a way as
       numbers. Here the effect is ludicrous, although the original idea resulted in a new
       and valuable tool of reasoning.

1J

Page 21

1   μία   Feminine form of εἷς, meaning 'one' (here = 'one and the same').

5   ἄριστος   An aristocracy is rule by the 'best' people.

11   δήπου   Like 'of course' in English, δήπου is often heavily sarcastic in its
     meaning.

Translation for 1I–J

RHAPSODE   But I am not stupid: I know many things.

DIKAIOPOLIS   How do you know many things? It is clear that you are uneducated,
              rhapsode. For you do not know whether our ship is 'black' or 'swift' or 'hollow'.

RHAP.   No, by Zeus, I am not uneducated about Homer. I know much because Homer
              knows much. For Homer knows matters of war, and matters nautical, tactical,
              strategic –

DIK.   So you also know matters of strategy?

RHAP.	Of course. It's my job.
DIK.	What? Are you then experienced in matters of strategy, rhapsode?
RHAP.	Yes. For Homer is experienced in matters of strategy, and I also am experienced [in them].
DIK.	Are then the skill of a rhapsode and the skill of a general one [and the same]?
RHAP.	One [and the same] skill, Dikaiopolis.
DIK.	So good rhapsodes are at the same time also good generals?
RHAP.	Yes, Dikaiopolis.
DIK.	And you are the best rhapsode of the Greeks?
RHAP.	Certainly, Dikaiopolis.
DIK.	Are you then, rhapsode, the best general of the Greeks?
RHAP.	Of course.
DIK.	What do you say, sailors? Is the rhapsode a fool or not?
SAILOR	By Zeus, the rhapsode is indeed a fool, Dikaiopolis. The fellow is, of course, the best general of the Greeks, but he does not know precisely whether the ship is 'black' or 'swift' or 'hollow'. So the best general of the Greeks is a fool.
RHAP.	It is clear, Dikaiopolis, that you are Socratising and joking with me. For Socrates always jokes in this way at his students.
DIK.	Yes. The Greeks are always children.

Grammar

Note carefully the conjugation of both irregular verbs εἰμί and οἶδα (*GE* p. 36, #44): it is essential to know both thoroughly – and although most of εἰμί has appeared in the Text, the plural forms of οἶδα have not. Nevertheless it is sensible to learn them now and it is worth learning them very carefully. You will, in fact, meet them in Test Exercise 1H–J.

EXERCISES FOR SECTION 1H–J

IRREGULAR VERBS

1H–J: 1

1. he/she/it is
2. we know
3. you (pl.) are
4. you (pl.) know
5. we are
6. you (s.) are
7. you (s.) know
8. they are
9. I am
10. they know

1H–J: 2

1. οἶδα
2. εἶ
3. εἰσί(ν)
4. ἐστί(ν)
5. ἴσασι(ν)
6. οἶδε(ν)

7. ἐσμέν

8. ἐστί(ν)

9. οἶδε(ν)

10. ἐστέ

1H–J: 3

1. You (s.) know about both seafaring and generalship.
2. We both know and see much.
3. You (pl.) both exist and do not exist (are and are not).
4. You know much (many things).
5. Do they know about both soldiering and generalship?

1H–J: 4

1. πολλὰ ἴσασιν.
2. ἔστι καὶ οὐκ ἔστιν.
3. οὐκ οἶδε τὰ στρατηγικά.
4. οἶδα καὶ οὐκ οἶδα τά τε ναυτικὰ καὶ τὰ στρατηγικά.
5. ἐσμέν τε καὶ ἴσμεν.

REVISION EXERCISES FOR SECTION 1H–J

A – VOCABULARY-BUILDING

1. I go away   I go round
   I go, come   I go (or come) round
   clear   I make clear, reveal
   I am   I am in
   a Greek person   Greek (adjective)
   I wait   I wait around
   a general   I command (an army)

B – WORD SHAPE

1. you (pl.) are   εἶ
   he/she knows   γιγνώσκουσι(ν)
   you (s.) know   ἴστε
   he/she is   εἰσί(ν)
   they know   οἶδε(ν)
   play! (s.)   παίζετε
   I am   ἐσμέν
   we know   οἶδα

C – SYNTAX

1. a. The rhapsode is a Greek.
   b. The Greek is a rhapsode.
   c. Rhapsodes (as a class of people*) are the best generals.
   d. The rhapsode is a fool.

e. The rhapsode is a captain.

f. The captain is a rhapsode/A rhapsode is captain.

This is where Greek uses the def. art. and English does not, to denote a class of people.

D – ENGLISH INTO GREEK

1. It is clear that Dikaiopolis is teasing the rhapsode.

   δῆλόν ἐστιν ὅτι ὁ ῥαψῳδὸς πολλὰ γιγνώσκει.

2. I am expert in many things.

   (σὺ) οὐκ ἔμπειρος εἶ περὶ τὸ ἔργον.

3. Rhapsodes are the best generals.

   ὁ ἄριστος στρατηγός ἐστι ῥαψῳδός.

4. Do you not know that the man is always joking?

   ἆρ᾽ οὐκ οἶδεν ὅτι ὁ ῥαψῳδὸς ἀκριβῶς λέγει;

5. You are not skilled, but foolish.

   ἀλλὰ μῶρος μὲν οὔκ εἰμι, πολλὰ δὲ γιγνώσκω.

Note: μῶρος δὲ μέν and μῶρος μὲν δέ are not permitted. μέν and δέ are never used side by side. Likewise οὐ δέ εἰμι is not on: μέν and δέ do not follow negatives.

E – TEST EXERCISE 1H–J

So the ship sails towards the Piraeus, but the sailors do not know where the ship is. So they ask the captain where it is. The captain says that the ship is near the harbour. Suddenly the rhapsode recites Homer. It is clear that the man knows much about Homer. Dikaiopolis teases the rhapsode.

DIKAIOPOLIS Do you know the business of a rhapsode, rhapsode?

RHAPSODE Of course. I also know the skills of a general.

DIK. What do you mean? (*Lit.* What are you saying?) For you are a rhapsode, not a general.

RHAP. Do you not know that the good rhapsode is at the same time also a good general?

DIK. No, but I know that you are a fool, rhapsode. For you are the best rhapsode of the Greeks and expert in Homer. On matters of strategy, however, you are not expert, nor do you know anything accurately.

Section Two: The glorious past

In this section you will practise a third variant of the contracted verbs that you met in Section 1. You will add -οω verbs *(GE* p. 20, #24) to -αω and -εω ones. It is easy to recognise which person the ending indicates. These are all in the *active voice.*

You will also meet a new pattern of verb in what is called the *middle voice* (*GE* pp. 43–46, #52–54). The active voice describes what the subject does to the object. The middle describes what the subject does for (or to) himself, or does for his own advantage, and it often does not have an object. The verbs you will meet in this section occur only in the middle and do not have an active voice.

You may want to make a chart of the present indicative middle and to add the new endings as you meet them, or you may just prefer to keep referring to *GE* pp. 44–45, #52–53.

You will also meet some more noun types (*GE* pp. 46–48, #55–58) which you will eventually have to learn, but you will be able to recognise what case they are in from the article used with them.

2A

After reading the English introduction, try reading through the whole of the first page (aloud, if circumstances permit!). Then try translating the paragraph, using the running vocabulary and the following notes for guidance if you need them.

Page 22

1 ἡ μὲν ναῦς   The article shows this is nominative; μέν warns you that there will be a contrast in the following clause or sentence marked by δέ, as in ὁ δὲ Δικαιόπολις. See *GE* p. 30, #43.
βραδέως   The ending in -ως shows that this is an adverb (see *GE* pp. 22–23, #28–29).
ἔρχεται   New ending; which person of the verb must it be? What should it mean? Sense demands a verb of motion – in fact, the verb can mean either 'come' or 'go', and is very common.

2 πρὸς ἀλλήλους   πρὸς should be known, ἀλλήλους – leave blank for a moment.

3 ἡδέως   Part of speech? (English 'hedonism' may guide you to the meaning of this word.)
διαλέγονται   Note the person ending; for meaning, English 'dialogue' may help; then back to ἀλλήλους = 'each other'.

4–5 διὰ τί ὁ ῥαψῳδὸς οὐ διέρχεται...;   Notice διὰ τί οὐ followed by a question
mark, 'Why doesn't ... ?' You will see the same pattern in 'διὰ τί οὐ λέγει...;'

4 διέρχεται   Both elements have been met – the ἔρχεται = 'come'/'go', δι- =
'through', hence 'go through' as in 'relate', 'recount'.
τὴν περὶ Σαλαμῖνα ναυμαχίαν   This is a phrase within a phrase as is shown
by the linking device connecting τήν with ναυμαχίαν; so the meaning is: **the
around-Salamis sea-battle**. See *GE* p. 49, #62. μάχη means 'battle' and ναῦς
'ship', hence ναυμαχία 'sea-battle'.

5 τί γίγνεται   The context should help, 'what happens';
ἐν τοῖς Μηδικοῖς   (literally) 'in the Medic (things)', Μηδικοῖς being neuter
plural; the Greeks used 'Medes' and 'Persians' almost interchangeably; the
phrase means 'in the Persian Wars'.

6 τίνα ἔργα τολμῶσι   The context should help you towards the general sense of
'what deeds they did'; τολμῶσι = 'dare' (τολμάω and its noun τόλμα are much
used later in this section).

9–11 The first three lines are mostly recapitulation of words/phrases occurring earlier.

10 ῥητορικά   Cf. 'rhetoric'.

11 ἄγε δή   *GE* gives 'come!' for ἄγε, but notice that here it is not used like
δεῦρο ἐλθέ, but more like English 'Come on!' – a spur to action and not
necessarily an instruction to move.

Page 23

12 ἐρχόμεθα   The verb has occurred earlier in the sense 'come', 'go'; ἡμεῖς
indicates the person.

15 ἡμετέραν   Possessive adjective, derived from ἡμεῖς ('we'), therefore = 'our'.
τόλμαν   See note earlier (line 6).
νικῶσιν   Here the verb is encountered for the first time. See also the noun νίκην.

20 οὐδὲν ἴσμεν ἀκριβῶς ἡμεῖς οἱ ναῦται   Notice the word order.

21 κάλλιστον ποίει τὸν λόγον   The word order shows that this means 'make the/
your story very beautiful', rather than 'make the very beautiful story'.

23 ἡσυχάζετε   Imperative. *GE* gives 'keep quiet', but note that as well as
meaning 'be silent', it can also mean something like 'settle down' or 'calm
down'.

Translation for 2A

*The ship goes slowly towards the Piraeus. Dikaiopolis and the sailors and the
captain and the rhapsode are talking happily to each other. The ship is already
going past Salamis and the captain says: 'Why does the rhapsode not relate the
sea-battle at Salamis, and why doesn't he tell what happened in the Persian Wars
and how the Greeks and Persians fought and what deeds they dared and how
many fell?' The rhapsode gladly relates the sea-battle.*

CAPTAIN   You, rhapsode, know much about Homer. You therefore know much about
rhetoric also (for Homer [is] rhetorical, [is he] not?). Come along then, come

over here and tell us the events at Salamis. For there is the island of Salamis, and we are going slowly past Salamis towards Athens. Tell us then the Persian Wars and the sea-battle at Salamis and our daring and victory. The Persians do not defeat us nor do they enslave us. Tell us what happened in the Persian Wars and how the Greeks and foreigners fought and how many fell. For you, my friend, know clearly the events at Salamis, and the sailors know nothing.

SAILORS   Yes. We sailors know nothing accurately. So we gladly listen. But speak, rhapsode, and make your story very fine.

RHAPSODE   Of course. I always make my stories very fine. Keep quiet then, sailors, and listen.

2B

Page 24

1 These lines are adapted from the opening lines of the *Iliad*, so they may present a few problems.

μῆνιν 'wrath' (acc.); this, in the *Iliad*, announces at the very outset a central theme of the poem – the wrath of Achilles, which dominates throughout and is finally resolved only in Book 24, the very last book.

ἄειδε Imperative, 'sing', the invocation of the Muse, goddess of memory, to help the poet in telling his story.

Θεά 'Goddess'.

Ξέρξου θείου βασιλῆος 'of Xerxes, the god-like king': in the original it is Πηληϊάδεω Ἀχιλῆος 'of Achilles, son of Peleus'.

οὐλομένην 'accursed': in the *Iliad*, because the quarrel of Agamemnon and Achilles led to near-disaster for the Greeks; here, because the invasion of Xerxes threatened the freedom of the Greeks.

3 ἀποροῦσι A verb for which there is no direct English equivalent: it means 'be in a state of not knowing what to do'. A common enough occurrence – it's surprising we have no verb for this, although nouns like 'perplexity', 'quandary', 'helplessness', etc. give the idea.

φοβοῦνται Another new verb: what are phobias?

πολλή 'much', 'many', 'large'.

4 στρατιά στρατηγός has been learnt (Section 1J); στρατιά was what the στρατηγός led, viz. an army.

ὀλίγοι 'small', 'few'. An oligarchy is rule by a few.

5–6 αἱ νῆες αἱ τῶν Ἀθηναίων Notice the repeated αἱ which adds a description, 'the ships, the ones of the Athenians'. See *GE* p. 49, #61.

7 κίνδυνος You have not yet been asked to learn this word, but it occurred on p. 16, line 16: 'We are safe, therefore we are not ἐν κινδύνῳ.'

ἀπορία The noun form of ἀπορέω (see above in line 3).

8 θυσίας Also above, 1G, line 9.

9 εὔχονται 'they pray'. This is not in the vocabulary for 2B, though it is in the Total Vocabulary.

10 ὑπὲρ τῆς ἐλευθερίας   A crucial phrase for a crucial concept to the Greeks, ὑπέρ = 'for', 'on behalf of'; τῆς ἐλευθερίας = 'freedom'. Herodotus describes the Persian Wars in terms that often sound surprisingly familiar, the struggle of the free peoples of the West against the totalitarian regime of the East.
ἀγαθόν   'good' – but neuter gender, whereas ἐλευθερία is feminine. This is a common idiom in Greek: 'freedom is a good thing'. Note that Greek uses the article with ἐλευθερία because it is a general idea, whereas English does not.

12 τόλμα   Not yet learnt, although the verb τολμάω has occurred (2A, line 6), and the accusative τόλμαν (p. 23, line 15).

13 ὅσαι   This means 'How much/many …' as used in exclamations.

14 ἱκετεῖαι   'supplications'.

16 τὴν Ἑλλάδα   Note the word order (the subject is after the verb); and this is the object. Notice also that it is accusative singular and feminine, so that it is not 'the Greeks', but 'Greece'.

18 ὕβριν   Difficult because not exactly like the English usage of 'hubris'. Here the sense is 'violence', 'aggression'.
τὸ πλῆθος   This is a neuter noun (of a type you have not yet met), so the accusative is the same as the nominative.

19 βεβαία … ἡ … σωτηρία   Cf. 1G, line 18.

Translation for 2B

'Sing, goddess, the destructive wrath of Xerxes the god-like king.' So the foreigners slowly approach the city, while the Athenians are at a loss and are afraid. For the Persian army [is] large, and the Athenians few. Many [are] the Persian ships, but few the ships of the Athenians. Great then [is] the danger of the Athenians, great their perplexity and great also their fear. So the Athenians sacrifice their sacrifices to the gods and pray much; they go quickly into their ships and fight for their freedom. For freedom [is] a good thing.

Finally the Persians arrive and the Greeks fight. Great [is] the daring of the Greeks and their generals. And in the sea-battle, how many are the shouts, how great the perplexities, how many the supplications to the gods! Finally the Athenians defeat the Persian fleet and the Persians fall and they do not enslave the Athenians. The Athenians free Greece and save their country through their daring. For courage and daring always defeat aggression and superior numbers. So thus the salvation of the Greeks becomes secure.

2C

Page 26

1 οὐδὲν λέγει   Literally 'says nothing', i.e. says nothing worth-while, talks rubbish.

4 οὐκ οἶσθα οὐδέν   Notice the reinforcing negative, 'you don't know *anything*'.

11 πολλάκις   The πολ- element should be familiar; here with the adverbial suffix -άκις or -κις it means 'many times', 'often'.

15 ὧδε   Means 'like this', when it refers to what is going to follow. οὕτως means 'like this', when it refers to what has gone before.

Page 27

20 ἔνθα καὶ ἔνθα   ἔνθα literally means 'then', 'there', 'when', 'where' according to context. Here it is used idiomatically to mean 'this way and that'.

21 ἅμα ἔῳ   Perhaps needs some explanation: ἅμα is an adverb meaning 'at the same time as'; ἔῳ is dative of a very irregular noun meaning 'dawn'. The phrase thus means 'at dawn'.

22 σάλπιγξ ἠχεῖ   Illustrated on *RGT* p. 26.

23 ἐκ ... πετρῶν   What is the meaning of the English name 'Peter'? Cf. Matthew 16.18, and note also 'petrol', 'petroleum' (='rock-oil').

25 This is taken from Aeschylus, *Persae* 353–5, completely unadapted.
  ἴτε   An irregular imperative (corresponds with Latin *ite*) meaning 'come!/go!'
  ἀγών   'struggle', as in English 'antagonist'.

Translation for 2C

The rhapsode is silent. The captain says that the rhapsode is speaking rubbish. Then the captain also relates the events at Salamis.

CAPTAIN   You are talking rubbish, friend, and you don't know anything. So you do not make your story very fine.

RHAPSODE   What are you saying? In what way am I not making my story very fine?

CAPT.   Consider. We are looking for the truth, and you are telling us falsehoods.

RHAP.   But how do you know whether I am telling the truth or falsehoods?

CAPT.   Listen, friend. My grandfather is a Salamis-fighter and he often tells me the events at Salamis truly, but not falsely, like you. For you perhaps tell us a fine story, my grandfather [tells] the facts. Be quiet then, and hear again, sailors, the fine deeds of the Greeks. For my grandfather tells the events at Salamis as follows.
  The sailors settle down.
  The Persian fleet arrives, and stays near Salamis, while we Greeks keep quiet. When night comes, the Persian ships sail slowly this way and that. But at dawn a shout arises (occurs) and when the trumpet echoes from the rocks, fear develops (occurs) at the same time in the foreigners. For they now clearly hear the shout:
    'O Children of the Greeks, go!
    Free your country, free your children, your wives!
    Now [is] the struggle for everything!'

2D

Page 28

2 θεᾶται   What one does in a θέατρον, viz. 'watches'.

3 ἀναχωροῦσιν   Both elements have been met: χωρεῖ 'go', ἀνά 'up', here combined in the sense of 'retreat', 'back water'.

4 φαίνεται ... φάσμα   φάσμα = 'apparition'. Cf. English 'phenomenon' which
is derived from φαίνομαι 'I appear'.

δεινόν   'terrible', occurring in English 'dinosaur', a 'terrible lizard' (σαῦρος).

7–9 ἐπιπλέω   ἐπι- in compounds often has the sense of 'against', so here 'sail
against'/ 'attack'; likewise ἐπέρχονται (line 1).

9 κόσμῳ   'order' – with interesting derivations: cosmos = 'ordered state of the
universe', cosmetic = 'ordered state of the dress/face'. κοσμέω also means 'I
decorate'.

10 τάξιν   'arrangement' – taxonomy is the classification, or arrangement, of
organisms into named groups (ὄνομα = 'a name'). In modern Greek ἐν τάξει
means 'in order', 'OK'.

ἀκόσμως ... ἀτάκτως   Opposites of the previous two words, α- being the
regular Greek negative prefix.

12 οἱ μὲν ... οἱ δέ ...   It means 'Of the Persians, some ... others ...'

22 μεταβολή   Means 'change'. Metabolism is the change of food into energy;
similarly, other 'meta-' compounds in English have a sense of 'change', e.g.
'metamorphosis'.

23 ὁμονοοῦσιν   The elements of the word may help, ὁμο- in compounds =
'same'; 'nous' has been adopted as a word for intelligence, actually itself the
Greek word for 'mind', which has the same root as the verb νοέω. So here it is
'be like-minded', or 'agree'.

μισοῦσιν   Again English compounds may help – as well as the context.
Clearly here the clause after ἀλλά is going to mean something contrasted with
the clause before it; and a few English compounds beginning 'mis-' may help
towards the meaning e.g. 'misanthrope', 'misogynist'.

25 φεῦ   Exclamation of despair or disgust.

τῶν Ἑλλήνων, τοῦ πολέμου   causal genitives.

Translation for 2D

CAPTAIN   So the enemy ships approach quickly for a sea-battle (Xerxes the king is
watching the sea-battle with pleasure), and I back water. And the other Greeks
retreat. Suddenly there appears the phantom of a woman, very terrible. I am
afraid of the phantom. But the phantom says: 'Friends, why are you still
retreating? Do not be afraid of the Persians but go to the rescue and be bold.'
And I quickly sail to the attack and am no longer afraid, and the rest of the
Greeks also sail swiftly to the attack and move against the Persians. Now we
are fighting in good order and in rank, while the foreigners are fighting in
disarray and out of rank since they are not bold like us.

Finally of the Persians, some flee, and others remain and fall. And of the
Greeks, some pursue the Persians, and others capture their ships and their sailors.
When the Athenians pursue the Persians, Xerxes also flees and no longer watches
the sea-battle. So the Greeks become free through their courage. In this way the
gods punish the aggression of the Persians and save the city. And the Persians do
not enslave the Athenians.

DIKAIOPOLIS   You speak well, captain. Now we know clearly and accurately about the
Persian Wars. But the change in events is now great: for at that time the Greeks
were friends with each other. Now they no longer agree, but hate each other
because of the war. Then there was agreement among the Greeks, and now
there is hatred. Alas, alas for the Greeks, alas for the war!

Grammar

Contracted verbs in -όω: there should be little difficulty in recognising the person
of these verbs from the endings you already know. Perhaps the most important
thing to notice is how -o- predominates throughout.

Much more important are the middle verbs in *GE* pp. 19–21 #23–25.

Feminine nouns: if you are doing English–Greek exercises, it is important to
notice the differences between the different types of feminine noun. (See *GE* pp.
46–47, #55–57.) For recognition of the **case** of the noun, it is enough to remember
the endings for the feminine of the definite article and the fact that nouns of the
first declension may have either -α- or -η- in the singular endings, while all the
plurals are the same. Notice also the masculine nouns (1d #58) which are slightly
different in some cases of the singular and the same as the feminines in the
plural.

Note also the extra vocabulary on p. 51, to be learnt before attempting the
exercises.

EXERCISES FOR SECTION 2A–D

MIDDLE VERBS

2A–D: 1

1. he/she/it becomes/
   happens/occurs
2. we are not going
3. they enslave
4. they are fighting
5. don't fight!
6. we are enslaving
7. go (s.)
8. go (pl.) and fight
   or you (pl.)are going and fighting
9. he/she/it is afraid
10. he/she is enslaving
11. he/she is watching
12. you (s.) are afraid
13. I am not watching
14. he/she/it shows

2A–D: 2

1. μὴ θεᾶσθε
2. ἔρχονται
3. οὐ φοβεῖται
4. γίγνεσθε
5. δουλοῦσθε
6. φοβοῦμαι
7. ἐρχόμεθα
8. φοβοῦνται
9. δουλοῦται
10. θεᾶται
11. οὐ γίγνονται
12. ἔρχῃ

NOUNS, TYPES 1a, 1b, 1c, 1d

2A–D: 3

1. τὸν ναύτην, νεανίαν
2. τῶν βοῶν, ἀποριῶν, θαλαττῶν, ναυτῶν, νεανιῶν
3. ταῖς βοαῖς, ἀπορίαις, θαλάτταις
4. ἡ βοή, ἀπορία, θάλαττα
5. τοὺς ναύτας, νεανίας
6. αἱ βοαί, ἀπορίαι, θάλατται
7. τοῖς ναύταις, νεανίαις
8. ὁ ναύτης, νεανίας
9. τὴν βοήν, ἀπορίαν, θάλατταν
10. τῷ ναύτῃ, νεανίᾳ

2A–D: 4

1. τὰς βοάς
2. τῷ ναύτῃ
3. ἡ τόλμα
4. τῶν ἀποριῶν
5. οἱ ναῦται
6. τῇ βοῇ
7. τὴν τόλμαν
8. τὸν νεανίαν

PREPOSITIONS

2A–D: 5

1. because of the war
2. against the barbarians
3. alongside the ship
4. away from the friends
5. because of the sailors
6. alongside the Athenians
7. against the enemy
8. because of the sea-battle
9. because of the perplexity
10. from the armies
11. alongside, beside the man
12. away from the Athenians

2A–D: 6

1. διὰ τὰς βοάς
2. ἐκ τῶν πλοίων
3. παρὰ τοὺς φίλους
4. ἐπὶ τὴν στρατιάν
5. διὰ τὴν ἐλευθερίαν
6. παρὰ τὰς θεάς
7. διὰ τὰς ὁμολογίας
8. ἀπὸ τῶν πολεμίων
9. ἐπὶ τοὺς ἀνθρώπους
10. διὰ τὴν νίκην

2A–D: 7

1. ἐν τοῖς βαρβάροις   among the barbarians/foreigners
2. ἐν τῇ ναυμαχίᾳ   in the sea-battle
3. ἐν τῷ ἔργῳ   in the deed/task
4. εἰς τὴν γῆν   into the land
5. ἐν τῷ Πειραιεῖ   in the Piraeus

REVISION EXERCISES FOR SECTION 2

A – VOCABULARY-BUILDING

true	the truth
accurately	accuracy
man	woman
a shout	I shout
experienced, expert	experience, expertise
work, task	I work, carry out a task
pleasantly	I am pleased, pleasure
bad	evil, wickedness
I fight	the warrior, the battle, unfightable
stupid	stupidity, folly
ship/I fight	I fight a sea-battle
victory/I win	unconquered, unconquerable
I make/do/create	the maker/creator/poet
war	the warrior/fighter, I make war
I am silent	silence
army	the army, I campaign, the soldier
I dare	the daring man, lacking courage, I lack courage
dear, a friend	I love, friendship/love
I fear	fear
falsely	I tell lies

B – WORD SHAPE

1.

we relate, go through	διέρχομαι
he/she fights	μάχονται
you (s.) fear	φοβεῖσθε
they watch	θεᾶται
You (pl.) enslave, enslave! (pl.)	δουλοῖ, δουλοῦ
you (pl.) watch or watch! (pl.)	θεᾶ or θεῶ
he approaches	προσέρχονται
they fear	φοβεῖται
I fear	φοβούμεθα
they happen	γίγνεται
you attack	ἐπέρχεσθε
you (pl.) fight or fight! (pl.)	μάχη, μάχου

2. ὁ ναύτης, τὴν τόλμαν, τῷ ναύτῃ, τὰς βοάς, αἱ νῖκαι, τῶν ναυτῶν, τὴν στρατιάν, τοῖς κυβερνήταις, τὴν νίκην, ἡ ἀπορία.

3. ἡ καλλίστη βοή, αἱ ἐμαὶ βοαί, τῇ ἐμῇ ἀπορίᾳ, τὴν πολεμίαν βοήν, ταῖς καλαῖς νίκαις

C – SYNTAX

1. a. τὰ ἔργα τὰ τῶν Περσῶν   The deeds of the Persians
      τὰ τῶν Περσῶν ἔργα

   b. ἡ στρατιὰ ἡ τῶν βαρβάρων   The army of the barbarians
      ἡ τῶν βαρβάρων στρατιά

   c. ἡ βοὴ ἡ ἐν τῷ λιμένι   The shout in the harbour
      ἡ ἐν τῷ λιμένι βοή

   d. οἱ ναῦται οἱ ἐν τῷ πλοίῳ   The sailors in the ship
      οἱ ἐν τῷ πλοίῳ ναῦται

   e. τὸ πλοῖον τὸ τῶν πολεμίων   The ship of the enemy
      τὸ τῶν πολεμίων πλοῖον

D – ENGLISH INTO GREEK

1. The ship goes towards the sea-battle.
   οἱ ναῦται πρὸς τὸν ῥαψῳδὸν διαλέγονται.

2. The best rhapsode always makes his stories very beautiful.
   ὁ κυβερνήτης ἡδέως διέρχεται τὴν ἡμετέραν ναυμαχίαν.

3. Then the Athenians fight, and the Persian generals are afraid.
   τέλος οἱ μὲν Ἀθηναῖοι νικῶσιν, οἱ δὲ τῶν Ἀθηναίων πολέμιοι πίπτουσιν.

4. Don't retreat, friends, but fight!
   μὴ φοβεῖσθε, ὦ ναῦται, ἀλλὰ μάχεσθε καὶ ἐλεύθεροι γίγνεσθε.

5. We know that the Greek army is approaching.
   ἴστε ὅτι οἱ τῶν Περσῶν στρατηγοὶ ἀναχωροῦσιν.

E – TEST EXERCISE 2

So when the Persian army and fleet are approaching, the Athenians quickly embark on their ships and sail towards Salamis. Then both the Athenians and the rest of the Greeks keep quiet. Finally the Persian fleet arrives, and, when night comes, their ships sail slowly up and down. And when the day comes, the Persians advance swiftly to battle, but the Greeks are at a loss and are afraid. Finally they are no longer afraid, but are daring and attack the foreigners. So they fight in good order and defeat the foreigners. So the foreigners flee, and Xerxes also flees. So in this way the Greeks become free through their courage.

3A

In this section you will meet the 3rd declension nouns formally. There are a number of variants which will be introduced gradually. It is not difficult to recognise the case if you are working from Greek into English, but if you want to feel really confident and to cope with English into Greek, you should learn each new noun, its gender and its stem and any peculiarities as you meet it. See *GE* pp. 54–56, #66–68.

A simplified form of the patterns can be summarised as follows:

	s.	m. + f. pl.	neut. pl.
Nominative	various	-ες	-α
Accusative	-α	-ας	-α
Genitive	-ος	-ων	-ων
Dative	-ι	-σι(ν)	-σι(ν)

This covers most of the forms you are likely to encounter in this section.

Page 30

1 πρὸς τὸν λιμένα   The phrase should be familiar, but attention now focuses on the ending of λιμένα. τόν indicates masculine accusative singular: the ending itself is -α, as above, which may be entered in a grid for 3rd declension endings.

2 λαμπάδα τινά   Another accusative singular. Notice that the indefinite τις, which regularly follows its noun, is also 3rd declension.

3 ἡ λαμπάς   The article indicates that this is nominative singular. Note that 3rd declension nouns have a number of different forms in the nominative. It is important to learn the stem to which the other case-endings are attached (as in Latin).

10–11 Note the way that Greek echoes the interrogative πόθεν by its indirect form ὁπόθεν in reply to the question.

13 τὰ πυρά   The article indicates neuter plural, as above. πῦρ, 'fire', gives us 'pyromaniac', 'pyrotechnics' etc. Enter neuter plural (nom. + acc.) in grid, both ending in -α (for neuter nouns in the nominative and accusative always have the same ending).

15 σῷζε ἡμᾶς εἰς τὸν λιμένα   Note the difference in usage in Greek and English. Literally, 'Save us into the harbour', but 'Bring us safely into the harbour' sounds better.

τίς not interrogative, but indefinite! The accent comes from enclitic ἐστιν (*GE* p. 30, #42b.)

20–21 εὖ οἶδα ὅτι   'I know that well.' This is an idiom. No clause follows the ὅτι.

21 τὰ πυρὰ δηλοῖ   Notice that

a. τὰ πυρά is neuter plural (as above in line 13)

b. neuter plural subjects have a singular verb (*GE* p. 26, #35)

c. δηλοῖ is here a verb, 3rd person singular (*GE* p. 20, #25).

23 σαφῶς δηλοῖ   The subject is τὰ πυρά (n. pl. subj. followed by singular verb) from the line before. 'They show clearly that ...'

νῆες   ναῦς is highly irregular (*GE* p. 64, #74 gives full forms), although the -ες ending is also the regular nom. pl. ending and may be entered on the grid.

Translation for 3A

Thus then the ship goes slowly towards the harbour. Dikaiopolis sees a light on Salamis. So the captain asks where the light is from. When he sees the light, he immediately hurries towards the harbour.

CAPTAIN   Come over here and look. We are now approaching the harbour.

DIKAIOPOLIS   *(Looks towards Salamis.)*

Look, captain: I see a light on the island.

CAPT.   What are you saying? Where is the light [coming] from?

DIK.   Where from? Look!

CAPT.   *(The captain also looks towards the island.)*

O Zeus! It is not a light you are seeing, but fire signals.

SAILOR   What are you saying? Do you say fire signals? O Zeus! Come along, captain, hurry, hurry and get us safe into the harbour.

CAPT.   But I am saving you. Don't be afraid. I am hurrying, and the ship is already turning into the harbour.

DIK.   But why are we hurrying? Is there some danger for us?

SAIL.   [Yes], by Zeus. We are in danger, Dikaiopolis, I know that well. We are hurrying because the fire signals show some danger.

DIK.   What do the fire signals show?

SAIL.   They show clearly that enemy ships are coming against us.

3B

New in this section is the word οὗτος 'this': so you may wish to have an empty grid ready to fill in its forms as they occur, or you may prefer to look at *GE* pp. 60–61, #69.

οὗτος can be used by itself as a pronoun to mean 'this man', or it can be used as a demonstrative adjective with a noun (οὗτος ὁ θόρυβος) to mean 'this din'. You will see that in the latter case the article is also used: 'this the din'. ἐκεῖνος 'that' (*GE* p. 61, #69) is used in the same way.

Page 32

1 οἱ ἐν τῷ Πειραιεῖ   See *GE* p. 49, #63; this is a very common type of phrase. 'The [people] in the Piraeus'. Here the article is followed by a prepositional phrase instead of a noun.

ταῦτα τὰ πυρά   Neuter plural of οὗτος; note the use of the article as well.

1–2 πολύς ... πολλαί   Both are parts of πολύς 'many' (as in English 'poly-' compounds). The full pattern is given in *GE* p. 63, #73. Notice that in the masc. and neuter nom. and acc. singular the stem is πολ- not πολλ- as in the rest of the cases.

3 ἐν ταῖς ὁδοῖς   There is just a small number of 2nd declension nouns which are feminine, and this is one of them.

8 μέγας   'big' (as in English 'mega-' compounds) has slight irregularities, like πολύς. See *GE* p. 63, #73. The stem μεγαλ- is the norm except in masc. and neuter nom. and acc. singular.

8–9 ἡ βοὴ ἡ ἐν τῷ λιμένι   Notice the repeated article, 'the shout, the one in the harbour'.

14, 15 Notice how ποῖ 'where to' is answered by οἴκαδε 'to my home', 'homewards'.

Page 33

20 τροπωτῆρα ... ὑπηρέσιον   There is no point in trying to guess these! The former is an 'oar-loop', to secure the oar to the thole-pin (a pin fixed in the port-hole) and/or the rower's wrist; the latter is a 'cushion' (usually tallowed underneath) to assist the rower in sliding backwards and forwards whilst rowing. Each member of the trireme's crew kept his own.

23 παῖς   This means 'child' or 'boy' but is frequently used with the meaning of 'slave' i.e. someone with no authority. This is the meaning given in the running vocabulary for 3B and is the meaning throughout this section.

Translation for 3B

When the people in the Piraeus see these fire signals, much confusion occurs in the harbour, and many shouts, and nowhere [is there] order. For it is night, and many men appear in the streets and watch the fire signals. Protarchos and Polos, his neighbour, see the men.

POLOS   *(Runs out of his house.)*
Tell me, what is this shouting? What is this confusion, neighbour? Do you know? For great is the confusion, great the shouting in the harbour.

PROTARCHOS   *(Runs homeward.)*
Come over here, neighbour, and look over there. Do you not see those fire signals? Look: it is clear that Salamis is in danger.

POL.   Tell me, neighbour, where are you running to?

PROT.   I am running home for my weapons. And then I am going quickly to my ship. For this danger is terrible and great. But why don't you come with me?

POL.   Indeed I am coming with you. But wait, friend.

PROT. But where are you running to?

POL.   I'm [going] home for my oar-loop and cushion. For it is clear that we are going to a sea-battle.

So Polos brings out his oar-loop and cushion, and Protarchos' slave brings out his weapons and his torch. Then the men go towards the harbour.

EXERCISES FOR SECTION 3A–B

THIRD DECLENSION NOUNS

3A–B: 1

1. τὸν ἄνδρα, γείτονα, λιμένα, παῖδα, σωτῆρα
2. οἱ ἄνδρες, γείτονες, λιμένες, παῖδες, σωτῆρες
3. τὰς λαμπάδας, νύκτας, πατρίδας
4. ἡ λαμπάς, νύξ, πατρίς
5. τοὺς ἄνδρας, γείτονας, λιμένας, παῖδας, σωτῆρας
6. αἱ λαμπάδες, νύκτες, πατρίδες
7. τὴν λαμπάδα, νύκτα, πατρίδα
8. ὁ ἀνήρ, γείτων, λιμήν, παῖς, σωτήρ

3A–B: 2

1. τῆς πατρίδος
2. τῶν παίδων
3. τοῦ σωτῆρος
4. τῷ ἀνδρί
5. τοῖς λιμέσι(ν)
6. τῶν γειτόνων
7. ταῖς νυξί(ν)
8. τῇ λαμπάδι

3A–B: 3

1. παρὰ τὸν λιμένα
2. εἰς τὴν πατρίδα
3. ἐπὶ τοὺς ἄνδρας
4. πρὸς τοὺς γείτονας
5. διὰ τὸν παῖδα
6. εἰς τοὺς λιμένας
7. ἐπὶ τὸν γείτονα
8. διὰ τὴν νύκτα
9. ἐπὶ τοὺς παῖδας
10. διὰ τὴν πατρίδα

PERSONAL PRONOUNS

3A–B: 4

1. We are fighting, but you (pl.) are keeping quiet/doing nothing.
2. I [can] see you (s.), but you cannot see me.
3. Our safety is in your (pl.) (hands), not in ours.
4. Which of you (pl.) or which of us is afraid of the men?
5. Your (pl.) freedom is in my hands/ is in my power/ is my responsibility.
6. The wicked men defeat you (pl.), but not us.
7. Don't chase us, men.
8. We are dying, but you (s.) do nothing, but watch us.

3A–B: 5

1. ἡμᾶς
2. ὑμεῖς ἡμεῖς
3. ἐν ἐμοί
4. πρὸς σέ

5. ἀπὸ ὑμῶν
6. ἡμῶν
7. ἐμὲ σέ
8. ἐν ἡμῖν

REVISION EXERCISES FOR SECTION 3A–B

A – VOCABULARY-BUILDING

1. a man	manly, brave
earth/work	farmer, I farm
I know	I do not know
to there	there, from there / thence
experienced	without experience
I watch	the spectacle, the spectator, the theatre
a din, commotion	I create a disturbance
the danger	I am in danger of, without danger
I learn	the student
house	belonging to the house or family, domestic
weapons	hoplite (heavy-armed soldier)
a child	education, I educate, uneducated
I appear	apparent, obvious

B – WORD SHAPE

1. a. τὸν ἔμπειρον ἄνδρα
   b. τὴν κακὴν νύκτα
   c. τὸν σῶον παῖδα
   d. τὴν καλὴν πατρίδα
2. a. ὁ ἀγαθὸς γείτων
   b. ἡ καλλίστη λαμπάς
   c. ὁ πολέμιος λιμήν
   d. ἡ ἐλευθέρα πατρίς
3. a. τοῦ ἐμπείρου ἀνδρός
   b. τῆς κακῆς νυκτός
   c. τοῦ σώου παιδός
   d. τῆς καλῆς πατρίδος

   a. τῷ ἐμπείρῳ ἀνδρί
   b. τῇ καλλίστῃ λαμπάδι
   c. τῷ πολεμίῳ λιμένι
   d. τῇ ἐλευθέρᾳ πατρίδι

C – SYNTAX

the expert man
the bad night
the saved child
the beautiful fatherland

the good neighbour
the most beautiful light/lamp
the enemy harbour
the free fatherland

3C

Page 34

4   δεινὸς ὁ ἐν Σαλαμῖνι κίνδυνος   Supply ἐστί.

7–8   πτώσσει ... ὥσπερ Ἀχαιὸς ὑφ' Ἕκτορι   The sailor is 'Homerising'.

10–11   μὴ ποίει τοῦτο μηδὲ φοβοῦ ...   Notice that the negatives οὐ and οὐδέ are used in negative statements, whereas μή, which will be followed by μηδέ, is used in negative commands or prohibitions.

17   οὐδεμία   Feminine of οὐδείς (*GE* p. 75, #86).

17–18   οὐκ ἀφικνεῖται Λακεδαιμόνιος οὐδείς, οὐδὲ λαμβάνει οὐδένα ...   Notice that additional compound negatives simply strengthen the negative sense (*GE* p. 75, #86).

21   τίνες οἱ λόγοι;   Supply εἰσί.

24   κρατοῦσι   κράτος is the Greek for 'power', from which we get our '-cracy' words, 'democracy', 'aristocracy', 'bureaucracy' etc.

26   Notice the contrast between ἐμπειρίαν τινά and οὐδεμίαν ... ἐμπειρίαν.

Page 36

28   καὶ δὴ καί   Often used at the end of a string of points as a final 'clincher': 'and what's more'.

29   γεωργοί   Compounded from γῆ 'land' and ἔργον 'work', hence 'farmer' (note Virgil's *Georgics* (farming matters) if that helps fix the meaning).

30   τὸ ... ναυτικόν   'the nautical thing', i.e. 'expertise at sea'.
     ταύτην   Refers back to τέχνη.

2   ἄλλως δὲ οὐδαμῶς   'otherwise nowise' i.e. 'otherwise there's no way [they can learn]'.

32–33   Notice the order of the words and the ideas, 'not easily, but with difficulty and with much practice ...'

34–35   φησί τις ὑμῶν   A typical rhetorical trick, the imagined interjection, 'says one of you'.

41   τριηράρχων   The -αρχ- element means 'ruler', τριηρ- 'of a trireme', hence 'captain of a trireme' or 'trierarch'.

Translation for 3C

Meanwhile Dikaiopolis and the sailors are still talking to each other.

DIKAIOPOLIS   O Zeus! Terrible is the danger in Salamis and great. Look, rhapsode: but where is the man? For I cannot see that man.

SAILOR   Look, this rhapsode 'is cowering' in the ship 'like an Achaean at Hector's mercy'. He's afraid of the Spartans.

DIK.   Tell me, rhapsode, what are you doing? What fear takes hold of you? For you are the best general of the Greeks. Don't do this, and don't be afraid of these Spartans. Look, we are already near the harbour. So don't be afraid.

RHAPSODE   What are you saying? Are the Spartans arriving? I am afraid of the Spartans, I am. For those men take sailors and kill them.

SAIL.   But no ship is arriving, my friend, and it is clear that not one of the Spartans is arriving, nor taking anybody, nor killing anybody. Do you not remember the words of Pericles?

RHAP.   What are the words? Tell me: for I do not remember.

SAIL.   Listen then to what Pericles says in the ecclesia (assembly) about the war and about nautical matters: 'Do not be afraid, Athenians, of the Spartans. For those men have supremacy on land, we [have supremacy] at sea. But we too have some experience on land, while they have no experience in nautical matters. And moreover, the Spartans do not easily learn nautical matters, I know that well, since they are farmers and not seafarers. Nautical [expertise] is a skill: and this "skill" men learn through practice, as they do other skills, and no other way. For you know well that not easily, but with difficulty and with much practice, do you learn this skill. "But the Spartans", one of you says, "do they not practise?" I reply "No, but we, since we have supremacy at sea, are preventing them."'

DIK.   And now see the harbour! How many torches [there are], how many warships, how much confusion, how many men! Look! Like ants, those sailors are swarming into the harbour. Great is the number both of ships and of trierarchs.

3D

Page 36

2 θόρυβος γίγνεται πολύς   Notice the word order. πολύς is delayed to the end to make it more emphatic.

3 κελευστής   Derived from κελεύω. 'The one who orders', translated in English above as 'boatswain' because he was the one who gave orders to the rowers.

Page 37

6 οἴκοι 'at home'. Cf. οἴκοθεν 'from home', and οἴκαδε 'to home'.
    που (Without an accent.) This is the indefinite form of ποῦ 'where'. It can mean 'somewhere', but it often makes the statement vague and tentative, like 'I suppose' in English.

14 παῖ 'Boy' is being used in the sense of 'slave'.

19–20 ἦ οὐχ οὕτως; 'or not thus?' (literally), i.e. 'or isn't he?' Greek will often add the alternative – and note the form of reply, οὕτως γε '[He] certainly [is] thus', γε emphasises οὕτως. The answer to questions is often given in the form of a positive statement: 'Is he there?' is more often answered by 'He is there' than by 'Yes'.

21 φέρε, ὦ παῖ φέρε is like ἄγε and means 'come on, do something'.

25 βάλλε εἰς κόρακας Literally, 'throw [yourself] to the crows' – a colloquial Greek expression meaning 'go to hell'.

Page 38

29 Κυδαθηναιεύς A member of the deme (roughly ward/parish in Attica) Kydathenaion, from which Polos came – a normal method of identification.

Translation for 3D

When Dikaiopolis and the rhapsode arrive on land, there is much confusion going on. The men keep quiet and watch the spectacle. Near the ship is a boat-swain, and this man is shouting.

BOATSWAIN   Tell me, where is our trierarch?

POLOS   Clearly at home, boatswain. He's asleep, presumably.

BOA.   Alas! Terrible is the danger of the Athenians, and that man is asleep at home. So hurry, Polos, and look for the trierarch and tell him about this danger in Salamis.

POL.   Of course, boatswain.
So Polos runs quickly towards the trierarch. Finally he arrives at the door.

POL.   Boy! Boy! What are you doing? Is the boy asleep? Boy! Boy!

BOY   Who is it? Who is shouting? Why are you calling me? Who are you looking for?

POL.   Tell me, is the trierarch inside? Or isn't he?

BOY   He is.

POL.   Come along then, boy, why are you still waiting? Why don't you call your master? For I am looking for him.

BOY   But it's impossible. The master is sleeping soundly.

POL.   What are you saying? Impossible? Go to hell! Don't joke with me. Why don't I knock on this door? Trierarch! Trierarch! I'm calling you!

TRIERARCH   Go to hell! But who's knocking at the door? What's this business? Who's calling me? Who's shouting?

POL.   Polos, from the deme Kydathenaion, is calling you – me!

TRI.   But I'm sleeping soundly –

POL.   But don't sleep, trierarch: Salamis is in danger. Come and look over there. Do you not see those fire signals?

TRI.   What are you saying? Are you joking with me?
(He sees the fire signals on the island.)
Alas! Wait, Polos. I'm coming quickly.

Page 39

6 ὠὸπ ὄπ   Not meaningful words – just a sort of 'in, out'.

7–8 τὰς εὐχὰς εὔχομαι   Greek likes these repetitive phrases; cf. σπονδὴν σπένδω, and θυσίας θύομεν. It would be the normal practice to pour a libation and to say a prayer at the start of a voyage.

16 κατακέλευε   Compound indicates giving time to rowers – 'Now call the time.

Translation for 3E

Finally the sailors and the boatswain embark on the ships, and the trierarch also embarks. And when he gives the order, the boat sails away.

TRIERARCH   Call the time, boatswain.

BOATSWAIN   In, out, in, out …

TRI.   Well done! Now I pour a libation to the gods and pray prayers.
(He prays his prayers.)
O Lord Poseidon – for you are the best saviour of sailors and we often sacrifice our sacrifices to you for our safety – get us safely back to our country.
(He pours the libation.)
Now call the time again, boatswain.

BOA.   In, out, in, out. Well done, men. Our ship is sailing away.

TRI.   Quickly now, boatswain. Give the order.

BOA.   In, out, in, out, in, out.

EXERCISES FOR SECTION 3C–E

ADJECTIVES/PRONOUNS: οὗτος, *this;* ἐκεῖνος, *that*

3C–E: 1

1.	τοῦτον τὸν λιμένα	this harbour
2.	αὗται αἱ λαμπάδες	these torches/lights
3.	οὗτος ὁ γείτων	this neighbour
4.	τούτους τοὺς παῖδας	these children
5.	ταύτην τὴν πατρίδα	this country
6.	τούτους τοὺς ἄνδρας	these men
7.	τοῦτο τὸ ἔργον	this deed/task
8.	αὗται αἱ νύκτες	these nights
9.	οὗτοι οἱ σωτῆρες	these saviours
10.	ταῦτα τὰ ὅπλα	these weapons

3C–E: 2

1.	ἐκεῖνοι οἱ λιμένες	those harbours
2.	ἐκείνας τὰς λαμπάδας	those lamps/lights

3. ἐκεῖνον τὸν γείτονα   that neighbour
4. ἐκεῖνοι οἱ παῖδες   those children
5. ἐκείνη ἡ πατρίς   that country/fatherland
6. ἐκεῖνοι οἱ ἄνδρες   those men
7. ἐκεῖνος ὁ σωτήρ   that saviour
8. ἐκεῖναι αἱ νύκτες   those nights
9. ἐκεῖνο τὸ ἔργον   that deed/task
10. ἐκεῖνα τὰ πυρά   those fire-signals

3C–E: 3

1. τούτου, ἐκείνου τοῦ γείτονος
2. ταύτῃ, ἐκείνῃ τῇ λαμπάδι
3. τούτων, ἐκείνων τῶν παίδων
4. τούτῳ, ἐκείνῳ τῷ λιμένι
5. τούτοις, ἐκείνοις τοῖς ἀνδράσι
6. ταύτης, ἐκείνης τῆς πατρίδος
7. ταύταις, ἐκείναις ταῖς νυξίν
8. τούτων, ἐκείνων τῶν ἔργων

MANY, GREAT: πολύς, μέγας

3C–E: 4

1. πολλοὺς λιμένας   many harbours
2. πολλαὶ λαμπάδες   many lights/lamps
3. πολλοὶ γείτονες   many neighbours
4. πολὺς πόλεμος   much war
5. πολλὰ ὅπλα   many weapons
6. πολλὰς νύκτας   many nights
7. πολλὴ ἀπορία   much perplexity

3C–E: 5

1. μέγαν λιμένα   a big harbour
2. μεγάλη λαμπάς   a great light
3. μεγάλοι γείτονες   big neighbours
4. μέγα ἔργον   a great deed
5. μεγάλας πατρίδας   large countries
6. μέγας ἀνήρ   a big man

3C–E: 6

1. πολλοῦ καὶ μεγάλου λιμένος
2. πολλῷ καὶ μεγάλῳ ἀνθρώπῳ
3. πολλῆς καὶ μεγάλης λαμπάδος
4. πολλῶν καὶ μεγάλων λόγων

5. πολλοῖς καὶ μεγάλοις ἐργοῖς
6. πολλῇ καὶ μεγάλη ἀπορίᾳ

IRREGULAR NOUNS

3C–E: 7

1. διὰ τὸν Δία
2. παρὰ τὰς ναῦς
3. εἰς τὴν ναῦν

4. πρὸς τὸν Δία
5. ἐπὶ τὰς ναῦς

REVISION EXERCISES FOR SECTION 3C–E

A – VOCABULARY-BUILDING

1. οὕτως 'thus', οὗτος 'this';
   βοηθέω 'I help', βοή 'a shout' + θέω 'I run' = 'I run to the help of';
   κελεύω 'I order', κατακελεύω 'I give the time', κελευστής 'orderer', i.e.
     (specifically in this chapter) 'boatswain';
   ὑμέτερος 'your' (belonging to lots of you), ὑμεῖς 'you' (pl.);
   σπένδω 'I pour a libation', σπονδή 'libation';
   ἐκεῖσε 'over there', ἐκεῖνος 'that (there)';
   ἔνδον 'inside', ἐν 'in';
   βοή 'a shout', βοάω 'I shout';
   ἔμπειρος 'experienced', ἐμπειρία 'experience';
   εὔχομαι 'I pray', εὐχή 'prayer';
   ἡμεῖς 'we', ἡμέτερος 'our'.

B – WORD SHAPE

1. a. τοῦτον τὸν ἄνδρα
   b. ταῦτα τὰ ἔργα
   c. ταύτην τὴν λαμπάδα
   d. τὰς βοὰς ταύτας
   e. τούτους τοὺς λιμένας
2. a. οὗτος ὁ γείτων
   b. αὗται αἱ λαμπάδες
   c. τὰ πυρὰ ταῦτα
   d. ἡ πατρὶς αὕτη
   e. οὗτοι οἱ ἄνδρες
3. a. μέγα τὸ ἔργον
   b. πολλὴν ἐμπειρίαν
   c. μέγαν λιμένα
   d. πολλὰ δεινά

C – SYNTAX

1. this man; these deeds; this lamp; these shouts; these harbours.
2. this neighbour; these lamps; these fire-signals; this country; these men.
3. great is the deed; the men have much experience in naval matters; the captain steers towards a great harbour; the sailor sees many strange things.

D – ENGLISH INTO GREEK

1. So the captain looks quickly towards Salamis.
   ἡ οὖν ναῦς πρὸς ἐκεῖνον τὸν λιμένα βραδέως πλεῖ.
2. For great is the danger of the Athenians, and great the confusion of the men.
   μέγας μὲν γὰρ ὁ θόρυβος, πολλαὶ δὲ αἱ βοαί, πολλοὶ δὲ (ἄνθρωποι/ ἄνδρες) φαίνονται.
3. Don't you know whether those men are sailors or not?
   οὐχ οἶδα πότερον ἐκεῖνος (ὁ ἄνθρωπος/ἀνήρ) στρατηγός ἐστιν ἢ οὔ.
4. This good captain does not hear these shouts.
   ἐκεῖνος ὁ μῶρος ῥαψῳδὸς φοβεῖται τούτους τοὺς Λακεδαιμονίους.
5. That man is stupid about many things, but this man [is stupid] about nothing.
   ἐκεῖναι μὲν γὰρ ἔμπειροι περὶ πολλά, αὕτη δὲ οὔ.

E – TEST EXERCISE 3C–E

While this ship is sailing past the island, Dikaiopolis sees a light on the island. The captain knows well that it is not a light but the fire signals. So he hurries into the harbour: for those fire signals reveal that the enemy are attacking the Athenians. The men in the harbour watch the fire signals and run home for their weapons. For they know that the danger is great. Great fear seizes the rhapsode. For he fears the Spartans. The sailors say that the Athenians are supreme at sea, and the Spartans by land. And the Spartans do not easily learn nautical technique. So when the ship arrives in the harbour, Dikaiopolis and the rhapsode go towards the ships. And it is clear that these ships are going to a sea-battle. For the boat-swains are looking for the trierarchs, but they are sleeping peacefully. Finally these trierarchs arrive at the harbour and get on board. Then they offer their sacrifices and pour their libations and put out to sea.

EXERCISE

Note: there are many more possible answers

1. εἰς τὸν λιμένα (3)   ἐπὶ τοὺς Ἀθηναίους (4)
2. ἐπέρχονται (4)   θεῶνται (4)   τρέχουσιν (5)
3. λαμπάδα ὁρᾷ (1)   θεῶνται τὰ πυρά (4, 5)
4. (a) μέγας (5)   (b) ναυτικήν (9)   (c) δῆλον (11)

In this Section, the new grammatical material includes the use of participles – of the verb 'to be' in Sections A–B, of active and middle verbs in Sections C–D.

Participles are very widely used in Greek: this means, in effect, that you should observe carefully the way they are used and not move on from Section 4 until you are quite happy with all the usages of participles encountered in this Section.

There are also more types of 3rd declension nouns, adjectives and pronouns (see *GE* pp.70–72, #77–80).

4A

Page 42

1 ὅσον πλῆθος   Once again the exclamatory use of ὅσος. πλῆθος is neuter (*GE* p. 71, #78) so the two agree. 'What a great crowd … !'

2 τὰ τείχη   τεῖχος is another neuter noun of the 3rd declension like πλῆθος. The Long Walls joined Athens to the Piraeus. See the map on page 38 of *RGT*.

3 πυράς τινας   The meaning should be clear (cf. τὰ πυρά in Section 3) but note that here we have the acc. pl. of another noun, ἡ πυρά 'funeral pyre'.

4 πρὸς τῶν θεῶν   'by the gods' – the case usage will be explained later.
δαίμων   English 'demon' is derived from this word, but note that the Greek has no 'bad' implications – it is a neutral term meaning 'god', 'divine spirit'.

6 κακοδαίμων   'ill-starred' is perhaps the closest English can get to this idea. It means the opposite of 'divinely favoured': some god is wishing evil upon you. This is a 3rd declension adjective (see *GE* p. 73, #82). The endings are just the same as in the nouns like λιμήν, which you have learned (see *GE* p. 54, #66).

8 Notice πρῶτον μὲν …, ἔπειτα δέ …, a common pairing.

10–11 ναύτης ὤν   'being a sailor'. This is the first example of the present participle. Participles have a wide range of usages in Greek (see *GE* p. 77–78, #88). When translating, it is often best to translate literally first, however un-English it may seem, then re-phrase more idiomatically. Here, for example, you might begin with 'he, being a sailor, likes Pericles' before modifying to another clause – 'because/as/since he is a sailor, he likes Pericles'.

11 Similarly, γεωργὸς ὤν 'because/as/since I'm a farmer'.

Page 43

12–13 Note how μέν and δέ are used to point the contrast between 'us' and the Lacedaemonians.

κρατοῦμεν As on p. 36 line 35, 'we are superior/supreme', and then understand κρατοῦσι in the next phrase.

13 καταλείπετε Note the -λειπ- element in the middle, with the basic sense of 'leave'. The policy of Pericles explained here was that it was not safe to risk a major land battle against the Spartans; therefore the countryside of Attica could not be defended and the advice was given to farmers to abandon their property and take refuge in Athens where the city, the Long Walls and Piraeus, could be defended, while Athens waged war by sea (Thucydides 2.13–17).

15–16 πόλις ... ἄνδρες Cf. Thucydides 7.77; 'It is men who make a city and not walls or ships with no men inside them.' See also Sophocles, *O.T.* 56–7.

19–20 τὰ δὲ πρόβατα ... διαπεμπόμεθα So that's what Dikaiopolis was doing over in Euboea way back in Section 1A!

Page 44

21 πολλοὶ ὄντες Another form of the participle. Deduce number, case and gender from πολλοί and enter in grid. See *GE* p. 77, #87 for the full paradigm of the participle. Notice that the endings are almost the same as the adjectives, but that the stem of the adjectives is -ov- and the stem of the participle is -οντ-. Also there is a separate feminine, as you will see in line 40 below.

23 οὔσας Use ὀλίγας to determine which form this is. This is the feminine form of the participle. The number, case and gender show that it agrees with τὰς οἰκήσεις.

24 νόσος Distinguish carefully from νῆσος. The English introduction, *RGT* p. 41, has already mentioned the plague which devastated Athens: νόσος generally means 'disease', here specifically 'the plague'.

25 οὖσα δεινή is here the clue to determining the form.

27 ὀλοφύρομαι You may be able to deduce the meaning of this from the illustration on p. 42.

28 τὸν ἐμὸν υἱόν, οὐκέτ' ὄντα 'my son, no longer being', 'my son who is no longer alive'. The verb 'to be' is often used in the sense of 'to be alive', 'to exist'.

29 οὖσαν Agreeing with τὴν ἐμὴν γυναῖκα, so which form?

30–31 κακοδαίμονα ὄντα, κακοδαίμονα ... οὖσαν, κακοδαίμονας ὄντας These show clearly the similarities and differences between the participle and the adjective. Note the adjective stem without a 'τ' and the participle stem with one, and that the adjective does not have a separate feminine form whereas the participle does.

31 τοὺς ἐν τῇ πόλει 'the people in the city' (remember *GE* p. 49, #63).

Translation for 4A

RHAPSODE   Heracles! What a lot of people! The walls seem full. Why has the city such a great crowd, Dikaiopolis? Alas! What's this? I see funeral pyres. Tell me, by the gods, what's the reason? Indeed it is clear that some evil god is punishing the city.

DIKAIOPOLIS   The city is indeed unfortunate, rhapsode, the crowd is unfortunate and the farmers in particular are unfortunate. The war is primarily responsible, and then also Pericles.

RHAP.   But Pericles [is] a very good general. For the sailor –

DIK.   But it is clear that that man likes Pericles because he's a sailor. But I'm not a sailor but a farmer. Since I'm a farmer, I think Pericles [is] responsible. For he says: 'We have supremacy at sea, but the Spartans [have supremacy] on land. So leave your homes, farmers, and your land, and bring your property into the city. Do not worry. For a city is not dwellings or land, but men.'

So, in this way Pericles persuades us, since he is a persuasive orator. We bring in from the country our children and our wives and the rest of our property. The flocks we transport across to Euboea.

When we – and there are many of us – arrive in the city, the situation becomes difficult. The city-people have the houses, which are few, and we live first in the Long Walls, then in the temples. After this the plague occurs; it is terrible and destroys many men, many women, many children. The plague also destroys my household. For I am still lamenting my own son, who is no longer, and my own wife, who is no longer. There you have the situation. You see me, rhapsode, who am ill-starred. You see the city, also ill-starred. You see the [people] in the city, also ill-starred.

4B

Page 45

2 βαρύς 'heavy', cf. English 'barometer' etc. You will not meet this type of 3rd declension adjective properly until Section 10.

3 νεκρός Cf. English 'necromancy', 'necrophilia'.
βαρὺν ὄντα This is accusative and refers to the νεκρός, which is now the object of φέρω. 'I carry it, being heavy, slowly.'

11 ὦ 'νθρωπε = ὦ ἄνθρωπε.

12 ὦ τῆς ὕβρεως The case is a genitive of exclamation. It will be explained later – for the present, 'What violence/aggression!' Similarly with ὦ τῆς ἀνομίας (15) and ὦ τῆς ἀσεβείας (16).

Page 46

21 σέβομαι Cf. ἀσέβεια, and τοὺς ἀσεβεῖς (line 28) and τοὺς εὐσεβεῖς (line 28). They are all from the same root.

25 ὥσπερ πρόβατα Our idiom is 'like flies'.

33 ἐφήμεροι   English 'ephemeral' helps, but note the literal meaning 'lasting for one day' (ἡμέρα 'day').

35 Pindar quotation, 'Man is the dream of a shadow', a comment on the transience of human existence. The young man is depicted here as exhibiting the sort of moral deterioration which Thucydides describes as one of the effects of the plague (Thuc. 2.53). He no longer sees any point in trying to observe the old religion and morality. The only deity he has any time for is Aphrodite.

39 ἡ θεός   There is a noun ἡ θεά, but θεός as a feminine form is more common.

Translation for 4B

YOUNG MAN   Look, a pyre. Come here, boy, quickly!

SLAVE   Wait, master, wait and don't hurry. For this corpse is heavy, and as it's heavy, I'm carrying it slowly.

DIKAIOPOLIS   What are you saying? You are carrying a corpse?

Y.M.   Come on, boy, throw the corpse onto this pyre.

DIK.   But what are you doing? Don't do this, by the gods, stop!

Y.M.   Don't get in my way, fellow.

DIK.   Foul [man]! Are you hitting me, a citizen? What aggressive behaviour! Don't hit [me].

OLD MAN   What's this? What are these shouts? You there, what are you doing? Are you hitting a citizen? What lawlessness! Stop! Alas, what's this? Are you throwing a corpse onto that pyre? What irreverence! Stop –

Y.M.   Don't get in my way, old man.

O.M.   But today I am burying my son, and it is my pyre.

Y.M.   I don't care.

O.M.   Do you not reverence the gods? Do you not honour the laws of man? Does nothing stop you, neither fear of the gods nor the laws of men?

Y.M.   What are you saying? Corpses are falling upon corpses, men are dying like flies in their homes and in the temples. And do you speak to me of gods and laws? You fool – the gods either don't exist or don't care about us, since the plague is destroying both the pious and the impious alike. Where are my mother and father, who were always pious? Now where is my brother, the most pious of men? Look.

And don't talk to me about laws and aggressive behaviour. For I'm not afraid of punishment. Don't you know that men are short-lived? What are we? What are we not?

'Man is the dream of a shadow.'

O.M.   Stop, stop! You are dishonouring the gods, though you are a mortal.

Y.M.   But I don't dishonour the gods. I honour Aphrodite particularly. She is a beautiful and kindly goddess. Since the goddess is beautiful and kindly, she makes life happy. So I'm turning to Aphrodite and pleasure, because they are fine.

DIK.   Are you surprised, rhapsode, that I hate the city because I am a farmer, and
         long for my own deme? For in the city there is nothing other than lawlessness
         and impiety and plague and a great quantity of corpses.

Grammar

Grammar for this part of Section 4 is given at *GE* pp. 70–72, #77–80 and pp.
73–76, #81–86.

Check that you know it and understand it.

There is also some vocabulary to be learnt (p. 70), before you try the exercises.

EXERCISES FOR SECTION 4A–B

TYPE 3 NOUNS

4A–B: 1

1. οἱ πρέσβεις
2. τὴν οἴκησιν, πόλιν, τάξιν
3. τὰ ἄστη, πλήθη, πράγματα, σκεύη
4. τοὺς πρέσβεις
5. τὰς οἰκήσεις, πόλεις, τάξεις
6. ὁ πρέσβυς
7. τὸ ἄστυ, πλῆθος, πρᾶγμα
8. τὸν πρέσβυν
9. ἡ οἴκησις, πόλις, τάξις
10. αἱ οἰκήσεις, πόλεις, τάξεις

4A–B: 2

1. τῷ πλήθει
2. τοῖς ἄστεσι(ν)
3. τῇ πόλει
4. τοῦ πράγματος
5. τῶν πρέσβεων
6. τῷ ἄστει
7. τοῦ πρέσβεως
8. τοῦ πλήθους
9. τῷ πράγματι
10. ταῖς πόλεσι(ν)

TYPE 3 ADJECTIVES, τις, τι, οὐδείς οὐδεμία οὐδέν

4A–B: 3

1. πλῆθος – εὔφρον, τι, οὐδέν
2. πόλιν – εὔφρονα, τινά, οὐδεμίαν
3. πρέσβεις – εὔφρονες, τινες, εὔφρονας, τινάς
4. ἄστυ – εὔφρον, τι, οὐδέν
5. οἰκήσεις – εὔφρονες, τινές, εὔφρονας, τινάς
6. τάξις – εὔφρων, τις, οὐδεμία
7. σκεύη – εὔφρονα, τινά

4A–B: 4

1. πλήθει – εὔφρονι, τινί, οὐδενί
2. πράγματος – εὔφρονος, τινος, οὐδενός
3. πρέσβεων – εὐφρόνων, τινῶν
4. τάξεως – εὔφρονος, τινός, οὐδενός
5. πόλει – εὔφρονι, τινί, οὐδενί
6. ἄστεσι – εὔφροσι(ν), τισι(ν)

Check that you understand *GE* pp. 76–78, #87–88 before trying the next exercises.

PRESENT PARTICIPLES

4A–B: 5

1. ὄντες
2. οὖσα
3. ὄντες, ὄντας
4. ὄντα
5. ὄντα
6. ὄντες
7. ὄν
8. οὖσαν
9. οὖσαι
10. ὤν

4A–B: 6

1. οὖσαν
2. ὄν
3. ὄντες
4. ὤν
5. οὖσαν

REVISION EXERCISES FOR SECTION 4A–B

A – VOCABULARY-BUILDING

Once again, do not be surprised if you cannot 'deduce' all the meanings.

Note that nouns which end in -σις normally express the doing of something, whereas nouns which end in -μα describe a thing done: e.g. ποίησις = 'making poetry', but ποίημα is 'a poem'.

1.	
Uneducated	education, lesson
I die, mortal	immortal, death
I become	origin, genesis
I reveal, show	revelation
I embark	embarkation
I ask	question
I seek	search
I watch	spectacle
I call	calling, summons

beautiful	beauty
I am powerful	strength, power
I learn	learning (the process), learning (the thing learned)
I make, do, create	poem, poetic art
general	stratagem
army	army, expedition
quickly	speed
I honour	honour, dishonoured
I dare	recklessness, daring deed
falsely	falsehood, lie

B/C – WORD SHAPE AND SYNTAX

1. a. κακοδαίμων ὤν / οὖσα (masc. or fem.) …

    b. ἡμεῖς ὀλίγοι ὄντες … ὑμᾶς πολλοὺς ὄντας.

    c. φίλαι οὖσαι, ὦ γυναῖκες …

    d. ἐγώ, Ἀθηναῖος ὢν καὶ εὐδαίμων, … σέ, Λακεδαιμόνιον ὄντα καὶ κακοδαίμονα.

    e. τίς ὢν σύ … ;

D – ENGLISH INTO GREEK

1. Since I am a mortal, I do not dishonour the gods.
    σὺ γεωργὸς ὢν οἶσθα τοὺς νόμους.

2. The Athenians defeat by sea those men who are experienced on land.
    ναῦται ὄντες, κατὰ θάλατταν κρατοῦμεν.

3. I do not honour the city, though it is beautiful.
    τὸ τῶν νεκρῶν πλῆθος, μέγα ὄν, οὐ φοβοῦμαι.

4. This general, since he is very good, is not afraid of the Spartans who are hostile.
    ἡ ἐμὴ γυνή, κακοδαίμων οὖσα, φοβεῖται τὴν νόσον, κακὴν οὖσαν.

5. The people, who are unlucky, honour the gods' laws, which are very good.
    τὸ πλῆθος, ἀγαθὸν ὄν, οὐκ ἀτιμάζει τοὺς θεούς, μεγάλους ὄντας.

E – TEST EXERCISE 4A–B

YOUNG MAN Come over here and tell [me]. Why are you lamenting, friend? Are you lamenting a son, who is ill-fated, or a daughter or a wife?

OLD MAN I am doing this because I am ill-fated, friend. For I am lamenting both my son, who is no more, and my daughter who is now a corpse.

Y.M. You seem to be ill-fated indeed. But what is the reason? How are the people dying?

O.M. Because of the plague, friend, corpses fall upon corpses and people die because they are ill-fated.

Y.M. We have many problems because of the plague. For I see the multitude of people are ill-fated, the city is in much perplexity and the people are short-lived and ill-fated.

O.M.   So do not dishonour the gods and do not commit irreverent acts against the city, but be resolute and honour the gods.

EXERCISE

1. ὄντα lines 2 and 4, m., s., agrees with υἱόν
    οὖσαν line 4, f., s., agrees with θυγατέρα [nb. there are more examples at lines 10 and 11]
2. ἔλθε εἰπέ line 1, sing.
    ἀτίμαζε, ἀσέβει, τόλμα, τίμα lines 13 and 14, sing.
3. κακοδαίμονες line 8
    ἐφημέρους line 11, κακοδαίμονας line 12
4. φίλε is vocative
    ἀπορίᾳ is dative

4C

This section introduces the present participle of active verbs: as above (Sections A–B), you may like to make an empty grid in which to fill in the various cases as they occur, using as your example the verb παύω. The endings are exactly the same as those for the verb 'to be' which are set out in *GE* p. 77, #87. You can also see the present participle of παύω set out on *GE* pp. 82–83, #90 followed by the participles of contract verbs GE #91.

Page 48

6 λανθάνει   A very awkward verb to translate as English has no direct equivalent. *GE* p. 86, #95 gives 'escape the notice of', which is the nearest English phrase: it means to do something either intentionally or accidentally unnoticed by yourself or another. The action that is 'not noticed' is expressed as a participle (in this case τρέχων). It is probably best to stick to the literal translation to begin with, 'Or does the man escape your notice running?' before trying to rephrase more idiomatically, 'Are you unaware of the man running?', 'Do you not notice the man running?'

7 προστρέχοντα   You can tell from the -οντα ending that it agrees with αὐτόν.

9 ἀποφεύγων τυγχάνει   τυγχάνω is another verb that is normally accompanied by a participle (see *GE* p. 86, #95). It means 'to happen to be doing something' or 'to be really doing something'.

10 ὁδοιπόρος   Both elements have been met, ὁδός 'road' and πορεύομαι 'I travel'. The noun means 'traveller'.

11 χλαμύδα   This is the garment worn in the illustration on p. 52 (not the hat or sticks!).

14 πάσχει   *GE* gives as 'suffer', 'experience', 'undergo'. The Greek usage is often not as strong as English 'suffer': here it's almost 'What's the matter with him?'

16 δῆλοί εἰσι διώκοντες   δῆλοι is used personally here, in place of δῆλον ὅτι. Literally, 'they are clear pursuing …' You will probably want to translate as 'it is clear that they are pursuing'; or 'they are clearly pursuing'.

18 φθάνει   Another awkward verb to translate and another of the group in *GE* p. 86, #95. *GE* gives as 'anticipate X (acc.) in -ing': the basic sense is usually of doing something either before another can stop you, or of doing it before they can do it. Here the former is more likely: the fugitive escapes into the sanctuary before the Eleven can prevent him from doing so. Once again it helps if you translate it literally, before turning your literal translation into acceptable English.

23 ὁ φεύγων   Literally 'the running away one', or 'the fugitive'.

28 τὸν φεύγοντα   As above, 'the fugitive', this time as the object.

καίπερ   'although' is always followed by a participle.

31–32   This quotation from Homer, *Odyssey* Book 6 can be found in its original context in *RGT* p. 260, lines 207–208.

Page 49

35 δυστυχής   The force of δυσ- in compounds is the opposite of εὐ- and often has the sense of 'with difficulty', 'hard' or 'bad'. Cf. English 'dyslexia', 'dyspepsia', 'dystrophy'.

Translation for 4C

Dikaiopolis and the rhapsode travel towards the city. Suddenly a man runs up to them.

DIKAIOPOLIS   Tell me, rhapsode, what's the din? What are those shouts? What's happening?

RHAPSODE   Look, Dikaiopolis, a man is running this way. Do you see the man? Or are you not aware of the man running this way?

DIK.   No, by Zeus. For I see him running towards [us]. But the situation is strange. Whoever is it?

RHAP.   Perhaps he is a slave and happens to be running away.

DIK.   But he is not a slave and he seems to be a traveller. Or do you not notice that the man has a cloak?

RHAP.   You speak rightly, Dikaiopolis. But perhaps he is a foreigner.

DIK.   Look! The man is running into the shrine of Heracles. What's the matter with him, that he's running into the shrine?

RHAP.   It's clear that he's turning in for sanctuary. And now some men are approaching. Clearly they are pursuing the man.

DIK.   But what's this situation? A herald is approaching and – the Eleven and the public slaves. But the man has anticipated the Eleven by running into the shrine.

SATYROS   Where is the Spartan fleeing to? Where is he? You there – do you know where the fugitive is? Or are you not aware of the man fleeing?

RHAP.   I am aware of him. But he's in that shrine, as a suppliant.

SAT.   Come here, slaves, into that shrine! Quickly lead away the stranger, as he's a Spartan.

DIK.   Don't drag away the fugitive, herald, although he's a Spartan. The stranger
         happens to be a suppliant, and he anticipated you by running into the shrine.
         Because he's a suppliant, he is sacrosanct.

RHAP.   'All strangers are under the protection of Zeus.'

HERALD   Don't worry about that, slaves, but lead the man away.

DIK.   What lawlessness! Indeed the stranger appears to be unlucky.

4D

Now the middle participles are introduced (*GE* pp. 84–85, #92–93) and the participles of the contracted verbs (*GE* p. 84, #93) and one further type of 3rd declension noun (*GE* p. 87, #97).

The middle participles are easily recognised.

παύομαι gives παυόμενος παυομένη παυόμενον, like καλός καλή καλόν

Page 50

  2 καθίζεται ... ἱκέτης ὤν   Illustrated at *RGT* p. 52, which may help towards
     meaning.
 11 ἀπόκοπτε τὰς χεῖρας   Sounds rather drastic, but such an event is recorded by
     Herodotus, 6.91.
 13 ὦνδρες = ὦ ἄνδρες.
 15 ἐπικαλούμενος   The first example of a middle participle. ἐπικαλοῦμαι is a
     contracted verb: the regular participle-ending is -όμενος, seen below in
     ὀλοφυρόμενος (18).
 19 τοὺς ... ἔχοντας   Article + participle 'the ones having ...'; often this is best
     translated by a relative clause, 'those who have ...'
 21 καθορᾶτε   This could be either indicative or imperative, 'you see' or 'see!'
     The context favours the latter.
21–22 τοὺς ἀσεβοῦντας   As above in line 19, 'those who ...'
     περὶ Δία ἱκέσιον καὶ ξένιον   Zeus was regarded as protecting suppliants as
     well as strangers and foreigners.
 23 τὸν τοὺς θεοὺς ἐπικαλούμενον   Notice that the participle can be itself an
     object, and govern an object, 'the man (obj.) calling upon the gods'.
 29 ναὶ τὼ σιώ   *GE* translates as 'by the two gods' (σιώ is Doric dialect for θεώ).
     The two gods are the twins Castor and Pollux, and the oath is a
     characteristically Spartan one.
 32 πρεσβευτής   As an ambassador he would of course (as today) be regarded as
     having diplomatic immunity.
35–36 πρὸς βασιλέα τὸν μέγαν   βασιλεύς (without the article) is regularly used of
     the King of Persia (contrast our usage: to emphasise, we would say '*the* king').
     Here the article is used to link the noun to the adjective μέγαν. The especial
     significance here is that throughout the Peloponnesian War, both Athens and
     Sparta at different times asked Persia for help, thinking that if they succeeded
     in obtaining Persian support they would be victorious. In fact, Sparta's later

success in securing Persian support undoubtedly contributed to her victory in
the end.

36–37   σὺ δὲ δῆλος εἶ φιλῶν τοὺς Λακεδαιμονίους   Literally 'But you are clear
loving the Lacedaemonians', or 'you are clearly in favour of the Spartans'.
Once again notice the personal use of δῆλος with the participle.

Page 51

43   νέμεσις μεγάλη   The concept of divine retribution for wrongdoing is common
in Greek Tragedy and in Herodotus (see Section 19 in *RGT* p. 230, line 1 for
one instance in the original context). Nemesis can fall upon the wrongdoer
himself or upon any one of his descendants. Here it is assumed that the extreme
ill-fortune of the stranger can only be explained by the belief that he is being
punished for the wrongdoing of one of his forebears. Cf. 'visiting the iniquity
of the fathers upon the sons unto the third or fourth generation' (Exodus 20.5).

47–48   εὐνομία and εὐπορία are contrasted with ἀνομία and ἀπορία. εὐνομία is the
opposite of ἀνομία; εὐπορία is the opposite of ἀπορία though here in a slightly
different meaning from 'perplexity' which you met before. ἀπορία can mean
'shortage of provisions', so εὐπορία means the opposite, 'abundance',
'plenty'.

49   Δυσνομία   A personified variation of ἀνομία, and the opposite of Εὐνομία.

50   In the second line of the quotation from Solon:
(a) ἀποφαίνει is active in form, therefore transitive, hence 'makes to appear',
'reveals'.
(b) εὔκοσμα and ἄρτια are neuter plural, agreeing with πάντα.

Translation for 4D

DIKAIOPOLIS   Look, rhapsode, do you see? What impiety! For the unfortunate stranger is
sitting on the altar, as a suppliant, but the public slaves are dragging him away
while the stranger is holding on to the altar and calling upon the gods. O city, city!

SATYROS   Drag away this man, since he's a Spartan, away from the altar.

STRANGER   I call upon the gods –

PUBLIC SLAVE   But the stranger is holding on to the altar, Satyros.

SAT.   Cut off his hands.

STR.   I call upon you, men!

DIK.   The stranger is calling upon us, rhapsode and doesn't stop calling upon us.

RHAPSODE   *(The rhapsode is silent, and finally speaks.)*
But nevertheless, be quiet yourself too, Dikaiopolis, and stop lamenting, and
don't do anything. Don't you see those public slaves, who have their daggers?

STR.   *(He does not stop calling upon the gods.)*
Oh gods, look down upon what I am suffering. Look down upon those who are
committing impiety against Zeus, god of suppliants and strangers.
The public slaves drag away from the altar the man who is calling upon the gods.

SAT.   Stop calling upon the gods, fellow. You, slaves, drag the fellow away to the
other Spartans.

STR.   Do you, Athenians, drag away those who flee into shrines? Do you kill those
       who turn aside for sanctuary? By the twain, you are clearly being unjust
       towards men and impious towards the gods.

DIK.   But who is that stranger?

SAT.   He happens to be an ambassador –

DIK.   What are you saying? An ambassador? What lawlessness! Are you killing
       ambassadors?

SAT.   He is an ambassador and happens to be travelling towards the great King.
       But you clearly love the Spartans. Shut up then and stop bewailing the
       Spartan.
       The public slaves drag the Spartan away towards the market-place. The
       stranger does not stop shouting and revealing what he is suffering at the hands
       of the Athenians.

DIK.   It is clear that the gods hate the man. For they are killing him, although
       he is an ambassador and a suppliant. Surely great retribution from the
       gods is coming upon him because of his ancestors and the aggression of his
       ancestors.

       But what's the matter with our city? What's happening? War seems to be a
       violent instructor, rhapsode. For in peacetime these things do not happen. In
       peacetime there is *good* order and plenty in the city, but in war there is
       lawlessness and shortage.

RHAP.   'So bad government brings very many evils to the city.
       But good government makes all appear well-ordered and perfect.'

Grammar

Check that you understand the participles (*GE* pp. 82–85, #89–93), including the
forms for the contracted verbs, and their various uses listed in *GE* pp. 85–86, #94,
95.

Notice also βασιλεύς (*GE* p. 87, #97), and the useful notes (*GE* pp. 87–88,
#98–100) on elision and crasis.

EXERCISES FOR SECTION 4C–D

MORE PRESENT PARTICIPLES

4C–D: 1

1. τρέχοντας, παυομένους
2. τρέχουσαι, παυόμεναι
3. τρέχων, παυόμενος
4. τρέχοντα, παυόμενον
5. τρέχοντες, παυόμενοι
6. τρέχουσαν, παυομένην
7. τρέχων, παυόμενος
8. τρέχον, παυόμενον

4C–D: 2

1. τρέχοντι, παυομένῳ
2. τρεχούσης, παυομένης
3. τρέχοντος, παυομένου
4. τρεχόντων, παυομένων

5. τρέχουσι(ν), παυομένοις
6. τρεχούσῃ, παυομένῃ
7. τρέχοντι, παυομένῳ
8. τρέχουσι(ν), παυομένοις

4C–D: 3

1. τὸν θεώμενον	the one watching	m. acc. s.
2. τὰς ὁρώσας	those/ the women seeing	f. acc
3. τοὺς ποιοῦντας	the ones doing	m. acc. pl.
4. αἱ δηλοῦσαι	the ones/the women showing	f. nom. pl.
5. οἱ φοβούμενοι	those afraid	m. nom. pl.
6. ἡ ποιοῦσα	the one/the woman doing	f. nom. s.
7. τὴν ὁρῶσαν	the one/the woman seeing	f. acc. s.
8. τὸ δηλοῦν	the one/it showing	n. nom./acc. s.

4C–D: 4

1. τοῖς θεωμένοις	to/for those watching
2. τῇ ὁρώσῃ	to/for the woman who sees
3. τῶν ποιούντων	of those doing, of the doers
4. ταῖς δηλούσαις	to/for the women who are showing
5. τοῦ φοβουμένου	of the one who is afraid
6. ταῖς ποιούσαις	to/for the women who are doing
7. τῷ ὁρῶντι	to/for the one who sees
8. τοῖς δηλοῦσι(ν)	to/for those who show

4C–D: 5

1. βαίνουσα
2. παίζων
3. φεύγων, βοῶντας
4. φεύγοντας
5. τρέχοντα

ELISION AND CRASIS

4C–D: 6

1. ὁ δ' ἀνήρ
2. ἆρ' ὁρᾷς;
3. ἀφ' ἡμῶν
4. ἐφ' ὑμᾶς
5. εἴμ' Ὀδυσσεύς

4C–D: 7

1. νῦν δὲ ἐπὶ οἰκίαν
2. ἀλλὰ ἐγώ
3. ἐν δὲ ἀπορίᾳ
4. κακός ἐστιν ὁ πόλεμος
5. ἆρά εἰμι ἔμπειρος;

REVISION EXERCISES FOR SECTION 4C–D

A – VOCABULARY-BUILDING

1 impiety   reverence
   temple, sacred thing   priest

a suppliant	I beseech
I hate	hated
stranger, guest, host	hospitality/I entertain
I happen/unlucky, unhappy	chance
offence	I assault, outrage

B/C – WORD SHAPE AND SYNTAX

1. a. Who is running? I do not see the man running, τὸν τρέχοντα
   b. Who are lamenting? Where are the people who are lamenting? οἱ ὀλοφυρόμενοι;
   c. I know who is escaping. The man escaping does not escape my notice (i.e. I am aware of the man who is escaping). ὁ ἀποφεύγων
   d. Who are fleeing? Do you see them fleeing? τοὺς φεύγοντας
   e. The king is running away and does not stop running away. ἀποτρέχων
   f. Women (in general) are always afraid. Why don't they stop being afraid? φοβούμεναι;

D – ENGLISH INTO GREEK

1. I do not see any Spartan escaping.
   ὁρῶμεν τοὺς ἀνθρώπους/ἄνδρας τρέχοντας.
2. Don't you see that the master has some gear?
   (Does the master escape your notice having some gear?)
   ἆρα λανθάνει σε ὁ δοῦλος τὸν ἱκέτην ἀφέλκων;
   (Does the slave escape your notice dragging away the suppliant?)
3. For the ambassadors anticipate the public slaves (by) running away.
   ὁ γὰρ Λακεδαιμόνιος φθάνει τοὺς διώκοντας τρέχων εἰς τὸ ἱερόν.
   (The Lacedaemonian anticipates the pursuers running into the shrine.)
4. The herald does not stop hating the strangers and being afraid.
   ὁ ξένος οὐ παύεται ἡμᾶς ἐπικαλούμενος καὶ βοῶν.
5. But you are clearly a suppliant and you happen to be lamenting the situation.
   ὁ δ' ἀνὴρ δῆλός ἐστι πρεσβευτὴς ὢν καὶ ἀποφεύγων τυγχάνει.

E – TEST EXERCISE 4C–D

A stranger happens to be running into the shrine of Heracles. The stranger is clearly suffering something dreadful, because some men are approaching quickly, pursuing him. The stranger eludes his pursuers [by] running into the shrine which is nearby. The pursuers arrive and ask the rhapsode where the stranger happens to be. For the rhapsode is clearly aware that the stranger is running away. (Lit. For it is clear that the stranger does not escape the rhapsode's notice running away.) When the pursuers see him in the shrine, they drag him away, although he is shouting and calling upon the gods. The stranger does not stop lamenting and revealing what he is suffering, but the rhapsode and Dikaiopolis keep quiet, as they are afraid of the Eleven.

So in this way lawlessness and impiety occur in the city of the Athenians.

EXERCISE

1. (a) m. s. nom.   (b) m. pl. nom.   (c) n. s./acc.   (d) m. pl. nom.
2. (a) 3rd pl.   (b) 3rd pl.   (c) 3rd s.   (d) 3rd pl.

Section Five: 'Socrates corrupts the young'

This is a vital section, in which you will meet new tenses of the verb; so far the narrative has been confined to the present tense alone.

In 5A–B the imperfect tense is introduced; and in 5C–D the future.

If you are not happy with the term imperfect, it may be helpful to look at the explanation in *GE* p. 93, #103.

Note: In Section 6 you will met another past tense called the aorist. The meaning of 'imperfect' in this context is 'incomplete', 'unfinished', while 'aorist' means 'undefined'. For example:

'I was going' indicates an event that was taking place and not necessarily completed (consider its likely context: 'I was going to the shop when …', where the 'when' clause is likely to explain why I never reached the shop).

'I went', by contrast, indicates a definitely completed action – but at an undefined time (yesterday / last week / ten years ago etc.).

Greek also has a perfect tense: this expresses a completed action in present time, 'I have just come in', 'I have shut the door'. It is much less common than the aorist, and it is not introduced until Section 13E.

Before beginning 5A you may find it helpful to write out the present tense (active and middle) of παύω, and another table for εἰμί, leaving room to the right of the table to enter imperfect endings as they occur. Or see *GE* p. 92, #102, and *GE* p. 98, #110.

A checklist of the active forms appears at the end of the notes to 5A, and a list of the middle forms and εἰμί at the end of 5B.

5A

Page 54

2 χρήματα   Illustrated at bottom of page 53.
  ὀφείλει   The root cause of Strepsiades' problem (see English note at top of page).
3 ἱππομανής   Break it up into its constituent parts: ἵππος (illustrated p. 53) + μανης (cf. English 'mania').
4 ὕπνος   Cf. English 'hypnosis' (and again note English at top of page).
6 τὸ χρῆμα τῶν νυκτῶν   Literally 'the business of the nights' – *GE* glosses χρῆμα here as 'length'.

12 δάκνει   Here = 'worry', though note its literal meaning is 'bite', which is used later in this section.

13 τουτονί   Adding the -ι to τοῦτον makes it even more demonstrative, 'this son of mine *here*'.

16 χθές   'yesterday', which indicates that ἦ is the past tense of εἰμί.

17 ἐκάθευδον   First example of the normal imperfect. Past tenses in Greek have ἐ- as a prefix. This is called the 'augment'. καθεύδων (9) and καθεύδει (9) indicate that 1st person singular of the present indicative must be καθεύδω. Note that the person is indicated by ἐγώ. Using these indicators, what would you deduce to be the 1st person singular of the imperfect of παύω?
ὅλην τὴν νύκτα   The accusative case without a preposition is used to express duration of time, 'for the whole night'. Similarly ὀλίγον χρόνον means 'for a short time'.

18 ἐδίωκον   Which person (οἱ χρῆσται is the subject)? You can confirm the formation by comparing ἐλάμβανον. Note that in the imperfect, the 1st person s. and the 3rd person pl. have the same ending.

20–21 ἔσῳζεν, ἐλάμβανεν   Identify the person of the verb by looking at the respective subjects (οὐδείς, ὁ υἱός) and use the endings to form the corresponding person of παύω.

23 ἦν   Past tense of εἰμί – person?

24 ἐλάμβανε   Compare ἐλάμβανεν (21). Can you explain the variation?
δι-ελέγετο   First example of a middle imperfect – which person? Note that when the verb has a preposition as a prefix the augment is attached to the verb stem and not to the preposition. See *GE* p. 95, #105.

25 ἤκουε   This is what happens when the augment merges with a vowel, ε + α = η. See *GE* p. 94, #105.

28 ἐπαυόμεθα   Which person? Notice that the subject is delayed and the verb comes first for emphasis: 'we never ceased...', and then you have to wait until the end of the sentence to find out what we never ceased doing.

30 γάμους   English 'monogamy', 'polygamy', etc. should help with the meaning.
πικρούς   'bitter'. Cf. 'picric acid'. Note that πικρόν is brought forward to emphasise it.

31–34 Note the contrast between rustic simplicity and urban extravagance – Aristophanes makes much more of this than the text here does.

Interim check: the imperfect so far. If you followed the suggestion above, your present + imperfect table (active only) could look like this. Note that the augment and the ending have been spaced so that you can see the stem clearly:

1st s.	παύω	ἔ -παυ -ον
2nd s.	παύεις	
3rd s.	παύει	ἔ -παυ -ε(ν)

1st pl.	παύομεν	
2nd pl.	παύετε	
3rd pl.	παύουσι (v)	ἔ -παυ -ον

Translation for 5A

Strepsiades happens to be lamenting because he owes a lot of money. For his son, being horse-mad, always takes much money. Now the son happens to be sleeping deeply, but the father cannot sleep (lit. *sleep does not hold the father*).

STREPSIADES   Alas, alas! O king Zeus! The length of the nights – how great it is! Day is not yet coming. See! My son is sleeping deeply and does not cease sleeping. Alas unhappy me! Deep sleep does not yet come to *(lit.* hold) me. I am unfortunate and sleepless. While I am sleepless, my debts which are heavy worry me. For I owe much money because of this son of mine, and because I owe [much money] my creditors pursue me and are always exacting their due.

But I am still sleepless and at a loss. And yesterday I was sleepless, for almost the whole night. For I was sleeping for a short while. But when I was sleeping, then my creditors kept on pursuing me in my dreams and kept on exacting their due because of my son. And while I was at a loss, nobody was saving me, but for the whole night I was always escaping from these lawsuits, and this son of mine kept on taking lots of money because he was horse-mad. And moreover even when sleeping the young man dreams of horses. Yes, certainly, even when a boy he kept dreaming of horses. Alas! Who was responsible? My wife [was] responsible, I know that well. For she always used to take her son and talk to him about horses. So her son always listened and learnt about horses.

But you, just as you are, sleep deeply! For the debts, as you well know, fall *(lit.* turn) onto my head. Alas! We never stopped arguing about the boy, my wife and I: we were always arguing. O king Zeus! Why do you make marriages so bitter? For always my wife makes my life bitter. How sweet was the country life! Marriage – how bitter! For my wife happens to be from the city, and being a city-woman she started to bring in much expense. This expense already then was ruining me. It is still ruining me even now.

5B

Page 56

2 ἅπτε λυχνόν   λυχνός is illustrated opposite, which should help with the meaning of this phrase.
4 ἔλαιον   'olive oil', a vital commodity for the Athenians.
5 κλαῖε   Literally 'weep'. Strepsiades intends to hit the slave, blaming him for the lack of oil – he should have filled the lamp.
8 ἀργούς   Compounded from ἀ- (negative prefix) + ἔργον, 'not working' i.e. 'lazy', 'idle'.

9 οὐ πείθονται   The middle of πείθω means 'I obey'.

ἦμεν   The past tense of εἰμί; ἡμεῖς indicates the person.

10 ἦσαν   The past tense of εἰμί – person?

11 τοὺς δεσπότας κακὰ ἐποίουν   ποιῶ here seems to take two objects. In fact, it does, because κακὰ ποιῶ ('I do bad things') was treated as a single idea, 'I harm', taking a direct object.

ἐπείθοντο   Imperfect middle ending. What would be the corresponding formation for παύομαι?

14 ἐμαυτόν and σεαυτόν (line 17) are reflexive pronouns: 'myself', 'yourself'.

By now the tables for παύομαι and εἰμί should look like this:

1st s.	παύομαι		εἰμί	ἦ(ν)
2nd s.	παύει		εἶ	
3rd s.	παύεται	ἐ -παύ -ετο	ἐστί(ν)	ἦν
1st pl.	παυόμεθα	ἐ -παυ -όμεθα	ἐσμέν	ἦμεν
2nd pl.	παύεσθε		ἐστέ	
3rd pl.	παύονται	ἐ -παύ -οντο	εἰσί(ν)	ἦσαν

For other persons, see *GE* p. 92, #102 and p. 98, #110.

Translation for 5B

STREPSIADES   But what do I owe? Slave! Come here! Light the lamp. For I can't see anything now; for it is deep night.

SLAVE   How can I light the lamp, master? Look! There is no oil in the lamp.

STR.   What are you saying? The lamp has no oil? Unhappy me! Come here and weep! How evil is the war! I no longer punish my slaves, although they are idle. For the war stops [me]. Alas for my troubles! For now we give orders, but they do not obey. But when we were young, then the old men always used to punish their slaves. So they were not idle, nor did they treat their masters badly, but were good and always obeyed. For they were afraid of punishment. But why don't I save myself and my son from our debts? Why don't I look for some scheme, and put an end to these debts? Now, Strepsiades, save yourself! Hurray, hurray! I have a plan! Now why don't I stop this young man sleeping?

EXERCISES FOR SECTION 5A–B

THE IMPERFECT

5A–B: 1

1. he/she was stopping   ἐπαύετο
2. I/they were carrying   ἐφερόμην, ἐφέροντο
3. you (s.) were taking   ἐλαμβάνου

4. we were learning   ἐμανθανόμεθα
5. you (pl.) were sacrificing   ἐθύεσθε

AUGMENTS

5A–B: 2

1. we hear   ἠκούομεν
2. they have   εἶχον
3. you (pl.) lament   ὠλοφύρεσθε
4. he owes   ὤφειλε
5. they pray   ηὔχοντο

5A–B: 3

1. he came down   καταβαίνει
2. you (s.) killed   ἀποκτείνεις
3. I/they drove away   ἀπάγω, ἀπάγουσιν
4. we were destroying   διαφθείρομεν
5. you (pl.) were bringing in   εἰσφέρετε

IMPERFECT OF CONTRACT VERBS AND VERB 'TO BE'

5A–B: 4

1. he was stopping
2. we were honouring
3. I was doing, they were doing
4. you (s.) were showing
5. you (s.) are punishing
6. he found out, learned
7. I was, he/she/it was
8. I was freeing, they were freeing
9. you (s.) were owing
10. he hears
11. we were remaining
12. he was doing

5A–B: 5

1. ἐτίμων
2. ἔπασχε(ν)
3. ὠφείλομεν
4. ἐκώλυον
5. ἐκελεύετε

ADDITIONAL IMPERFECT PATTERNS

5A–B: 6

1. he was ceasing
2. you were obeying
3. they were conversing
4. we are afraid
5. they were
6. they were showing
7. he was afraid
8. they are fighting
9. I was calling to witness
10. we were turning
11. you (s.) were seeming
12. he was lamenting

5A–B: 7

1. ἐπείθοντο
2. ἐφοβεῖτο
3. ἐμαχόμεθα

4. ἐφαινόμην
5. διελέγεσθε

5A–B: 8

1. ἐκώλυε
2. ἐπαύετο
3. ἐπεκαλούμεθα
4. ὤφειλες
5. ἤκουον

6. ἐβοᾶτε
7. ἐδουλοῦντο
8. ἐτίμων
9. ἐποιεῖτο
10. διελέγοντο

REVISION EXERCISES FOR SECTION 5A–B

B/C – WORD SHAPE AND SYNTAX

1. a. I am sleeping, but these men are still pursuing me.
   ἐκάθευδον ... ἐδίωκον.
   b. Who is responsible? My wife. For she always takes her son and talks to him about horses.
   ἦν ... ἐλάμβανε ... διελέγετο.
   c. How bitter is marriage! For my wife always makes our marriage bitter.
   ἦν ... ἐποίει.
   d. We are young and punish the house-slaves. For in this way the house-slaves become good.
   ἦμεν ... ἐκολάζομεν ... ἐγίγνοντο.
   e. The slaves do not fear their masters nor do they obey them.
   ἐφοβοῦντο ... ἐπείθοντο.

2. we were conversing   διελεγόμην
   we were watching   ἐθεώμην
   they were bringing in   εἰσέφερεν
   you (s.) owed   ὠφείλετε
   we were in   ἐνῆ
   you (pl.) were watching   ἐθεῶ
   you (s.) used to obey   ἐπείθεσθε
   they were afraid   ἐφοβεῖτο
   I was calling upon   ἐπεκαλούμεθα
   I was stopping   ἐπαύομεν
   he/she was   ἦσαν
   you were afraid   ἐφοβεῖσθε
   he/she was watching   ἐθεῶντο

D – ENGLISH INTO GREEK

1. The young man was shouting, but the sailor did not stop chasing.
   βαθέως ἐκάθευδον ἀλλ' ὁ υἱὸς οὐκ ἐπαύετο βοῶν.
2. The farmers always used to honour the gods.
   ὁ πατὴρ ἀεὶ ἐκόλαζε τὸν υἱόν.
3. The sons owed much money.
   οἱ νεανίαι χρηστοὶ (ἀγαθοὶ) ἦσαν καὶ ἐπείθοντο.
4. We used to pray to the goddess, but we did not make sacrifices.
   ἡμεῖς μὲν ἐκελεύομεν, οἱ δὲ δοῦλοι (οἰκέται) ἡμᾶς κακὰ ἐποίουν.
5. You (s.) stopped the woman punishing the household slaves.
   ἐβοῶμεν καὶ τοὺς δούλους (οἰκέτας) ἐπαύομεν διαλεγομένους.

5C

In this section you will meet the future tense. In almost all verbs the distinguishing mark is a '-σ-', although when this is merged with a consonant stem it is not always apparent. See *GE* pp. 102–103, #112–114.

Page 58

1 Φειδιππίδιον Note the diminutive form – affectionate?
5 αὔριον 'tomorrow'; this should alert you to what tense is coming next!
  φιλήσεις The first example of the future – note ending -σ-εις.
6 φιλήσω ... παύσομαι 1st person singular of active and middle respectively.
  Note the -σ- inserted between present stem and person-ending. (With φιλήσω,
  φιλήσεις there is an additional point to note: contracted verbs lengthen the
  vowel at the end of the stem before adding the same endings as uncontracted
  verbs; see *GE* pp. 103–104, #115–116
6 τουτονί τὸν ἵππιον Pheidippides swears by Poseidon, god of horses (as well
  as god of the sea). The point will be further developed later.
9 πείθου This is the middle imperative, 'obey!'
10 πείσομαι Also future. Note that verb-stems ending in dentals -τ/-δ/-θ/-ζ lose
  the final consonant of the stem before adding -σ- and regular endings.
12 πείσῃ 2nd s. future middle of πείθω, 'Will you obey?'
13 Obediently, Pheidippides changes his oath to swear by Dionysus.
17 ἀκούσομαι Some verbs change from present active to future middle with no
  change in meaning.
20 λέξω Verbs with stems ending in -γ/-κ/-χ combine the final consonant of the
  stem with the -ς- to form -ξ-. See *GE* p. 103, #114.
22 σώσει See note above on p. 58 line 10.

Translation for 5C

STREPSIADES Pheidippides, Pheidippidikins!
PHEIDIPPIDES What, father?

STR.	Tell me, son, do you love me?
PHEI.	I [do], and I don't ever stop [loving you].
STR.	Will you love me tomorrow?
PHEI.	By Poseidon here, god of horses, I shall love you tomorrow and I shan't stop ever.
STR.	Don't ever mention that horsey one, son – for that one has the responsibility for my troubles – but listen and obey.
PHEI.	Look, I am listening and obeying and I shall always obey. So speak then! What are you ordering?
STR.	I shall order a small thing, my son, a very small thing. For I have a plan and I am planning something. Will you obey?
PHEI.	I will obey, by Dionysus. Don't worry, father.
STR.	Were you listening? Or weren't you listening? Or am I speaking in vain? I'll stop you sleeping.
PHEI.	Yes. I was listening and I am listening and I shall listen. What were you telling me?
STR.	I was telling you that I have an idea.
PHEI.	What is your idea? What have you in mind and what are you planning? Were you saying?
STR.	No, but I will [tell you]. For perhaps this idea will stop us somehow from our debts. I'm planning something big.
PHEI.	Tell [me]. What is your plan, father? What will you order? How will your idea save us? How shall we stop from our debts?
STR.	You will do it?
PHEI.	I will do it, by Dionysus.

5D

Page 60

1 οἰκίδιον   The diminutive form of οἶκος/οἰκία.

3 φροντιστήριον   An Aristophanic coinage, constructed from φροντίζω 'I think', 'I consider' with the suffix -ηριον, which corresponds to English '-ery' suffix in e.g. 'bakery', 'brewery' – the place where something is done. Hence φροντιστήριον means 'thinkery'.

5 πνιγεύς   Ilustrated on next page – these are bowl-shaped, earthenware ovens.

   ἄνθρακες   English 'anthracite' may help towards meaning: 'coals'.

6–7 Notice the implication that Socrates and his associates are well paid for their teaching – something which Socrates always vigorously denied.

9 μαθήσονται   The future of μανθάνω (μαθ-). Some irregular verbs use the stem given in brackets to form the future. See *GE* p. 105, #120 for a list of 'important futures'.

13 λόγον   Always a difficult word to translate. Here perhaps 'argument' fits the meaning most closely. Socrates is depicted as having two 'arguments' in his

'thinkery' (in the original play these 'arguments' actually appear as characters): the 'right' argument, which argues correctly, and the 'wrong' argument, which, by verbal trickery etc., can make the weaker argument appear the stronger. Hence Strepsiades' interest in the latter argument.

16 σοφισταί   Originally a neutral term for philosophers, but later acquiring pejorative overtones – hence the disgusted reaction from Pheidippides.

18 ὠχρούς ... ἀνυποδήτους   Ochres are pale yellowish shades, which gives the meaning of ὠχρούς. To be pale was a sign of spending too much time indoors, and was hence a derogatory description for a man. ἀν-(negative) ὑπο- ('under') -δητους ('bound'): 'unbound-under' meant 'shoeless'; here it is also derogatory, as a sign of poverty. In addition, Socates went unshod.

23 οἱ ἔνδον   'those inside'.

24 σὺ δὲ διὰ τί οὐκ εἰσέρχῃ μαθητής;   'But you, why don't you go in (as) a student?'

27 διαφθερεῖ   One of only two examples in this section of a grammatical point that is easily overlooked (see *GE* p. 104, #117). Verbs with a present stem ending in -λ-, -μ-, -ν- or -ρ- do not insert -σ- to form future, but have a contracted future in -έω.

28 λήψονται   The future of λαμβάνω (λαβ-), is again based on the bracketed stem but with the vowel lengthened.

29 ἄριστε ἀνθρώπων   Strepsiades reverts to his wheedling.

32 εἴσειμι   The irregular future of εἰσέρχομαι. This is doubly confusing because εἶμι ('I shall go') is identical in spelling with εἰμί ('I am'). However, the accent distinguishes the two when not prefixed.

34 οὔκουν πείσῃ;   'Won't you obey?'

35 γενήσομαι   The future of γίγνομαι (γεν-), again based on the bracketed stem. See *GE* p.104, #117.

36–38 εἴσει, εἴσεισι, εἴσιμεν   The future of εἰσέρχομαι again (cf. note on line 32).

Page 62

41 ἐκβαλῶ   βάλλω has shortened the present stem to βαλ- and added -έω to form future (see *GE* p. 104, #117).

50 γνώσομαι   The future of γιγνώσκω (γνω-), based on the bracketed stem. See *GE* p. 105, #120.

57 κόψω   Notice how the -σ- in the future can combine with a labial consonant stem (κοπ-) to produce -ψ-. See *GE* p. 103, #114.

Translation for 5D

STREPSIADES   Look over here. Do you see this door and the house?

PHEIDIPPIDES   I see it. What is it, Father?

STR.   This is the thinkery of wise souls. Inside live wise men, and speaking they persuade their pupils that the heaven is a bell-oven and this bell-oven is around us and we are the coals. These men persuade their pupils, always teaching and receiving a lot of money. And by Zeus no one of them will stop receiving much money from their pupils.

PHEI. But what do the men teach? What will young men learn, becoming [their] pupils?

STR. The pupils will learn arguments.

PHEI. Which arguments do you mean, Father?

STR. Which? I mean the just and unjust argument.

PHEI. The students will learn these arguments?

STR. [Yes], by Zeus. And what's more in lawsuits they will always defeat their opponents.

PHEI. Who are these men? What is the name of the men?

STR. I do not know the name. But they are fine, noble sophists.

PHEI. Yuck! Awful [people], I know. You mean the pale shoeless [people], wretched Socrates and Chaerephon.

STR. Hey, hey, be quiet! Will you not listen?

PHEI. I will listen. What will you tell me?

STR. But as I was saying, those inside have two arguments, the just and the unjust. Why do you not go in as a student? For this way we shall stop ourselves from our debts.

PHEI. What will I learn?

STR. The unjust argument. For the unjust argument will put a stop to our debts, the just one won't. So learn: in this way the creditors will not recover any of these debts. Why don't you go into the thinkery, best of men?

PHEI. What are you saying? I, [go] into the thinkery? By Poseidon, god of horses, I won't do this. I'm not going in today, I won't go in tomorrow and I won't do so in any way. For I love horses, not sophists.

STR. Won't you obey and do this?

PHEI. I won't obey and I won't do this. I shall become pale, being a student.

STR. But if you won't go in, who will go in? Shall we go in together, you and I?

PHEI. I won't.

STR. Then I'll chase you out of the house and send you to hell!

PHEI. I'll run away. I'll go into the house, but not into the thinkery of the sophists.

STR. What shall I do? Pheidippides will not win, but I shall become the winner. I know: I myself will go into the thinkery and will become a pupil of the sophists and I will learn the unjust argument. In this way I shall stop those creditors taking their money. But how shall I, an old man and slow in exact arguments, learn philosophy? All the same I'll go in. Why don't I knock at this door and shout? I'll do this and I'll knock at the door and shout.

Grammar

Do not neglect the very useful table of indefinites and interrogatives in *GE* p. 109, #125. And learn to decline Σωκράτης in *GE* p. 110, #127a.

At this point you may find it useful to revise the different formations of the future tense, before you go on (*GE* pp. 102–103, #112–114). You may find it helpful to make a chart like this, leaving the third column free to add the first person of the aorist tense as you learn it in the next section.

	Present	*Future*	*Aorist*
Vowel stems	παύω	παύσω	
Consonant stems			
κ, γ, χ	εὔχομαι	εὔξομαι	
π, β, φ	κόπτω	κόψω	
τ, δ, θ	πείθω	πείσω	
most ζ	θαυμάζω	θαυμάσω	
μ, ν, λ, ρ	διαφθείρω	διαφθερῶ (έω)	
most –ιζω	νομίζω	νομιῶ (έω)	
Contracted verbs	ποιέω	ποιήσω	
	τιμάω	τιμήσω	
	δηλόω	δηλώσω	

The future of contracted verbs has ordinary, not contracted, endings: -ω, -εις, -ει … , but the stem vowel is lengthened.

Irregular verbs	μανθάνω	μαθήσομαι
	λαμβάνω	λήψομαι
	γιγνώσκω	γνώσομαι
	γίγνομαι	γενήσομαι

EXERCISES FOR SECTION 5C–D

THE FUTURE TENSE

5C–D: 1

1. they will hinder — κωλύουσι
2. he will order — κελεύει
3. we shall travel — πορευόμεθα
4. you (s.) will cease — παύῃ
5. you (s.) will prevent — κωλύεις

CONSONANT STEMS

5C–D: 2

1. they pray — εὔξονται
2. he hits — τύψει
3. you (s.) keep quiet — ἡσυχάσεις
4. we turn — τρεψόμεθα
5. you (s.) persuade — πείσεις

CONTRACT VERBS

5C–D: 3

1. we shall defeat   νικῶμεν
2. he will love   φιλεῖ
3. I shall hold power over   κρατῶ (έω)
4. you (pl.) will seek   ζητεῖτε
5. they will set free   ἐλευθεροῦσιν

ADDITIONAL FUTURE PATTERNS

5C–D: 4

1. he will stop, you (s.) will cease
2. they will obey, they will suffer
3. they will persuade
4. you (s.) are knocking
5. we shall pray
6. you (s.) were ordering
7. you (pl.) will do
8. they will destroy
9. we prevent
10. he will converse
11. he will consider
12. I shall show

5C–D: 5

1. κελεύσουσι(ν)
2. πείσει
3. πείσεται
4. τιμήσω
5. ποιήσετε

IRREGULAR FUTURES

5C–D: 6

1. he will take
2. they will become
3. we shall be
4. you (pl.) will learn
5. they will find out
6. he/she/it will be
7. they will go
8. they will be
9. I shall go
10. you (s.) will know
11. he will become, it will happen
12. he/she will go

5C–D: 7

1. ἴασι(ν)
2. ἔσται
3. γνωσόμεθα
4. γενήσῃ
5. εἶσι(ν)
6. λήψονται
7. μαθήσομαι
8. ἔσεσθε
9. ἴμεν
10. ἔσεσθε

5C–D: 8

1. πρὸς τὰς τριήρεις οὔσας, ἰούσας.
2. τῶν μητέρων οὐσῶν, ἰουσῶν.

3. ἀπὸ τοῦ Περικλέους ὄντος, ἰόντος.
4. τὸν Σωκράτη ὄντα, ἰόντα.
5. οἱ πατέρες ὄντες, ἰόντες.
6. ταῖς θυγατράσιν οὔσαις, ἰούσαις

REVISION EXERCISES FOR SECTION 5C–D

A – VOCABULARY-BUILDING

1.

responsible/cause	I blame			
I teach	the teacher	teaching, instruction	to do with teaching	
justice/ right	just	the contestant in a lawsuit	unjust	
	I do wrong	the juror	I judge	
unfortunate	I am unfortunate			
I learn	the pupil	ignorant	to do with learning	
mind/sense	I consider	an idea	I think	I understand
a household slave	a little house	the house	I live in	
	the household or house	belonging to the house or family		
wise	wisdom	a sophist	philosophy	I love

B/C – WORD SHAPE AND SYNTAX

1. a. The father orders his son. κελεύσει
   b. What are you saying, sir? λέξεις
   c. We do not teach the teachers. διδάξομεν
   d. The men receive much money. δέξονται
   e. We do not hear the words. ἀκουσόμεθα
   f. I am wise, this (man) does not defeat me. ἔσομαι … νικήσει
   g. The son does not love his father. φιλήσει
   h. The idea saves us. σώσει
   i. I knock at the door and shout. κόψω … βοήσομαι
   j. Who wins the lawsuits? νικήσει
   k. The pupils do not stop learning. παύσονται
   l. Who are the wise men? ἔσονται

D – ENGLISH INTO GREEK

1. The sophists will teach you tomorrow.
   οἱ νεανίαι τήμερον μαθήσονται τὸν ἄδικον λόγον.
2. I shall never hate the gods.
   ὁ ἀγαθὸς υἱὸς ἀεὶ φιλήσει τὸν πατέρα.

3. The sailors will not stop looking for the captain.
    οὗτος ὁ ἵππος οὐ παύσεται τρέχων.
4. The master will punish the slave.
    ὁ μαθητὴς εἴσεισιν εἰς τὸν οἶκον/τὴν οἰκίαν.
5. The women will listen to the words.
    οἱ σοφοὶ ἔσονται δίκαιοι.

E – TEST EXERCISE 5

DIKAIOPOLIS   Slave, slave, come here.

SLAVE   Who is this? Who won't stop calling me?
         You there! Who was shouting?

DIK.   Who? I was shouting, boy. But tell me: is Euripides in?

SLAVE   He is not in and he is in, if you get the idea.

DIK.   How do you mean, boy? How can a man be in and not in? It is clear that you are talking nonsense.

SLAVE   I was speaking correctly/ the truth. His mind is collecting words and is not in, but the man is in, writing a tragedy.

DIK.   O thrice blessed Euripides, in having such a clever slave. How beautifully he speaks! But now, stop teasing me, and call him, boy.

SLAVE   But it is impossible.

DIK.   Why is it impossible? Call Euripides.
        I won't go away. No, by Zeus, but I will knock on the door and call Euripides again.
        Euripides, dear Euripides. Don't you hear? It's me, Dikaiopolis calling you, from the deme of Cholleidae.

EXERCISE

1. (a) imperfect   (b) imperfect   (c) future   (d) present
2. (a) m., s., nom.   (b) m., s., nom.   (c) m., s., acc.   (d) n., s. nom.

Section Six

In this section the aorist tense is introduced (if you are uncertain of terminology, please refer back to the note at the beginning of Section 5). You may want to look at *GE* pp. 115–118, #128–138. You will find that in most cases the aorist adds a sigma before the ending, just like the future; but, as it is a past tense, it will also have an augment, like the imperfect.

6A

Page 63

3 ἔκοψε, ἐβόησεν   The first examples of the aorist. Note (a) the augment ἐ- (as for imperfect); (b) -σε in the ending; note also that π + ς = ψ. The contracted verb lengthens the stem vowel before adding the ending, just as in the future.

5 ἔκοψα, ἐβόησα   1st person singular (as ἐγώ indicates). Note ἐ- (augment), -σα (person-ending).

6 τίς ὢν σὺ τοῦτο ἐποίησας   Literally 'You being who did this?' or 'Who are you that you did this?' (2nd singular aorist indicated by σύ). Again, ἐ- (augment), -σας (person-ending), and the lengthening of the stem vowel.

10 ποιήσω, κόψω   What tense?

12 τίς ὁ κόπτων;   'Who is the one knocking?' Note the use of the participle.
ἐπαύσατο   The first example of the middle aorist. Note ἐ- (augment), -σατο (person-ending).

Page 64

17 ἐπαυσάμην   Which person do you think this is? Cf. ἐπαυόμην.
ὦ 'γαθέ = ὦ ἀγαθέ.

19 μόνοι   'alone'. Cf. 'monopoly', 'monarchy', 'monoplane' etc.

22 ψύλλα ... ὀφρύν   There is no point in trying to guess here! ψύλλα is 'a flea'; δάκνει has occurred at the beginning of the section 5A (p. 54, line 12), and is here used in its basic sense of 'bite'; and ὀφρύς is 'an eyebrow'. To explain the humour of the situation, the scholiast (ancient commentator) informs us that Chaerephon had shaggy eyebrows and that Socrates was bald.

25–26 ὁπόσους ... πόδας   'how many of its own feet', i.e. how many 'flea-feet'?

30–31 πρῶτον μὲν ... εἶτα ... τέλος δέ ...   Three stages of the experiment.

35 ἐμβάδας   Illustrated below, though in the experiment something slightly less monstrous is envisaged: 'slippers', perhaps.

40 ἐποίησαν   Resumption of aorist endings. ἐ- (augment) and -σαν (person-ending).

42 ὡς ἔλεγον   'as I was saying'. Notice the difference between the imperfect tense and the aorists which follow, 'they made the wax warm etc.'

Page 65

46–47 If the apparent lack of connection here is confusing, it is designed to convey the ignorance of Strepsiades. 'Knowing the flea's leap' = 'being educated', and if he's educated, then he's sure to win his lawsuits.

Translation for 6A

Strepsiades knocks at the door and shouts

STREPSIADES   Boy! Young boy!

STUDENT   Go to hell. Who knocked at the door? Who shouted?

STR.   I knocked at the door and I shouted.

STU.   Who are you that you did that? Some ignoramus, I know well.

STR.   Strepsiades, from the deme Kikynna.

STU.   Go to hell, again.

STR.   Alas! What shall I do? Well, I'll knock again.
(He knocks at the door again.)

STU.   Who's that knocking? Why did this fellow not stop knocking, when I told him to? Why are you knocking again? What do you have in mind? You've knocked away my thought [by] doing that.

STR.   But I've just stopped, my dear fellow. For you told me to. Don't throw me out, although I'm a rustic and ignorant. But what was your thought? Tell me.

STU.   It isn't right. Only the students learn these thoughts of the sophists.

STR.   Tell me then. For I have come to the thinkery as a student of the sophists.

STU.   I will tell you. A flea bites Chaerephon's eyebrow. When it jumps onto Socrates' head, the men converse as follows.

SOCRATES   Look, Chaerephon. The flea does not escape my notice being worthy of an Olympic crown. But tell [me], how many of its own feet did the flea leap?

CHAEREPHON   I do not know, Socrates. But why don't we measure the distance?

SOC.   How shall we measure it, Chaerephon?

CHA.   Look. First I take some wax, then I make the wax warm. Finally I put the flea's feet into the wax.

SOC.   What then?

CHA.   Now the wax is becoming cold. Look, Socrates: for the flea has slippers.

SOC.   But what are you doing now?

CHA.   Now I am loosing the slippers. Look!

STR.   O king Zeus! Oh the wisdom of the men! But tell me, whatever did the men do, student?

STU.   You don't escape my notice being a rustic, Strepsiades, not knowing anything. But as I was saying, first they made the wax warm. Then they put the flea's feet into the wax. Finally they loosed the slippers and measured – of course – the distance.

STR.   O king Zeus! The men appear to be wise. Why then do we marvel at that [famous] Thales? Indeed I shall easily escape justice. For I shall know the flea's leap. Open, open the door!

6B

Page 66

1 θηρία   *GE* gives 'beasts' – perhaps 'monsters' conveys the sense better.

4 οἱ ... βλέποντες   As before: article + participles = relative clause.

5 τὰ κατὰ γῆς   As before: a very common idiom, using neuter plural of article + adjective/adjectival phrase. Literally 'the things beneath the earth'. Here something like 'subterranean phenomena' might convey the meaning.

6 Strepsiades, of course, takes the words at face value: 'They must be looking for truffles.'

7 πρωκτός   If the students are bent double, what is pointing towards the heavens?

12 ἀστρονομία   Possibly in the original production represented by some elaborate instrument. Likewise γεωμετρία (14).

15 The explanation of the original meaning of 'geometry', from γῆ 'land' and μετρέω 'measure'.

19 περίοδος   Both elements are known, ὁδός 'journey', περί 'round', hence the meaning 'map'.

23 A stock joke in comedy was that Athens was litigation mad. Hence, to Strepsiades' over-literal mind, a map couldn't represent Athens without depicting a lawcourt and jurors.

30–31 Another over-literal interpretation: on the map Sparta looks too close, so Strepsiades suggests moving it further away.

35 κρεμάθρας   See stage directions (line 34).

36 αὐτός   'Himself', 'The Master'.

Translation for 6B

STREPSIADES   Heracles! What are these monsters?

STUDENT   Hey you! Why are you amazed? Why did you yell again? Are you amazed at these students?

STR.   Yes, by Zeus, I am amazed. But what are these ones doing, who are looking into the ground?

STU.   These are investigating subterranean phenomena.

STR.   Then they are looking for truffles. Don't worry about it any more, monsters: I know where there are some lovely big ones. But who's this? Why is his bottom looking towards the sky?

STU.   Because his bottom is studying astronomy.

STR.   Look! What's this? Tell me!

STU.   This is astronomy.

STR.   And what's this?

STU.   Geometry.

STR.   And what use is this? Tell [me]!

STU.   With this we measure the land. This is a map of the world.
            Do you see? This is Athens.

STR.   What are you saying? I don't believe [you]: I don't see any one of the jurors
            sitting. Where is my deme?

STU.   It's here. Do you see Euboea?

STR.   I see [it]. But where does Sparta happen to be?

STU.   Where? Here.

STR.   Alas! Go away, go away! How near us Sparta is. But why don't you drag this
            away from us a very long way?

STU.   Impossible.

STR.   By Zeus, you'll regret it. But tell me, who's this who is in the basket?

STU.   Himself.

STR.   Who's Himself?

STU.   Socrates.

Grammar

At this point your chart should look like this:

	Present	*Future*	*Aorist*
Vowel stems	παύω	παύσω	ἔπαυσα
Consonant stems			
κ, γ, χ	εὔχομαι	εὔξομαι	ηὐξάμην
π, β, φ	κόπτω	κόψω	ἔκοψα
τ, δ, θ	πείθω	πείσω	ἔπεισα
most ζ	θαυμάζω	θαυμάσω	ἐθαύμασα
μ, ν, λ, ρ	διαφθείρω	διαφθερῶ (έω)	διέφθειρα
most -ιζω	νομίζω	νομιῶ (έω)	ἐνόμισα
Contracted verbs	ποιέω	ποιήσω	ἐποίησα
	δηλόω	δηλώσω	ἐδήλωσα
	τιμάω	τιμήσω	ἐτίμησα

Note once again that the aorist of contracted verbs has 'ordinary' endings -α, -ας,
-ε ... You will meet the aorists of the irregular verbs in the next section.

EXERCISES FOR SECTION 6A–B

THE AORIST

6A–B: 1

1. ἔθυσε(ν)   he sacrificed   ἔθυσαν   they sacrificed
2. ἐκέλευσε(ν)   he ordered   ἐκέλευσαν   they ordered

3. ἐκώλυσε(ν)   he hindered   ἐκώλυσαν   they hindered
4. ἔλυσε(ν)   he set free   ἔλυσαν   they set free

6A–B: 2

1. you (pl.) pray   ηὔξασθε
2. they hit   ἔτυψαν
3. he keeps quiet   ἡσύχασε(ν)
4. we turn   ἐτρεψάμεθα
5. I persuade   ἔπεισα

6A–B: 3

1. we defeated   νικῶμεν
2. he loved   φιλεῖ
3. I held power over   κρατῶ (έω)
4. you (pl.) sought   ζητεῖτε
5. they set free   ἐλευθεροῦσι(ν)

6A–B: 4

1. ἤκουσε(ν)   he heard   8. ἐδίδαξε(ν)   he taught
   ἤκουσαν   they heard   ἐδίδαξαν   they taught
2. ἀνεχώρησε(ν) he retreated   9. ἐθαύμασε(ν)   he marvelled
   ἀνεχώρησαν   they retreated   ἐθαύμασαν   they marvelled
3. ἠτίμασε(ν)   he dishonoured   10. ἔθυσε(ν)   he sacrificed
   ἠτίμασαν   they dishonoured   ἔθυσαν   they sacrificed
4. ἔβλεψε(ν)   he looked   11. ἐνίκησε(ν)   he defeated
   ἔβλεψαν   they looked   ἐνίκησαν   they won
5. ἐβόησε(ν)   he shouted   12. ἐθεάσατο   he watched
   ἐβόησαν   they shouted   ἐθεάσαντο   they watched
6. ἐδέξατο   he received   13. ἐτρέψατο   he turned
   ἐδέξαντο   they received   ἐτρέψαντο   they turned
7. ἐλύσατο   he ransomed   14. ἔκοψε(ν)   he knocked
   ἐλύσαντο   they set free   ἔκοψαν   they knocked
                                   15. ἐχώρησε(ν)   he went
                                       ἐχώρησαν   they went

6A–B: 5

1. ἠκούσαμεν   6. ἐβοήσατε
2. ἐδέξαντο   7. ἐνόμισε(ν)
3. ἀνεχώρησας   8. ἐδήλωσα
4. ἐδίωξε(ν)   9. ἔμειναν
5. ἐκόλασαν   10. διέφθειραν

REVISION EXERCISES FOR SECTION 6A–B

B/C – WORD SHAPE AND SYNTAX

1. a. Who is knocking at the door? ἔκοψε(ν)
    b. Who is going into the thinkery? ἐχώρησε(ν)
    c. But I knock again and do not stop knocking. ἔκοψα, ἐπαυσάμην
    d. I will tell you. ἔλεξα, εἶπον
    e. Finally we shall release the slipper. ἐλύσαμεν
    f. Why do we admire that Thales? ἐθαυμάσαμεν

2. a. The flea leaps onto Socrates' head. ἐπήδησεν
    b. But how will you measure, Chaerephon? ἐμέτρησας
    c. Finally we measure the distance. ἐμετρήσαμεν
    d. These are seeking things below the ground and do not stop seeking. ἐζήτησαν, ἐπαύσαντο
    e. What does the matter reveal, Socrates? ἐδήλωσε(ν)

3. a. αὐδάω   they spoke   f. ὠθέω   I pushed
    b. ἐλπίζω   you (s.) hoped   g. ἐρωτάω   they asked
    c. ὁμολογέω   you (pl.) agreed   h. οἰκέω   I lived, dwelt
    d. ἡγέομαι   I considered, led   i. ἀσπάζομαι   they greeted
    e. ἄρχομαι   they began   j. ἐκπέμπω   he sent out

4.

present	imperfect	future	aorist
κελεύω	ἐκέλευον	κελεύσω	ἐκέλευσα
κωλύω	ἐκώλυον	κωλύσω	ἐκώλυσα
παύομαι	ἐπαυόμην	παύσομαι	ἐπαυσάμην
βλέπω	ἔβλεπον	βλέψω	ἔβλεψα
κόπτω	ἔκοπτον	κόψω	ἔκοψα
κρύπτω	ἔκρυπτον	κρύψω	ἔκρυψα
δέχομαι	ἐδεχόμην	δέξομαι	ἐδεξάμην
διώκω	ἐδίωκον	διώξω	ἐδίωξα
πράττω	ἔπραττον	πράξω	ἔπραξα
ἀτιμάζω	ἠτίμαζον	ἀτιμάσω	ἠτίμασα
κολάζω	ἐκόλαζον	κολάσω	ἐκόλασα
σπεύδω	ἔσπευδον	σπεύσω	ἔσπευσα
διαφθείρω	διέφθειρον	διαφθερέω	διέφθειρα
μένω	ἔμενον	μενέω	ἔμεινα
ἀπορέω	ἠπόρουν	ἀπορήσω	ἠπόρησα
δηλόω	ἐδήλουν	δηλώσω	ἐδήλωσα
μισέω	ἐμίσουν	μισήσω	ἐμίσησα
νικάω	ἐνίκων	νικήσω	ἐνίκησα

D – ENGLISH INTO GREEK

1. The woman looked for her son.

   ὁ γεωργὸς ἐβόησε καὶ ἔκοψε τὴν θύραν.

2. Don't they know that you did this job easily?

   ἆρ' οὐκ ἴσασιν ὅτι σὺ/ὑμεῖς ἡδέως ταύτην τὴν γνώμην
   ἐδέξω/ἐδέξασθε;

3. The suppliant did not respect/honour the goddess.

   ὁ σοφιστὴς οὐκ ἔπεισε τοὺς σοφοὺς νεανίας.

4. Even though they were wicked, the neighbours did not punish the young
   man.

   ὁ δίκαιος, καίπερ σοφὸς ὤν, ἐθαύμασε τὸν ἄδικον λόγον.

5. She stopped looking at the stranger.

   ἐπαύσαντο βλέποντες τοὺς ἵππους.

6C

New in this section is the second aorist; see *GE* pp. 124–126, #144–146. As you
meet them, make a list of these verbs with their principal parts (present, future,
and aorist).

The aorist tense in Greek is formed in one of two ways:

1. First aorist, which has an augment at the beginning of the word and suffix
   at the end – compare English 'regular' past tenses adding '-d' or '-ed' to
   the present stem (e.g. 'walk', 'walked'). This is the sort you have just
   learned.

2. Second aorist, which still has the augment but it is added to a stem changed
   in some way – compare English 'irregular' past tenses (e.g. 'sleep',
   'slept'). The endings are the same as those for the imperfect, but the
   imperfect uses the present stem, while the aorist has its own stem which is
   always different from the present stem.

Note that, again as in English, most verbs have *either* a first *or* a second aorist:
they are not alternative forms for the same verb.

Page 68

2 ἐλθέ   You have met this already (in fact, three of the most irregular past stems
   have been introduced). ἐλθ- is the second aorist stem of ἔρχομαι.

6 ὦ ἐφήμερε   ἐφήμερος has been met in section 4A (p. 46, line 33) with the
   meaning 'ephemeral', 'short-lived'. Here Socrates uses it for comic effect.
   ἦλθες   2nd singular of the second aorist.

8 εἰπέ   εἰπ- is the second aorist stem of λέγω.
   Notice the word order in πῶς δ' ἤκουσάς με ὡς σοφός εἰμι; Literally,
   'How did you hear me that I am wise?' or 'How did you hear that I was
   wise?'

11–16 The content is repeated from earlier in the chapter, but note the presence of second aorists – ἔδακε (second aorist of δάκνω), ἤρου (second aorist of ἐρωτάω), ἐλάβετε (second aorist of λαμβάνω), ἐγένετο (second aorist of γίγνομαι), and ἔθετε (aorist of τίθημι, a verb which you have not yet learned in detail).

18 εἶδον ἰδ- is the second aorist stem of ὁράω.

19–20 πόθεν ὢν τυγχάνεις 'Where do you happen to come from?'

27 ἐξευρίσκεις εὑρίσκω has perfect tense ηὕρηκα, familiar from Archimedes' cry on discovering the principle of displacement. Second aorist stem εὑρ- is met in the next line.

29–30 ἔμαθον, ἔτυχε Second aorists respectively of μανθάνω, τυγχάνω.

Translation for 6C

The student goes away. Strepsiades calls Socrates.

STREPSIADES   Socrates! Dear little Socrates! Come here!

SOCRATES   Who called? Who forced his way into the thinkery of the sophists?

SRT.   I shouted, Strepsiades from the deme Kikynna. But I didn't force my way into the thinkery.

SOC.   Why call'st thou me, O creature of the day? For what purpose have you come?

STR.   I have come as a student into the thinkery. For I have already heard that you are wise.

SOC.   Tell me, who said that? How did you hear that I was wise?

STR.   One of the students said this.

SOC.   What did the student say? Tell [me].

STR.   The student said that a flea bit Chaerephon's eyebrow. Then it jumped onto your head. You asked Chaerephon how many of its own feet the flea leapt. You measured it thus: first you took the flea and put it into warm wax. When the wax became cold, the flea had Persian slippers. Then you measured the distance. I have never seen anything so wise.

SOC.   You have never seen anything so wise? But where do you actually come from?

STR.   Kikynna.

SOC.   You did not escape my notice being a rustic, and ignorant.

STR.   Don't blame me. But tell me, what are you doing in that basket, Socrates?

SOC.   I am walking on air and contemplating the sun.

STR.   Why are you doing that from a basket and not from the ground? What are you discovering or learning, being in a basket?

SOC.   I never discovered meteoric phenomena nor learnt anything, looking from the ground. For the earth happened to prevent thought.

Grammar

The second part of your verb chart should now look like this:

Irregular verbs	**present**	**future**	**aorist**
	μανθάνω	μαθήσομαι	ἔμαθον
	λαμβάνω	λήψομαι	ἔλαβον
	γίγνομαι	γενήσομαι	ἐγενόμην

and you should also have added:

	ἔρχομαι	εἶμι	ἦλθον
	ὁράω	ὄψομαι	εἶδον
	εὑρίσκω	εὑρήσω	ηὗρον

Remember to add other verbs with second aorists to the list as you meet them.

6D

This section contains mainly further practice in second aorist stems: these have been given in vocabularies so (it is hoped) they should pose few problems.

Page 70

3–5   πάσχεις ... ἔπαθον   The question–answer format may help to link these two.

4   ἔλαθον   Second aorist of λανθάνω, cf. λαμβάνω, ἔλαβον.

6   λήψονται   Irregular future of λαμβάνω.

7   ἕτερον   'one of two'. Cf. line 8 πότερον 'which of two?'

10–12   τί δράσω   'What shall I do?' is answered by ὅ τι; 'What?'

12   κατακλίνηθι   An irregular imperative form. The -κλιν- (Latin *clin-*) stem may guide you towards the meaning 'lie down' ('recline'), and the noun κλίνη is anticipated in the stage directions 'couch'.

20   λήσω   Irregular future of λανθάνω.

28   ἔχεις τι   'Do you have something?' meaning 'Have you an idea/suggestion?', but the literal translation is probably better to lead into the vulgarity which follows.

38   γυναῖκα φαρμακίδα   'a woman sorceress', a 'witch' in the sense of a woman with supernatural powers.

38–43   In ancient Greece the months were lunar, and interest was due at the start of the month when the moon rose. Thus no moon = no month = no interest due. In the original, Socrates is more impressed with Strepsiades' reasoning than the abrupt termination to this chapter would suggest.

Translation for 6D

STREPSIADES   But, Socratikins, why don't you come down? For I have come into the thinkery because, owing much money, I am in debt.

SOCRATES	But how did you become a debtor? How do you suffer this?
STR.	I escaped my own notice having a horse-mad son. So I became a debtor. And I suffered this through horse-fever and my son. For my creditors always exact justice, and unless I do something they will always exact [justice]. So teach me one of your arguments.
SOC.	One of my arguments? Which do you mean? The greater or the lesser?
STR.	I mean the unjust one, the lesser, the one stopping debts. For this argument will win lawsuits, the greater won't. What shall I do?
SOC.	What? First lie down on the couch. Then think out some way out of your affairs.
STR.	Alas for me! The bedbugs will exact their penalty today.
SOC.	You there, what are you doing? Aren't you thinking?
STR.	I? [Yes] by Poseidon.
SOC.	And what did you think?
STR.	Whether I shall escape the bedbugs, which are biting me terribly.
SOC.	You are talking rubbish. But the fellow's silent. What's he doing? *(He addresses Strepsiades.)* You there, are you asleep?
STR.	By Apollo, I am not.
SOC.	Do you have something?
STR.	By Zeus, I haven't.
SOC.	Nothing at all?
STR.	I have my penis in my right hand.
SOC.	To hell with you! Don't joke, fellow.
STR.	Socratikins!
SOC.	What, old man?
STR.	I have an idea.
SOC.	Tell [me] your idea.
STR.	I shall take a witch woman and I shall steal the moon by night.
SOC.	What are you saying? You will steal the moon? Tell [me] – how is this useful?
STR.	How? Listen. The creditors lend money by the month. So I will steal the moon. The moon will no longer rise. How then will the creditors take their money?
SOC.	To hell with you! You are a peasant and ignorant. I will not teach you any longer, since you are ignorant.

EXERCISES FOR SECTION 6C–D

THE SECOND AORIST

6C–D: 1

1.	εἶπε(ν), εἶπον	he, they spoke
2.	ἔλαβε(ν), ἔλαβον	he, they took
3.	ἔμαθε(ν), ἔμαθον	he, they learned
4.	ἦλθε(ν), ἦλθον	he, they went

5. ἐγένετο, ἐγένοντο   he, they became
6. ἔδραμε(ν), ἔδραμον   he, they ran
7. ηὗρε(ν), ηὗρον   he, they found
8. εἶδε(ν), εἶδον   he, they saw
9. ἔτυχε(ν), ἔτυχον   he, they happened to…
10. ἔσχε(ν), ἔσχον   he, they had

6C–D: 2

1. ἐγένοντο   5. ἤλθετε
2. εἴδομεν   6. εἶπες
3. ηὗρες   7. ἔμαθον
4. ἔλαβε(ν)   8. ἔδραμον

REVISION EXERCISES FOR SECTION 6C–D

B/C – WORD SHAPE AND SYNTAX

1. βιασα- ἐβιασάμην
    κλεψα- ἔκλεψα
    θαυμασα- ἐθαύμασα
    διδαξα- ἐδίδαξα
    δεξα- ἐδεξάμην
    φιλησα- ἐφίλησα
    δηλωσα- ἐδήλωσα
2. μαθ- ἔμαθον
    ἐλθ- ἦλθον
    ἐξευρ- ἐξηῦρον
    διελθ- διῆλθον
3. I saw (ὁράω)
    I said (λέγω)
    I escaped notice (λανθάνω)
    I found (εὑρίσκω)
    I learned (μανθάνω)
    I went (ἔρχομαι)
    I became (γίγνομαι)
    I suffered (πάσχω)

D – ENGLISH INTO GREEK

1. The sailors said that the captain had finally learned the truth.
    ὁ μαθητὴς εἶπεν ὅτι ἐξηῦρεν ὁπόσον ἐστὶ/ἦν τὸ χωρίον.
2. The young men happen to be suffering terribly.
    ὁ γεωργὸς ἔτυχεν ἀμαθὴς ὤν.
3. The suppliants ran into the temple/shrine.
    ὁ γέρων ἀπῆλθεν εἰς τὴν πόλιν.

4. The women saw the moon.
    ὁ πατὴρ ἄδικος ἐγένετο.
5. You (pl.) took the money because of your debts.
    οὐκ ἔλαθές με ἄγροικος ὤν.

SUMMARY EXERCISES FOR SECTION 6

A – VOCABULARY-BUILDING

1. | | | | |
    | --- | --- | --- | --- |
    | impossible | power | I am able | |
    | I force | forceful | force | |
    | I do | drama | | |
    | I am amazed | amazing | wonder | wonderful |
    | horse-mad | I am mad | madness | |
    | horse | horsey | horsemanship | horseman |
    | I steal | thief | theft | |

2. All in the right-hand column are diminutives.

old man	little old man
child	baby
door	little door
house	little house
father	daddy
Socrates	Socratikins
Pheidippides	Pheidippidikins

B/C – WORD SHAPE AND SYNTAX

When the Persian army and fleet approach (προσῆλθον), the Athenians quickly embark (εἰσέβαινον) on their ships and sail (ἔπλευσαν) towards Salamis. Then the Athenians and the other Greeks keep quiet (ἡσύχαζον). Finally the Persian fleet arrives (ἀφίκετο) and when night comes (ἐγένετο), the ships sail (ἔπλευσαν) slowly this way and that. And when day comes (ἐγένετο), the Persians approach (προσῆλθον) quickly for a sea-battle, the Greeks are at a loss (ἠπόρησαν) and afraid (ἐφοβοῦντο). Finally they are no longer afraid (ἐφοβοῦντο) but are daring (ἐτόλμων) and advance (ἐπῆλθον) against the barbarians. So they fight (ἐμάχοντο) in good order and defeat (ἐνίκησαν) the barbarians. And Xerxes also flees (ἔφυγε). In this way the Greeks become (ἐγένοντο) free through their courage.

D – ENGLISH INTO GREEK

γέρων δέ τις καὶ ὁ υἱός, νεανίας ὤν, διελέγοντο περὶ χρημάτων. ὁ δὲ νεανίας ἔτυχεν ὀφείλων πολλὰ χρήματα. καὶ διὰ ταῦτα, οἱ χρῆσται οὐκ ἐπαύοντο διώκοντες τὸν πατέρα. ὁ δὲ πατὴρ οὐκ ἐκόλαζε τὸν υἱόν (ἡ γὰρ μήτηρ ἔπαυεν αὐτὸν κολάζοντα) ἀλλὰ διενοεῖτο μηχανήν/γνώμην δεινήν τινα. ἐπεὶ οὖν ὁ πατὴρ ἔπεισε τὸν υἱόν, ὁ νεανίας πειθόμενος ἦλθε πρὸς τοὺς σοφιστὰς καὶ πολλὰ ἔμαθεν. οἱ γὰρ σοφισταὶ ἀεὶ ἔπειθον αὐτόν, καὶ πολλὰ καὶ σοφὰ

ἐδίδασκον καὶ πολλὰ χρήματα ἐδέχοντο. οὗτος οὖν ὁ υἱὸς μανθάνων ταχέως
τὸν δίκαιον καὶ τὸν ἄδικον λόγον, ἀεὶ τὰς δίκας ἐνίκα, ἀλλὰ ἐπεὶ ὁ υἱὸς
ἐπανῆλθεν οἴκαδε, αὕτη ἡ γνώμη οὐκ ἔπαυε τὰ χρέα τὰ τοῦ πατρός. ὁ γὰρ
νεανίας οὐκ ἐφίλει τὸν πατέρα, ἄγροικον ὄντα, ἀλλὰ ἐμίσει. καὶ οὐκ ἐπαύετο
παίζων πρὸς τὸν πατέρα. τέλος δὲ ὁ γέρων ἐξέβαλεν αὐτόν.

E – TEST EXERCISE 6

*A young man happened to owe much money because of his horse-fever. So, while
the father was always defending the lawsuits of his creditors, the creditors
pursued him and did not stop exacting their dues. So the father and mother
converse.*

FATHER   You, wife, appear to be responsible for my troubles. For who took our son and
talked to him about horses, except you? Who made our son horse-mad, except
you? Now what shall I do? How shall I stop our debts?

MOTHER   You are responsible, husband. As you are ignorant and a yokel, the young man
does not love you or obey you, but since I am from the city he loves me
particularly.

But don't worry about it. For I have an idea. I will persuade and teach our
son, and by persuading [him] I will stop [him] from his horse-madness.

*But [despite] teaching and persuading, the mother did not stop the young man,
nor did their son stop being horse-mad. Finally the young man went into the
thinkery of the sophists and became a student. He saw and heard many wise
things, and the sophists taught him much. When the son learnt the just and the
unjust argument, the father said:*

FA.   Hurrah hurrah! For now the creditors will not get their money any longer. For
my son will win the lawsuits through the unjust argument, which is stronger,
and we shall escape our creditors.

EXERCISE

1. (a) aorist   (b) imperfect   (c) imperfect
    (d) present   (e) aorist   (f) future
    (g) aorist
2. (a) m. pl. nom.   (b) f. s. acc.   (c) m. s. acc.
3. (a) vocative   (b) genitive

Section Seven: Socrates and intellectual inquiry

This is another very important section which introduces some more extremely valuable grammar: infinitives in 7A (*GE* pp. 134–135, #150–152), and then in 7D the aorist participle is introduced (*GE* pp. 142–145, #162–166).

You will find the style of these passages, which are only slightly adapted from the original, rather different from the style you have met before. In the first (7A–C), taken from Plato's version of Socrates' defence at his trial (see Introduction), you will find some rhetorical features mixed with a discursive, almost colloquial style. In the second (7D–F) you will meet the typical style of the Platonic dialogue, reflecting a technical philosophical argument, and in the third (7G–H) you will meet the narrative style that Herodotus uses in his *History*.

You may find that it takes you a little while to get used to these changes of style and at first the Greek may seem more difficult. But once you adapt, you will enjoy the variation and will have acquired a new skill.

Make sure that you read the 'Introduction' to each passage so that you understand the context.

7A–C Plato: *Apology* 20c–23b

7A

Page 74

1 ἐρωτῶσιν οὖν τινες   'some people ask, therefore …': a typical rhetorical device which allows the speaker to pose the question which he wants to answer.

3 οὐ βουλόμεθα διαβάλλειν σε   'we don't want to slander you': βούλομαι + the infinitive – a very common pattern.

4 διέβαλον, ἐγένοντο   Tense?

6 φανοῦμαι   Tense?
   ὅτι οὐδὲν ἄλλο ἢ τὴν ἀλήθειαν λέγειν βούλομαι   'that I want to speak nothing other than the truth'.

8 εἰδέναι   Learn carefully to distinguish the three infinitives εἶναι, ἰέναι, εἰδέναι, *GE* p. 135, #152.

10 ἀνάγκη ἐστί …   See *GE* p. 135, #153.

11 που   The particle means something like 'I suppose', although it is literally the indefinite form of ποῦ 'where?'

14 σοφώτερος ἤ … 'wiser than …' See *GE* p.136–138, #155–160 for comparison of adjectives.

σοφώτατος 'wisest'.

14–15 τί οὖν ποιεῖν με δεῖ 'What is it necessary for me to do? 'What must I do?'

17 ᾔει What verb does this come from? See vocabulary and *GE* pp.138–139, #161.

18 μὴ θορυβεῖτε The jurors are reacting unfavourably. This is a frequent plea by orators who are battling to be heard.

ὦνδρες = ὦ ἄνδρες.

Translation for 7A

Some people therefore are asking 'But, Socrates, why are these men slandering you? What do they have in mind? From where do these slanders arise and this reputation of yours? Speak, then, and explain to us. For we do not want to slander you.' Therefore I want to explain to you and tell you why these men slandered me and from where the slanders and this reputation arose. Listen then. And know well that I do not want to joke with you, for perhaps I shall appear to be joking, but you must be assured (know well) that I wish to speak nothing but the truth.

For, gentlemen of Athens, I happen to have this reputation on account of some kind of wisdom. Do you want to know what this wisdom is? As witness, I want to bring the god at Delphi. For the god at Delphi will bear witness to my wisdom. And indeed it is necessary for the god to speak the truth.

You know Chaerephon, I suppose. He was my companion from childhood, and you know how impetuous Chaerephon was about everything. And Chaerephon once reasoned thus to himself. 'That Socrates is wise, I know well. But I want to know if anyone is wiser than Socrates. For perhaps Socrates is the wisest of men. What then must I do? It is clear that I must go to Delphi and consult the oracle. For there is great necessity for the god to speak the truth.'

So Chaerephon went to Delphi and he obtained this oracle in the presence of the god. Do not make a din, gentlemen! For, indeed, he asked whether there is anyone wiser than Socrates, and the Pythia answered that no one is wiser.

7B

Page 76

1–2 λέγει … λέγων You may want to translate this as 'What does the god *mean* when he *says*?'

5 πολὺν μὲν χρόνον 'for a long time'. Accusative of duration of time.

ἠπόρουν What verb? What tense?

ἐτραπόμην Second aorist middle of τρέπω. Lit.: 'I turned myself towards'.

9 πολιτικόν τινα ὄντα Agrees with τοῦτον τὸν σοφόν and refers to him. We might say 'who was a politician'.

10 ᾤμην Tense? Verb? The vocabulary will tell you.

ἔδοξέ γε σοφὸς εἶναι, οὐκ ὤν 'He thought he was wise, not being.' Note the use of the participle. 'He thought he was wise, though, in reality, he was not.'

ἐπειρώμην 'I tried': the imperfect of πειράομαι.

10–11   ἀποφαίνειν αὐτὸν δοκοῦντα σοφὸν εἶναι, οὐκ ὄντα   'to show him that he thought he was wise, though when he wasn't'. Cf. line 13.

11   πολλοὶ τῶν παρόντων   'many of those present'.

12–13   οὗτος δοκεῖ τι εἰδέναι, οὐδὲν εἰδώς   'this man thinks he knows something, though he knows nothing'. Cf. lines 10 and 11.
εἰδώς -οτος   This is the participle of οἶδα.

16   ᾖα   Cf. note on 7A line 17, if you are stuck.
ἐπὶ τοὺς ἄλλους τοὺς δοκοῦντάς τι εἰδέναι   Cf. line 11.

21–22   τοὺς δὲ λόγους τούτους οὐκ ἴσασιν ὅ τι νοοῦσιν   'they do not know these words what they mean' – 'they do not know what these words mean.' This is a very common pattern of word order in Greek, which can be difficult for speakers of English. See p. 77, note on 6C line 8.

23   ἀπῆα   What verb? What tense?

Translation for 7B

When I heard this, I reasoned in this way to myself: 'What does the god wish to say? For I know that I am not wise. What then does the god mean when he says that I am the wisest and that no one is wiser? It cannot be that he is lying; for it is not lawful for him. It is necessary for the god to speak nothing but the truth.' And for a long time I was at a loss to know what he meant, and then I turned to a search [to find out] whether the god was speaking the truth or not. For I did not want to be in doubt about the oracle.

Therefore I went to a wise man (at least he thought he was wise). For I wanted to test the oracle and to show that 'You, Apollo, said that I was the wisest, but this man is wiser.' Therefore I spoke with this wise man, who was a politician. And the man, as I thought, considered himself to be wise, though he was not. And when I tried to show him that he considered himself to be wise, though he was not, he and many of those present began to hate me. So, to myself, I reasoned that 'I am wiser than this man. For this man thinks that he knows something, though he knows nothing. but I, though I know nothing, do not think that I know anything.' From there, I went to another wise man and he too thought that he knew something, though he knew nothing. As a result of this (from this) that man and others of those present hated me.

After this, I went to the others who thought that they knew something. And, by the dog, those who thought that they knew something were more foolish, as I thought, while those who thought they knew nothing were wiser. For after the politicians, I went to the poets. And I am ashamed to tell the truth, gentlemen, but nevertheless I must tell it. For the poets do not make up their poems by wisdom, but by instinct and inspiration, like the prophets and soothsayers. For indeed they say many beautiful things, but they do not know what these words mean. And, at the same time, the poets thought that they had knowledge, through their poetry, though they had none, and they thought they were the wisest of men, though they were not. So I went away from there thinking that I was wiser than the poets.

Page 78

4   τοιοῦτον πάθος ἐφαίνοντο οἱ ποιηταί πάσχοντες   'such an experience the poets seemed to be suffering'. τοιοῦτον πάθος is the object of πάσχοντες: 'such was the experience they seemed to be experiencing'.

9–10   εὑρίσκουσι πολὺ πλῆθος τῶν δοκούντων μέν τι εἰδέναι, εἰδότων δ' ὀλίγα ἢ οὐδέν   'They find a large number of those who ...' Note μέν ... δέ making the contrast between what people think they know, and what they actually know.

13–14   ἔχουσι μὲν οὐδὲν λέγειν ἐκεῖνοι   'they have nothing to say', 'they can say nothing'.

17   κατάδηλοι   'obvious' – the prefix κατα- sometimes simply adds emphasis.

Translation for 7C

Finally I went to the craftsmen (artists). For I knew that I knew nothing and that the craftsmen knew many beautiful things. Therefore, knowing many things the craftsmen were wiser than I. But, as I thought, they considered that because of their skill/art they were the wisest in many other respects, though they were not. Such was the experience which both the poets and the craftsmen were clearly experiencing.

From this search, gentlemen of Athens, arose the slanders against me, which are serious, and my reputation. And, moreover, the young men, who are wealthy and have most leisure, enjoy listening to my words and often try to examine others in the way that I do. For young men are arrogant and very much enjoy examining their elders. And, as I think, in the course of examining them, they discover a great number of those who consider that they know something, but know little or nothing. Therefore, as a result of this, those who think that they know something become angry and say that 'Socrates is a most disgraceful person and corrupts the young men.' But I want to ask 'How does Socrates corrupt the young men? What does he do or what does he teach to corrupt them?' And they have nothing to say, but not wishing to seem to be at a loss, they say that, like the other sophists, Socrates teaches 'the things in the air and the things beneath the earth' and 'not to believe in the gods' and 'to make the weaker argument the stronger'. For they do not wish, as I think, to tell the truth, that they have been revealed as thinking that they know something, when, in fact, they know nothing.

Grammar

Do not forget to learn εἶναι, ἰέναι, εἰδέναι, *GE* p. 135, #152 and the past tense of εἶμι 'I shall go', *GE* p.139, #161.

Note also the irregular comparative forms, *GE* p. 137, #159.

EXERCISES FOR SECTION 7A–C

PRESENT INFINITIVE

7A–C: 1

1. διαβάλλειν	7. παρεῖναι	13. θαυμάζειν
2. εὑρίσκειν	8. νομίζειν	14. πείθεσθαι
3. πειρᾶσθαι	9. ἰέναι	15. δέχεσθαι
4. εἰδέναι	10. κλέπτειν	16. ποιεῖν
5. δηλοῦν	11. ἀπιέναι	17. μανθάνειν
6. λογίζεσθαι	12. βιάζεσθαι	18. λαμβάνειν

7A–C: 2

1. βούλομαι ἰέναι	5. δεῖ με, ἡμᾶς, ὑμᾶς παρεῖναι
2. βούλονται πιστεύειν	6. τὸν Σωκράτη δεῖ διδάσκειν
3. φαίνεται νομίζειν	7. ἀνάγκη ἐστὶν ἀπιέναι
4. φαίνονται διαβάλλειν	8. ὑμῖν ἀνάγκη ἐστὶ μανθάνειν

COMPARATIVE AND SUPERLATIVE OF ADJECTIVES

7A–C: 3

1. τόν πολεμιώτερον, πολεμιώτατον ναύτην
   the more hostile, most hostile sailor
2. τοὺς βεβαιοτέρους, βεβαιοτάτους λιμένας
   the safer, safest harbours
3. τὴν ἀμείνονα, ἀρίστην θεάν
   the better, best goddess
4. αἱ πλείονες, πλεῖσται νῆες
   more ships, most ships (αἱ technically makes this 'the great majority of',
   'the huge majority of')
5. οἱ μείζονες, μέγιστοι βασιλῆς
   the greater, greatest kings
6. τὰς κακίονας, κάκιστας γυναῖκας
   the more wicked, the worst women
7. τὸ κάλλιον, κάλλιστον ἄστυ
   the more beautiful, most beautiful city
8. ἡ δηλοτέρα, δηλοτάτη ἀνομία
   the clearer, most obvious lawlessness

7A–C: 4

1. τῷ πολεμιωτέρῳ, πολεμιωτάτῳ ναύτῃ
   to, for the more hostile, most hostile sailor
2. τῶν βεβαιοτέρων, βεβαιοτάτων λιμένων
   of the safer, safest harbours
3. τῆς ἀμείνονος, ἀρίστης θεᾶς
   of the better, best goddess

4. τοῖς μείζοσι, μεγίστοις βασιλεῦσι
   to, for the greater, greatest kings

5. τῇ κακίονι, κακίστῃ γυναικί
   to, for the worse, worst woman

6. τοῦ καλλίονος, καλλίστου ἄστεως
   of the more beautiful, most beautiful city.

PAST OF εἶμι *I SHALL GO*

7A–C: 5

1. ἦμεν	7. εἰσί(ν)
2. ἦμεν	8. ἦμεν
3. ἴασι(ν)	9. ἦτε
4. ἐστί(ν)	10. ἤεισθα
5. ἤει	11. ἐσμέν
6. εἶσι(ν)	12. ἦσαν

REVISION EXERCISES FOR SECTION 7A–C

B/C – WORD SHAPE AND SYNTAX

1a.

1. λέγειν	6. διαφθείρειν
2. διαβάλλειν	7. εὑρίσκειν
3. δοκεῖν	8. ἰέναι
4. ἀποφαίνειν	9. εἶναι
5. διαλέγεσθαι	10. εἰδέναι

1b. a. δεῖ ὑμᾶς τὴν ἀλήθειαν λέγειν, καὶ μὴ διαβάλλειν Σωκράτη.
      You must tell the truth, and not slander Socrates.

   b. οὐ βουλόμεθα δοκεῖν ἄριστοι, ἀλλ᾽ εἶναι.
      We do not want to seem the best, but to be the best.

   c. οἱ σοφοὶ δοκοῦσί τι εἰδέναι, οὐκ εἰδότες.
      The wise men seem to know something, although they do not.

   d. ἀνάγκη ἦν Σωκράτη ἰέναι πρὸς τοὺς σοφοὺς καὶ διαλέγεσθαι περὶ
      σοφίας.
      It was necessary for Socrates to go to the wise men and talk about
      wisdom [with them].

   e. Σωκράτης, ὡς ἐγὼ οἶμαι, οὐ πειρᾶται διαφθείρειν τοὺς νέους.
      Socrates, as I see it, is not trying to corrupt the young men.

   f. Σωκράτης ἐβούλετο εὑρίσκειν πότερον τὴν ἀλήθειαν λέγει ὁ ἐν
      Δελφοῖς θεὸς ἢ οὔ. καὶ πολλάκις ἐπειρᾶτο Σωκράτης δηλοῦν τὸν θεὸν
      οὐ τἀληθῆ λέγοντα.
      Socrates wanted to discover whether the god in Delphi was telling the
      truth or not. And Socrates often tried to show that the god was not telling
      the truth.

2.   ἀγαθός ἀμείνων ἄριστος
     βέβαιος βεβαιότερος βεβαιότατος
     δεινός δεινότερος δεινότατος
     κακός κακίων κάκιστος
     καλός καλλίων κάλλιστος
     μέγας μείζων μέγιστος
     μῶρος μωρότερος μωρότατος
     πολέμιος πολεμιώτερος πολεμιώτατος
     πολύς πλείων πλεῖστος
     φίλος φίλτερος φίλτατος
     χρήσιμος χρησιμώτερος χρησιμώτατος

D – ENGLISH INTO GREEK

1. The farmers must go to the city.
     ἔδει με πρὸς τοὺς ποιητὰς ἰέναι.
2. We must make sacrifices and pray to the gods.
     δεῖ σε ἐξετάζειν ἐμὲ καὶ ἀκριβῶς σκοπεῖν.
3. The women are trying to watch the play.
     πειρῶμαι εὑρίσκειν ὅπως οἱ ποιηταὶ τὴν σοφίαν ἀποφαίνουσιν.
4. We know that the king wanted to punish the herald.
     οἶσθα/ἴστε ὅτι ἐβούλου/ἐβουλόμεθα διαβάλλειν ἐμέ.
5. You seem to be stupid, although you are a teacher.
     ἐντεῦθεν οὖν ἐδόκουν τοὺς νέους διαφθείρειν, καίπερ οὐδὲν εἰδώς.

7D–F Plato: *Euthydemos* 275–277c

Here you meet the dialogue style of Plato, and the aorist participle, *GE* pp. 142–145, #162–166. Note that the aorist participle is formed from the aorist stem.

7D

Page 79

5 ἦν δ᾽ ἐγώ   'I said' these phrases only occur in direct speech and are very common in Platonic dialogue
6 ἢ οὔ;   'or not?' In Platonic dialogue most questions are asked in the form 'Is X true, or not?'
7 ἦ δ᾽ ὅς   'he said'

Page 80

8 εἶεν   'so be it', 'well all right then'. Another very common feature of dialogue style.
17 ἀκούσας   Nom. s. masc. aor. part. act., *GE* p.142, #162. Note the 'echo' effect: <u>ἄκουε</u> οὖν, ὦ Κλεινία, <u>ἀκούσας</u> δέ … 'Listen then, Kleinias, and *having listened* …'

18 ἀποκρινοῦμαι   Tense? Cf. ἀποκρίνομαι.
21 πότεροι … ἤ …   A double question, 'are they … or …?'
23 … ἠπόρησεν. ἀπορήσας δ' …   Cf. line 17.
27 … ἐγέλασεν, γελάσας δέ …   Cf. lines 17 and 23.

Translation for 7D

Yesterday I went to the Lyceum, Kriton, and I found Euthydemos and Dionysodoros conversing with many others. And you know that both these men have a good reputation, turning men to philosophy. Therefore, wanting to hear their arguments, I said: 'Do you, Dionysodoros, have a reputation for turning people to philosophy and virtue or not?'

'We certainly seem to, Socrates', he said.

'So be it', I said. 'Then you must turn this young man to philosophy and virtue. They call him Kleinias. He is young. But why don't you question the young man closely, talking here in front of us?'

Euthydemos immediately answered boldly: 'We are certainly willing to talk here, Socrates. But the young man must answer.'

'But', I said, 'the fact is that, Kleinias, enjoys answering. For his friends often go to him, asking questions and discussing, and they always question him closely while he is speaking and answering.'

And Euthydemos said: 'Listen then, Kleinias, and answer when you have listened.'

Kleinias said: 'I will do this and answer. For I enjoy answering. Speak then, Euthydemos, and question me. For it is by speaking and questioning that a sophist turns his students to virtue.'

And Euthydemos said: 'Tell me then, which people learn, the clever or the ignorant?'

And the young man – for it really was a big question – was at a loss. And being at a loss he looked at me and blushed.

I, seeing him blush, said: 'Don't worry, and don't be afraid, but answer boldly.'

And at this moment Dionysodoros laughed and with a laugh said: 'Indeed I know very well that Euthydemos will defeat him in discussion.'

I did not answer. For while Dionysodoros was saying this, Kleinias happened to answer that the people who learn are the clever people.

7E

Page 81

3 ὡμολόγει   'he agreed'. ὁμολογέω is another common word in Plato.
6 ἧστε   What verb does this come from? See vocab., and *GE* p.146, #167.
7 ᾖσμεν   Cf. line 6.
10 ἀμαθεῖς   You can work out the meaning from μανθάνω and then make it negative with ἀ-, thus ἀ-μαθεῖς.
11 πάνυ γε   'certainly'.

12 ἄρα   This particle shows that you are reaching the climax of the argument
– see also in line 14.

Translation for 7E

And Euthydemos said: 'But who teaches those who learn, the teacher, or someone
else?'

He agreed that the teacher teaches those who learn.

'And when the teacher was teaching you as children, were you pupils?'

He agreed they were.

'And when you were pupils, you knew nothing yet?'

'No, by Zeus! For since we were pupils we knew nothing.'

'Were you then clever, when you knew nothing?'

'No, indeed, we were certainly not clever since we knew nothing', said
Kleinias.

'Therefore, if you were not clever, were you ignorant?'

'Certainly.'

'So then, when you were pupils you knew nothing, but being ignorant you were
learning?'

The young man agreed.

'Then it is the ignorant who learn, Kleinias, but not the clever, as you believe.'

7F

Page 82

2 ἐπήνεσαν   From ἐπ-αινέω.

ὥσπερ σφαῖραν   'just like a ball', σφαῖρα = 'sphere'.

2–3 ἐξεδέξατο … ἐκδεξάμενος δὲ …   Aor. mid. indic… . aor. mid. part… .

4–5 πότεροι … ἤ …   'are they … or …?':   a double question.

7 ἄρα   Climax again.

Translation for 7F

So said Euthydemos. The students, making a din and laughing at the same time,
praised this cleverness. And Dionysodoros at once caught up the argument, like a
ball, and, having received it, he said: 'What then, Kleinias? Let's suppose the
teacher speaks some words. Who learns these words, the clever or the ignorant?'

'The clever,' said Kleinias.

'Then it is the clever who learn, but not the ignorant, and you did not answer
well just now.'

At this point the students, laughing vigorously and making a din, immediately
praised this cleverness. But we, falling into perplexity, were silent.

Grammar

Do not forget to learn ᾔδη, the past tense of οἶδα (see *GE* p. 146, #167), and φημί,
ἔφην 'I say', 'I said' (*GE* pp. 146–147, #168).

EXERCISES FOR SECTION 7D–F

AORIST PARTICIPLES

7D–F: 1

1. m. pl. nom.   παύω
2. m. pl. acc.   λύω
3. m. s. nom.   ζητέω
4. f. pl. acc.   ζητέω
5. f. s. nom.   δέχομαι

6. m. pl. nom.   βλέπω
7. f. s. nom.   δηλόω
8. m. s. acc.   πείθω
9. m. s. nom.   βοάω
10. m. pl. acc.   τρέπομαι

7D–F: 2

1. βλέψασαν
2. θαυμάσας
3. τρεψάμενον
4. διωξάσας
5. ποιήσαντες

6. βιασάμενοι
7. κολάσαντας
8. μισήσασα
9. δουλωσαμένους
10. δεξαμένη

7D–F: 3

(a) With one look at Penthesilea, Achilles burned with passion.
(b) While he gazed at Penthesilea, Achilles burned with passion.

ᾖδη *I knew, and* φημί *I say*

7D–F: 4

1. ἴσμεν
2. ἔφασαν
3. ᾔδει
4. φαμέν
5. οἶσθα

6. ἔφη
7. ᾔδη
8. φησίν
9. ἔφατε
10. ᾔδεσαν, ἦσαν

REVISION EXERCISES FOR SECTION 7D–F

B/C – WORD SHAPE AND SYNTAX

1.
   1. βλέψας
   2. φροντίσας
   3. ῥίψας
   4. σώσας
   5. παυσάμενος

   6. δεξάμενος
   7. βιασάμενος
   8. λογισάμενος
   9. μαχεσάμενος
   10. ἀποκρινάμενος

2.
   1. ποιήσας
   3. βοηθήσας
   4. ἀπορήσας

   4. ἐλευθερώσας
   5. τολμήσας
   6. θεασάμενος

3.

   a. ἀποροῦντες
   b. βλέψας
   c. ἀκούσαντες
   d. γελῶν
   e. ἐκδεξαμένη
   f. ἀποκρινόμενος

D – ENGLISH INTO GREEK

1. The students said in answer that lawlessness is not just.
   ὁ διδάσκαλος ἀποκρινόμενος εἶπεν ὅτι ἀρετή τις ἐστὶν ἡ
   φιλοσοφία.
2. Socrates, hearing the argument, laughed.
   ὁ Διονυσόδωρος γελῶν/γελάσας τὸν λόγον ἐξεδέξατο.
3. The suppliants hurried to the shrine and prayed to the gods.
   ὁ σοφιστής, πρὸς ἐμὲ βλέψας, ὡμολόγησεν.
4. With a glance at me, the woman was silent.
   ἐπαινέσας αὐτοὺς 'προτρέπετε', ἦν δ' ἐγώ, 'εὐθύς αὐτούς.'
5. Having stolen the money the young man shouted loudly.
   ἀπορήσας ὁ μαθητὴς ἐπειρᾶτο φεύγειν.

E – TEST EXERCISE 7D–F

'You, Socrates,' I said, 'question [me] carefully, and I shall reply.'

   'Consider then,' said Socrates, 'and if you have anything to object, make your objection, and I, for my part, shall obey.'

   'You seem to speak well,' I said, 'as I think.'

   'Well then,' he said, 'does a philosopher who says that we must not praise all the opinions of men speak the truth? What do you say? Do you think he is speaking the truth (*lit.* does he seem to you to speak the truth) in saying this, or not? Answer.'

   'The truth,' I said.

   'So should we praise and honour good opinions, but not bad ones?'

   I agreed.

   'Come then,' said Socrates, 'when the plague fell upon the city and destroyed it, where did you go, to your friends or to the doctor?'

   'I went to the doctor,' I said, 'and my friends went there too. For the doctor knew about the plague, being more skilled than the others.'

   'The doctor seemed to be most skilled, then,' said Socrates. 'So did you have to go to the doctor, and to no one else?'

   'I did,' (*lit.* it was necessary) I said.

   'So we shouldn't praise and respect the opinions of the many about the plague, but that of any skilled doctor who happens to be [available]. Do we agree so or not?'

   'We do by Zeus,' I said.

EXERCISE

1. (a) present indicative   (b) future indicative
    (c) imperfect indicative   (d) imperfect indicative
2. (a) acc.   (b) acc.
    (c) acc.   (d) nom.
    (e) m. acc.   (f) s.

7G–H Herodotus: *Histories* 4.110–116, the Amazons

Now we change to Herodotus and the narrative style. You will often find that the sentences are longer, but the syntax will usually follow the sequence of events, with a series of participles leading on to the final event in the main verb.

Aorist participles are frequent, for where in English we would write 'they attacked them and fought them', the Greeks preferred to have only one main verb and to say 'having attacked them, they fought them'.

The second aorist participle has the same endings as the present participle, but has the aorist stem, *GE* pp. 151–152, #169–171: e.g. λαμβάνων present participle, λαβών aorist participle.

7G

Page 83

1 εἰσπεσόντες   Nom. pl. masc. aor. part, of εἰσπίπτω (second aor. ἔπεσον).
2 αὐτάς   'them', see *GE* p. 153, #172–173. There are other uses and meanings (*GE* pp. 153–155, #174–176) which will be gradually introduced.
2–3 τὰς ἐκ τῆς μάχης περιούσας   περιούσας agrees with τὰς Ἀμαζόνας and is the acc. pl. fem., participle of περίειμι 'I survive'.
    ἔλαβον. λαβόντες δ' αὐτάς   Note the 'echo' effect. Cf. 7D lines 17 and 23 and 7F lines 2–3.

Page 84

5 ἰδοῦσαι   εἶδον (second aorist of ὁράω) drops the augment to give the stem ἰδ-, therefore the participle is ἰδών, ἰδοῦσα, ἰδόν.
6 ἀποκτείνασαι   Cf. ἀπέκτειναν line 5.
8–9 ἀφικόμεναι ... ἀποβᾶσαι   Remember that the Amazons are feminine. Note: participle ... participle ... main verb.
10–12 Note the structure: οἱ δὲ Σκύθαι / οὐ γιγνώσκοντες τὴν φωνὴν / καὶ ἄνδρας νομίζοντες τὰς Ἀμαζόνας / ἐμπεσόντες καὶ μαχεσάμενοι / τοὺς νεκροὺς ἀνεῖλον (subject / pres. part. / pres. part. / aor. part. and aor. part. / main verb).
12 ἀνελόντες   What verb is this from? ἀν-αιρέω, second aorist εἷλον, stem ἑλ-.
13 γνόντες   From γιγνώσκω, second aorist ἔγνων; the aorist participle is γνοὺς γνόντος.
    ἐξ αὐτῶν   'from them'.

14 τοὺς ἑαυτῶν νεανίσκους   'their own young men' (lit. the young men of themselves).

ἔπεσθαι   Note the rough breathing. It is from ἕπομαι 'I follow'.

15 εἵποντο   What verb? What had they been told to do?

16 ἀπῆλθον ... ἀπελθοῦσαι   The pattern as before.

Translation for 7G

When the Greeks came upon the Amazons and were fighting them, they defeated them in the battle. And having defeated them, they captured the Amazons who survived the battle. And having captured them, they went away in three ships. They did not, however, arrive at their native land. For while they were on the sea they did not guard the Amazons. And the Amazons, seeing that the men were not guarding [them], killed [them]. But the Amazons were not experienced in seafaring, and so, having killed the men, they sailed where the wind carried [them].

Finally having arrived at the land of the Scythians and having disembarked from the ships, they found a herd of horses, and taking the horses they laid waste the land of the Scythians. But the Scythians, not knowing the language, and think-ing the Amazons were men, attacked and having fought a battle (*lit.* having attacked and fought) took up the corpses. Thus, then, they discovered that they were women, on taking up the corpses.

Having discovered this, and not wanting to kill [them] any more, but to have children by them, they sent their own young men to them, ordering them not to fight, but to follow and to make camp near the Amazons. So, coming near, the young men followed [them] and made camp. And first the Amazons went away, but on going away they saw the men following. So the Amazons gave chase, and the men fled. Seeing the men fleeing, the Amazons became quiet. In this way, then, having learned that the men were not hostile, they did not worry about them any longer.

7H

Page 86

3 εἰς τὸ αὐτὸ χωρίον   'to the same place', αὐτός preceded by the article always means 'the same'. See *GE* pp. 153–155, #172–176 for the different uses of αὐτός. Be careful to distinguish between αὐτόν 'him' and ἑαυτόν (or αὑτόν) reflexive 'himself'.

4 τὸ αὐτό   'the same thing'.

ἄξει   What tense? What verb?

5 τῇ δ' ὑστεραίᾳ   'on the next day'. Dative of time when.

αὐτός   'himself', emphatic; agrees with the subject: 'coming himself ...'

6 τὴν Ἀμαζόνα αὐτήν   'the Amazon herself' (emphatic).

8 ἐποίουν τὸ αὐτὸ καὶ αὐτοί   Cf. lines 4 and 5 'they did the same thing themselves also'.

9 συνῴκουν If you cannot identify it, try taking it apart: συν- preposition, -ῳ- = ε + οι (i.e. augmented οι), therefore the stem is οἰκ- from οἰκέω.

14–15 οὐ γὰρ οἱ αὐτοὶ οἵ τε ἡμέτεροι νόμοι καὶ οἱ τῶν Σκυθῶν 'For our customs and the Scythians' customs are not the same (οἱ αὐτοί).'

18–19 δεῖ ὑμᾶς There are two sets of actions which they must perform: (i) ἐλθόντας … μέρος and (ii) καὶ ἔπειτα … ἡμῶν.

Grammar

Don't forget to learn δύναμαι, *GE* p. 156, #177, and make sure that you understand *GE* pp. 153–155, #172–176, αὐτός / ἑαυτόν / ὁ αὐτός.

Translation for 7H

So then a young man, on coming across an Amazon who was alone, immediately had intercourse with her. And the Amazon did not prevent [him]. And she was not able to speak [his language], but by means of a sign she ordered the young man to come to the same place on the next day and to bring another young man, giving a sign that she herself would do the same thing and would bring another Amazon. And the young man went away and told this to the others, and on the next day, on coming himself to the same place, bringing another young man, he found the Amazon herself who had brought another Amazon. The two young men, on finding the Amazons and having had intercourse with them, went away. But the rest of the young men, on learning what had happened, did the same thing themselves also.

After this the Scythians and the Amazons began to live together. The men could not learn the language of the Amazons, but the women learned that of the Scythians. At last the young men said to them: 'We have parents and possessions. Why, then, don't we go away to our people? We shall have you as our wives and no others.' But they said to this: 'We cannot live with your women. For our customs and the Scythians' customs are not the same. For we use bows and arrows and ride horses, and we have not learned women's tasks. But your women do none of these things, but do women's tasks, staying in the wagons and not using bows and arrows or riding horses. But if you want to have us as your wives, you must go to your parents and obtain [your] portion of the possessions, and then come back and live with us.'

Having said these things, they convinced the young men. So the young men, on obtaining their portion of the possessions, came back again to the Amazons. So the Amazons said to them: 'But a great fear holds us. For we cannot live in this region, having laid waste the land. But if you want to have us as your wives, why don't we get up and go off from this land and, crossing the river Tanais, live there?' And the young men obeyed these things too. So having got up and left, and having arrived at the place, they inhabited it.

EXERCISES FOR SECTION 7G–H

SECOND AORIST PARTICIPLES

7G–H: 1

1. τὸν λαβόντα
2. τοὺς ἐλθόντας
3. τὴν μαθοῦσαν
4. αἱ ἰδοῦσαι

5. οἱ γενόμενοι
6. τὰς ἀφικομένας
7. τὸ πεσόν
8. ἡ ἑλοῦσα

7G–H: 2

1. τῷ μαθόντι
2. τῆς τυχούσης
3. ταῖς δραμούσαις
4. τοῦ ἀφικομένου

5. τῇ εἰπούσῃ/λεξάσῃ
6. τοῖς γενομένοις
7. τῷ εὑρόντι
8. τοῦ λαβόντος

ADJECTIVES/PRONOUNS: αὐτός-ή-όν

7G–H: 3

1. I saw the man
2. I saw him
3. I saw the man himself
4. I myself saw the man himself

5. I myself saw the same man
6. I myself saw the same man
7. He himself saw him (someone else)
8. He himself did the same thing

7G–H: 4

1. τὸν αὐτὸν ἄνδρα
2. ἆρ' εἶδες αὐτάς;
3. αὐτὴ ἦλθεν
4. ἔλαβεν αὐτόν

5. αὐτοὶ ἀφίκοντο
6. τὴν γυναῖκα αὐτήν
7. οἱ αὐτοὶ νόμοι
8. εἶδεν αὐτό

REVISION EXERCISES FOR SECTION 7G–H

B/C – WORD SHAPE AND SYNTAX

1. 1. ἐγενόμην γενόμενος
   2. ἔμαθον μαθών
   3. εἶδον ἰδών
   4. ἀφικόμην ἀφικόμενος
   5. ἦλθον ἐλθών
   6. ἔλαβον λαβών
   7. ηὗρον εὑρών
   8. εἶλον ἑλών
   9. ἔπεσον πεσών

2. a. The young men went away and said these things to the rest.
      ἀπελθόντες
   b. The Amazons came across the young men and conversed with them.
      καταλαβοῦσαι
   c. The young man saw the Amazon and went towards her.
      ἰδών

    d. The Scythians find the Amazons and come closer. εὑρόντες

    e. The young men came closer and pitched camp. ἀφικόμενοι

    f. The Scythians, having picked up the corpses and found them to be women, were amazed. ἀνελόντες, μαθόντες

3. a. αὐτούς

    b. ὁ αὐτός

    c. αὐτή

    d. τὴν αὐτήν

    e. αὐτός

    f. περὶ τὰ αὐτά

    g. αὐτός

    h. αὐτοὺς τοὺς νεανίας

    i. αὐτάς, αὐτούς

D – ENGLISH INTO GREEK

1. The women, seeing the old man, went away.
οἱ ἄνδρες ἀνελόντες τοὺς τῶν γυναικῶν νεκροὺς ἀπῆλθον.

2. Saying this/with these words, the sailor laughed
εὑρόντες ταύτας τὰς γυναῖκας, οἱ νεανίαι ἐθαύμασαν.

3. Having become pupils, the young men wanted to learn.
φίλοι γενόμενοι, οἱ νεανίαι δύνανται διαλέγεσθαι πρὸς ἐκείνας τὰς γυναῖκας.

4. On discovering the men, the women stopped worrying.
ταῦτα εἰποῦσαι αἱ γυναῖκες ἔπεισαν τοὺς νεανίας.

5. After this the boy ran into the house and looked for his father.
διὰ δὲ ταῦτα οἱ νεανίαι πρὸς τὰς οἰκίας ἐπανελθόντες τὰ κτήματα ἔλαβον.

SUMMARY EXERCISES FOR SECTION 7

A – VOCABULARY-BUILDING

1.
necessity, necessary, I compel
I laugh, laughter, laughable
I cross, the crossing
I destroy, the destruction
I am able, powerful, force/power
I praise, the praise
a possession, I possess, the (act of) possessing
I reason, the reasoning
I agree, the agreement
I try, the attempt
I guard, the guard (person), the guard (act of guarding), unguarded

2.

μάχη battle, μάχομαι I fight; ἀληθής true, ἀλήθεια truth; διαβάλλω I slander,
διαβολή slander; σοφία wisdom, σοφός wise; ἀποφαίνω I reveal, φάσμα
apparition, φαίνομαι I appear; λόγος word, argument, λογίζομαι I reason;
ἡδέως with pleasure, ἥδομαι I have pleasure; νέος young, νεανίας young man;
οἰκέω I live, οἰκία house; δοκέω I seem, δόξα reputation

D – ENGLISH INTO GREEK

αἱ δ' Ἀμαζόνες τοὺς Ἀθηναίους ἀποκτείνασαι πρὸς τὴν τῶν Σκυθῶν γῆν
ἀφίκοντο. ἀφικόμεναι δὲ καὶ ἵππους εὑροῦσαι πρὸς τοὺς Σκύθας ἐμαχέσαντο.
οἱ δὲ Σκύθαι αὐτὰς νικήσαντές τε καὶ περὶ αὐτῶν γνόντες φίλοι γίγνεσθαι
ἐβούλοντο. οἱ οὖν νεάνιαι πλησίον ἑπόμενοι οὐκ ἐμαχέσαντο. αἱ δ' Ἀμαζόνες
ταῦτα ἰδοῦσαι αὐταὶ ἡσύχαζον. τέλος δὲ φίλοι γενόμενοι συνῴκησαν ἀλλήλοις,
ἀλλὰ ἔδει τούς τε νεανίας καὶ τὰς γυναῖκας διὰ τὸν ποταμὸν διαβαίνειν καὶ
ἄλλην τινὰ χώραν οἰκεῖν. 'τὴν γὰρ ὑμετέραν γῆν', ἔφασαν αἱ Ἀμαζόνες, 'οὐ
βουλόμεθα οἰκεῖν, ἐπειδὴ ἀφικόμεναι πρὸς ὑμᾶς ἐμαχεσάμεθα.'

E – TEST EXERCISE 7

Some Amazons arrived in the land of the Scythians and disembarked from their
boats, and falling on the land they laid it waste. The Scythians defeated them in
battle, and taking up their corpses and finding them to be women, wanted to have
children by them. So they ordered their young men never to fight, but to go closer
and become friends, and they sent them towards the Amazons. The Amazons, on
seeing them following close by but not fighting, no longer worried about them.
Then a Scythian, coming across an Amazon who was on her own, and becoming
friendly [with her], advised the others to do the same, and, if they came on any
Amazons, to become friends. So the others obeyed, and eventually the Scythians
and the Amazons began to live together. But the Amazons did not wish to go back
to the mass of the Scythians. 'For', they said, 'we cannot live with your women.
For our customs and those of the Scythians are not the same.' So, taking their
possessions and crossing the river, they found a land near by and lived in it.

EXERCISE

1. (a) aorist   (b) aorist   (c) present   (d) aorist
    (e) present   (f) aorist
2. (a) imperfect (b) aorist   (c) imperfect (d) aorist

Section Eight: Aristophanes' *Birds*

Now we return to Dikaiopolis and the rhapsode, and to an episode based on another play of Aristophanes, where he escapes into fantasy from the bitter realities of life in Athens during the Peloponnesian War. The social comment, however amusingly expressed, is deeply serious.

This section introduces the genitive case formally. You have already met it frequently, but now all forms of it are laid out (*GE* pp. 160–161, #178–179) and the main uses are listed (*GE* pp. 163–165, #180). You will also meet other forms of the comparative (*GE* pp. 165–167, #181–182) as well as the optative mood (*GE* pp. 167–169, #183–186).

8A

Page 90

1 Look for the subject and the two aorist participles before you go on to the main verb.

4 ἀπιόντα   Remember the difference between ὤν ('being') and ἰών ('going'). The 'going' verb has an iota, the 'being' verb does not.

3–4 καθορᾳ̃ ..., κατιδών   If you remove the prefix, καθ-, κατ-, you should be able to recognise the verb. ἰδ is the stem of the second aorist εἶδον.

8 λαμβάνεται τοῦ ἱματίου   He takes hold of his tunic. The genitive is used because he takes hold of part of his tunic (not the whole thing). This is called a partitive genitive.

Page 91

11 τίς ὤν σύ ...   Note the idiomatic use of the participle, 'Who are you to take hold of...?'

13 τυγχάνω + participle   'happen to be ...'

19 ὑμῶν ἕνεκα   ἕνεκα follows the word it governs.

20 περιμενοῦμεν   Tense? Cf. περιμένομεν: which is future and which is present and how can you tell? See *GE* p. 104, #117.

21 φθάνω + participle   'to do something before someone else'. See *GE* p. 86, #95.

23 ποῖ δὴ καὶ πόθεν;   You will need to supply verbs in English, but the meaning should be clear.

25 κυρία ἐκκλησία   There was a 'sovereign' assembly once a month unless
additional emergency ones were needed. κύριος is a word with a wide range of
meanings, all of which are concerned with authority or power. The head of the
family is ὁ κύριος, and the word is also used in the New Testament for Jesus
Christ.

Page 92

27–28 μῶν εἰς κόρακας;   Joke! Cf. 6A line 4 βάλλ' εἰς κόρακας.

29 ἀνιστάμεθα   See *GE* p. 170, #187.

30 λέγοιτ' ἄν   This is a new mood, called the optative (*GE* pp. 167–169,
#183–186). Don't try to learn it now, but you may want to start making a
chart to fill in. You can usually recognise it easily because of -οι- in the
ending. The optative + ἄν means 'could' or 'would'. It is called the *potential
optative*.

31 ἄν ἀκούοιμι   Another one.

32 λέγοιμι ἄν   And another.

ἀπράγμονα   ἀ-πράγμων = 'not busy' or more often 'not meddlesome', or
'trouble-free'. It is the opposite of πολυπράγμων 'meddling'. Cf. πράττω and
πρᾶγμα.

Translation for 8A

*Dikaiopolis, having observed the lawlessness of the Eleven and having heard the
words of the suppliant, goes away through the crowd of citizens towards the
agora with the rhapsode. And Euelpides the son of Polemarchos sees him going
away with the rhapsode towards the market-place. Having seen them, he sends
his slave to them. Thus Euelpides' slave approaches Dikaiopolis and shouts, as
he comes up.*

SLAVE   Wait, Dikaiopolis, wait!
DIKAIOPOLIS   What shout is that? Who is responsible for that shout?
             The slave runs up and grabs his tunic.
SL.   I was the cause of the shouting.
DIK.   Who are you, and why are you holding my tunic, my good fellow?
SL.   I am a slave.
DIK.   But whose slave are you? Who sent you?
SL.   I am the slave of Euelpides, and he happened to send me. For Euelpides, the
             son of Polemarchus, greets you.
DIK.   But where is he?
SL.   Here he is, he is coming up behind. Do you not see him, running through the
             crowd of people? And a friend of his is following with him, Peisetairos, the son
             of Stilbonides. It is clear that he is running after you. But wait!
DIK.   We will wait.
             *Euelpides runs up, holding a basket in his hand. He gets there before
             Peisetairos and taking Dikaiopolis' hand he greets him.*

EUELPIDES   Greetings, my dear Dikaiopolis, where are you going and where have you come from?

DIK.   From the Piraeus, my friend, and I am on my way to the assembly. It will be a sovereign assembly today.

Meanwhile Peisetairos comes up, with a crow on his wrist.

DIK.   Greetings to you too, Peisetairos, but where on earth are you going with that crow? Could it be that you are going to the crows?

PEISETAIROS   Of course! We are leaving the country, our fatherland.

DIK.   But why do you want to leave like this, my friends? Please tell me, for I would be very glad to know the reason.

EU.   I will tell you. We are looking for a peaceful place. We shall go there, and when we get there, we shall settle in a peaceful city.

DIK.   But why do you want to carry that crow on your wrist?

EU.   This crow is guiding us, and we are following it. For who can lead us to the crows better than a crow?

DIK.   He is certainly the best guide.

8B

Page 94

1   μείζονα   Comparative. See *GE* pp. 136–138, #154–160 for more forms. Note that there are two ways of saying more … than …: *GE* pp. 137, #158 and *GE* p. 164, #180(e).

4   εὐδαιμονεστέραν   This is another form of the comparative; see *GE* p. 166, #182. It is easily recognisable, as is the superlative which follows in the next line.

9   τί παθόντες   Aorist participle of πάσχω, second aor. ἔπαθον. Literally 'having experienced what, and wanting what, are you leaving?'

13   τοιοῦτον τὸ πάθος   πάθος is a neuter noun 3c. τοιοῦτον = 'such'.

13–14   εἰς τὸ δικαστήριον   Note the -ηριον ending which denotes a place where an activity takes place. Cf. φροντιστήριον.

16   κατεψηφίσαντο   ψηφίζομαι means 'I vote'. καταψηφίζομαι means 'I condemn', ἀποψηφίζομαι means 'I acquit'.

20   οἱ μὲν γὰρ τέττιγες …   For the Athenian love of litigation see also Section 6B lines 23–24, where Strepsiades cannot believe that it is Athens on the map because there are no jurors sitting.

30   ἀποκρινοῦμαι   What is the tense? Cf. ἀποκρίνομαι.

Translation for 8B

DIKAIOPOLIS   Are you looking for a greater city than Athens?

EUELPIDES   No, by Zeus, I do not mean that. There is no greater city than this one. For, in the name of Zeus, Athens is clearly the greatest.

RHAPSODE   Are you looking for a wealthier city than this one?

EU.   There is no city wealthier than this one. For Athens is the wealthiest.

DIK.   What then? What do you have in mind? Do you perhaps hate the city?

PEISETAIROS   No, by Zeus, we do not hate the city itself.

DIK.   Tell me then, my friends, what happened to you, or what is it that you want that makes you leave the city?

EU.   Peisetairos here and I have had a terrible experience, Dikaiopolis, and so we want to go away. For we find the affairs of the city hard to bear, especially the lawcourts. So great was the misfortune we suffered when we entered the lawcourts.

RHAP.   What sort of misfortune? What had you done, or what wrong did you do so that you suffered this misfortune?

EU.   We did nothing and we did no wrong, but the jurors condemned us, even though we were innocent, because of the false testimony of the witnesses.

DIK.   I am not surprised that you are setting off to find another city, since you give a just account of the lawcourt and the jurors. For the crickets sing for a little while in the branches, but the Athenians sing all the time in their lawsuits. You are doing this with reason. And it is with reason that I shall not do this. For I, like the orators, love the city and I shall never cease to love the city.

PEI.   Dikaiopolis, what are you saying? Do you really think that the orators love the city?

DIK.   I do. Why not?

PEI.   But how do the orators show their love for the people? Consider. The war drags on, everywhere there is lamentation and funeral pyres because of the plague: everywhere there are corpses, there is much lawlessness. Do the orators show pity for the people? Do they pity them or not? Tell me. Why are you silent? You will not say? They do not pity them, but they will destroy the city, you know it well. I will answer for you. The land is full of their audacity, the assembly is full of it and the lawcourts are full of it, but the people are full of distress.

8C

Page 96

3–4 οἴκοι μέν ... ἐν δὲ τῇ ἐκκλησίᾳ ...   Note the contrast.

13 βελτίους   Not what it seems at first glance – see *GE* p. 166, #181.

15 χείρους   What case is it?

16 βελτίους   What case is it?

    κλοπήν   Pericles was suspended from his office of strategos and ordered to submit his accounts for inspection. They were found to be five talents adrift and he was convicted. His conviction was largely a political move, and he was re-elected the following year.

21 τὸ ἀγαθόν   Plato's lectures on 'The Good' were said to be the ultimate in obscurity. But the remark was made by a slave in comedy, and should not perhaps be taken too seriously.

23 γνούς   Aorist participle of γιγνώσκω, from the second aorist ἔγνων.

25 δύναται   *GE* p. 156, #177.

25–26 οἱ μέν ... οἱ δέ ...   'some ... others ...'

27–30 A rather touching personal view. It shows Aristophanes' sympathy with 'honest country folk', and a glimpse of the pre-war Athens.

32 ἂν βουλοίμην   ἄν + optative again – 'could', 'would'.
ἀναπείσω   What verb does this come from? Try πείθω.

33 εἶμι   (not εἰμί) 'I shall go'.

34 ἄλλο τι πλήν ...   'anything else but ...'

42–44 Note ἄν + optative repeatedly.

Page 97

46 A quotation from Homer, *Odyssey* 1.267.

48–49 Two lines from the *Homeric Hymn to Demeter* 216–217. The vocabulary should give you all the help you need.

Translation for 8C

DIKAIOPOLIS   You seem to speak the truth, Peisetairos. But who will save the city, since the orators seem to be worth nothing? Perhaps the people themselves?

EUELPIDES   O Herakles, don't say that! For the people are most skilled at home, but absolute idiots in the assembly.

RHAPSODE   But if Pericles –

DIK.   Don't speak of Pericles!

RHAP.   What do you mean, my friend? Pericles seemed to be the best of them all, so they say.

PEISETAIROS   But the good citizen makes the citizens better instead of worse. Did Pericles do this or not?

RHAP.   He did it, by Zeus!

PEI.   When Pericles began to speak in the assembly, therefore, were the Athenians worse, and when he died were they better?

RHAP.   It is probable that they were. For the good citizen makes the others better.

PEI.   But we know clearly, you and I, that at first Pericles was well thought of when the Athenians were, as you say, worse; but when they became better, because of him, they condemned him for theft, and it is clear that he was a villain.

DIK.   You speak the truth, I know it well. Who will save the city? A man who loves the city will save it and not destroy it. What must we do?

RHAP.   Dikaiopolis, you must seek the good of the city.

DIK.   But what is the good, rhapsode? For I don't know what it is that is the good [of the city].

RHAP.   You don't know what 'the good' is? But on the ship you seemed to be some sort of a philosopher, knowing their jargon.

DIK.   Don't mock me, rhapsode! For the philosophers search, as I hear, for 'the good', but no one can discover it. Some think that it is virtue, and others think that it is justice, but they do not know. But the farmers know what is good. They have found it in the fields. It is peace. For war is full of events, perplexity and plague and fitting out ships; but peace is full of weddings, feasts, relations, children, friends, wealth, health, food, wine and pleasure. I do not know if anyone else wants to make a treaty and to live at peace, but I would like to, myself. But how shall I alone persuade the people? What shall I say or shout or order, if I am going to make a treaty? But I shall go, ready to shout and abuse anyone who speaks about anything else except peace. Come on now, Dikaiopolis, off to the assembly!

EU. + PEI.   Yet we are setting off for a place that is peaceful. Farewell!

RHAP.   I think these men are stupid. I wouldn't do that. I wouldn't hurry off to the assembly, nor would I want to flee from my own country. Don't they know that the poet spoke truly who said

'These matters lie in the lap of the gods'

For we must accept the gifts of the gods with resignation, both the bad and the better.

'We men must endure the gifts of the gods,
though grieving. For the yoke lies
upon our necks.'

EXERCISES FOR SECTION 8

THE GENITIVE CASE

8A–C: 1

1.	lawlessness	τῆς ἀνομίας, τῶν ἀνομιῶν
2.	peace	τῆς εἰρήνης, τῶν εἰρηνῶν
3.	market-place	τῆς ἀγορᾶς, τῶν ἀγορῶν
4.	assembly	τῆς ἐκκλησίας, τῶν ἐκκλησιῶν
5.	battle	τῆς μάχης, τῶν μαχῶν
6.	voice	τῆς φωνῆς, τῶν φωνῶν
7.	virtue, courage	τῆς ἀρετῆς, τῶν ἀρετῶν

8A–C: 2

1.	citizen	τοῦ πολίτου, τῶν πολιτῶν
2.	juror	τοῦ δικαστοῦ, τῶν δικαστῶν
3.	poet	τοῦ ποιητοῦ, τῶν ποιητῶν
4.	a sophist	τοῦ σοφιστοῦ, τῶν σοφιστῶν

8A–C: 3

1.	trireme	τῆς τριήρους, τῶν τριηρῶν
2.	Socrates	τοῦ Σωκράτους
3.	relation, kinsman	τοῦ συγγενοῦς, τῶν συγγενῶν
4.	Pericles	τοῦ Περικλέους

8A–C: 4

1. food   τοῦ σίτου, τῶν σίτων
2. a philosopher   τοῦ φιλοσόφου, τῶν φιλοσόφων
3. the people   τοῦ δήμου, τῶν δήμων
4. lawcourt   τοῦ δικαστηρίου, τῶν δικαστηρίων
5. time   τοῦ χρόνου, τῶν χρόνων
6. river   τοῦ ποταμοῦ, τῶν ποταμῶν
7. young man   τοῦ νεανίσκου, τῶν νεανίσκων
8. heaven, sky   τοῦ οὐρανοῦ, τῶν οὐρανῶν

8A–C: 5

1. worthy   τοῦ ἀξίου, τῆς ἀξίας, τοῦ ἀξίου, τῶν ἀξίων
2. that   ἐκείνου τοῦ, ἐκείνης τῆς, ἐκείνου τοῦ, ἐκείνων τῶν
3. right   τοῦ δεξιοῦ, τῆς δεξιᾶς, τοῦ δεξιοῦ, τῶν δεξιῶν
4. ready   τοῦ ἑτοίμου, τῆς ἑτοίμης, τοῦ ἑτοίμου, τῶν ἑτοίμων
5. himself   τοῦ αὐτοῦ, τῆς αὐτῆς, τοῦ αὐτοῦ, τῶν αὐτῶν
6. difficult   τοῦ χαλεποῦ, τῆς χαλεπῆς, τοῦ χαλεποῦ, τῶν χαλεπῶν
7. your (pl.) τοῦ ὑμετέρου, τῆς ὑμετέρας, τοῦ ὑμετέρου, τῶν ὑμετέρων
8. greatest   τοῦ μεγίστου, τῆς μεγίστης, τοῦ μεγίστου, τῶν μεγίστων
9. best   τοῦ βελτίστου, τῆς βελτίστης, τοῦ βελτίστου, τῶν βελτίστων
10. your (s.) τοῦ σοῦ, τῆς σῆς, τοῦ σοῦ, τῶν σῶν
11. much   τοῦ πολλοῦ, τῆς πολλῆς, τοῦ πολλοῦ, τῶν πολλῶν
12. this   τούτου τοῦ, ταύτης τῆς, τούτου τοῦ, τούτων τῶν

8A–C: 6

1. suffering   τοῦ πάθους, τῶν παθῶν
2. number, crowd   τοῦ πλήθους, τῶν πληθῶν
3. wall   τοῦ τείχους, τῶν τειχῶν

8A–C: 7

1. thing, affair   τοῦ πράγματος, τῶν πραγμάτων
2. herald   τοῦ κήρυκος, τῶν κηρύκων
3. possession   τοῦ κτήματος, τῶν κτημάτων
4. speaker   τοῦ ῥήτορος, τῶν ῥητόρων
5. old man   τοῦ γέροντος, τῶν γερόντων
6. foot   τοῦ ποδός, τῶν ποδῶν
7. thought   τῆς φροντίδος, τῶν φροντίδων
8. thing, object   τοῦ χρήματος, τῶν χρημάτων
9. god   τοῦ δαίμονος, τῶν δαιμόνων
10. woman   τῆς γυναικός, τῶν γυναικῶν

8A–C: 8

1.	ill-fated	κακοδαίμονος, κακοδαίμονος, κακοδαιμόνων
2.	going	ἰόντος, ἰούσης, ἰόντος, ἰόντων
3.	being	ὄντος, οὔσης, ὄντος, ὄντων
4.	better	βελτίονος, βελτίονος, βελτιόνων
5.	having set free	λύσαντος, λυσάσης, λύσαντος, λυσάντων
6.	worse	χείρονος, χείρονος, χειρόνων
7.	someone	τινός, τινός, τινῶν

8A–C: 9

1.	Zeus	τοῦ Διός
2.	I	ἐμοῦ, μου, ἡμῶν
3.	ship	τῆς νεώς, τῶν νεῶν
4.	king	τοῦ βασιλέως, τῶν βασιλέων
5.	you	σοῦ, σου, ὑμῶν
6.	eyebrow	τῆς ὀφρύος, τῶν ὀφρύων
7.	old woman	τῆς γραός, τῶν γραῶν

8A–C: 10

1.	juror	τοῦ δικαστοῦ, τῶν δικαστῶν
2.	child, slave	τοῦ παιδός, τῶν παίδων
3.	sun	τοῦ ἡλίου, τῶν ἡλίων
4.	dwelling	τῆς οἰκήσεως, τῶν οἰκήσεων
5.	possession	τοῦ κτήματος, τῶν κτημάτων
6.	plan	τῆς διανοίας, τῶν διανοιῶν
7.	temple, shrine	τοῦ ἱεροῦ, τῶν ἱερῶν
8.	city	τοῦ ἄστεως, τῶν ἄστεων

8A–C: 11

1.	μετὰ τοῦ Σωκράτους	8.	ἄξιος τῆς ἀρετῆς
2.	ἀπὸ τῆς ἐκκλησίας	9.	αἴτιος τῆς ἀνομίας
3.	διὰ τοῦ πλήθους	10.	μετὰ τοῦ κήρυκος
4.	ἐκ τοῦ πλοίου	11.	διὰ τοῦ ποταμοῦ
5.	καταδικάζω τοῦ ἀνθρώπου	12.	περὶ τοῦ νόμου
6.	ἀκούω τῆς γυναικός	13.	ἀπὸ τῶν Ἀθηνῶν
7.	λαμβάνομαι τοῦ πολίτου	14.	ἐκ τῆς οἰκίας

ALTERNATIVE COMPARATIVE FORMS

8A–C: 12

1.	τὸν βελτίονα, βελτίω ναύτην	the better sailor
2.	τοὺς βελτίονας, βελτίους λιμένας	the better harbours

3. τὴν βελτίονα, βελτίω θεάν   the better goddess
4. αἱ βελτίονες, βελτίους νῆες   the better ships.
5. οἱ βελτίονες, βελτίους γεωργοί   the better farmers
6. τὰς βελτίονας, βελτίους γυναῖκας   the better women
7. τὸ βέλτιον ἄστυ   the better city
8. τὰ βελτίονα, βελτίω πλοῖα   the better ships

COMPARING ADJECTIVES LIKE εὔφρων

8A–C: 13

1. ὁ εὐδαιμονέστερος, εὐδαιμονέστατος ναύτης
   the more fortunate, most fortunate sailor
2. τὸ κακοδαιμονέστερον, κακοδαιμονέστατον ἄστυ
   the more unfortunate, most unfortunate city
3. τὴν εὐφρονεστέραν, εὐφρονεστάτην θεάν
   the more gracious, most gracious goddess
4. τὰς κακοδαιμονεστέρας, κακοδαιμονεστάτας γυναῖκας
   the more unlucky, most unlucky women
5. ἡ εὐδαιμονεστέρα, εὐδαιμονεστάτη νῆσος
   the more fortunate, most fortunate island
6. τοὺς κακοδαιμονεστέρους, κακοδαιμονεστάτους διδασκάλους
   the more unfortunate, most unfortunate teachers

THE OPTATIVES

8A–C: 14

1. they find   εὑρίσκουσιν   εὑρίσκοιεν
2. he/she examines   ἐξετάζει   ἐξετάζοι
3. we reckon   λογιζόμεθα   λογιζοίμεθα
4. he/she becomes   γίγνεται   γίγνοιτο
5. you (s.) marvel   θαυμάζεις   θαυμάζοις

8A–C: 15

1. you (s.) love   φιλεῖς   φιλοίης
2. they intend   διανοοῦνται   διανοοῖντο
3. he conquers   νικᾷ   νικῴη
4. he/she tries   πειρᾶται   πειρῷτο
5. they dare   τολμῶσιν   τολμῷεν

ἄν + OPTATIVE

8A–C: 16

1. φέροιεν ἄν   4. πέμποιμι ἄν
2. διαλεγοίμεθα ἄν   5. δέχοιο ἄν
3. σκοποίη ἄν   6. ἀδικοῖεν ἄν

7. ὁρῷη ἄν   9. φυλάττοιμεν ἄν
8. πείθοιτε ἄν   10. πείθοιντο ἄν

ἀνίσταμαι, *I LEAVE, EMIGRATE*

8A–C: 17

1. you (s.) leave   6. they are able
2. he/she is able   7. being able
3. leaving (n.m.s.)   8. he/she leaves
4. to be able   9. we are able
5. you (pl.) leave, leave! 10. to leave

SUMMARY EXERCISES FOR SECTION 8

A – VOCABULARY-BUILDING

1. I wrong   the wrongdoing
    I stand up   the awakening,
                           resurrection
    worthy   important
    people/I am   the power of the
      powerful   people
    leader   the leadership
    I am powerful   most powerful
    I send   the procession
    citizen   constitution   I engage in   political/to do with the
                                               government   city
    difficult   I am difficult/angry
    hand   I set my hand to
                           something, I try

B/C – WORD SHAPE AND SYNTAX

1.

A   But who is responsible for this war and this perplexity? (τούτου τοῦ
    πολέμου, ταύτης τῆς ἀπορίας)

B   The orators are responsible for this matter, I know it well. For the city is
    full of noise and shouting because of the war and the boldness of the
    orators. For who does not know about their boldness? (τούτου τοῦ
    πράγματος, θορύβου, βοῆς, τῶν ῥητόρων, τῆς τόλμης, αὐτῶν)

A   But I don't think the orators are responsible for these matters, but [I
    consider them] the best of men. For they always fight for the people and
    the city, as they themselves say. (τούτων τῶν πραγμάτων, ἀνθρώπων, τοῦ
    πλήθους, τῆς πόλεως)

B   Yes. But they tell lies. For the mass of these men is bad and no
    one is worse than an orator. For the orators seize the assembly and the

lawcourt, (τούτων τῶν ἀνδρῶν, ῥήτορος, τῆς ἐκκλησίας, τοῦ δικαστηρίου)

2.   1. μένοις ἄν You could wait   5. ἀποκρίνοιο ἄν You could answer
     2. λέγοιμι ἄν I might speak   6. κελεύοις ἄν You would order
     3. βουλοίμεθα ἄν We would like to   7. παυοίμην ἄν I could stop
     4. πείθοισθε ἄν You would obey   8. φέροιμεν ἄν We would carry

3.   a. (i) The foreigner sits on the altar. (ἐπί + gen.)
        (ii) The ship goes towards the enemy. (ἐπί + acc.)
     b. (i) I shall go tomorrow into the agora with my friends. (μετά + gen.)
        (ii) After this I shall go back home. (μετά + acc.)
     c. (i) The ship sails past the island. (παρά + acc.)
        (ii) The sophist receives much money from the pupils. (παρά + gen.)
     d. (i) The slave ran towards us, forcing his way through the crowd. (διά + gen.)
        (ii) My wife is afraid of the city because of the plague. (διά + acc.)

4.   1. Διονυσόδωρος καλλίων ἐστὶν Εὐθυδήμου
        ἢ Εὐθύδημος
     2. Διονυσόδωρος μείζων ἐστὶν Εὐθυδήμου
        ἢ Εὐθύδημος
     3. Διονυσόδωρος κακοδαιμονέστερός ἐστιν Εὐθυδήμου
        ἢ Εὐθύδημος
     4. Διονυσόδωρος εὐφρονέστερός ἐστιν Εὐθυδήμου
        ἢ Εὐθύδημος
     5. Διονυσόδωρος ἀμείνων ἐστὶν Εὐθυδήμου
        ἢ Εὐθύδημος
     6. Διονυσόδωρος μωρότερός ἐστιν Εὐθυδήμου
        ἢ Εὐθύδημος
     7. Διονυσόδωρος σοφώτερός ἐστιν Εὐθυδήμου
        ἢ Εὐθύδημος

D – ENGLISH INTO GREEK

1.
     1. The herald's son listens to the speaker.
        ὁ παῖς ὁ τοῦ ἀνδρὸς τῆς τοῦ ῥαψῳδοῦ χειρὸς λαμβάνεται.
     2. Who is responsible for this lawlessness, which is so dreadful?
        τίς ἐστιν αἴτιος ἐκείνων τῶν βοῶν, μεγίστων οὐσῶν;
     3. Since we are Athenians we are worth much.
        σοφιστὴς ὤν, οὐδενὸς ἄξιος εἶ.
     4. Why do you say that no one is wiser than Socrates?
        διὰ τί οἱ ῥήτορες πλουσιώτεροί εἰσιν ἢ τὸ τῆς πόλεως πλῆθος;/[no ἢ]
        τοῦ τῆς πόλεως πλῆθος; εἰπέ μοι.
     5. We made our way through the city of the Lacedemonians.
        πολλὰ κακὰ παθόντες πρὸς τοὺς Πέρσας ἐμαχεσάμεθα ὑπὲρ τῆς ἐλευθερίας.

2.

ΔΙΚΑΙΟΠΟΛΙΣ   ἰδού, ὁρῶ γὰρ παῖδά τινα πρὸς ἡμᾶς προστρέχοντα. τίνος εἶ σὺ παῖς;

ΔΟΥΛΟΣ   παῖς ὢν τυγχάνω τοῦ Εὐελπίδου, τοῦ σοῦ φίλου.

εἴποις ἂν ὅτι βούλῃ, καὶ τί βουλόμενος πρὸς ἐμὲ προσέδραμες;

ΔΟΥ.   ὅ τι; εἴποιμι ἄν. δεῖ γὰρ ἐμέ, ὡς ἐκέλευσεν ὁ Εὐελπίδης, κελεύειν ὑμᾶς μένειν.

ΔΙΚ.   μενῶ οὖν. χαίρετε, ὦ Εὐελπίδη καὶ Πεισέταιρε. τί βουλόμενοι ἀπὸ τῆς πόλεως ἀπέρχεσθε; ποῖ διανοεῖσθε ἀπιέναι;

ΠΕΙΣΕΤΑΙΡΟΣ   πρὸς πόλιν τινὰ νέαν καὶ χρησιμωτέραν δεῖ ἡμᾶς ἀπελθεῖν.

E – TEST EXERCISE 8

A slave, going through the crowd of citizens, ran towards Dikaiopolis and, taking hold of his hand, asked him to wait. Then those who had sent the slave, Euelpides and Peisetairos, who were friends of Dikaiopolis, came towards Dikaiopolis and greeted him. He, however, since he did not know what their object was in leaving the city, asked them where they intended to go and for what reason. They answered that they had to look for Cloud-Cuckooland, and, when they had found it, to live there. Dikaiopolis thought that Athens was the most prosperous, and that no city was better than Athens. So at first he could not understand why they were leaving, then having heard about the dikasts and the lawcourt and the politicians, he agreed. For the dikasts seemed to be wronging the good men, and the politicians (as it seemed) were actually destroying the people and not pitying them. So Dikaiopolis' friends went away. But he, finding the affairs of the city and the people hard to bear and thinking that peace was best, decided to make a treaty in the assembly. But the rhapsode, who thought that the men were ignorant and stupid, did not himself want to accompany him, but went away alone.

EXERCISE

1. (a) aorist   (b) aorist   (c) present   (d) aorist
    (e) aorist   (f) present   (g) present   (h) present
2. (a) genitive   (b) genitive   (c) accusative (d) nominative
    (e) genitive   (f) accusative

Section Nine: Aristophanes' *Wasps*

This is a long section with a lively story which introduces several important items of grammar, the dative case (*GE* pp. 176–180, #189–190), the aorist infinitive (*GE* pp. 187–189, #195–197), the aorist imperative (*GE* pp. 189–191, #198–200), γιγνώσκω (*GE* p. 201, #209), and the principal parts of common and very irregular verbs (*GE* p. 202, #211). None of this is difficult, but it pays to learn the new grammar carefully after each section in which it is introduced.

Before you start you may like to look at the table (*GE* pp. 176–177, #103) where the forms of the dative are set out. Notice the predominance of ι:

in -ᾳ -ῃ -ῳ -ι -ει in the singular

in -αις -οις -σι in the plural

The various uses of the dative are well described in *GE* pp. 179–180, #190.

9A

Page 100

10 τί βουλόμενος   As before, 'wanting what, do you … ?'

ἀπολεῖς με …   'you will destroy me', 'you will be the death of me'. The future of ἀπόλλυμι.

11 βοῇ χρῶμαι   χράομαι ('I use') takes the dative (*GE* p.180, #190 (e)). The meaning is the same as if βοῷ had been written.

17 ἐμπεσεῖται   Future of ἐμπίπτω – πίπτω πεσοῦμαι ἔπεσον.

18 τυγχάνεις εἰδώς   εἰδώς -ότος is the participle of οἶδα; the infinitive is εἰδέναι.

20 οὑτοιί   οὗτος αὕτη τοῦτο + ι is even more demonstrative. 'These spectators *here*'. (Note that the neuter is τουτί ταυτί.)

20–21 κάτειπε…. τοῖς θεαταῖς, πολλοῖς δὴ οὖσιν   'Tell the spectators, being many indeed'. What part of the verb is οὖσιν? Can you recognise it? It is the dative plural of the participle ὤν οὖσα ὄν.

22 καταλέξω   From καταλέγω. What tense?

Translation for 9A

In front of the house are two slaves. They first converse with each other, then with the spectators.

SOSIAS   Hey you, what is the matter with you? (what are you suffering?) Hey you, what is the matter with you? I'm talking to you, Xanthias.

113

XANTHIAS   What's the shouting? To whom are you speaking, Sosias? Wanting what do you shout thus? You will destroy me by shouting.

SOS.   I'm talking to you, unlucky Xanthias, and it's for your sake that I'm shouting. But what are you suffering?

XAN.   I'm sleeping with pleasure.

SOS.   You're sleeping? But I would like to say something to you, ill-favoured man that you are, and unlucky.

XAN.   What would you like to say to me?

SOS.   I'd like to say to you that a great evil will befall you. For the master will kill you. So don't sleep. Don't you happen to know what sort of beast we are guarding?

XAN.   I certainly think I know.

SOS.   But these spectators here don't know. So tell the story of the play to the spectators, who are many.

XAN.   All right, I'll tell the large number of spectators the story of our play.

9B

Page 101

1   ἐκεινοσί   Compare οὑτοιί (line 20). 'That is our master *there*.'

4   τῷ δὲ δεσπότῃ   Possessive dative, see *GE* p. 180, #190 (b).

5   κελεύοντι ἐπιθόμεθα   πείθομαι takes the dative; ἐπιθόμην is the second aorist. 'We obeyed him ordering.'

6   ἐνέπεσεν   For the principal parts of πίπτω see 9A line 17.
     ἔγνω   What is it? Aorist of γιγνώσκω γνώσομαι ἔγνων: see *GE* p. 201, #209.

9   ὑμεῖς δ᾽ ἀποκρίνεσθε ἡμῖν ἐρωτῶσιν   Note the dative plural of the participle agreeing with ἡμῖν. 'You answer us asking.'

16   οὗτος δέ μοι ἐρομένῳ ἀποκρίνεται   'This man answers me, having asked.' Note the aorist participle ἐρόμενος from ἐρωτάω ἐρωτήσω ἠρόμην.

18   φιλόξενος … Φιλόξενος   This is the joke we have been working up to, with all the words beginning φιλ-, a pun on the name of Philoxenos.

Translation for 9B

XANTHIAS That is our master there, who is sleeping above peacefully. Can't you see him sleeping? So this is our master here. But the master has a very old father. The master ordered us to guard his father, and we obeyed his orders. For the master fell into perplexity about his father, since he knew that he was more wicked than the others in the city, and responsible for many evils. For the master's father has a certain illness. So I ask you, spectators, what happens to be the name of this illness? You answer us asking. Come now, what does this man say?

SOSIAS   He in answering us thinks that the old man is 'a lover of dice'. But I say to the man that it is clear that he is speaking nonsense, answering such things. None the less 'love-' is the beginning of this evil.

XAN.	Yes, the old man loves something. But what does this man say?
SOS.	This man answers me, having asked, that he thinks the father is 'a lover of sacrifices' or 'a lover of strangers'.
XAN.	By the dog, old fellow, he is not a lover of strangers (philoxenos), since Philoxenos, at any rate, is a homosexual.

9C

Page 102

1 ἐξευρήσετε   What tense? What verb? If you do not know, look up εὑρίσκω in the list of irregular verbs (*GE* pp. 436–442, #389). You will find this very helpful when you need to hunt for an unfamiliar form or if you are not quite sure which verb it comes from.

2 ἐμπεσοῦσα   What verb does this come from? What is it? Try the aorist participle of πίπτω.
ὑμῖν ἐν ἀπορίᾳ οὖσι   Note that οὖσι agrees with ὑμῖν 'you being in perplexity'.

4–5 τῆς μὲν ἡμέρας ... τῆς δὲ νυκτός   Genitive of the time within which, 'during the day and during the night'. See *GE* p. 181, #191 for time phrases.

8–9 ἐπεὶ τὸν πατέρα ἔμαθεν φιληλιαστὴν ὄντα   'When he learned that his father was φιληλιαστής'. Verbs of knowing and perceiving are often followed by a participle, 'learned his father being ...' The rest of the story will explain why his father's mania was such a bad thing.

12 παύσῃ   Can you recognise this? (2nd person singular future indicative middle.)
πείσῃ   Can you recognise this? It comes from πείθω.

13 ὁ δὲ πατήρ   'But his father did not obey him (αὐτῷ) persuading (ἀναπείθοντι) him not to go out.'

14 ἐκορυβάντιζεν   We do not know why he enrolled his father as a Korybant. Was it just to take his mind off being a juror, or does Aristophanes say this simply for the ridiculous picture of him sitting in court banging his tambourine?

15 ἐμπεσών   What is it? It should be familiar by now! If not see 9A line 17, and learn the principal parts of πίπτω.

Translation for 9C

XANTHIAS   You will never find [it] out, spectators. Indeed, if you want to know what the illness is that has befallen the father, be silent now. For I shall tell you, being in perplexity, the illness of the old man. He is a lover of being a juror in the court of the Eliaia, like no man. For he is always being a juror and loves the lawcourt, sitting in the lawcourt during the day and dreaming of cases during the night. Indeed, lovers write on a door 'Demos is beautiful', but this man, on seeing and approaching, writes alongside near by 'Kemos (a voting funnel) is beautiful.' So we are guarding this man, having shut him in with these bars which are many and big. For when his son learned that his father was a lover of being a juror in the lawcourt of the Eliaia, finding the illness hard to bear, first he tried to persuade him not to go out of the house, saying such things: 'Why', he said, 'do you always judge cases, Father, in the lawcourt? Won't you stop being a juror in the Eliaia court? Won't you obey your son?'

But the father didn't obey him persuading [him] not to go out. Then the son introduced the father into the Korybantic rites. But the father, having fallen [head-long] into the lawcourt, was a juror, drum and all. From that time, having shut him inside, we have been guarding him with these nets. The name of the old man is Philokleon, while the name of this son is Bdelykleon.

9D

Page 104

6 τίσι   Dative plural of τίς. 'To whom is the man speaking?'

7 ὡς ἐμοί δοκεῖ   This is the impersonal use of δοκεῖ, 'as it seems to me'.

8 ἐντυχών   τυγχάνω takes the dative in the sense of 'finding', 'happening upon', 'meeting with'.

11 λόγῳ μέν ... ἔργῳ δέ ...   'in word ... in deed ...'; 'in theory ... in practice ...' a very frequent contrast.

20 καπνῷ ἐξιόντι οὐχ ὅμοιος εἶ   ὅμοιος takes the dative ('like to'): 'You are not like smoke coming out, but more like ...'

22 οὐδενὶ ... ἤ ...   'He seems to me to be more like *to no one* than Philokleon.'

Translation for 9D

BDELYKLEON   *(Shouts to the slaves from the roof.)*
Xanthias and Sosias, are you asleep?

XANTHIAS   Oh dear, poor me!

SOSIAS   What is it?

XAN.   The master is no longer sleeping, but is already standing and shouting.

SOS.   But to whom is the man speaking?

XAN.   Bdelykleon is saying something to us, as it seems to me. And our master, on happening upon us sleeping, will destroy [us].

SOS.   He seems to me too to be saying something, Xanthias. But wanting what are you standing up/what need makes you stand up, master?

BDEL.   What need? In theory my father is quiet, Sosias, but in practice he wants to go out. And my father always uses audacity when he wants to go out. But now, as it seems to me at any rate, my father, having gone into the oven, is seeking a hole with great zeal. Lord Poseidon, whatever noise is the chimney making?
Out of the chimney comes Philokleon.
You, who are you?

PHILOKLEON   Me, I'm smoke coming out.

BDEL.   Smoke? But you are not like smoke coming out, as it seems to me, but more like Philokleon. What do you think, Xanthias?

XAN.   He seems to me to be more like to no one than Philokleon, master.

BDEL.   Here now, look for some other scheme.

9E

Page 105

6 νουμηνία   The first day of the month was market day.

11 τὸν ἡμίονον   The 'half-donkey' is a mule, offspring of a horse and a donkey.

12 αὐτοῖς τοῖς κανθηλίοις   'pack-saddle and all'. See *GE* p. 180, #190 (h).

15 ἄμεινον ἢ σύ   Both this phrase and σοῦ ἄμεινον in the next line have the same meaning.

17 εἰσιών, ἔξαγε   Note the prefixes, 'going *in*, bring *out* …'

20–21 εἰ μὴ φέρεις Ὀδυσσέα τινά   'If you are not carrying an Odysseus'. The picture of Odysseus escaping from the Cyclops under a ram should make the reference clear.

Page 106

25 Οὖτις   Odysseus also tricked the Cyclops by telling him that his name was Οὖτις 'Nobody'. (See Homer, *Odyssey* 9 for the story.)

27 Ἰθακήσιος   Odysseus came from Ithaka, but he was not 'the son of runaway horse'!

31 γιγνώσκω γάρ σε πάντων πονηρότατον ὄντα   'I know you are (participle) the most wicked of all men.'

35 λίθων   From λίθος we get 'monolith', 'megalith', 'lithograph', etc.

37 ἐνέπεσε   What tense? What verb? Try πίπτω.

41 φθήσεται   The future of φθάνω. For the meaning of φθάνω and of λανθάνω + participle see *GE* p. 86, #95.

Translation for 9E

PHILOKLEON   But open the door.

BDELYKLEON   By Poseidon, Father, never at all.

PHIL.   But it is the first of the month today.

BDEL.   This man is preparing a great mischief, as it seems to me at any rate. What do you think, Xanthias?

XANTHIAS   It seems so to me too.

PHIL.   By Zeus, not at all, but I am coming out, since I want to sell the mule in the market-place, pack-saddle and all.

BDEL.   You want to sell the mule, pack-saddle and all? But I could do this.

PHIL.   I could do this better than you.

BDEL.   No, by Zeus, but I [could do it] better than you.

PHIL.   Well, go in and lead out the mule.

BDEL.   But suffering what are you groaning, mule? Is it because today we are going to sell you? But don't groan any longer, mule. What is this affair? Why are you groaning, if you are not carrying an Odysseus?

SOSIAS   But by Zeus it is carrying this certain someone underneath, at any rate.

BDEL.   Who is the mule carrying? Who are you, fellow?

PHIL.   Nobody by Zeus.

BDEL.   You, Nobody? From which country are you?

PHIL.   An Ithakan, the son of runaway horse.

BDEL.   Drag him from beneath. O most foul man. I know you are the most wicked of all men. For my father is most like Odysseus, as it seems to me at any rate. But, Father, push the mule and yourself into the house with, all urgency. You then, Sosias, push many of the stones towards the door with your hands.

SOS.   Alas poor me! What is this? From wherever did the clod of earth fall on me?

XAN.   Look, master. The man is becoming a sparrow.

BDEL.   Alas wretched me! For it does not escape my notice that my father is becoming a sparrow. But he will anticipate us by escaping. Where, where is my net? Shoo, shoo, shoo back!
         (He pursues the father with the net.)

SOS.   Come now. Since we have shut him in, and the old man will not again give trouble to us who have shut him in and are guarding him, nor will he escape our notice by running away, why don't we sleep for a little while?

EXERCISES FOR SECTION 9A–E

DATIVE CASE

9A–E: 1

1. sea   τῇ θαλάττῃ, ταῖς θαλάτταις
2. perplexity   τῇ ἀπορίᾳ, ταῖς ἀπορίαις
3. freedom   τῇ ἐλευθερίᾳ, ταῖς ἐλευθερίαις
4. safety   τῇ σωτηρίᾳ, ταῖς σωτηρίαις
5. goddess   τῇ θεᾷ, ταῖς θεαῖς
6. victory   τῇ νίκῃ, ταῖς νίκαις
7. harmony   τῇ ὁμονοίᾳ, ταῖς ὁμονοίαις
8. daring   τῇ τόλμῃ, ταῖς τόλμαις

9A–E: 2

1. spectator   τῷ θεατῇ, τοῖς θεαταῖς
2. poet   τῷ ποιητῇ, τοῖς ποιήταις
3. captain   τῷ κυβερνήτῃ, τοῖς κυβερνήταις
4. sophist   τῷ σοφιστῇ, τοῖς σοφισταῖς

9A–E: 3

1. trireme   τῇ τριήρει, ταῖς τριήρεσιν
2. Socrates   τῷ Σωκράτει
3. relation   τῷ συγγενεῖ, τοῖς συγγενέσιν

9A–E: 4

1. mule   τῷ ἡμιόνῳ, τοῖς ἡμιόνοις
2. ship   τῷ πλοίῳ, τοῖς πλοίοις
3. man   τῷ ἀνθρώπῳ, τοῖς ἀνθρώποις
4. lawcourt   τῷ δικαστηρίῳ, τοῖς δικαστηρίοις
5. time   τῷ χρόνῳ, τοῖς χρόνοις
6. friend   τῷ φίλῳ, τοῖς φίλοις
7. word   τῷ λόγῳ, τοῖς λόγοις
8. god   τῷ θεῷ, τοῖς θεοῖς

9A–E: 5

1. wicked   τῷ πονηρῷ, τῇ πονηρᾷ, τῷ πονηρῷ,
                 τοῖς πονηροῖς, ταῖς πονηραῖς, τοῖς πονηροῖς
2. that   ἐκείνῳ τῷ, ἐκείνῃ τῇ, ἐκείνῳ τῷ, ἐκείνοις τοῖς,
                 ἐκείναις ταῖς, ἐκείνοις τοῖς
3. disgraceful   τῷ μιαρῷ, τῇ μιαρᾷ, τῷ μιαρῷ,
                 τοῖς μιαροῖς, ταῖς μιαραῖς, τοις μιαροῖς
4. like   τῷ ὁμοίῳ, τῇ ὁμοίᾳ, τῷ ὁμοίῳ
                 τοῖς ὁμοίοις, ταῖς ὁμοίαις, τοῖς ὁμοίοις
5. bad   τῷ κακῷ, τῇ κακῇ, τῷ κακῷ
                 τοῖς κακοῖς, ταῖς κακαῖς, τοῖς κακοῖς
6. safe   τῷ σώῳ, τῇ σώᾳ, τῷ σώῳ
                 τοῖς σώοις, ταῖς σώαις, τοῖς σώοις
7. greatest   τῷ μεγίστῳ, τῇ μεγίστῃ, τῷ μεγίστῳ
                 τοῖς μεγίστοις, ταῖς μεγίσταις, τοῖς μεγίστοις
8. clear   τῷ δήλῳ, τῇ δήλῃ, τῷ δήλῳ
                 τοῖς δήλοις, ταῖς δήλαις, τοῖς δήλοις
9. your (s.)   τῷ σῷ, τῇ σῇ, τῷ σῷ, τοῖς σοῖς, ταῖς σαῖς, τοῖς σοῖς
10. much   τῷ πολλῷ, τῇ πολλῇ, τῷ πολλῷ
                 τοῖς πολλοῖς, ταῖς πολλαῖς, τοῖς πολλοῖς
11. this   τούτῳ τῷ, ταύτῃ τῇ, τούτῳ τῷ
                 τούτοις τοῖς, ταύταις ταῖς, τούτοις τοῖς
12. such   τοιούτῳ, τοιαύτῃ, τοιούτῳ
                 τοιούτοις, τοιαύταις, τοιούτοις

9A–E: 6

1. suffering   τῷ πάθει, τοῖς πάθεσιν
2. crowd, mass   τῷ πλήθει, τοῖς πλήθεσιν
3. wall   τῷ τείχει, τοῖς τείχεσιν

9A–E: 7

1. drama, play   τῷ δράματι, τοῖς δράμασιν
2. lord, king   τῷ ἄνακτι, τοῖς ἄναξιν

3. name   τῷ ὀνόματι, τοῖς ὀνόμασιν
4. thing, (pl.) money   τῷ χρήματι, τοῖς χρήμασιν
5. neighbour   τῷ γείτονι, τοῖς γείτοσιν
6. lamp, torch   τῇ λαμπάδι, ταῖς λαμπάσιν
7. night   τῇ νυκτί, ταῖς νυξίν
8. fatherland   τῇ πατρίδι, ταῖς πατρίσιν
9. leader, guide   τῷ ἡγεμόνι, τοῖς ἡγεμόσιν
10. woman   τῇ γυναικί, ταῖς γυναιξίν

9A–E: 8

1. better   ἀμείνονι, ἀμείνοσιν
2. going   ἰόντι, ἰούσῃ, ἰόντι, ἰοῦσιν· ἰούσαις, ἰοῦσιν
3. being   ὄντι, οὔσῃ, ὄντι, οὖσιν, οὔσαις, οὖσιν
4. having sacrificed   θύσαντι, θυσάσῃ, θύσαντι, θυσᾶσι, θυσάσαις, θυσᾶσιν
5. fortunate   εὐδαίμονι, εὐδαίμοσιν
6. someone   τινί, τισίν

9A–E: 9

1. Zeus   τῷ Διί
2. I   ἐμοί, μοι, ἡμῖν
3. ship   τῇ νηί, ταῖς ναυσίν
4. king   τῷ βασιλεῖ, τοῖς βασιλεῦσιν
5. you (s.)   σοί, σοι, ὑμῖν
6. eyebrow   τῇ ὀφρύι, ταῖς ὀφρύσιν
7. old woman   τῇ γραί, ταῖς γραυσίν

9A–E: 10

1. juror   τῷ δικαστῇ, τοῖς δικασταῖς
2. boy, slave   τῷ παιδί, τοῖς παισίν
3. river   τῷ ποταμῷ, τοῖς ποταμοῖς
4. dwelling   τῇ οἰκήσει, ταῖς οἰκήσεσιν
5. possession   τῇ κτήματι, τοῖς κτήμασιν
6. battle   τῇ μάχῃ, ταῖς μάχαις
7. temple, shrine   τῷ ἱερῷ, τοῖς ἱεροῖς
8. city   τῷ ἄστει, τοῖς ἄστεσιν

9A–E: 11

1. δοκεῖ τῷ Σωκράτει
2. ἕπομαι ὑμῖν
3. ἐντυγχάνω τῷ βασιλεῖ
4. ἐν ταῖς ναυσί(ν)
5. δοκεῖ ἡμῖν
6. πρὸς τοῖς θεαταῖς
7. σὺν ἡμῖν
8. χρῶμαι σοί
9. ἕπομαι αὐτοῖς
10. ἐν τῷ πλήθει
11. ἐπὶ τῇ νίκῃ
12. λόγῳ μὲν … ἔργῳ δέ

TIME PHRASES

9A–E: 12

1. We went away in the night.
2. The suppliant stayed in the shrine for two days.
3. I shall go within two days.
4. He met the man on the first day.
5. He was shouting all night.

PRINCIPAL PARTS OF VERBS

9A–E: 13

1. λήσει
2. ἤροντο, ἠρώτησαν
3. δύναιτο ἄν
4. ἐροῦμεν
5. ἔλαθεν
6. ἀνισταῖτο ἄν
7. ἤρετο, ἠρώτησεν
8. ἐροῦσι(ν)
9. δύναιντο ἄν
10. ἠρόμεθα, ἠρωτήσαμεν

REVISION EXERCISES FOR 9A–E

B/C – WORD SHAPE AND SYNTAX

1. He is my father, a very wicked man. ἡμῖν
2. A great evil will befall you, since you are accursed. ὑμῖν, κακοδαίμοσιν οὖσιν
3. In theory no one in the city is better than your father, but in fact no one is worse. ἐν ταῖς πόλεσιν.
4. Tell the spectator the plot of the play with full (all) enthusiasm. τοῖς θεαταῖς
5. We shout loudly (use great shouts). μεγάλῃ βοῇ
6. The sailors happened to be on the ships. ἐν τῷ πλοίῳ
7. We must obey those who give orders. τῷ κελεύοντι
8. What is the name of the king? τοῖς βασιλεῦσιν
9. Why do you (pl.) try to persuade me with this argument? τούτοις τοῖς λόγοις
10. On the next day the son chased his father back into the house with the big nets. τῷ μεγάλῳ δικτύῳ

D – ENGLISH INTO GREEK

1. This woman's plan is dangerous/terrible.
   τὸ ὄνομα τούτῳ τῷ θεατῇ ἐστι Φιλόξενος.
2. They are speaking to us and our children/slaves.
   λέγει ὑμῖν καὶ τοῖς θεαταῖς.
3. He was bringing the man on to the ship with the help of the sailors.
   χαλεπῶς οἴσουσι καθίζοντες ἐν τῷ δικαστηρίῳ.

4. I stole the money with (using) my right hand.
    ἐνέκλεισα τὸν πατέρα πολλοῖς δούλοις χρώμενος.
5. He is destroying Socrates with a wicked slander.
    καλοῖς λόγοις ἔπεισαν τὸν δῆμον οἱ ῥήτορες.

9F

Page 107

2 ἐάσω   The future of ἐάω 'I allow'.
3 λήσεις   The future of λανθάνω.
5 οὐκ ἐάσας   What is this? Compare it with εἴασας. Remember that the aorist indicative has an augment. The participle has not.
7 πιθέσθαι   Aorist infinitive from ἐπιθόμην (second aorist of πείθομαι). For aorist infinitives see *GE* pp. 187–189, #195–197. Here the aorist is used to emphasise the aspect. 'You must (χρή) stay here (present infinitive = all the time, a process) and obey me [now] (aorist infinitive denotes a single event).'
10 δικάσαι   First aorist infinitive active from δικάζω.
    δυνήσῃ   The future of δύναμαι: 'you will be able'.
11 μοι ... ἐνθάδε μένοντι   Note the agreement: 'How will it be possible *for me remaining* here to be a juror?' 'How will it be possible ... if I stay here?'

Page 108

16 παύσασθαι   First aorist infinitive middle.
17 κατάσκοπον   κατά, σκοπέω. Cf. the various English '-scope' words. Most relevant here is 'episcopal', from ἐπίσκοπος an 'overseer' or a 'bishop' in Christian Greek.
    γενέσθαι   What is this? What are the principal parts of γίγνομαι?
19 ἐξευρεῖν   What is it? Try the principal parts of εὑρίσκω. Remember that the infinitive does not have an augment.
    λαβεῖν   What is it? Try the principal parts of λαμβάνω.
25 λήψῃ   What tense? What person? What verb? Try the future of λαμβάνω.
28 ποιῆσαι   ποιέω ποιήσω <u>ἐποίησα</u>. Therefore aorist infinitive active.
40 ἐξήνεγκον   For the principal parts of φέρω see *GE* p. 202, #211.
47 ἐσθίειν   Another very irregular verb: ἐσθίω ἔδομαι ἔφαγον 'I eat'.

Translation for 9F

Bdelykleon speaks to the father.

BDELYKLEON   Listen, Father, I shall not allow you to go out to the courtroom any longer, nor will you escape my notice by trying to go out.

PHILOKLEON   What's this? But you will destroy me, not allowing me to go out.

BDEL.   You must stay here, Father, and obey me.

PHIL.   But nevertheless I want to be a juror.

BDEL.   Get up, Father, since today you will be able to be a juror.

PHIL.   But how will it be possible for me to be a juror if I stay here?

BDEL.   There will be a courtroom for you in your own house and you will be able to judge the members of the household.

PHIL.   What do you say? But in what way and about what?

BDEL.   About many things. Come then. For you have many household slaves, but you know well that the slaves do not want to stop doing wrong, but are responsible for many bad things. So you must become a spy of the affairs which happen in the house. And it will be possible for you being a spy to discover these evils today, and having discovered them to exact justice. So wouldn't you like to do this, and to force the household slaves to cease from their evils and become better?

PHIL.   I certainly would like to. For you convince me with your words. But you have not yet said this, from where I shall be able to get the pay. Wouldn't you like to reveal the matter?

BDEL.   You will get it from me.

PHIL.   You speak well.

BDEL.   And you would be willing to do this?

PHIL.   I would do this.

BDEL.   Hold on now. For I shall come quickly bringing the things of the lawcourt in my hands. By Zeus, I shall bring everything out.

The old man waits around, but the son goes into the house. After a short while Bdelykleon, on coming out, carries the things of the lawcourt in his hands with difficulty.

BDEL.   Look. For at last I have brought out the things of the lawcourt.

PHIL.   Indeed, have you brought out everything?

BDEL.   [Yes] by Zeus, I think at any rate that I have brought everything. And I have brought out this fire, at least. Look, near the fire there is some lentil soup for you.

PHIL.   Hurrah, hurrah! For it will be possible for me to eat the lentil-soup while I am judging. And by Zeus I shall eat it, as it seems to me, with all eagerness, being clever at eating. But wanting what have you brought out the cockerel?

BDEL.   What? The cock will be able to wake you up with its voice. For the speeches of the prosecutors are long, and you are clever at sleeping, although sitting in the lawcourt.

Grammar

Make sure that you have learned the principal parts of the irregular verbs you have met in this section before you go on further, and check that you can recognise the aorist infinitives active and middle.

9G

Page 110

4 ἄκουσον   What is it? 2nd person singular of the aorist imperative. See *GE* p. 189, #198. Note this form of the aorist imperative active in -σον.

5 ἴθι   See *GE* p. 191, #201 for the imperatives of εἰμί, εἶμι and οἶδα.
λέξον   Another aorist imperative.

11 κάδων ἕνεκα   There were two voting-urns, one for guilty and one for innocent. Jurors placed their pebbles in one or the other.

12 μὴ ἄπιθι μηδαμῶς, ἀλλ' ἐμοὶ πιθοῦ καὶ ἄκουσον, ὦ πάτερ   More imperatives. Note πιθοῦ, the 2nd person singular second aorist middle imperative from ἐπιθόμην.

14 ἔασον   The -σον ending again from the aorist imperative of ἐάω.

17 παῦσαι   2nd person singular of the aorist imperative middle of παύω. The spelling is exactly the same as the aorist infinitive active παῦσαι from ἔπαυσα, but the context will almost always make the meaning clear.

Page 111

24 ἡ κλεψύδρα   The water clock was used to measure the time allowed for the prosecution speech and the defence speech.

32 παῦσαι   See the note on line 17 above. Note all the other aorist imperatives that follow. The 2nd persons plural are much easier to recognise than the 2nd persons singular, because they are like the 2nd person plural of the aorist indicative, though without the augment.

34 κατηγορεῖτε   The κατά- prefix suggests 'I speak against', 'prosecute', 'accuse'.

Translation for 9G

BDELYKLEON   Does everything please you, Father? Tell me.

PHILOKLEON   Everything does indeed please me, know that well.

BDEL.   Therefore sit down, father. Look, I am calling the first case.

PHIL.   Don't call the case, child, but listen.

BDEL.   Well, all right, I'm listening. What do you say? Go on, Father, speak.

PHIL.   Where are the voting-urns? For I cannot place the vote without voting-urns, know it well.

The old man begins to run out.

BDEL.   Hey, you, where are you hurrying?

PHIL.   I'm running out because of the urns.

BDEL.   Don't go away in any way, but obey me and listen, Father.

PHIL.   But, child, I must look for the voting-urns and place my vote. But let [me].

(Again begins to run out.)

BDEL.   Stop running out, Father, since I happen to have these cups. So don't go away.

PHIL.   Fine! For everything of the lawcourt is here – except –

BDEL.   Speak; what is it?

PHIL.   Except the water clock. Where is the water clock? Bring it to me.

BDEL.   Look!

(He shows his father's chamber-pot.)

Speak, what is this? Do you not think that this chamber-pot is an excellent water clock? Everything is now here.

Sit down, then, Father, and stop worrying. Listen, slaves, and obey me, and bring out the fire. You pray to all the gods, and after praying, prosecute.

After bringing out the fire all the slaves go away, while those present pray to the gods.

Grammar

Make sure that you know these forms of the imperative before you go on to the next section.

EXERCISES FOR SECTION 9F–G

AORIST INFINITIVES

9F–G: 1

1.	to learn	μαθεῖν
2.	to run out	ἐκδραμεῖν
3.	to begin	ἄρξασθαι
4.	to lead out	ἐξαγαγεῖν
5.	to make, do	ποιήσασθαι
6.	to wrong (someone)	ἀδικῆσαι
7.	to consider	νομίσαι
8.	to guard	φυλάξαι
9.	to turn towards	προτρέψαι
10.	to sacrifice	θῦσαι

9F–G: 2

1.	to make, do	aorist	7.	to judge	aorist
2.	to conquer	present	8.	to see	aorist
3.	to speak	present	9.	to begin	present
4.	to set free	aorist	10.	to become	aorist
5.	to learn	present	11.	to go	aorist
6.	to run	aorist	12.	to lead, drive	present

AORIST IMPERATIVES AND MORE PRESENT IMPERATIVES

9F–G: 3

1.	learn (pl. aor.)	7.	become (s. aor.)
2.	speak (s. pres.)	8.	receive (s. aor.)
3.	speak (s. aor.)	9.	obey (s. aor.)
4.	stop (s. aor)	10.	find (pl. aor.)
5.	seek (s. pres.)	11.	stop (pl. aor.)
6.	stay (pl. aor.)	12.	let go, loose (s. aor.)

VOCATIVES

9F–G: 4

1.	voc.	7.	nom.
2.	nom., voc.	8.	nom., voc.
3.	nom.	9.	voc.
4.	nom., voc	10.	voc.
5.	voc.	11.	voc.
6.	nom., voc.	12.	voc.

πᾶς παντ- *ALL, WHOLE, EVERY*

9F–G: 5

1. Be, know
2. All of you women, go!, all you women are going
3. It was possible for you all to bear everything
4. Everyone be brilliant at selling. *(Only the accent shows it is imperative)*
5. All of you leave and do not remain but go
6. It will be possible for all to leave
7. Everybody come and carry everything
8. It is not possible for me to carry all these things
9. Get up and go (s)
10. Go (pl.) and carry all the equipment

REVISION EXERCISES FOR SECTION 9F–G

B/C – WORD SHAPE AND SYNTAX

1.

ἐπαυσάμην	παύσασθαι			
ἤκουσα	ἀκοῦσαι			
ἐποίησα	ποιῆσαι			
ἠδίκησα	ἀδικῆσαι			
εἶπον	εἰπεῖν			
ἤνεγκον	ἐνεγκεῖν	*or*	ἤνεγκα	ἐνέγκαι
ἐγενόμην	γενέσθαι			
ἔμαθον	μαθεῖν			
ἔλαβον	λαβεῖν			
ἀφικόμην	ἀφικέσθαι			
εἶδον	ἰδεῖν			
ἐπιθόμην	πιθέσθαι			
ἔπεσον	πεσεῖν			

2.
1. run away, flee (pl., pres.)
2. know, be (s., pres.)
3. look, see (s., pres.)
4. show (s., aor)
5. arrive (pl., aor.)
6. bring (s., aor.)

7. go (s., pres)   9. look (s., aor.)
8. be afraid (pl., pres)   10. cease (s., aor)

3. 1. I want to be a juror in the house, but my son does not allow me to be a juror here. δικάσαι δικάζειν
    2. We must all go out into the market-place. ἐξιέναι
    3. What must you do? ποιῆσαι
    4. It is permissible for Philokleon to prosecute. κατηγορεῖν
    5. The son did not allow his father to go out to the lawcourt. ἐλθεῖν
    6. How shall I persuade you, father, to listen to all the speeches? ἀκοῦσαι
    7. Why aren't you willing to bring out Philokleon, mule? ἐξενεγκεῖν
    8. You (s.) must become a juror in the house. γενέσθαι
    9. They must learn the words of the play. μαθεῖν
    10. He himself wants to keep taking the whole fee from his son. λαμβάνειν
    11. I shall not allow him to reach the lawcourt. ἀφικνεῖσθαι
    12. It is possible for me both to take the whole reward here and eat it. λαβεῖν, φαγεῖν

D – ENGLISH INTO GREEK

1. General, we must stay here and fight.
   ὦ πάτερ, δεῖ σε μένειν ἐνθάδε καὶ δικάζειν.
2. It is possible for me to listen to the orators.
   ἐξέσται πᾶσιν ὑμῖν πωλεῖν τοὺς ἡμιόνους.
3. I learn many things, but I do not understand everything.
   πάντα πάρεστιν ἐνθάδε πλὴν τοῦ πυρός.
4. Look at the ships, boys/slaves.
   ἐξενέγκετε τὰ πυρά/τάς λαμπάδας, ὦ παῖδες.
5. 'Tell me, what did you want when you knocked on the door?' 'What did I want? The master.'
   'εἰπέ μοι, τί βουλόμενος ἐξέδραμες;' 'ὅ τι; τὰ πάντα.'

9H

This section introduces the 3rd person of the imperative, which we have to translate as 'let him/her …' or as 'let them …' See *GE* pp. 197–199, #206–207 for the full paradigm.

The 3rd person endings of the imperative are easy to recognise:

	Active		*Middle*	
Singular	-έτω	-άτω	-έσθω	-άσθω
Plural	-όντων	-άντων	-έσθων	-άσθων

But it is easy to confuse the active endings -όντων and -άντων with the genitive plural of the present and aorist active participles which are the same in spelling. Once again only the context will help you.

Page 112

1, 3 εἰσίτω and προσίτω   Note the 3rd s. imperative of εἶμι 'I go'.

   3 ὁ φεύγων   'the defendant'. Cf. ὁ διώκων 'the prosecutor' in line 11.

   5 ἀκούσατε   'Listen to ...' This must be imperative because there is no augment. Compare ἠκούσατε 'you heard'.

   7 Λάβης   From λαμβάνω. The dog is called 'Grabber'. There is probably a topical reference here to a case which Kleon, the politician, may have been intending to bring against a man called Lakhes.

11–12 ἐξαπατήσειν μ' ἐλπίζεις   ἐλπίζω is normally followed by a future indicative: 'You hope to deceive me.'

   14 Dogs say αὖ αὖ, and sheep say βῆ βῆ. This is part of the evidence for the pronunciation of vowel sounds in the fifth century BC.

   16 'This seems to me to be another Labes (i.e. Grabber, i.e. thief).'
      λόγῳ μέν.... ἔργῳ δέ ...   Note the contrast. Cf. 8D line 11.

Page 114

   18 ἀναβάς   This is the aorist participle. Note the principal parts βαίνω βήσομαι ἔβην.

   19 ἀναβῆναι   Aorist infinitive of ἀναβαίνω.

   23 οὗτος ὁ ἀδικήσας 'the one having done wrong', 'the criminal', ἀδικήσας is the aorist participle of ἀδικέω.

   24 ὅτε   'When'. Cf. τότε 'then', and do not confuse it with ὅτι 'that', 'because'.
      ᾔτησα   From αἰτέω αἰτήσω ᾔτησα 'I ask'.

   25 οὐ παρεῖχέ μοι αἰτοῦντι   'did not give it to me asking'. Note that αἰτοῦντι agrees with μοι.

   27 ἑλεῖν αἱρέω αἱρήσω εἷλον. This usually means 'to take' (middle 'to choose'), but in the context of a lawcourt it will usually mean 'to convict'.

29–30 δεῖ σε ...   'You must hear them both, and, having heard them, on that basis (οὕτω) cast your vote.' σε is accusative after δεῖ, and ἀκούσαντα is accusative agreeing with σε. The two infinitives are governed by δεῖ.

   31 ὡς ὄντα ...   'as being ...' 'on the grounds that he is ...'
      κυνῶν ... ἄνδρα   An intentional absurdity, like μονο-φαγίστατον. Note μονο- and φαγ- and the superlative ending.

   35 προσιόντων πάντες   What is προσιόντων? What makes sense in the context? See introduction to 9H.

   40 κατάβηθι   'get down'. Note that the 2nd s. aorist imperative of βαίνω is βῆθι.

Translation for 9H

BDELYKLEON   If any juror happens to be outside, let him come in and make haste.

PHILOKLEON   Who is the defendant? Let him come forward.

The defendant, who is a dog, comes forward.

BDEL.　Listen now to the charge. Dog of the deme Kydathenaion has indicted dog Labes of the deme Aixone for theft. For the defendant has done wrong by eating up the cheese on his own. And indeed the defendant Labes here is present.

PHIL.　Let him come forward. O foul one here, I know that you are a thief. But you hope to deceive me, I know it. But where is the prosecutor, the dog from the deme of Kydathenaion? Come, dog.

DOG　Woof woof!

BDEL.　He is here.

XAN.　This one seems to me to be another Labes, who is in word innocent, but in deed himself also a thief, and good at eating all the cheese.

BDEL.　Be quiet, sit down. But you, dog, come up and prosecute.
But the dog, not wanting to come up, runs away.

PHIL.　Hurrah. For at last the dog has come up. But I, at the same time as judging, will eat all the lentil soup, and I shall listen to the prosecution while eating.

DOG　You have heard the charge, men of the jury. For this dog, the one who has done wrong, escaped my notice by going off alone and eating all the cheese. And when I asked for a share, he did not give [it] to me asking. I shall stop prosecuting. Judge.

PHIL.　But, good fellow, the matter is clear. For it cries out. So I must cast my vote, and convict him.

BDEL.　Come, father, by the gods, obey me and don't prejudge. For you must hear both, and having heard on that basis place your vote.

DOG　Punish him, since he is moreover much the most selfish eater of all dogs, and convict him.

BDEL.　Now I for my part shall call in the witnesses. Let all the witnesses of Labes come in, the cup, the cheese-grater, the cooking-pot, and all the other equipment. Come, dog, come up, make the speech for the defence. Suffering what are you silent? You should speak. For it is possible; and indeed you must make the speech for the defence.

PHIL.　But this one at least is not able, as it seems to me. For he doesn't know how to speak.

BDEL.　Get down, dog. For I intend to make the speech for the defence, as I know well about legal matters.

91

Page 116

2　This is a typical beginning for a speech in a lawcourt. ὦνδρες = ὦ ἄνδρες 'gentlemen'.
τοσαύτης διαβολῆς　'such a great slander'. Do not confuse τοσοῦτος 'so great' with τοιοῦτος 'of such a kind'.

3　γιγνώσκω αὐτὸν ...　γιγνώσκω is followed by accusative and participle.

7 ἑλεῖν ... ἑλόντα ...   From αἱρέω meaning 'convict'. See *RGT* 9H line 27.

9 'Able to guard many sheep'. This is a character reference. It was normal, and indeed expected, in the Athenian courts to smear your opponent's character and to build up your own. As most cheese was made of sheep's milk, this is not a completely irrelevant characteristic. The better the sheep are guarded, the more milk, and the more cheese.

10 ὑφαιρεῖται   The prefix ὑφ- suggests stealth. The middle of αἱρέω means 'to take for oneself'.

12 κιθαρίζειν γὰρ οὐκ ἐπίσταται   Literally 'he does not know how to play the lyre'. The meaning is 'he is not educated', or even, 'he has not had a good education'.

30 ποῦ τὰ παιδία;   It was normal practice in an Athenian lawcourt to parade the children of the defendant, weeping to arouse the pity of the jurors. In this case, the children are, of course, puppies.

Translation for 9I

Bdelykleon speaks, beginning the defence.

BDELYKLEON   It is difficult, gentlemen, to reply on behalf of a dog who has met with such a great slander, but none the less I shall speak. For I know that he is good and chases the wolves.

PHILOKLEON   No, rather this one seems to me to be a thief and worthy of death. So I must convict him as a thief, and having convicted him, judge another case as well.

BDEL.   By Zeus, but he is the best of all the dogs now [alive], since he is able to guard many sheep.

PHIL.   So what is the use, if he steals the cheese and, having stolen it, eats it up?

BDEL.   What use? For he also guards the door. But if he stole the cheese, forgive him. For he does not know how to play the lyre. Listen, my good fellow, to the witnesses. Come up, cheese-grater, and speak loudly. For you happened to be guarding the cheese.

The cheese-grater comes up.

Answer clearly; did you grate the cheese for both the dogs? She says that she grated it all for both.

PHIL.   By Zeus, but I know she is lying.

BDEL.   But, good fellow, pity those who suffer evil things. For this Labes never stays in the house, but goes out of the house looking for food. But the other dog only guards the house. For by staying here he hopes to steal the food from the others. And when he steals nothing, he bites.

PHIL.   Arghh! Whatever evil is this? An evil surrounds me, and the speaker persuades me with his words.

BDEL.   Come, I beg you, pity him, Father, who has suffered evil things, and acquit him. Where are the children? Come up, wretched ones, ask and plead weeping.

PHIL.   Get down, get down, get down, get down.

BDEL.   I shall get down. And yet, this 'get down' deceives many very much. For the jurors order the defendant to get down, then when he has got down, they find him guilty. But none the less I shall get down.

9J

Page 118

2   ἀπεδάκρυσα   Philokleon cannot bear to admit that he could pity a defendant, so he has to blame the lentil soup. It must have disagreed with him.

7   βελτίω = βελτίονα. Did you recognise this form of the comparative? τά should have provided a useful clue.

9   ὑστέρῳ   Juries filed past two urns: the one they came to first (the earlier or nearer) was for condemnation and the next (the later or further) for acquittal.

14   περίπατον   Cf. 'peripatetic'.

21   οὐχ ἑκών   'not willingly'. This has the same meaning as ἄκων 'unwillingly' (line 34).

22   ἠγωνισάμεθα,   See ἀγωνίζομαι. Here it is almost in the sense of 'to settle a contest'.

27   ἔπαιρε σεαυτόν   'Lift yourself up' from αἴρω ἀρῶ ἦρα 'I raise'.
ἀνίστασο   2nd persons. imperative of ἀνίσταμαι.

33   πείσομαι   Can be the future of either πάσχω or πείθομαι. See *GE* p. 202, #211. The context will give you the right meaning here.

Translation for 9J

PHILOKLEON   Go to hell. How bad (not good) I consider the lentil soup. For I burst into tears as I ate this lentil soup.

BDELYKLEON   The dog is acquitted, then?

PHIL.   It is difficult for me to know.

BDEL.   Come, Daddy dear, turn to better things. Taking this voting-pebble in your hand, put it into the further voting-urn, and acquit (him), Father.

PHIL.   No indeed. For I do not know how to play the lyre.

BDEL.   Come now, let me take you round this way.
(*So taking him round a big walkabout, he walks to the further voting-urn first.*)

PHIL.   Is this the nearer?

BDEL.   This is it. Place the voting-pebble.

PHIL.   This voting-pebble is in here.

BDEL.   (*Speaks to himself.*)
Hurrah! I have deceived him. For Philokleon has acquitted the dog unwillingly, by putting the voting-pebble in the further voting-urn.

PHIL.   How then have we contested?

BDEL.   I intend to reveal [it]. You have been acquitted, Labes. Father, Father. What are you suffering? Alas, where is water? Lift yourself up, stand up.

PHIL.   Now tell me that, has he really been acquitted? You will destroy me with the word.

BDEL.   [Yes] by Zeus.

PHIL.   Then I am nothing.

BDEL.   Don't worry, my good fellow, but stand up.

PHIL.   But did I acquit the man who was the defendant with the voting-pebble? What do I suffer? Whatever shall I suffer? But, O much-honoured gods, forgive me, because I did that by placing my voting-pebble involuntarily and not convicting.

EXERCISES FOR SECTION 9H–J

THIRD PERSON IMPERATIVES

9H–J: 1

1. let him/her hear
2. let them retreat
3. let him/her converse
4. let him/her learn
5. let them be silent
6. be victorious (pl.)
7. let him/her carry
8. let them release
9. let him/her/it begin
10. let them turn

9H–J: 2

1. let him/her/it be.
2. It is possible to see everything in the house.
3. let him/her learn everything.
4. let every one arrive.
5. let them leave and let them not remain/ let them leave without waiting.
6. let him/her/it go.
7. let everyone carry the man out.
8. let it be impossible to find these things in the harbour.
9. let him/her know.
10. put all these things here.

FUTURE INFINITIVES

9H–J: 3

1. κελεύσειν   to be about to order
2. κωλύσειν   to be about to hinder
3. ζητήσειν   to be about to seek
4. πείσεσθαι   to be about to obey
5. δέξεσθαι   to be about to receive
6. ἐξαπατήσειν   to be about to deceive

7. ἀπολογήσεσθαι   to be about to defend oneself
8. κατηγορήσειν   to be about to accuse
9. γράψεσθαι   to be about to write/ indict
10. βιάσεσθαι   to be about to use force

IRREGULAR PRINCIPAL PARTS

9H–J: 4

1. αἱρήσω
2. ἐπίστανται πείθειν
3. ἐλπίζει αἱρήσεσθαι
4. εἷλον
5. ἔβη
6. πείσονται

7. ὑπισχνεῖται ἀπιέναι
8. ἔπαθον
9. ἔπεισαν
10. εἵλετο
11. εἷλεν
12. ἔβης

REVISION EXERCISES FOR SECTION 9H–J

B/C – WORD SHAPE AND SYNTAX

1. Present: πλεῖν, ἀποχωρεῖν, σπεύδειν, ὀφείλειν,
   Aorist: βοηθῆσαι, μαχέσασθαι, ἀφικέσθαι, κρατῆσαι,
              βιάσασθαι
   Future: φροντιεῖν, διώξειν, ἔσεσθαι, μαθήσεσθαι, ὀλοφυρεῖσθαι,
              ποιήσειν, παύσεσθαι, δέξεσθαι, λήψεσθαι.

2. δέξαι, δέξασθαι, δεξάμενος -η -ον
   δρᾶσον, δρᾶσαι, δράσας -ασα -αν
   ἐλθέ, ἐλθεῖν, ἐλθών -οῦσα -όν
   γενοῦ, γενέσθαι, γενόμενος -η -ον
   κώλυσον, κωλῦσαι, κωλύσας -ασα -αν
   ἐπαίνεσον, ἐπαινέσαι, ἐπαινέσας -ασα -αν
   βάλε, βαλεῖν, βαλών -οῦσα -όν
   παῦσον, παῦσαι, παύσας -ασα -αν

3. λήσειν   escape notice (fut. inf.)   λανθάνω
   λάβετε   take (aor. imperative pl.)   λαμβάνω
   ἑλεῖν   take (aor. inf.)   αἱρέω
   ἰδών   see (aor. part. m. s. nom.)   ὁράω
   λαθών   escape notice (aor. part. m. s. nom.) λανθάνω
   ἐλθέ   go (aor. imperative s.)   ἔρχομαι
   λήψεσθαι   take (fut. inf.)   λαμβάνω
   ἀπέθανε   die (aor. 3 s. indic.)   ἀποθνῄσκω
   γενήσεσθαι   become (fut. inf.)   γίγνομαι
   ἐρόμενος   ask (aor. part. m. s. nom.)   ἐρωτάω
   μαθόντες   learn (aor. part. masc. pl. nom.)   μανθάνω
   γένεσθε   become (aor. imperative pl.)   γίγνομαι
   δραμεῖν   run (aor. inf.)   τρέχω

οἴσει	will carry (3 s. fut.indic.)	φέρω
τυχούσῃ	happen (aor. part. fem. s. dat.)	τυγχάνω
ἐνέγκατε	carry (aor. imperative pl.)	φέρω
εἶναι	be (pres. inf.)	εἰμί
ἰόντος	go (fut. part. masc./neut. gen. s.)	εἶμι
ᾔδεσαν	know (past indic. 3 pl.)	οἶδα
ᾔεισθα	go (impf. 2 s.)	εἶμι
βαλεῖν	throw (aor. inf.)	βάλλω
εἰδότες	know (pres. part. masc. nom. pl.)	οἶδα
εὑρήσειν	find (fut. inf.)	εὑρίσκω
πεσόντι	fall (aor. part, masc./neut. dat. s.)	πίπτω
σχές	have/hold (aor. imperative s.)	ἔχω
πεσοῦμεν	fall (fut. part, masc./neut. dat. s.)	πίπτω
ἕξειν	have (fut. inf.)	ἔχω

D – ENGLISH INTO GREEK

1. Let the children play.
   εἰσελθόντων οἱ κύνες.
2. Let the herald enter the city.
   ὁ κλέπτης ὑφελέσθω τὸ μέρος τὸ τούτου τοῦ κυνός.
3. He expects/hopes to pursue/prosecute the wicked citizen.
   ἐλπίζω τοὺς φεύγοντας καλῶς ἀπολογήσεσθαι.
4. This woman intends to listen to the stranger.
   οὗτος ὁ δικαστὴς τὸν θάνατον μέλλει καταδικάσειν τοῦ κυνός.
5. Let the suppliants pray to the gods.
   ὁ διώκων ἀρχέσθω κατηγορεῖν.

SUMMARY EXERCISES FOR SECTION 9

A – WORDS

I take	I destroy
I write down	letter
I hope	hope
I know how to	knowledge, understanding
witness	evidence, I bear witness
name	I name
wretched	wretchedness

D – ENGLISH INTO GREEK

1.

νεανίᾳ τινὶ ἦν πατήρ, γέρων ὤν. τὸ δ' ὄνομα τῷ μὲν νεανίᾳ ἦν Βδελυκλέων,
τῷ δὲ γέροντι Φιλοκλέων. ὁ δὲ γέρων ἐτύγχανεν ἔχων νόσον τινὰ δεινήν.
οὐδέποτε γὰρ ἐπαύσατο βουλόμενος δικάζειν ἐν τοῖς δικαστηρίοις. ὁ δὲ

νεανίας ἐπειρᾶτο αὐτὸν πεῖσαι μὴ δικάζειν, ὁ δὲ γέρων αὐτῷ οὐκ ἐπείθετο
καίπερ πολλὰ πείθοντι. τέλος δὲ ὁ μὲν νεανίας αὐτὸν ἐν τῇ οἰκίᾳ ἐνέκλεισεν,
ὁ δὲ ἀπορῶν ἐπειρᾶτο φεύγειν, πολλοῖς λόγοις χρώμενος. ἀλλὰ οὐκ ἐδύνατο
λαθεῖν τοὺς δούλους τοὺς τὴν οἰκίαν φυλάττοντας.

2.

ΒΔΕΛΥΚΛΕΩΝ   ἄκουσον γάρ, ὦ πάτερ, καὶ ἐμοὶ πιθοῦ. οὐ γὰρ ἐάσω σε λιπόντα τὴν
οἰκίαν ἐν τῷ δικαστηρίῳ δικάζειν.

ΦΙΛΟΚΛΕΩΝ   ἀλλὰ διὰ τί οὐκ ἐάσεις ἐμέ; ἐλπίζω γὰρ σέ μοι πάντα λέξειν.

ΒΔΕΛ.   διότι πονηρότατος εἶ τῶν ἐν τῇ πόλει.

ΦΙΛ.   τί οὖν ἐάσεις με ποιεῖν; τί μέλλεις ποιήσειν;

ΒΔΕΛ.   ἔξεσται σοι δικάζειν ἐνθάδε ἐν τῇ οἰκίᾳ. ταῦτα δὲ βούλοιο ἂν ποιῆσαι;

ΦΙΛ.   βουλοίμην ἂν ἔγωγε. εἰπέ μοι ταχέως, τί δεῖ με ποιεῖν;

ΒΔΕΛ.   μεῖνον ἐνθάδε. ἐξοίσω γὰρ τὰ τοῦ δικαστηρίου.
(ἐκφέρει μὲν τὰ σκεύη. τὸ δὲ δικαστήριον ποιεῖται.)
προσελθέτω ὁ ἀντίδικος. ἡ δὲ δίκη ἀρχέσθω. ποῦ ἐστιν ὁ κατήγορος; δεῦρο
ἐλθέ, ὦ κύον, καὶ κατηγόρησον. ἀνάβηθι καὶ εἰπέ. λέγε ἡμῖν τίς καὶ τί
βουλόμενος τὴν γραφὴν ἐγράψατο. ὦ πάτερ, ἐλπίζω σε προσέξειν τὸν
νοῦν.

ΦΙΛ.   μὴ φρόντιζε. ἄγε δή, ὦ κύον, εἰπὲ δή.

E – TEST EXERCISE 9

PHILOKLEON   Come, all [my] friends, come. For I hear you singing, but am not able to
sing myself. What shall I do? For these men are guarding me, although I want
to come with you to the lawcourt and make some trouble. But, O Zeus, stop
giving me troubles and become my friend and pity my suffering. Save me, O
Zeus. Either make me suddenly into smoke, or indeed make me a stone, on
which they count the votes. Lord, dare to save me.

JURORS   Who is it who is shutting you in? Speak, we beg you.

PHIL.   My son, know it well. But don't shout. For he's actually to be asleep here in
front.

JUR.   Why isn't it possible for you to come along with us and listen to the prosecutors
and those defending themselves?

PHIL.   Men, my son doesn't allow me to pass judgement or to do anything bad. But
look for some device, I beg you. For I intend to hear both the prosecutors and
the defendants today.

JUR.   We can't save you, friend. For all the members of your family are guarding
you, and it is not possible for you to escape.

PHIL.   Therefore I must pray to the gods, in hope of escaping. May the gods hear,
then, and help. O lord Lykos, neighbouring hero – for you love the lawcourt
– pity me and save me in my perplexity.

JUR.   You too, slaves, run and shout and tell Kleon this and order him to come. For
Bdelykleon says that it is necessary not to pass judgement on cases. So let
Kleon come and become a saviour to the old man.

EXERCISE

1. (a) 2nd s., aor.   (b) 2nd s., aor.   (c) 2nd s., aor.   (d) 2nd pl., pres.
    (e) 2nd pl., pres.   (f) 3rd pl., pres.   (g) 2nd s., aor   (h) 3rd s., aor
2. (a) voc.   (b) acc.   (c) voc.   (d) nom.
    (e) voc.   (f) dat.

Section Ten: Aristophanes' *Lysistrata*

We now embark on one of Aristophanes' most famous and delightful plays. With its female lead (though played by a man, of course), it brings back women into the text, alive and very decidedly kicking.

The grammatical input here is challenging, consisting of the aorist optative active and middle (*GE* pp. 210–211, #212), δίδωμι (*GE* pp. 212–214, #214), ἀμελής and γλυκύς (*GE* pp. 214–215, #215) and the relative pronoun (*GE* pp. 216–219, #216–219). It is worth mastering this material very thoroughly. δίδωμι, of which *GE* says comfortingly that 'there is little here that is difficult to recognise', is the valuable gateway to a family of verbs which end in -μι.

10A

Page 120

1 ἥ   Your first relative pronoun: feminine because it goes with Lysistrata, nominative because it is the subject of the verb in its clause.

3 καταλύσασαι   What part of the verb is this? Women are the subject of the sentence.

5 ἴδοιμι   From ὁράω. The second aorist is εἶδον, the aorist stem is ἰδ- and this is the aorist optative.

6–7 καὶ Κλεονίκη … κἀμοί = καὶ ἐμοί;   what does καί mean in both these phrases?

8 οὔσαις   What part of the verb? It's a participle, and we are still talking about women.
οἵ   What gender, what case? Why? See *GE* p. 216, #216. Note that in the nominative case m.s., f.s., and pl. the relative pronoun has an accent, whereas the article has none.

11 ἀναγκάσειν   What infinitive? Cf. ἀναγκάζειν.

12 λέξον   Aorist imperative from λέγω. ἔλεξα is an alternative form for the aorist.
ἐκεῖνο ὅ   Literally 'that which'.

15 τῶν ἀφροδισίων   Cf. Aphrodite, the goddess of sex, and 'aphrodisiac'.

16 οὕς   You have now met seven forms of the relative pronoun. Learn it (*GE* p. 216, #216).

19 ποιήσαιμι   We now meet the first aorist optative. Note that -σαι- is a characteristic element of this. Contrast with -οι- in the present optative (and in

137

the second aorist optative – see *GE* pp. 210–211, #212 and cf. ἴδοιμι in line 5 on this page). Don't overlook the ἄν.

ἑρπέτω   What part of the verb is this? See *GE* pp. 197–198, #206–207.

20 κέλευσον   If you cannot recognise this, see *GE* p. 189, #198 .

21 ἐθελήσαιμι   1st person singular aorist optative. Note the ἄν.

μᾶλλον ... ἤ   'rather than ...'

25 ποιήσειας   Which part of the aorist optative is this? (*GE* p. 210, #212).

Page 121

27 ποιήσειε   Which part of the aorist optative is this?

29–30 συμψηφίσαιο, σώσαιμεν   Look at the aorist optatives active and middle of παύω (*GE* pp. 210–212, #212) and learn them. Note that the endings of the second aorist optative are identical with those of the present optative.

31 ναὶ τὼ σιώ   This is a particularly Spartan oath. 'The Two' are Castor and Pollux, the divine brothers of Helen of Troy, who were born in Sparta to Leda in an egg, as the result of her liaison with Zeus in the guise of a swan.

Translation for 10A

Lysistrata, who is an Athenian woman, comes forward and speaks.

LYSISTRATA   Do you hope, women, to bring the war to an end with me? For you know well that once we have brought the war to an end we shall see peace again.

MYRRHINE   *(Myrrhine, who is a friend of Lysistrata, agrees.)*
By the gods, I would gladly see peace after bringing the war to an end.

KLEONIKE   *(Kleonike, who is another friend, also agrees.)*
To me also it seems a good idea to bring the war to an end. But how is this possible for us, women that we are? Do you have some plan? For it is necessary that the men, who fight the battles, should bring the war to an end and make a treaty.

LYS.   Let me speak. For one mustn't keep silent. But, women, if we are going to force the men to make peace, we must refrain from ...

MYR.   From what? What is the plan? Say what you have in mind.

LYS.   So will you do what I order?

MYR.   We shall do everything you tell us to.

LYS.   Then we must refrain from sex.
All the women, after hearing the words which Lysistrata says, begin to go away.

LYS.   Where are you going? Why are you weeping? Will you or won't you do what I order? Or what do you intend?

MYR.   I couldn't do what you say, Lysistrata; instead let the war take its course.

KLE.   By Zeus, I won't either; instead let the war take its course. Order me to go through fire. I would be willing to do that rather than to refrain from sex. For nothing is like sex, my dear Lysistrata. I won't do it – no way.

LYS.   What about you then? Would you do what I tell you?

MYR.	I too would be willing to go through fire. No, by Zeus, I would not do it.
LYS.	Oh how totally lascivious is all of our sex! Will no one do what I propose? But, my dear Spartan, would you vote with me? For if so, we might still save the whole business.
LAMPITO	By the two gods, it's difficult for us to sleep without sex. But we must bring the war to an end and have peace. I would vote with you.
LYS.	O you my dearest friend and the only true woman among them.
MYR.	Then if these things seem good to you, they seem a good idea to us too.

10B

Page 122

2   πεῖσαι   What part of the verb? *GE* pp. 187–188, #195–196. Triremes and the silver to finance them were the basis of Athenian naval power.

5–6   αὐτῷ τῷ ἀργυρίῳ   'with silver and all'. The Athenian reserves of silver were kept in the treasury on the Acropolis.

9   τῆς θεοῦ   Don't worry about the apparently masculine ending of θεοῦ. The word θεός can refer either to a god or to a goddess.

16   ὡς   'to', 'towards', normally only with persons.

21   ἔγνω   The paradigm for this aorist (of γιγνώσκω) is in *GE* p. 201, #209. Learn it.

22   ᾤμωξε   Take the augment out of this (so that ω becomes o) and put the iota subscript back above the line (οἰ-). You should then be able to identify the word.

24   γνῶναι   The aorist infinitive of γιγνώσκω, *GE* p. 201, #209.

27   συνοικεῖς   This is the normal word for a man and woman living together in marriage.

Translation for 10B

LAMPITO	So we shall persuade our husbands and force them to make peace. In what way will you be able to persuade your men, who have the triremes and the silver? By money or gifts or by doing what?
LYSISTRATA	Oh, but we have prepared this well too, because today we shall take the Acropolis, by seeming to be sacrificing. Having taken it we shall guard it, money and all.
	Suddenly Lampito hears a shout and, having heard it, she speaks to Lysistrata.
LAM.	Who shouted? Who was responsible for the shout?
LYS.	This is what I was talking about. For the old women, who had to take the Acropolis of the goddess, now hold it. But, Lampito, you go off home and put affairs among you [Spartans] in good order, while we go into the Acropolis, which the old women have just taken, and guard it.
	Lampito, going away, walks along the road which leads to Sparta, while the other women go into the Acropolis and guard it. Suddenly Lysistrata shouts having spotted a man who is approaching.
LYS.	Oh, oh, women! Come here to me quickly.
KLEONIKE	What is it? Tell me, what is the shout?

LYS.   I see a man approaching, a man. Look. Does any one of you recognise the man
            who is approaching?

MYRRHINE   My god!

KLE.   It's clear, Lysistrata, that Myrrhine has recognised him. For after seeing him
            and recognising him she cried 'My god!'

LYS.   Speak, Myrrhine. Does Kleonike speak the truth? Have you recognised the
            man? For to me as well you seem to recognise the man.

MYR.   By Zeus, I do recognise him. For he is Kinesias, whose wife I am.

LYS.   It's your job now to trick and love and not to love this man who you live with.

MYR.   I shall do these things.

LYS.   Look, I'll join you in tricking him by waiting here after sending away the old
            women whose job it is to guard the Acropolis.

10C

Page 124

2   σπασμός   *GE* gives 'discomfort'. Presumably Kinesias' problem was a
    massive erection. Comic actors wore a padded costume with a large phallus
    attached, so Kinesias' condition would be clear for all to see.

7   ἀνὴρ δῆτα   'Indeed I am a man.' Kinesias confirms the obvious.

12 πρὸς ἑαυτὸν λέγων   'speaking to himself'. Remember the reflexive ἑαυτόν or
    αὑτόν.

13–14 οἱ θεοί, οἷς εὔχομαι ...   'the gods to whom I pray ...'
    δώσουσι   'will grant'. δίδωμι now makes many appearances. Learn *GE* pp.
    134–136, #131.

18 ἐκ-κάλεσον   'call out', aorist imperative from ἐκ-καλέω.

22 εὐξαμένῳ   Agrees with μοι: 'to me having prayed'.

26 The gift of an apple could be an erotic token.

27 τοῦτ' ἂν διδοίην   You should be able to work out that this is an optative and
    to guess what verb it comes from.

30 νὴ τὴν Ἀφροδίτην   Who else would she swear by?

Page 125

54 οἷον τὸ τεκεῖν   'What it is to be a mother!', literally 'What a thing it is to bear
    a child!'

Translation for 10C

The old women go away while Kinesias arrives, and as he approaches, he laments.

KINESIAS   Oh, poor me, what discomfort tortures me!

LYSISTRATA *(Speaking from the wall.)*
            Who is this man who has forced his way through the guards without our
            noticing?

KIN.   It's me.

LYS.	Are you a man?
KIN.	Yes, a man.
LYS.	Won't you get the hell out of here then?
KIN.	Who are you, who are chucking me out?
LYS.	A guard.
KIN.	My god!

KIN. *(Speaking to himself.)*
It's clear that I must, unlucky as I am, pray to all the gods. Perhaps the gods, to whom I am praying, will grant that I can see my wife.
(The man prays.)
O all you gods, grant that I may see my wife.
(Again he addresses Lysistrata.)
By the gods, call Myrrhine out here now.

LYS. Who are you?

KIN. Her husband, Kinesias of the deme Paionis, with whom she lives.
(Speaking to himself.)
Hurrah! Because I've prayed, the gods have granted that I can see Myrrhine.

LYS. Hello, dearest Kinesias. For we too know your name well. For you are always on your wife's lips. Taking an apple, she says, 'How gladly would I give this to Kinesias.'

KIN. Oh by the gods, am I the man to whom Myrrhine wants to give apples?

LYS. [Yes] by Aphrodite. Indeed, even yesterday, when some discussion concerning men arose, your wife said, 'I consider Kinesias the best of all.'

KIN. Then go and call her.

LYS. What then? Will you give me something?

KIN. By Zeus, I'll give you something. I have this. So what I have I give you. So you, to whom I give this, call her.
(He gives what he has in his hand to Lysistrata.)

LYS. Well then, I'll go down and call her for you.
(She goes down from the wall.)

KIN. Quickly.

MYRRHINE *(Inside.)*
Don't you call me to him, Lysistrata. For I don't want to go down.

KIN. Myrrhine baby, why are you doing this? Come down with all haste and come here.

MYR. By Zeus, I won't. I'll go away instead.

KIN. Don't go away, but listen to our baby at any rate.
(He speaks to the baby, which a servant carries.)
You there, won't you call mummy?

BABY Mummy mummy mummy.

KIN. You there, what's up with you? Don't you pity the baby, which is unwashed?

MYR. In that case I do pity it.

KIN. Come down then, my dear lady, for the sake of our baby.

MYR. What it is to be a mother. I must go down.

10D

Page 126

3ff. γλυκύς and ἀμελής are used frequently. Learn these adjectives either now or at the end of this section (*GE* p. 215, #215). For γλυκύς cf. 'glucose'.

11 πιθομένη   Second aorist participle middle from πείθω, 'having obeyed', or 'having been persuaded by'.
τοιαύταις   'by such women'.

13 παῦσαι   The context will tell you whether this is aorist imperative middle or aorist infinitive active.

15 βαδιῇ   (What part of the verb is this?). Many -ιζω verbs have futures of this type. This one is middle, βαδιοῦμαι, as in the next line.

19 κατακλίνῃ   Notice also κλινίδιον 'bed'. Cf. 'recline', 'incline'.

20 ἐρῶ   'I shall say', ὡς here means 'that'.

Translation for 10D

Myrrhine, coming down and reaching the gate, speaks to the baby.

MYRRHINE   My child, how sweet you are. Come, I'll kiss you. For your mother's kiss is sweet. Your mother is sweet too; but you do not have a sweet father, but an uncaring one. I find fault with your father since he's uncaring. Child, how unlucky you appear to be because of your father.

KINESIAS   But do you call your husband uncaring? For there's no one more uncaring than you and no one more unlucky than me.
(Stretching out his hand to his wife, he speaks.)
What is it that you want, you bad woman, that you do these things, obeying such women?

MYR.   Stop, you vilest of men, and don't stretch out your hand to me.

KIN.   Won't you come back home?

MYR.   By Zeus, I won't go home. Before I do, the men must cease from the war and make a treaty. Will you do this?

KIN.   Why won't you lie down with me for a short time?

MYR.   No. And yet I won't say that I don't love you.

KIN.   You love me? So why don't you lie down?

MYR.   You silly fellow, in front of the baby?

KIN.   [You're right] by Zeus. Manes, take the baby home.
The servant, who is carrying the baby, goes off home.
Look, the baby is out of the way, so won't you lie down?

MYR.   But where should one do this? For first I must bring a little couch.

KIN.   Not at all, since it is possible for us to lie down on the ground.

MYR.   By Apollo, I shan't allow you to lie down on the ground despite the state you're in.
(She goes out.)

KIN.   Oh what good luck! It's clear that my wife loves me.

10E

Page 127

11 προσκεφάλαιον   How does this word come to mean 'pillow'?

Page 128

17 ἀνίστασο   'stand up'.

19 Literally 'Now I have all things, as many as I need' (δέομαι takes the genitive), i.e. 'Now I've got everything I want.'

32 ἀμέλει   This is, strictly speaking, an imperative of ἀμελέω, so 'Never mind', but it comes to be used as if it were an adverb: 'of course'.
   ταχύ   The neuter (singular or plural) of the adjective is often used in place of the adverb, 'quickly'.

35 ἡ ἄνθρωπος   This is a derogatory expression here.

Page 129

40 μυριῶ   Future of μυρίζω.

46 διατριβῆς   'delay'. The verb διατρίβω means 'I wear away something', hence 'I spend time', 'waste time' and thus 'delay'.

50 ἔα   From ἐάω 'I allow' or 'let pass'. Perhaps translate 'Forget it!'
   κάκιστ' ἀπόλοιτο   There is no ἄν with this optative, so it must express a wish. 'May he perish most wretchedly, who first …'

52 νὴ τὴν Ἄρτεμιν   An ominous change of oath from the goddess of love to the virgin huntress, goddess of chastity.

53 ψηφιεῖ   From ψηφίζομαι. You should now be able to recognise the tense, and ὦ φίλτατε should help you to recognise the person.

55 ψηφιοῦμαι   See above.

57–58 τί πάσχω; τί πείσομαι;   Present followed by future.

Translation for 10E

Myrrhine returns bringing a little couch.

MYRRHINE   Look, I'm undressing. And yet I must bring a mattress.

KINESIAS   What kind of mattress? Don't bother just for me. Let me kiss you instead.

MYR.   There.
   (After kissing her husband she goes out again. She comes back very quickly bringing a mattress.)
   Look, a mattress. Why don't you lie down? And indeed I'm undressing. And yet you don't have a pillow.

KIN.   But I don't need one.

MYR.   By Zeus, but I need one.
   (She goes out again. She returns bringing a pillow.)
   Stand up, jump up.

KIN.	I've now got everything I need.
MYR.	Everything?
KIN.	Come here then, Myrrhine baby.
MYR.	Now I'm untying my sash. But take care not to cheat me over the treaty which we recently discussed.
KIN.	By Zeus, may I die [if I cheat you].
MYR.	(Suddenly she stops undressing.) You don't have a blanket.
KIN.	By Zeus, I don't need one, but I want to screw you.
MYR.	Of course you'll do this. For I'm coming back quickly. (She goes out.)
KIN.	The creature will kill me with her blankets. Myrrhine returns bringing a blanket. Now I'll love you. Look.
MYR.	Hang on. Shall I anoint you with myrrh?
KIN.	By Apollo, not me.
MYR.	By Aphrodite, I shall do this. Stretch out your hand and take what I shall give you and anoint yourself.
KIN.	The myrrh which you have given me is not pleasant. For it smells of delay, but it doesn't smell of marriage.
MYR.	Poor me, I've brought the myrrh from Rhodes.
KIN.	Good. Let it be, my dear lady. May the man who first made myrrh die very horribly. But lie down and don't bring me anything.
MYR.	I'll do this, by Artemis. I'm undoing my shoes at any rate. But, my dearest husband, will you vote to make a treaty?
KIN.	I'll vote.

Myrrhine runs away.

What's going on here? The wife's gone off and left me. Oh dear, what am I suffering? What shall I suffer? Oh dear, the wife will destroy me. Who shall I screw now? Alas! I'm the unluckiest man alive.

Grammar

Now learn *GE* p. 219, #219 to master two further forms of the relative pronoun, ὅσπερ and ὅστις. You have met them a few times. Notice that both parts of ὅστις decline.

EXERCISES FOR SECTION 10

AORIST OPTATIVE

10: 1

1.	he saved	σῴζοι, σώσειεν
2.	they make/do	ποιοῖεν, ποιήσειαν
3.	they refrained from	ἀπέχοιντο, ἀπόσχοιντο

4.	he finishes	καταλύοι, καταλύσειεν
5.	we lived together	συνοικοῖμεν, συνοικήσαιμεν
6.	I voted	ψηφιζοίμην, ψηφισαίμην
7.	we cease	παυοίμεθα, παυσαίμεθα
8.	you compelled	ἀναγκάζοις, ἀναγκάσειας
9.	he blamed	μέμφοιτο, μέμψαιτο
10.	I flee	φεύγοιμι, φύγοιμι

δίδωμι

10: 2

1. you were giving
2. he/she gives
3. he/she gave
4. to give (aor.)
5. giving (m. s. pres. part.)

6. give!
7. giving (f.s. pres. participle)
8. you (s.) will give
9. to give (pres.)
10. they were giving

10: 3

1. ἔδοτο
2. δώσεται
3. δοίη
4. δώσουσι
5. δότε, ἔδοτε

6. δώσομαι
7. δούς
8. δώσετε
9. δοῖτο
10. δώσεσθαι

ἀμελής *and* γλυκύς

10: 4

1. τοὺς ἀμελεῖς, γλυκεῖς φύλακας
2. τῆς ἀμελοῦς, γλυκείας μητρός
3. τὰ ἀμελῆ, γλυκέα παίδια
4. τοῖς ἀμελέσι, γλυκέσιν ἀμφοτέροις
5. οἱ ἀμελεῖς, γλυκεῖς μάρτυρες
6. τῶν ἀμελῶν, γλυκέων υἱέων

7. ἀληθεῖς, βραχεῖς
ἀληθοῦς, βραχείας
ἀληθῆ, βραχέα
ἀληθέσι, βραχέσι
ἀληθεῖς, βραχεῖς
ἀληθῶν, βραχέων

THE RELATIVE PRONOUN

10: 5

1.	who	ὅς, ὅστις
2.	whom	οὕς, οὕστινας
3.	whose	ἧς, ἧστινος
4.	to whom	αἷς, αἷστισι(ν)
5.	whom	ἅς, ἅστινας
6.	who	οἵ, οἵτινες
7.	(those) whom	οὕς, οὕστινας, ἅς, ἅστινας, ἅ, ἅττα
8.	whose	ὧν, ὧντινων, ὅτων

9. what   ὅ, ὅτι ἅ, ἅτινα, ἅττα
10. what   ὅ, ὅτι, ἅ, ἅτινα, ἅττα

10: 6

1. ᾗ, ᾗτινι
2. ὧν, ὧντινων, ὅτων
3. ὧν, ὧντινων, ὅτων
4. ᾧ, ᾧτινι, ὅτῳ
5. ὧν, ὧντινων, ὅτων

REVISION EXERCISES FOR SECTION 10

A –WORDS

1. uncaring   it concerns
   I give   I give back   the act of giving   giving in return,
                                              (dose)   repayment (antidote)
   a gift   the gift, bribe   I give a present,
                                              I bribe
   a scheme   I plan, contrive
   zeal, haste   I am zealous, busy   eager, serious,
                                              important
   I live with   a living together,
                     marriage
   a wall   I fortify

B/C – MORPHOLOGY AND SYNTAX

1. a. You could speak to me. προσαγορεύσαις
   b. I would gladly give up the war. παυσαίμην
   c. We should like to make a truce with great eagerness. ἐθελήσαιμεν
   d. I could not do this, Mother. ποιήσαιμι
   e. I could see the city. ἴδοιμι
2. a. Will you give me what you have? δώσεις
   b. He was giving the money to the woman. ἐδίδου
   c. Why are you not willing to give me what I ask for? διδόναι
   d. Why are you giving me this apple, Myrrhine? δίδως
   e. Suddenly giving (aorist participle) the woman the money which she demanded, the man went away. δούς
3. a. Kinesias is the husband of Myrrhine. Kinesias goes to the Acropolis.
      Κινησίας, ὃς ἀνήρ ἐστι Μυρρίνης, βαδίζει πρὸς τὴν ἀκρόπολιν.
   b. The women are on the Acropolis. The women are shouting.
      αἱ γυναῖκες, αἵ εἰσιν ἐν τῇ ἀκροπόλει, βοῶσιν.
   c. The men are fighting the battles. The men do not in any way want to end the war.

οἱ ἄνδρες, οἳ τὰς μάχας μάχονται, οὐκ ἐθέλουσιν οὐδαμῶς τὸν
πόλεμον καταλῦσαι.

d. What is this? What do you want to say?

τί ἐστι τοῦτο ὃ ἐθέλεις λέγειν;

e. The women want to hear the words. Lysistrata speaks the words.

αἱ γυναῖκες ἐθέλουσιν ἀκούειν τοὺς λόγους οὓς λέγει Λυσιστράτη.

f. The old women hold the Acropolis. I can see the old women.

αἱ γρᾶες ἔχουσι τὴν ἀκρόπολιν ἃς ἐγὼ ἰδεῖν δύναμαι.

g. Where is Kinesias? Myrrhine is his wife.

ποῦ ἐστι Κινησίας οὗ Μυρρίνη ἐστὶν ἡ γυνή;

h. Where are the old women? It is their task to guard the money.

ποῦ αἱ γρᾶες ὧν τὸ ἔργον ἐστὶ φυλάττειν τὰ χρήματα;

i. Do you recognise the man? The man is approaching.

ἆρα γιγνώσκεις τὸν ἄνδρα ὃς προσέρχεται;

j. We must keep peace. Peace is the cause of many good things.

δεῖ ἡμᾶς εἰρήνην ἄγειν ἣ αἰτία ἐστὶ πολλῶν καλῶν.

D – ENGLISH INTO GREEK

1.

1. ἆρα αἱ γυναῖκες ἀφέξονται τῶν δώρων ἃ οἱ ἄνδρες δώσουσιν
αὐταῖς;

2. οὗτοι οἱ φύλακες, ἀμελεῖς ὄντες, οὐδεμίᾳ σπουδῇ φυλάττουσιν.

3. αἱ γρᾶες μηχανὴν μηχανῶνται ᾗπερ τὰ τείχη λήψονται.

4. δοκεῖ ἡμῖν, αἳ γυναῖκές ἐσμεν (γυναιξὶν οὔσαις), καταλῦσαι τὸν
πόλεμον.

5. ἆρ' οὐδεὶς ἀναγκάσει τοὺς ἄνδρας παύεσθαι τοῦ πολέμου;

2.

ΛΥΣΙΣΤΡΑΤΗ δεῖ ἡμᾶς, τὸν πόλεμον καταλυσάσας, σπονδὰς ποιεῖσθαι, καὶ πείσομεν
τοὺς ἄνδρας, ὧν τὸ ἔργον ἐστὶ μάχεσθαι, ποιεῖν ἃ ἐθέλομεν.

ΓΥΝΗ κἀγὼ δὴ ἐθελήσαιμ' ἄν. ἀλλὰ πῶς (τίνι τρόπῳ) ἔξεστιν ἡμῖν, γυναιξὶν
οὔσαις, τοῦτο ποιεῖν; εἰπέ μοι ἃ ἐν νῷ ἔχεις.

ΛΥΣ. ἆρα ποιησαιτ' ἂν ἃ κελεύω;

ΓΥΝΑΙΚΕΣ ποιήσαιμεν ἄν, νὴ Δία.

ΛΥΣ. χαλεπὴ οὖσα τυγχάνει ἡ μηχανή, ἣν ἐν νῷ ἔχω. ἀκούετε οὖν τοὺς λόγους
οὓς λέγω, καὶ πίθεσθε. δεῖ τοίνυν ἡμᾶς ἀπέχεσθαι πάσας τῶν ἀφροδισίων.

ΜΥΡΡΙΝΗ οὐ ποιήσω τοῦτο οὐδαμῶς.

ΚΛΕΟΝΙΚΗ οὐδ' ἐγώ.

ΛΥΣ. ἆρ' ἐστὶν ἥτις ποιήσει ἃ κελεύω;

ΛΑΜΠΙΤΩ ἀλλὰ δεῖ ἡμᾶς εἰρήνην ἄγειν, παυσάσας τοὺς ἄνδρας οἳ τὰς μάχας
μάχονται. ἐγὼ οὖν συμψηφιοῦμαί σοι.

ΛΥΣ. ἀλλ', ὦ φίλη Λαμπιτώ, δός μοι τὴν χεῖρα.

ΛΑΜ. ἰδού.

ΛΥΣ. ἄπιθι δῆτα πρὸς τὴν Λακεδαίμονα, καὶ πεῖσον τοὺς Λακεδαιμονίους.

ΛΑΜ. εὐθὺς δ' ἄπειμι.

F – TEST EXERCISE 10

LACEDAEMONIAN   Where is the Athenian Council? I would like to report something
new.

ATHENIAN   Who are you who come here to the wall, walking with such great eagerness?

LAC.   I am a herald, by the twin gods, and I have just come from Sparta about peace.

ATH.   What is this thing of yours which you have got in your hands?

LAC.   It is a Spartan code-staff.

ATH.   I know what you mean. But what is happening in Lacedaemonia? Could you
say?

LAC.   I would gladly tell you. For a great evil has befallen us; and Lampito is
responsible, who came back from Athens and persuaded the women to refrain
from sex.

ATH.   And how are you getting on? You are suffering severely, from what you say.

LAC.   I am really suffering severely, by the twin gods. Therefore, we must obey the
women and make the truce, which they themselves will tell us to make, and end
the war.

ATH.   Why then don't we call Lysistrata, who alone could make a treaty for us? For
we too have suffered this evil.

LAC.   Yes, by the twin gods! Who could tell us where Lysistrata is?

ATH.   Oh, there is no need for us to call her; for here she is herself, coming, having
heard what we were saying.

LYSISTRATA   Come, men. Listen to the words which I speak. I am a woman, but I have
sense. Why are you fighting now in this way, and why do you not cease from
your nastiness, you who have the same altars and the same sacrifices? Why do
you destroy Greek men and cities, when instead of this it is possible for you
(*lit.* 'to whom it is possible …') to see peace and to be friends and allies?

LAC. & ATH.   And yet we ask for no other gift than to be able to make love.

LYS.   All of you, therefore, make a treaty and end the war. And then let each one take
his own wife and go off home.

Section Eleven: Aristophanes' *Akharnians*

There is relatively little grammatical input in this section. You learn the present and imperfect tenses passive (*GE* pp. 226–227, #220), which are the same as the middle, the genitive absolute (*GE* p. 228, #222), comparative adverbs (*GE* pp. 229–230, #225) and the optative of φημί (*GE* p. 231, #227).

The concept of the passive will present no problem to Latinists. *GE* p. 227, #221 will be useful.

Aristophanes' comedy *Akharnians* tells us much about Athenian politics and the feelings of the countrymen of Attica cooped up inside the city during the Peloponnesian War. It holds out a tantalising vision of peace.

11A

Page 132

1 κυρία ἐκκλησία   See *RGT* p. 91, Section 8A line 25 and the map on *RGT* p. 92.

2 ἡ Πνὺξ αὑτηί   αὑτηί is the extra demonstrative form. Cf. οὑτοσί.
   ἐρῆμος   Why no feminine ending? It's a two-termination adjective, i.e. it has no separate feminine ending. Compound adjectives (e.g. ἀ-θάνατος, εὐ-δόκιμος) mostly fall into this category, as well as a number of other adjectives. See *GE* pp. 230–231, #226.

5 σχοινίον   A rope with vermilion dye was swept across the agora to push people towards the Pnyx (the hill on which the ecclesia was held). The Assembly itself was proclaimed by a trumpet call; any citizen arriving with vermilion dye, and therefore touched by the rope, could be fined for arriving late.
   ἥξουσιν   This is a future tense. To find out what the present stem is, remove the ς from the ξ and you will be left with three possibilities, ἥκω, ἥγω or ἥχω. If you now check with the vocabulary or a dictionary, you will find ἥκω 'I come'.

10 The Prytaneis: 'presidents' acting as chairmen for the meetings of the assembly. The ten tribes between them subdivided the year into ten parts, each tribe having a spell of providing these presidents.
   οὑτοί   See note on line 2 about the extra demonstrative.

13 ἐντὸς τοῦ καθάρματος   A purification ceremony was held before each meeting of the βουλή and the ἐκκλησία. It involved the sacrifice of a pig.

14   παρελθόντων ... πάντων   The genitive absolute – see *GE* pp. 228–229, #222–223 – 'all having come forward', i.e. 'when all had come forward'. Don't worry too much about this construction. It occurs mainly in stage directions in this section and is thoroughly revised in Section 12.

18   μένοντος ... Ἀμφιθέου   Another genitive absolute – 'Amphitheos remaining', i.e. 'since Amphitheos stays there'.

26   Amphitheos claims to be a god, but he complains that the prytaneis are not granting him his travel expenses.

31   οἱ τοξόται   'the bowmen': these were Scythian mercenaries, hired by the state, who obeyed the orders of the state executives. One of their duties was keeping order in the ἐκκλησία.

32   ἀπαγόντων ... αὐτῶν   'them leading him away', i.e. 'as they lead him away'.

Translation for 11A

DIKAIOPOLIS   But what's this? For I know that the sovereign assembly is going to be held today. But the Pnyx here is empty. The men in the agora are talking to each other as they run from the rope all over the place. The prytaneis will come in late, I know it well. But nobody thinks how peace will happen. But I always come into the assembly and sit down first, and on my own I look out to the country, loving peace but hating the city and longing for my own deme. But here are the prytaneis coming in late. This is precisely what I was saying.

HERALD   *(He makes a proclamation.)*
Come forward to the front. Come forward inside the purified place.
All those present come forward to the front. When all have come forward, suddenly someone called Amphitheos addresses the herald.

AMPHITHEOS   Has anyone spoken yet?
Amphitheos waits, but the herald doesn't answer. As Amphitheos waits he continues his proclamation.

HER.   Who wishes to speak?

AMP   *(Again he addresses the herald.)*
I do.

HER.   Who are you?

AMP.   Amphitheos.

HER.   Not a man?

AMP.   No, but an immortal whom the gods have ordered to make a treaty with the Spartans. But since I'm an immortal, gentlemen, I don't have the travelling expenses which I need. For the prytaneis don't give them to me. So I hope to receive the travelling expenses ...

A SPEAKER   Know well, Athenians, that I am well disposed to the people. So don't listen to this man unless he speaks about war.
The Athenians praise this and raise a clamour.

HER.   Archers!

The archers come in and lead off Amphitheos. As they are leading him off,
Dikaiopolis becomes angry.

DIK.   Prytaneis, you wrong the assembly by leading off the man who was going to
make a treaty for us.

HER.   Shut up and sit down.

DIK.   By Apollo, I won't, but you do business about peace.

HER.   The ambassadors from the king.

11B

Page 134

1   ὄλοιντο   Note the stem ὀλ- (cf. ἀπόλοιντο in line 4). What verb?
Note that there is no ἄν with the optative and therefore this is a
wish.

4   'For we are always being deceived and wronged and ruined by them.' The
verbs are passives. Write out this sentence in English with the verbs in the
active beginning with 'For they …'

At this stage all passives are used with ὑπό + gen. meaning 'by' when it is a
person, or with the dative when it is a thing.

5   ἀδικουμένοις   Passive participle: 'being wronged'.

6–7   πειθόμενος, θωπευόμενος, ἐξαπατώμενος, διαφθειρόμενος   These are
passive participles: the first one means 'being persuaded'. What do the others
mean?

10   φαίη   Optative of φημί. Learn *GE* p. 231, #227.

12   ἔστω   'so be it'.

13ff.   A further statement of Pericles' policy at the beginning of the Peloponnesian
War.

14   ἄκοντες   'unwilling', the opposite of ἑκόντες.
ἀπολλύμενοι   Present passive participle of ἀπόλλυμι: 'being destroyed by …'
The datives here mean 'by' (dative of instrument).

22   ἐξισταμένοις   What verb?: Hint: -στα-. *GE* p. 170, #187.

23ff.   This is quite a complicated looking sentence, but the structure is clear: γνούς (a
participle, 'realising') followed by acc. and participle (twice) ἐμαυτὸν … ὄντα,
and οὐκ ἀναγκαζόμενον … ποιεῖν ἃ μὴ ἐθέλω, then a genitive absolute τῶν
ἄλλων πολεμούντων, then the main clause ἐγὼ … οὐ πολεμήσω, ἀλλ' εἰρήνην
ἄξω (future of ἄγω).

25   μοι   This is an ethic dative, sometimes called the dative of the person concerned.
You could translate it 'please tell me'.

28, 31   δούς, τοῦ Δικαιοπόλεως δόντος   Note the aorist participles of δίδωμι.

33   πρεσβεύεσθε, ἐκδικάζετε, χρηματίζετε   Indicative or imperative?

36   δεῖται + genitive = 'needs'.

Translation for 11B

DIKAIOPOLIS   Death to all the Athenians who praise and obey what the prytaneis say, and the worst death of all to those speakers who flatter the people and always deceive them. For what do we farmers not suffer at their hands? For we are always being deceived and wronged and ruined by them. But what can we do when we are always being wronged by them in this way? For the people seem to enjoy being persuaded by the speakers and being flattered and cheated and ruined by their words. For the man who says 'I am well disposed to the crowd' is always honoured by the people, but the good man who gives good advice is never honoured by them.

But perhaps someone may say, 'So what? The people are free and rule themselves and are not ruled by any other. If they want to be deceived and persuaded and flattered by the speakers, so be it.'

But I answer, 'And yet the sailors have power in the assembly while the farmers are forced against their will to live in the city, being destroyed by the way they live, their lack of provisions and the plague.'

Perhaps this man might answer 'But aren't you free? So don't worry at all, either about the people or the speakers or the war or the written or unwritten laws. For in this city nobody is ever forced by anyone to do what he doesn't want. I consider utterly free the horses and the mules in the city, who as they go along the roads love to bump into the travellers who don't get out of their way.'

All right, then. Realising that I am free and not being forced by anyone to do what I don't want to, while the others are making war, I myself shall not make war but shall live in peace. Amphitheos, come here. But please, where is Amphitheos?

AMPHITHEOS   Here I am.

DIK.   *(Giving to Amphitheos eight drachmas.)*

You take these eight drachmas and make a treaty with the Spartans for just me and my children.

After Dikaiopolis has given him the travelling expenses, Amphitheos goes away.

You deal with ambassadors, then make judgements, then do business about the war and about ways of raising money and about making laws and about allies and about triremes and about dockyards and about sacrifices. But the city needs neither triremes nor dockyards if it is going to be happy, nor great numbers nor great size, without peace.

11C

Amphitheos is now back from Sparta. He is being hotly pursued by Akharnians, angry old men eager to go on with the war because their vineyards are being burnt by the Spartans.

Page 136

2   Δικαιοπόλεως δὲ ταῦτα εἰπόντος   Genitive absolute, 'when Dikaiopolis had said this …'

9   Genitive absolute, 'the Spartans having destroyed our land', i.e. 'although the Spartans have wrecked our land'. Note how, in the genitive absolute construction, we often have to supply a word (e.g. 'when', 'since', 'although') in English and create a clause.

9–10   λίθους δὲ λαβόντων αὐτῶν   See note above. What English word should we supply here?

11   βοώντων   *GE* #206–207.

23   ὀξύτατα   Superlative adverb, 'most sharply'. Learn the comparative and superlative adverbs. *GE* pp. 229–230, #225.

Page 137

26   The Rural Dionysia was a festival held in winter. The central feature was a procession bearing a phallus to promote the fertility of the autumn-sown crops. In *Akharnians* Dikaiopolis emerges from his house leading his family in a mini-procession of the Rural Dionysia.

Translation for 11C

DIKAIOPOLIS   But here's Amphitheos back from Sparta. Greetings, Amphitheos.
            Though Dikaiopolis has said this, Amphitheos keeps running.

AMPHITHEOS   Not yet, Dikaiopolis. For I must flee and escape from the Akharnians.

DIK.   What's up?

AMP.   I was hurrying here bringing a treaty for you. But I didn't evade the Akharnians. Those old men, being fighters at the battle of Marathon, the moment they spotted me bringing the treaty, all shouted, 'You foulest of creatures, are you bringing a treaty when the Spartans have destroyed our land?' And they took up stones. And when they took up stones, I ran away. But they were following me and shouting.

DIK.   Let them shout, then. But are you bringing the treaty?

AMP.   I'll say. Here are three samples.
       (He gives him one sample.)
       This is for five years. Take it and taste.

DIK.   *(After Amphitheos has given it him, Dikaiopolis tastes it.)*
       Yuk!

AMP.   What is it?

DIK.   It doesn't please me because it smells of equipping of ships.

AMP.   *(Giving him another sample.)*
       You take this ten-year treaty instead and taste it.

DIK.   It smells too – very pungently of ambassadors to the cities.

AMP.   But here is a thirty-year peace by both land and sea.

DIK.   O festival of Dionysos, this smells of ambrosia and nectar. I'll choose this with the greatest pleasure, bidding a long farewell to the Akharnians. Ceasing from war and its evils I intend to go in and celebrate the country Dionysia.

AMP.   *(Seeing the Akharnians approaching.)*
And I'll run away from the Akharnians.

EXERCISES FOR SECTION 11

THE PASSIVE

11: 1

1.	κηρύττεται, ἐκηρύττετο	it is/was being announced
2.	φιλῇ, ἐφιλοῦ	you (s.) are/were being loved
3.	ἄρχονται, ἤρχοντο	they are/were being ruled
4.	ἐλευθερούμεθα, ἠλευθερούμεθα	we are/were being freed
5.	τιμᾶσθε, ἐτιμᾶσθε	you (pl.) are/were being honoured
6.	δίδοται, ἐδίδοτο	he is/was being given
7.	ἀναγκάζομαι, ἠναγκαζόμην	I am/was being compelled
8.	καταλύεται, κατελύετο	it is/was being ended
9.	διώκονται, ἐδιώκοντο	they are/were being pursued
10.	ἐξαγόμεθα, ἐξηγόμεθα	we are/were being driven out

11: 2

1. ἐφιλοῦντο ὑπὸ τοῦ κήρυκος, ὑπὸ τῶν ἀνδρῶν.
   they were loved by the herald, by the men.
2. κηρύττεται ὑπὸ τοῦ κήρυκος, τοῖς λόγοις.
   it is announced by the herald, with the words.
3. ἐφυλαττόμην ὑπὸ τῶν φυλάκων, τῷ τείχει.
   I was guarded by the guards, by the wall.
4. ἐκωλυόμεθα ὑπὸ τοῦ διδασκάλου, ὑπὸ τῶν ἀνδρῶν.
   we were prevented by the teacher, by the men.
5. ἐξεφέρετο ὑπὸ τῶν ἀνδρῶν, ὑπὸ τῶν φυλάκων.
   it was carried out by the men, by the guards.
6. πείθονται τοῖς λόγοις, τῇ ἀληθείᾳ.
   They are persuaded by the arguments, by the truth

   N.B. There are a number of possible answers in this exercise, but the important thing is that *agents* (people) are in the genitive with ὑπό, while *instruments* are translated by the dative alone, without a preposition.

GENITIVE ABSOLUTE

11: 3

1. ἡμῶν φυγόντων εἰς τὴν ἀκρόπολιν
2. τῶν ῥητόρων ἀκουσάντων τῶν λόγων

3. σοῦ δόντος ἡμῖν τὰ σῖτα
4. τῶν δούλων ἐλευθερουμένων
5. τῶν σοφιστῶν τοὺς νεανίσκους διδαξάντων
6. λαβόντων τῶν Περσῶν τὰς ναῦς
7. ἐλθόντος ἐμοῦ πρὸς τὴν πόλιν
8. τοῦ δώρου διδομένου τῇ γυναικί

REVISION EXERCISES FOR SECTION 11

A – WORDS

1. I perceive   perception
    unwilling   willing
    the prytanis (see vocab. for 10A)   the prytaneion (the building in
                                          which the prytaneis lodged during
                                          their term of office. It was called the
                                          tholos.)

B/C – MORPHOLOGY AND SYNTAX

1. a. The people honour good men.
        οἱ χρηστοὶ τιμῶνται ὑπὸ τοῦ δήμου.
    b. Lysistrata compels us to make peace.
        ἀναγκαζόμεθα σπονδὰς ποιεῖσθαι ὑπὸ τῆς Λυσιστράτης.
    c. The orators/politicians wrong the city.
        ἀδικεῖται ἡ πόλις ὑπὸ τῶν ῥητόρων.
    d. The politician deceives the people.
        ἐξαπατᾶται ὑπὸ τοῦ ῥήτορος ὁ δῆμος.
    e. We flatter the assembly with our words/speeches.
        ἡ ἐκκλησία θωπεύεται τοῖς ἡμετέροις λόγοις.
    f. You persuade the citizens to maintain peace.
        οἱ πολῖται πείθονται ὑφ᾽ ὑμῶν εἰρήνην ἄγειν.
    g. The gifts/bribery persuaded the people.
        ἐπείθετο τοῖς δώροις ὁ δῆμος.
    h. The speeches of the politicians were unjust to / wronged the assembly.
        ἡ ἐκκλησία ἠδικεῖτο τοῖς λόγοις τοῖς τῶν ῥητόρων.
    i. The walls used to guard the city.
        ἡ πόλις ἐφυλάττετο τοῖς τείχεσιν.
    j. The schemes of the women compelled the men to make a truce.
        ταῖς μηχαναῖς ταῖς τῶν γυναικῶν ἠναγκάζοντο οἱ ἄνδρες σπονδὰς
        ποιεῖσθαι.
2. a. The men went away, but we went on towards the city.
        ἀπελθόντων τῶν ἀνδρῶν, ἡμεῖς πρὸς τὴν πόλιν ἐπορευόμεθα.
    b. The woman gave me the money, and I went away.
        δούσης μοι τὸ ἀργύριον τῆς γυναικός, ἀπῆλθον.

c. The god is waiting, but the Athenians do not want to listen.

τοῦ θεοῦ μένοντος, οἱ Ἀθηναῖοι οὐ βούλονται ἀκούειν.

d. The rest are at war, but I shall not go to war.

τῶν ἄλλων πολεμούντων, ἐγὼ οὐ πολεμήσω.

e. The city is wronged by the politicians. but the Athenians do not care.

τῆς πόλεως ἀδικουμένης ὑπὸ τῶν ῥητόρων, οἱ Ἀθηναῖοι οὐδὲν φροντίζουσιν.

f. The assembly was discussing/doing business about the war but Dikaiopolis did not care.

τῆς ἐκκλησίας περὶ τοῦ πολέμου χρηματιζούσης, ὁ Δικαιόπολις οὐδὲν ἐφρόντιζεν.

g. The assembly is ruled by no one and the people do what they like.

τῆς ἐκκλησίας ὑπ’ οὐδενὸς ἀρχομένης, ὁ δῆμος ποιεῖ ἃ ἐθέλει.

h. The Akharnians picked up (aorist) stones. I started to run away (imperfect).

τῶν Ἀχαρνέων λίθους λαβόντων, ἐγὼ ἔφευγον.

i. Amphitheos presented treaties, and Dikaiopolis received them.

τοῦ Ἀμφιθέου δόντος τὰς σπονδάς, ὁ Δικαιόπολις ἐδέξατο.

j. The herald made a proclamation, but the god was silent.

τοῦ κήρυκος κηρύξαντος, ὁ θεὸς ἐσίγησεν.

D – ENGLISH INTO GREEK

1.

1. τοῦ κήρυκος κηρύττοντος, οἱ πρυτανεῖς εἰσέβαινον εἰς τὴν ἐκκλησίαν.
2. ὁ δῆμος ἐπείθετο πολεμεῖν ὑπὸ τῶν ῥητόρων, τῶν γεωργῶν πρὸς τοὺς ἀγροὺς βλεπόντων.
3. λέγεται ὅτι οἱ ῥήτορες εὖνοί εἰσι τῇ πόλει.
4. ἡμῶν ὑπὸ τῶν ῥητόρων ἐξαπατωμένων, οἱ Λακεδαιμόνιοι διαφθείρουσι τὴν γῆν.
5. ἡ ἐκκλησία ὑπ’ οὐδενὸς ἄρχεται.

2. ἀλλ’ οἱ πρυτάνεις οὑτοιὶ ἥκουσιν. καὶ ἡκόντων αὐτῶν, εὖ οἶσθ’ ὅτι οἱ ῥήτορες παρίασι, λέγειν βουλόμενοι. ἡμεῖς δέ, γεωργοὶ ὄντες, ἡσυχίαν ἄξομεν, εἰς τοὺς ἀγροὺς βλέποντες, ἄκοντες μὲν γὰρ ἀναγκαζόμεθα ἀκούειν τὰ ὑπ’ αὐτῶν λεγόμενα. οἱ δὲ τἀληθῆ οὐ λέξουσιν. ἀεὶ γὰρ λέγουσιν ὅτι ἡ πόλις ἄρχεται αὐτὴ ὑφ’ αὑτῆς φιλουμένη ὑπὸ πάντων τῶν ῥητόρων, οἱ δὲ οὐδενὶ ἄλλῳ ἢ ἑαυτοῖς εὖνοι ὄντες τυγχάνουσι. τῆς δὲ πόλεως ὑπ’ αὐτῶν διαφθειρομένης, οὐδεὶς ἑκὼν χρηματιεῖ οὔτε περὶ τούτων οὔτε περὶ τῆς εἰρήνης. οὐκ ἀρέσκει μοι οὐδαμῶς τὸ πρᾶγμα.

E – TEST EXERCISE 11

This is a difficult passage based on a later extract from the Akharnians when Dikaiopolis has persuaded the chorus to listen to his anti-war argument. He also refers to an occasion when Kleon had indicted Aristophanes for abusing the

Athenian people in public when there were foreigners in the audience. That was at the City Dionysia, the big spring festival; this is at the Lenaia, a festival held in winter when few foreigners could sail to Athens.

DIKAIOPOLIS   Don't make a noise, spectators, if I come as a beggar and begin speaking among Athenians about the city, even though I am taking part in a comedy. For even comedy knows what justice is. And I shall tell you terrible but just things. For Kleon will not now abuse me for speaking ill of the city when strangers are present. For we are on our own, and no strangers are here yet. I hate the Lacedaemonians very much. May they perish, themselves, their wives and their children. My vineyard is being cut down by them, and we are shut up in the city against our will, being destroyed by the plague and always gazing out at our fields. But (for you who are here are friends) how are the Lacedaemonians responsible for these disasters? There are men among us (I do not mean the city, remember this, that I do not mean the city) who are responsible, most particularly Pericles, the Olympian, who proposed the law that Megarians must not remain on land, nor in the market, nor on the sea, nor on the mainland. And, though the Megarians and the Lacedaemonians often asked and begged us to withdraw the decree, we were not willing to do so. For it was not pleasing to Pericles.

This was the start of the war.

The next three sections are taken from a lawcourt speech, with imaginary conversations between three jurors at intervals, which ingeniously reinforce the new points of grammar and syntax that have been introduced. Rhetorical Greek is often elaborately structured and you may find that you have to analyse the sentences carefully as a whole, before you can translate them in detail.

The case is also fairly confusing, so it is well worth reading the introduction before you start. The speech throws some interesting light on the position of women in Athenian society.

A great deal of new grammar and syntax is introduced in these sections and so it is wise to do the exercises when they occur to consolidate your learning with practice, or, if you find that makes you lose track of the story, finish reading Section 12 and then go back to revise the grammar and do the exercises.

Section Twelve: Neaira as slave

12A

Page 144

1–2 ἄλλος ἄλλον ὡς ὁρῶσιν ἥκοντα   'as they see one another coming'.
3 οὗ   'where', relative. Cf. ποῦ 'where?' interrogative.
   μέλλουσι δικάσειν   μέλλω + future infinitive, 'I am about to do something'.
9 οὐκ ἤλπιζον ἐντεύξεσθαι   ἐλπίζω + future infinitive, 'I did not expect to meet.'
9–10 Στρυμοδώρῳ ... διατρίβοντι ... νέῳ ὄντι καὶ ἀπείρῳ   All agree.
11 ἐξέσται   The future of the impersonal verb ἔξεστι: 'it will be possible'.
15 ὄλοιο   2nd. s. aorist optative of ὄλλυμι: 'may you perish'.

Translation for 12A

When the herald summons them the dikasts come into the courtroom. And as they see one another coming in, they immediately greet one another, shaking hands. When Komias and Euergides come into the lawcourt – where they are going to judge a case about Neaira – they greet one another.

EUERGIDES   Greetings, Komias.

KOMIAS   And [greetings] to you too, Euergides. What a big crowd! But who is this? It's not really our neighbour Strymodoros, is it? Yes, by Zeus, it is indeed the man himself. Oh what luck! But I did not expect to meet Strymodoros spending his time in the lawcourt, since he is a young man and without experience in judicial matters.

EU.   Why don't you call him over here? It will be possible for him to sit with us.

KOM.   A good suggestion (you speak well) and we will call him. Strymodoros, Strymodoros!

STRYMODOROS   Greetings, neighbours. Oh the size of the crowd!
(He is pushed by a juror who is holding his tunic.)
You, what did you mean by holding my tunic? To hell with you! (May you perish!)

EU.   Well done. Sit down.

Page 145

5   οὐδὲν διαφέρει   'it makes no difference'.

Page 146

12   πάνυ δεινὸν λέγειν   'very clever at speaking', an idiomatic use of δεινός + the infinitive.
ὁ διώκων = 'the pursuer', 'prosecutor'; ὁ φεύγων = 'the fleer', 'the defendant'.

16   οὐκ ἂν σιγῴης καὶ προσέχοις τὸν νοῦν;   ἄν + optative expresses a polite request, 'Won't you be quiet and concentrate?'

19   ὅπως σιωπήσεις   ὅπως, ὅπως μή + future indicative expresses a caution 'see that you …' (*GE* p. 260, #245).

20   καὶ προσέξεις τὸν νοῦν   See above on line 16.

Translation for 12B

Apollodoros the prosecutor comes in.

STRYMODOROS   But who is that, who is approaching the rostrum, walking quickly?

KOMIAS   This happens to be the prosecutor in the trial, whose name is Apollodoros, and he has a meddlesome nature.

EUERGIDES   But it makes no difference if his nature is meddling or not. For we must show common goodwill for the contestants and listen in the same way to the arguments which each of them uses, according to the oath which we swore. And indeed Apollodoros seems to himself and to many others to be benefiting the city and making the laws valid by bringing a charge against Neaira for being an alien.

KOM.   Perhaps Apollodoros is naturally patriotic. But I know that you, Euergides, as a prosecutor are very clever at speaking. For such things are always said by the accusers. And Apollodoros, I know it well, will say the same things; 'I did not begin the enmity', he will say, and 'The defendant did me the greatest injustice', and 'I want to be revenged on him.' But I am not always persuaded by such statements.

EU.   Reasonably. But now won't you be quiet and concentrate? For Apollodoros is already clearing his throat, as people do who are starting to speak, and he is standing up.

KOM.   I shall be silent, Euergides. But see that you are silent too, Strymodoros, and concentrate.

12C

Page 146

2 ἠδικήθην   1st s. aorist passive of ἀδικέω: 'I was wronged' (*GE* pp. 236–237, #228).

2–3 οὗ γυνή ἐστιν ...   'Whose wife is ...' οὗ = 'whose', genitive of ὅς.

3 κατέστην   From the verb ἵστημι. Some tenses are transitive and have an object, some have not and are intransitive. If it has an object it will mean 'place', 'set up'; if it does not have an object it will mean 'stand', 'be set up', 'set myself up'. Similarly, καθίστημι εἰς + object means 'I put someone into a state'; but καθίσταμαι εἰς (without an object) means 'I get into a state'. See *GE* p. 242, #234.

ἀδικηθείς   Nom. s. m. aorist passive participle of ἀδικέω.

7 ἀδικηθέντες   Nom. pl. m. aorist passive participle of ἀδικέω.

11–12 τίς γὰρ οὐκ ἂν βούλοιτο ...   'Who would not want?' Potential expressed by ἄν + optative.

Page 147

14 ὅπως μὴ ... πιστεύσεις   'See that you don't trust ...' (see note on 12B, line 19).

17 ἡδέως ἄν τι μάθοιμι   Cf. line 21, potential ἄν + optative. 'I would gladly learn something.'

Translation for 12C

Apollodoros speaks.

APOLLODOROS   For many reasons, gentlemen of Athens, I wanted to bring this charge against Neaira, which I am now pursuing, and to come before you. For I was greatly wronged by Stephanos whose wife this Neaira is. And having been wronged by him, I was placed in extreme danger, not only myself, but my daughters and my wife. It is therefore for the sake of revenge that I am engaging in this contest, having been placed in such danger. For I did not begin the enmity, but Stephanos did, [although] he had not been wronged in any way yet by us in word or deed. I want to give you a preliminary outline of everything we suffered and [to tell you] how, having been wronged by him, we were placed in extreme danger of poverty and loss of citizen rights.

STRYMODOROS   Apollodoros, who was wronged by Stephanos, is a clever speaker, as it seems. I feel goodwill towards him because it was Stephanos who began the enmity. For who would not want to take vengeance on an enemy? Everyone wants to do good to their friends and harm to their enemies.

KOMIAS   Take care that you do not easily trust the contestants, Strymodoros. For when they stand up in court the contestants use every art to win the goodwill of the jurors.

STR.   But I would gladly learn something. For Apollodoros says that being wronged by Stephanos he was placed in danger of poverty. What did Stephanos do to bring Apollodoros into this danger?

EUERGIDES   Listen. For Apollodoros is continuing to speak about the beginning of the conflict.

12D

Page 148

3   ἑλών   Nom. s. m. aorist participle of αἱρέω from εἷλον.
ᾔτησε   3rd s. aorist indicative from αἰτέω.

4   ὃ οὐχ οἷός τ' ἦ ἐκτεῖσαι   'Which I was not able (οἷός τ' ἦ) to pay'.

7–9   μοι ... καταστάντι ... οὐ δυναμένῳ ... ὀφείλοντι   Note the agreement of all the participles with μοι.

9   οἳ οὐκ ἐπείσθησαν   'who were not persuaded'. Aorist passive.

Page 149

19–21   φάσκω Στέφανον τοῦτον συνοικεῖν ... εἰσαγαγεῖν ... ἐγγυᾶν ... ἀσεβεῖν   'I allege that Stephanos does ...' (a series of things in the infinitive). The grammar of this is explained later in *GE* pp. 247–249, #235–236.

Translation for 12D

When I was acting as a member of the Council I proposed a decree which I brought before the people. But this Stephanos indicted my decree as illegal, and thus began our enmity. For, having secured a conviction against the decree, and having brought false witnesses, he asked for a large fine which I could not pay. For he was seeking, having placed me in extreme embarrassment, to deprive me of my citizen rights, because I owed money to the state and was unable to pay.

Therefore we were all going to be placed in poverty. The disaster and the disgrace was going to be great for me in regard to my wife and daughters if I had been bankrupted and could not provide a dowry and owed the amount of my fine to the state. I am deeply grateful to the jurors who were not persuaded by Stephanos, but who inflicted a lesser penalty on me.

Stephanos therefore became the cause of such great evils for us all, though he had never been wronged by me. And now with all my friends encouraging me and urging me to take vengeance on Stephanos, by whom I was so wronged, I bring this case before you. For my friends reproach me and call me the most cowardly of men if I do not exact vengeance on behalf of my daughters and my wife.

Therefore I bring this Neaira before you and charge her, she who is irreverent to the gods, insulting to the city and contemptuous of your laws. For Stephanos was trying to deprive me of my family against the laws. Thus I have come to you and I declare that this Stephanos is living with a foreign woman contrary to the law, and that he has introduced alien children into the phratries and to the demesmen, and that he gives in marriage the daughters of prostitutes as if they were his own daughters, and that he is committing sacrilege against the gods.

That I was formerly wronged by Stephanos you know well. That Neaira is an alien and that she is living with Stephanos against the laws, this I want to prove to you clearly.

Grammar

You should now learn the grammar for 12A–D before you go on.

1. The aorist passive (*GE* pp. 236–237, #228–229) indicative and participle. This is easy to recognise because of 'θ' but make sure you also read the notes!
2. The verb ἵστημι 'I set up'. This is difficult and seems complicated at first. It may be helpful if you look back over the passage you have just read in this section and see how it has been used, then go on and try the exercises to confirm your understanding.
   See *GE* pp. 238–242, #230–233. Below is a simplified version in chart form.

The verb ἵστημι

	Transitive		Intransitive
Pres. Act.	ἵστημι (ἱστάς) I am setting up	*Pres. mid.*	ἵσταμαι (ἱστάμενος) I am standing up
Fut. Act.	στήσω (στήσων) I will set up	*Fut. mid.*	στήσομαι (στησόμενος) I will stand up
Imperf. Act.	ἵστην I was setting up	*Imperf. mid.*	ἱστάμην I was standing up
1st aor. act.	ἔστησα (στήσας) I set up	*2nd. aor. act.*	ἔστην (στάς στᾶσα στάν) I stood up
1st aor. mid.	ἐστησάμην (στησάμενος) I set X up for myself	*2nd. aor. act. (intrans.) has taken place of 1st aor. mid., so 1st aor. mid. becomes transitive and 'true' middle.*	

Note on καθίστημι

In its transitive forms it means 'I put someone in a certain position', 'elect', e.g. κατέστησα αὐτὸν εἰς πενίαν 'I reduced him to poverty' ('I placed him in poverty').

In its intransitive forms it means 'I am put in a certain position' or 'I am elected', 'I am made', 'I become', e.g. κατέστην εἰς πενίαν 'I was reduced to poverty' ('I was placed in poverty').

Examples

12C (pp. 146–147)

3   εἰς κινδύνους τοὺς ἐσχάτους *κατέστην*.
5   *καταστὰς* εἰς τοιοῦτον κίνδυνον ...
8–9   εἰς τοὺς ἐσχάτους κινδύνους *κατέστημεν* περί τε τῆς πενίας καὶ περὶ ἀτιμίας.
17–18   ἀδικηθεὶς ὑπὸ τοῦ Στεφάνου, εἰς κίνδυνον *κατέστη* περὶ τῆς πενίας.
18–19   τί ποιῶν ὁ Στέφανος κατέστησε τὸν Ἀπολλόδωρον εἰς τοῦτον τὸν κίνδυνον;

EXERCISES FOR SECTION 12A–D

THE AORIST PASSIVE

12A–D: 1

1.	ἐκωλυθήσαν	they were prevented
2.	ἐπέμφθημεν	we were sent
3.	ἐλύθη	he/she was set free
4.	ἐπείσθητε	you (pl.) were persuaded
5.	ἐδόθην	I was given
6.	ἐφυλάχθη	he was guarded
7.	ἐδιώχθης	you (s.) were chased
8.	ἐγράφησαν	they were indicted/ written
9.	ἐτιμήθη	he/she was honoured
10.	ἐποιήθητε	you (pl.) were made

12A–D: 2

1.   τοὺς πολεμίους πεισθέντας
2.   τῷ δούλῳ λυθέντι
3.   τῶν χρημάτων δοθέντων
4.   αἱ γυναῖκες κελευθεῖσαι
5.   τοῦ ἀνδρὸς ἀδικηθέντος

12A–D: 3

1.	ἵσταμεν	we are setting up
2.	ἱστάναι	to set up

3. ἵστης   you (s.) were setting up
4. ἱστᾶσα   setting up (n.f.s. pres. part.)
5. ἱσταίη   may he set up

12A–D: 4

1. ἵστασθαι   to be being set up
2. ἵσταντο   they were setting themselves up/being
                            set up
3. ἱστάμενοι   being set up (n.pl.m. pres. part.
                            pass.)
4. ἐστάθη   he/it was set up
5. ἵσταται   he/she/it is being set up

12A–D: 5

1. he/she/it stood up
2. they were setting up for themselves, they were being set up
3. setting up for himself, being set up
4. set up! (2.s.1st aor. imperative.)
5. we are setting up, we were setting up (if iota is long)
6. stand up! (you pl. 2 aor. imperative), set yourselves up
7. they will set themselves up
8. he set up for himself
9. I set myself up, I stood up
10. to set up for oneself (1st aor. infinitive active)

REVISION EXERCISES FOR SECTION 12A–D

B/C – MORPHOLOGY AND SYNTAX

1. Apollodoros wronged me greatly and placed (κατέστησεν transitive) us all
   in great despair. For, having set up (ἀναστήσας trans.) lying witnesses in
   the lawcourt, he convicted me and asked for a large fine. I, therefore,
   owing the fine to the city, and being placed (καταστάς intrans.) in the
   position of loss of citizen's rights, emigrated (ἐξανέστην intrans.) from the
   city. Then, having left (ἀναστάς lit. having got up from) my fatherland,
   I went to Megara, where, reduced (καταστάς intrans.) to a state of poverty,
   I remained for two years.
2. a. For my daughter is getting into a state of poverty because of this case.
      κατέστη
   b. Therefore the Athenians move the Aeginetans from Aegina.
      ἀνέστησαν
   c. But you, gentlemen of the jury, are placing my daughters in great
      despair by condemning (having condemned) me.
      κατεστήσατε

d. This prosecutor stands up in court and terrifies (brings to fear) the defendant. ἀνέστη κατέστησεν

3.

ἐκλήθησαν	they were called	καλέω
ἐλήφθη	he was taken	λαμβάνω
ἠπορήθην	I was at a loss	ἀπορέω
κατεδικάσθητε	you (pl.) were condemned	καταδικάζω
ἐξηλέγχθης	you (s.) were convicted	ἐξελέγχω
ἐξεδόθημεν	we were given in marriage	ἐκδίδωμι
ὑβρίσθη	he was insulted	ὑβρίζω
διηλλάχθησαν	they were reconciled	διαλλάττομαι
ἐγράφην	I was written	γράφω
ὠργίσθητε	you (pl.) were made angry	ὀργίζομαι
ἐλέχθη	it was said	λέγω
ἐβιάσθημεν	we were forced	βιάζομαι
κατηγορήθη	he was accused	κατηγορέω
ἀπελύθης	you were acquitted, released	ἀπολύω
ἀπεπέμφθησαν	they were sent away	ἀποπέμπω
ἐξηπατήθης	you (s.) were deceived	ἐξαπατάω
ἐπείσθην	I was persuaded	πείθω

4. a. The jurors were not persuaded by the defence, and I was condemned. ὁ μὲν δικαστὴς οὐκ ἐπείσθη ... ἡμεῖς δὲ κατεδικάσθημεν

b. But indeed it makes no difference to me if you were not acquitted but condemned. ἀπελύθητε κατεδικάσθητε

c. For this speech was made by the opponent. οὗτοι οἱ λόγοι ἐλέχθησαν

d. You were greatly wronged by this man. σὺ δὲ ἠδικήθης

5. a. I am well disposed towards the man who was wronged by Stephanos. ἀδικηθέντα

b. We, being persuaded by the opponent, exacted the penalty. πεισθέντες

c. Since the woman had been deceived by the one who had lost his citizen's rights, her husband despised her. ἐξαπατηθείσης

d. When I was forced to introduce the child to the clan, my daughter became hostile. βιασθέντος

e. My friends helped me when I lost my citizen's rights and was in despair. ἀπορηθέντι

f. We gave many drachmas to the old men who had been deceived by Kleon. ἐξαπατηθεῖσι

D – ENGLISH INTO GREEK

1. ὁ Ἀπολλόδωρος ἠδικήθη μεγάλα ὑπὸ Στεφάνου καὶ Νεαίρας.
2. τίμημά τι μέγα ᾐτήθη ὑπὸ Στεφάνου.
3. ὁ Ἀπολλόδωρος ἔμελλε καταστήσεσθαι εἰς τὴν ἐσχάτην ἀπορίαν.

4. ὁ Στέφανος κατέστησε τὸν Ἀπολλόδωρον εἰς κίνδυνον μέγαν.
5. ὁ Ἀπολλόδωρος ἐπείσθη τιμωρεῖσθαι τὸν Στέφανον.

12E

This section introduces the accusative (or nominative) and infinitive construction to express an indirect statement after verbs of saying and thinking (*GE* pp. 247–249, #235–236).

Page 150

3   φησὶ γὰρ ὁ Ἀπολλόδωρος   Followed by the accusative (τὸν Στέφανον) and infinitive (ἄρξαι) construction, and then the nominative (αὐτός) and infinitive (ἀγωνίζεσθαι) construction. 'Apollodoros says that Stephanos began the enmity, and that he (Apollodoros) is bringing the case for the sake of revenge ...'

6–7   ἀλλ' ἡγοῦμαι ...   Introduces more accusative and infinitive: 'I think that Apollodoros ...'

7–9   πρῶτον μὲν γὰρ ἔφη Ἀπολλόδωρος ... καταστῆναι ... οὐ δυνήσεσθαι ...   This time the construction is nominative and infinitive with the nominative left out: 'Apollodoros said that he (Apollodoros) had been in danger ...'

11ff.   ἄν + the optative. A series of potential optatives ('could' or 'would'). 'How could Apollodoros not be ashamed ...?'

Translation for 12E

KOMIAS   Don't you see? This is just what I was saying. The contestants always say such things. But I am not persuaded by them, myself.

STRYMODOROS   Rightly, indeed. For Apollodoros says that Stephanos began the enmity and that he himself is bringing the action for revenge because he has been wronged by him. All this is what you said, Komias.

EUERGIDES   These things were said by Apollodoros, but I think that perhaps Apollodoros is saying something important. For first of all Apollodoros said that he had been put in danger of poverty and loss of citizen rights, and that he would not be able to give his daughters in marriage. Then he said that Stephanos and Neaira were contemptuous of the laws and irreverent to the gods. Who would not be concerned about this?

STR.   No one, by Zeus. For how could Apollodoros not feel ashamed at having unmarried daughters? And who would marry a woman from such a father who did not have a dowry?

EU.   But perhaps Komias would not agree?

KOM.   About poverty I would agree, of course. But about the laws and the gods I do not know clearly. When trustworthy evidence is brought by Apollodoros we shall find out in detail.

EXERCISES FOR SECTION 12E

INDIRECT SPEECH USING THE INFINITIVE

12E: 1

1. I said to be about to arrive.
    I said I would arrive.
    'I will arrive.'
2. I said that man to be about to arrive.
    I said that man would arrive.
    'That man will arrive.'
3. He thought himself to be wise.
    He thought he (himself) was wise.
    'I am wise.'
4. He thought him to be wise.
    He thought he (someone else) was wise.
    'He is wise.'
5. We think not to be able to see.
    We think we cannot see.
    'We cannot see.'
6. They thought Stephanos not to have deceived the woman.
    They did not think that Stephanus had deceived the woman.
    'Stephanos did not deceive the woman.'

REVISION EXERCISES FOR SECTION 12E

B/C – MORPHOLOGY AND SYNTAX

1. The prosecutor is the most eager of men.
    φημὶ τὸν κατήγορον σπουδαιότατον εἶναι τῶν ἀνθρώπων.
    I say that the prosecutor is the most eager of men.
    ἔφην τὸν κατήγορον σπουδαιότατον εἶναι τῶν ἀνθρώπων.
    I said that the prosecutor *was* the most eager of men.
2. I was placed in great danger.
    φησὶν ἐμὲ εἰς μέγαν κίνδυνον καταστῆναι.
    He says that I *was placed* in great danger.
    ἔφη ἐμὲ εἰς μέγαν κίνδυνον καταστῆναι.
    He said that *I had been placed* in great danger.
3. The antagonists always say something dreadful/clever.
    ἡγοῦμαι ἀεὶ λέγειν τι δεινὸν τοὺς ἀντιδίκους.
    I consider that the antagonists always *say* something clever.
    ἡγούμην ἀεὶ λέγειν τι δεινὸν τοὺς ἀντιδίκους.
    I considered that the antagonists always *said* something clever.
4. Stephanos introduced the alien children to the brotherhood.
    φασὶ τὸν Στέφανον εἰσαγαγεῖν εἰς τοὺς φράτερας τοὺς ἀλλοτρίους παῖδας.

They say that Stephanos *introduced* the alien children to the brotherhood.

ἔφασαν τὸν Στέφανον εἰσαγαγεῖν εἰς τοὺς φράτερας τοὺς ἀλλοτρίους παῖδας.

They said that Stephanos *had introduced* the alien children to the brotherhood.

5. Neaira is not ashamed of despising the laws.

τίς οὐκ ἂν οἴοιτο τὴν Νέαιραν οὐκ αἰσχύνεσθαι καταφρονοῦσαν τῶν νόμων;

Who would not think that Neaira *is not ashamed* of despising the laws?

τίς οὐκ οἴεται τὴν Νέαιραν οὐκ αἰσχύνεσθαι καταφρονοῦσαν τῶν νόμων;

Who does not think that Neaira *is not ashamed* of despising the laws?

6. We wanted to be revenged on our enemies at that time.

φαμὲν βούλεσθαι τότε τιμωρεῖσθαι τοὺς ἐχθρούς.

We say that we *wanted* to be revenged on our enemies at that time.

ἔφαμεν βούλεσθαι τότε τιμωρεῖσθαι τοὺς ἐχθρούς.

We said that we *wanted* to be revenged on our enemies at that time.

12F

Page 151

2–4 ὅτι … τοῦθ’   '*That* Neaira is not only … *this* is what I want to prove.'

Page 152

9   ἔδοξεν αὐτῷ   'It seemed good to him to', 'he decided to'.

10 βουλομένῳ   Dative in apposition to αὐτῷ in line 9.

13 ἠσχύνετο γὰρ τὴν γυναῖκα   'He felt ashamed in respect of his wife.'

16–18 ὡς οὖν ἀληθῆ λέγω, ὅτι …, τούτων ὑμῖν αὐτὸν τὸν Φιλόστρατον μάρτυρα καλῶ   'that (ὡς) I am speaking the truth [when I say] that (ὅτι) … I call Philostratos himself as witness to you of these things (τούτων)'. Note that the main clause is delayed to the end of the sentence.

Translation for 12F

Apollodoros continues.

Now then, you have heard the law, judges, this law which does not allow an alien woman to live with a male citizen nor a female citizen to live with an alien man, nor to have children. That Neaira is not only an alien but also a slave and a prostitute, I want to prove to you in detail from the beginning.

For Neaira was first of all a slave of Nikarete in Corinth. She had been brought up by her from the time when she was a small child. And this is clear and reliable proof of this. For Nikarete had another slave called Metaneira, whose lover, the sophist Lysias, paid many drachmas for her. But since all the money which he had paid for her had been taken by Nikarete, he decided to make her an initiate and to spend a lot of money on the feast and on the ceremonies, wanting to spend his money on Metaneira and not on Nikarete. And Nikarete was persuaded to go to the mysteries taking Metaneira. When they arrived, Lysias did not take them to his own house (for he felt shame before the wife whom he had and his mother, who was an old woman and lived in the house). Lysias established them in the house of Philostratos, who was still a bachelor and was a friend of his. Neaira came with them to Athens, being herself also the slave of Nikarete and already working with her body, but being somewhat younger. That I am telling the truth and that Neaira was the property of Nikarete and came with her, I call Philostratos himself as witness.

Grammar

You now need to learn τίθημι (very important), *GE* pp. 251–253, #237–238 and δείκνυμι (less important) *GE* pp. 254–255, #239.

EXERCISES FOR SECTION 12F

τίθημι

12F: 1

1.	he gives	τίθησι(ν)	he puts
2.	you (pl.) were putting	ἐδίδοτε	you (pl.) were giving
3.	we gave	ἔθεμεν	we placed
4.	he was placed	ἐδόθη	he/it was given
5.	to give (aor.)	θεῖναι	to put, to have put
6.	he placed	ἔδωκε	he gave
7.	having given (n.pl.)	θέντες	having put
8.	put (s.)	δός	give! (s.)
9.	to give (pres.)	τιθέναι	to place
10.	you (pl.) will place	δώσετε	you (pl.) will give

δείκνυμι

12F: 2

1.	you (pl.) are placing	δείκνυτε	you (pl.) are showing
2.	we shall show	θήσομεν	we shall put
3.	they placed	ἔδειξαν	they showed
4.	he was showing	ἐτίθη	he was placing
5.	placing (n.pl.f.)	δεικνῦσαι	showing

12F: 3

ἐδείχθημεν	we were shown
ἐτέθησαν	they were placed
ἐδεικνύμεθα	we were being shown (could be middle)
δειχθέντες	having been shown (n.pl.m.)

REVISION EXERCISES FOR SECTION 12F

B/C – MORPHOLOGY AND SYNTAX

1. a. The sophist pays many drachmas on behalf of Metaneira. ἔθηκε
   b. Although the sophist was paying money on behalf of Metaneira, Nikarete did not give her anything, but she was reducing the girl to despair. θέντος δίδωσι κατέστησεν
   c. But then, when the girl had been reduced to despair, the sophist decided to pay many drachmas for the mysteries. καθισταμένης θεῖναι
   d. 'But', he said, 'acting thus, I shall put down this money on behalf of Metaneira herself.' ἔθηκα
   e. Lysias, having gone to Athens and paid many drachmas, establishes Nikarete and Metaneira at Philostratos' house. τιθείς κατέστησε

D – ENGLISH INTO GREEK

1. ὁ Στέφανος φήσει τὸν Ἀπολλόδωρον ὑπάρξαι τῆς ἔχθρας.
2. ὁ Ἀπολλόδωρος ἔφη βούλεσθαι τιμωρεῖσθαι τὸν Στέφανον.
3. ὁ Ἀπολλόδωρος οὐ* φήσει ἀδικῆσαι τὸν Στέφανον.
4. πολλοὶ πολλὰ χρήματα ὑπὲρ τῆς Νεαίρας ἔθεσαν.
5. ὁ Ἀπολλόδωρός φησι τὸν Στέφανον δούλη συνοικεῖν ὡς γυναικί.
*The negative is always attached to φημί (GE p. 247, #224).

12G

This section introduces conditional ('if') sentences with ἄν + the optative (GE pp. 257–258, #240–241) and ἄν + the imperfect indicative (GE pp. 258–259, #243). Wishes for the future are expressed by the optative without ἄν and wishes for the past (GE p. 259, #244) by the imperfect indicative. Note also GE p. 260, #245: ὅπως, ὅπως μή + future indicative expresses a caution, 'see to it that ...' 'take care that you don't ...'

Page 154

1 ἀπολοίμην　The optative is used to express a wish 'may 'I perish' Cf. 'I am damned if I can remember' (GE p. 212, #213).

6–7 βουλοίμην μεντἄν　μεντἄν = μέντοι ἄν. Therefore we have the optative + ἄν and therefore the meaning is potential: 'I would like, however ...'

7 εἴθε μνημονεύοιμι　'Would that I could remember'. εἴθε + optative expresses a wish (GE p. 259, #244).

8 πῶς γὰρ ἄν δικαίως τιθεῖτό τις　'For how could anyone justly cast his vote?' Potential ἄν + optative.

9 μὴ μνημονεύσας τοὺς λόγους;　'If he does not remember the arguments?' Note that a participle is used instead of an 'if' clause: 'not having remembered'. Note also μὴ, the proper negative in a conditional clause.

10 χαλεπὸν δή ἐστι τῷ δικαστῇ διακρίνειν τὴν δίκην, μὴ μνημονεύοντι
μνημονεύοντι agrees with τῷ δικαστῇ: 'It is difficult for a juror to judge the
trial, if he does not remember (*lit.* not remembering).'

11–13 εἰ μέντοι σοφιστὴς γένοιο σύ, ῥαδίως ἂν μνημονεύσαις ... καὶ οὐκ ἂν
ἐπιλάθοιο 'If you became a sophist you would easily remember ... and
would not forget.' A conditional sentence with optative and ἄν. See *GE*
pp. 258–259, #151. This is called a remote future condition.

15 εἴθε Ἱππίας γενοίμην ἐγώ   cf. *RGT* 12G p. 154 line 7. εἴθε + optative (no ἄν)
expresses a wish.

16 εἰ νῦν Ἱππίας ἦσθα, οἷός τ’ ἂν ἦσθα 'If you were Hippias, you would be
able', ἄν + the indicative expresses an unfulfilled condition (*GE* p. 167, #242).
The imperfect indicative is used to express present time and the aorist
indicative to express past time.

19 εἴθε μνημονεύσαιμι   A wish.

20 εἰ πάντες οἱ σοφισταί με διδάσκοιεν, οὐκ ἂν οἷοί τ’ εἶεν 'If all the sophists
taught me, they would not be able'. A remote future condition.

21–22 ἀλλ’ εἰ Ἱππίας ἡμῖν νῦν συνεγίγνετο, πῶς ἂν ἐδίδασκέ με, καὶ τί ἂν
ἔλεγεν; καὶ πῶς ἂν ἐμάνθανον ἐγώ; ἄν + imperfect indicative. A
series of unfulfilled conditions in present time. 'If Hippias were with us
now, how would he teach me, and what would he be saying, and how would I
learn?'

23 εἴθε ταῦτα εἰδείην   A wish.

23–24 εἰ ταῦτα ἤδη ἐγώ, πλούσιος ἂν ᾖ τὸ νῦν   An unfulfilled condition in present
time. 'If I knew this, I would be rich now.'

26–27 εἰ δέ τις ἐπιλάθοιτο, πῶς ἂν δικάσειε   What sort of condition?

28–29 οὐ γὰρ ἂν γένοιτο ... εἰ μὴ μνημονεύσειε   What sort of condition?

Page 155

30 ἀλλ’ ὅπως προθύμως προσέξεις τὸν νοῦν   ὅπως + future indicative (*GE*
p. 260, #245), 'see that you ...', 'take care that you ...'

33 ἀπόλοιντο ...   'May they perish!'

Translation for 12G

STRYMODOROS   I'm damned (May I perish!) if I can remember –

KOMIAS   You seem to me to be in some perplexity, Strymodoros. Don't cover up your
perplexity, feeling ashamed in front of Euergides, but tell me what is
perplexing you.

STR.   I will tell you, Komias, what is perplexing me. Why did Apollodoros mention
Lysias and Metaneira? For I don't remember. And, by Zeus, I would like to
remember what the contestant says. Would that I could remember everything
he says, and I am damned if I can remember. For how could anyone cast his
vote justly, if he cannot remember the arguments?

KOM.   It is difficult for the juror to judge the case if he can't remember everything
which the prosecutor says. If you were a sophist, you would easily remember

all the arguments, Strymodoros, as it seems, and you would not forget the things that have been said. But, like a Hippias, you would remember everything, having heard it once.

STR.   Like Hippias? Would that I were Hippias!

KOM.   If you were Hippias now, you would be able to list all the archons from Solon. For Hippias, having heard them once, used to remember fifty names.

STR.   What skill! Would that I could (if only I could) remember so much! But I am not clever by nature. If all the sophists taught me, they would not be able to make me a sophist. But if Hippias were here, how would he be teaching me, and what would he be saying? And how would I learn?

KOM.   I wish I knew this, Strymodoros! For if I knew that I would be rich now, and not a poor man and a juror.

STR.   Oh dear! For, like an old man, I forget everything I hear, of the laws and the arguments and the evidence. If anyone forgets so much, how could he judge the case and cast his vote?

KOM.   I do not know, Strymodoros. For he would never be a good juryman if he could not remember the things said by the prosecutor ... But see to it that you concentrate on the arguments and the laws and the evidence. For by doing this the jurors cast their votes easily.

STR.   May they perish, whoever are jurors and forget what the contestants say.

EXERCISES FOR SECTION 12G

CONDITIONAL SENTENCES AND WISHES

12G: 1

1. εἰ μὴ ἀκούοις, οὐκ ἂν μένοιμι.
2. εἰ ὑμεῖς ἐκελεύετε, ἐπειθόμην ἂν ἐγώ.
3. εἰ μὴ φιλοίης, φιλοίην ἂν ἐγώ.
4. εἰ μὴ ἐτρέχομεν, οὐκ ἂν ἐφεύγομεν.
5. εἰ μὴ ζητήσειας, οὐκ ἂν εὕροις.

12G: 2

1. εἰ γὰρ ἐξεφεύγομεν
2. εἴθε ἔδωκε, ὤφελε δοῦναι
3. εἰ γὰρ ἔστη, ὤφελε στῆναι
4. εἴθε ἐτίθεσαν
5. εἴθε ἀπεθνῇσκον

ὅπως + FUTURE INDICATIVE

12G: 3

1. ὅπως μὴ εἶ, See to it that you (s.) do not go.
2. ὅπως ἀκούσεσθε, See to it that you (pl.) listen.

3. ὅπως κολάσεις, See to it that you (s.) punish.
4. ὅπως μὴ γενήσῃ, See to it that you (s.) do not become.
5. ὅπως εἴσῃ (fut. οἶδα 'know') or ὅπως ἔσῃ (= fut. εἰμί 'be'), see to it that you (s.) know/see to it that you (s.) are.

12G: 4

1. εἰδείης, ἴοις
2. εἶεν, ἴοιεν
3. εἶμεν, εἰδεῖμεν
4. εἰδείη, ἴοι
5. εἴην, εἰδείην

REVISION EXERCISES FOR SECTION 12G

B/C – MORPHOLOGY AND SYNTAX

1. a. I want to be appointed as a juror and to cast my vote.
       εἴθε δικαστὴς καθισταίμην καὶ τιθείμην τὴν ψῆφον.
    b. You want to be a sophist.
       εἴθε σοφιστὴς γένοιο.
    c. I want you to put down money for me.
       εἴθε θείης χρήματα εἰς ἐμέ.
    d. I do not want to perish.
       μὴ ἀπολοίμην.
    e. I don't want you to know this.
       ταῦτα μὴ εἰδεῖτε.
    f. He wants to make the boy a sophist.
       σοφιστὴν τὸν παῖδα ποιήσειεν.
    g. I want him to remember the evidence.
       εἴθε μνημονεύσειε τὴν μαρτυρίαν.
    h. I want them to forget these arguments.
       ἐπιλάθοιντο τούτων τῶν λόγων.
    i. You (pl.) want to be rich.
       εἴθε πλούσιοι εἶτε (εἴητε).
    j. I don't want my family to be rich.
       εἴθε οἱ ἐμοὶ οἰκεῖοι μὴ πλούσιοι εἶεν.
2. a. I receive a big fine / the opponent exacts the penalty.
       εἰ ἐτίμων τίμημα μέγα, δίκην ἐλάμβανεν ἂν ὁ ἀντίδικος.
       εἰ τίμημα μέγα τιμῷην, δίκην λαμβάνοι ὁ ἀντίδικος.
    b. The jurors are persuaded by the prosecutor / they condemn the defendant.
       εἰ οἱ δικασταὶ πείθοιντο ὑπὸ τοῦ κατηγόρου, τοῦ φεύγοντος ἂν καταδικάζοιεν.
       εἰ ἐπείθοντο οἱ δικασταὶ ὑπὸ τοῦ κατηγόρου, τοῦ φεύγοντος ἂν κατεδικάζον.

c. You begin the enmity / the evidence is clear.

εἰ ὑπήρχετε τῆς ἔχθρας, τὰ τεκμήρια ἂν ἦν φανερά.

εἰ ὑπάρχοιτε τῆς ἔχθρας, φανερὰ ἂν εἴη τὰ τεκμήρια.

d. You mention the citizens / the accuser does not forget.

εἰ μνείαν ποιοίης τῶν ἀστῶν, οὐκ ἂν ἐπιλανθάνοιτο ὁ κατήγορος.

εἰ ἐποίεις μνείαν τῶν ἀστῶν, οὐκ ἂν ἐπελανθάνετο ὁ κατήγορος.

e. The citizens have children from the prostitutes / we know clearly.

εἰ οἱ ἀστοὶ ἐξ ἑταιρῶν ἐπαιδοποιοῦντο, σαφῶς ἂν ᾖσμεν.

εἰ παιδοποιοῖντο οἱ ἀστοὶ ἐξ ἑταιρῶν, σαφῶς ἂν εἰδεῖμεν.

f. The rich men do not have dealings with prostitutes / those women welcome the poor men.

εἰ μὴ οἱ πλούσιοι ταῖς ἑταίραις συγγίγνοιντο, τοὺς πένητας ἀσπάζοιντ᾽ ἂν ἐκεῖναι.

εἰ μὴ οἱ πλούσιοι ταῖς ἑταίραις συγγίγνοντο, τοὺς πένητας ἠσπάζοντ᾽ ἂν ἐκεῖναι.

3. a. Concentrate your mind and listen.

ὅπως προσέξεις τὸν νοῦν καὶ ἀκούσῃ.

b. Don't flatter the jurors.

ὅπως μὴ θωπεύσετε τοὺς δικαστάς.

c. Don't forget the arguments.

ὅπως μὴ ἐπιλήσῃ τῶν λόγων.

d. Recite the plot of the play.

ὅπως κατερεῖς (καταλέξεις) τὸν τοῦ δράματος λόγον.

e. Remember the words.

ὅπως μνημονεύσεις τοὺς λόγους.

f. Don't have children from prostitutes.

ὅπως μὴ παιδοποιήσεσθε ἐκ τῶν ἑταιρῶν.

g. Arrange the affair well.

ὅπως εὖ θήσεις τὸ πρᾶγμα.

h. Don't despise your friend.

ὅπως μὴ καταφρονήσεις τοῦ ἑταίρου.

12H

This section introduces accusative (or nominative) and participle construction after verbs of knowing or perceiving (*GE* pp. 264–265, #247), and the future passive (*GE* pp. 265–266, #248).

Page 156

1 ᾤχετο   Past tense of οἴχομαι.

4 ᾤετο   Past tense of οἶμαι.

12 ᾔδει γὰρ   'For she knew': a verb of knowing followed by three participles.

14 δοῦσα ... πάντα τὰ αὑτῆς   'Giving all her own things (*lit.* the things of herself)'.

Translation for 12H

Apollodoros resumes.

Phrynion, then, having paid the money on behalf of Neaira for her freedom, went to Athens, taking her with him. But when he arrived in Athens, he treated her disgracefully, and he used to go to dinners everywhere, taking her, and always went to riotous parties with her. Neaira, since she was being treated like dirt in a shameful way by Phrynion, and since, as she thought, she was not loved, collected all Phrynion's belongings from the house, and the clothes and the gold jewellery which Phrynion had given her. Taking all these, and two slave girls, Thratta and Kokkaline, she ran away to Megara. She spent two years in Megara but she could not make an adequate income for the management of the household (to meet the household expenses). Then this Stephanos travelled to Megara and lodged with her, as she was a hetaira. Neaira, having described the whole affair and the insolence of Phrynion, gave Stephanos all the things she had brought with her when she came from Athens, being very eager to live here, but being afraid of Phrynion. For she knew that Phrynion had been wronged by her and was angry with her, and that he had a pompous and contemptuous character. Neaira therefore gave everything she had to Stephanos and made him her protector.

121

Page 158

1 τῷ λόγῳ 'by his word', 'by his promise'.
2 ἐκόμπαζε Followed by accusative and infinitive: 'He boasted that Phrynion would not touch her', and then by nominative (αὐτός) and infinitive (ἕξειν) 'that he would have her as his wife'.
3–4 ἔφη δὲ 'he said that he', followed by infinitive (the nominative is omitted), but at ἀδικηθήσεσθαι αὐτήν the subject of the clause is someone else, and so appears in the accusative.
4 ὡς αὑτοῦ ὄντας 'as being his own children'. Note that αὑτοῦ = ἑαυτοῦ 'of himself' i.e. belonging to the subject of the sentence. There are several more examples of this usage in this passage.
7–8 παρὰ τὸν ψιθυριστήν 'next door to the Whisperer'. This was the title of a statue of Hermes.
10–11 εὖ γὰρ ᾔδει Στέφανος ... Followed by nominative and participle 'For Stephanos knew very well that he had no other income, unless he ...'
12–14 Note the structure of the sentence: ὁ δὲ Φρυνίων, πυθόμενος ... (followed by accusative and participle), παραλαβὼν ... ἦλθεν ... ὡς ἄξων αὐτήν (ὡς + the future participle expresses purpose, 'in order to take her').
14–15 ἀφαιρουμένου δὲ ... εἰς ἐλευθερίαν A genitive absolute. ἀφαιρεῖσθαι τινα εἰς ἐλευθερίαν has the technical meaning 'to claim as free'. So this awkward sentence will mean 'Although Stephanos claimed her as free according to the

laws, Phrynion compelled her to give securities to the polemarch, believing that she was his own (αὐτῷ) slave, since he had paid money for her.' καταθέντι (dative) agrees with αὐτῷ.

Translation for 12I

Apollodoros goes on speaking.

This Stephanos filled Neaira with great hope in Megara by this promise. For he boasted that Phrynion would never touch her, and that he himself would take her as his wife. And he said that her children would be introduced into the phratries as if they were his own, and they would become citizens, and she would not be harmed by anyone. Having said this he arrived here from Megara, bringing her with him and her three children with her, Proxenos and Ariston and a girl child who is now called Phano.

And he brought her and the children to a little house which he had in Athens next to the Whisperer Hermes, between the house of Dorotheos the Eleusinian and the house of Kleinomachos. He came with her for two reasons: so that he would have a beautiful hetaira for free and so that she would work and look after his household. For Stephanos knew very well that he had no other income or livelihood, unless he earned something by informing. But Phrynion, having found out that Neaira was living in Athens and with Stephanos, took young men with him and went to the house of Stephanos to take her away. Although Stephanos claimed her as free in accordance with the law, Phrynion compelled her to give securities before the Polemarch, regarding her as his slave since he had put down money on her behalf.

EXERCISES FOR SECTION 12H–I

INFINITIVE AND PARTICIPLE IN REPORTED SPEECH

12H–I: 1

a. I know I am wise.
b. I know you are not foolish.
c. We learned they were fleeing.
d. They heard that we had gone.

12H–I: 2

1. We say that politicians do not speak the truth.
    ὅτι + indicative clause.
2. He said he would be present.
    nom. + infinitive construction.
3. He found out the enemy had fled.
    acc. + participle construction.
4. They hoped to arrive quickly/they hoped they would arrive quickly.
    nom. + fut. infin. after verb of hoping or expecting.

5. He knew that they (the women) had obeyed.
    acc. + participle construction

THE FUTURE PASSIVE

12H–I: 3

1.	ἀκουσθήσομαι	I shall be heard
2.	δουλωθήσεται	he will be enslaved
3.	δοθήσονται	they will be given
4.	τεθήσεται	he/she/it will be placed
5.	σταθήσεται	it will be set up

REVISION EXERCISES FOR SECTION 12H–I

B/C – MORPHOLOGY AND SYNTAX

1. I shall be brought into   εἰσάγω
    we shall be convicted   ἐξελέγχω
    you (s.) will be compelled   ἀναγκάζω
    he will be angry   ὀργίζομαι
    to be going to be fined   ζημιόω
    they will be wronged   ἀδικέω

2. a. The woman will be wronged by no one.
        οὔ φαμεν τὴν γυναῖκα ἀδικηθήσεσθαι ὑπ' οὐδενός.
        We say that the woman *will* not be wronged by anyone.
        οὐκ ἔφαμεν τὴν γυναῖκα ἀδικηθήσεσθαι ὑπ' οὐδενός.
        We said that the woman *would* not be wronged by anyone.

    b. The prostitute's children will become citizens.
        οἴεται τοὺς τῆς ἑταίρας παῖδας πολίτας γενήσεσθαι.
        He thinks that the prostitute's children *will* become citizens.
        ᾤετο τοὺς τῆς ἑταίρας παῖδας πολίτας γενήσεσθαι.
        He thought that the prostitute's children *would* become citizens.

    c. Stephanos and Neaira will arrive in Athens from Megara.
        ἡγεῖται τὸν Στέφανον καὶ τὴν Νέαιραν ἀφίξεσθαι ἐκ τῶν Μεγάρων
        Ἀθήναζε.
        He thinks that Stephanos and Neaira *will* arrive in Athens from
        Megara.
        ἡγήσατο τὸν Στέφανον καὶ τὴν Νέαιραν ἀφίξεσθαι ἐκ τῶν Μεγάρων
        Ἀθήναζε.
        He *thought* that Stephanos and Neaira *would* arrive in Athens from
        Megara.

    d. I shall be compelled to take Neaira away from Phrynion.
        φησὶν ἐμὲ ἀναγκασθήσεσθαι παρὰ Φρυνίωνος τὴν Νέαιραν
        ἀφαιρεῖσθαι.
        He says that I *will* be compelled to take Neaira away from Phrynion.

ἔφη ἐμὲ ἀναγκασθήσεσθαι παρὰ Φρυνίωνος τὴν Νέαιραν
ἀφαιρεῖσθαι.

He said that I *would* be compelled to take Neaira away from Phrynion.

3. a. Phrynion was wronged by me and was angry with me.

οἶδα τὸν Φρυνίωνα ἀδικηθέντα ὑπ' ἐμοῦ καὶ ὀργισθέντα ἐμοί.

I know that Phrynion *was* wronged by me and *was* angry with me.

ἤδη τὸν Φρυνίωνα ἀδικηθέντα ὑπ' ἐμοῦ καὶ ὀργισθέντα ἐμοί.

I knew that Phrynion *had been* wronged by me and *had been* angry with me.

b. Neaira was living in town (imperfect) and went to Stephanos.

ὁρᾷ τὴν Νέαιραν ἐπιδημοῦσαν καὶ ἐλθοῦσαν ὡς Στέφανον.

He sees that Neaira *is* resident in the town and *has gone* to Stephanos.

εἶδε τὴν Νέαιραν ἐπιδημοῦσαν καὶ ἐλθοῦσαν ὡς Στέφανον.

He saw that Neaira *was* resident in the town and *had gone* to Stephanos.

c. We were wronged by the prosecutor and condemned by the jurors.

αἰσθάνονται ἡμᾶς ἀδικηθέντας ὑπὸ τοῦ κατηγόρου καὶ
καταδικασθέντας ὑπὸ τῶν δικαστῶν.

They perceive that we *were wronged* by the prosecutor and *condemned*
by the jurors.

ᾔσθοντο ἡμᾶς ἀδικηθέντας ὑπὸ τοῦ κατηγόρου καὶ καταδικασθέντας
ὑπὸ τῶν δικαστῶν.

They perceived that we *had been wronged* by the prosecutor and *had
been condemned* by the jurors.

d. You wronged the city and despised the laws and were irreverent to the
gods.

γιγνώσκετε ἀδικήσαντες τὴν πόλιν καὶ τῶν νόμων καταφρονοῦντες
καὶ ἀσεβοῦντες εἰς τοὺς θεούς.

You know that you *have wronged* the city and *are despising* the laws
and *are being irreverent* to the gods.

ἔγνωτε ἀδικήσαντες τὴν πόλιν καὶ τῶν νόμων καταφρονοῦντες καὶ
ἀσεβοῦντες εἰς τοὺς θεούς.

You knew that you *had wronged* the city, *were despising* the laws and
were being irreverent to the gods.

e. You are a prostitute and you are having children by citizens.

οἶσθα ἑταίρα οὖσα καὶ παιδοποιουμένη ἐξ ἀστῶν.

You know you *are* a prostitute and that you *are having* children by citizens.

ᾔδεισθα ἑταίρα οὖσα καὶ παιδοποιουμένη ἐξ ἀστῶν.

You knew you *were* a prostitute and that you *were having* children by
citizens.

D – TRANSLATE INTO GREEK

1. Sentences

1. εἴθε μνημονεύσαιμι τοὺς λόγους τοὺς τοῦ κατηγόρου.
2. εἰ σοφιστὴς ἦν, ἐμνημόνευον ἂν τούτους τοὺς λόγους.
3. εἰ δυναίμην μνημονεύειν τὰς μαρτυρίας, δικαίως ἂν θείμην τὴν ψῆφον.

4. ὁ Φρυνίων ᾔδει τὴν Νέαιραν ἐπιδημοῦσαν καὶ τὰ χρήματα ἔχουσαν.

5. ὁ Στέφανός οὔ φησι τὴν Νέαιραν ἀδικηθήσεσθαι ὑπ' οὐδενός.

2. Prose

ὁ δὲ Ἀπολλόδωρος, ἀδικηθεὶς ὑπὸ τοῦ Στεφάνου καὶ εἰς κίνδυνον καταστάς, ἀγωνίζεται ταύτην τὴν δίκην. οὐ γὰρ ἐῶσιν οἱ νόμοι ἑταίρᾳ ὡς γυναικὶ συνοικεῖν ἀστῶν οὐδένα. καὶ ὁ Ἀπολλόδωρος λέγει ὅτι σαφῶς ἐπιδείξεται τὸν Στέφανον αὐτὰ ταῦτα ποιεῖν. εἰ γὰρ ὁ Στέφανος ταῦτ' ἐτύγχανε ποιῶν, χαλεπώτατον ὂν ἂν ἐφαίνετο. ἐντεῦθεν οὖν ἐλπίζω ἔγωγε τὸν Ἀπολλόδωρον νικήσειν τὴν δίκην. εἰ γὰρ καὶ νικώῃ οὗτος, ἀγαθὸν ἂν εἴη τῇ πόλει.

E – TEST EXERCISE 12

But I shall tell you what came next (the things after this). See that you listen carefully, gentlemen of the jury. For when this Timarkhos here was released from Antikles, he used to spend his days in the gambling-den. One of the gamblers is a certain Pittalakos, a slave of the city. This man, seeing Timarkhos in the gambling-den, took him to his home and kept him with him.

And, as for the outrages, which I know clearly were inflicted on Timarkhos by this man, by Zeus the Olympian, I would not dare to speak of them before you. By Zeus, may I perish most miserably, if I mention such things. For, if I were to speak in your presence of the things that this man did, I would not be able to go on living.

Meanwhile Hegesandros is sailing here from the Hellespont, Hegesandros, whose character you know even better than I do, to be unjust and disdainful. He went regularly to visit Pittalakos who was a fellow-gambler, and first seeing Timarkhos there, wanted to take him to his own home. For he thought that he was close to his own nature.

When Timarkhos had been detached from Pittalakos and taken up by Hegesandros, Pittalakos was angry, realising that he had spent so much money on Timarkhos in vain, and he kept visiting the house of Hegesandros. But when Hegesandros and Timarkhos got angry with him for coming so often, they forced their way during the night into the house where Pittalakos lived, and they first of all smashed up the furniture, and finally beat up Pittalakos himself for a long time. On the next day, Pittalakos, being angry about the affair, went naked into the market-place and sat on the altar of the mother of the gods. When a crowd ran up, Hegesandros and Timarkhos hurried to the altar and standing beside it they kept begging Pittalakos to get up, claiming that the whole affair had been a drunken brawl. And Timarkhos himself kept declaring that everything would be done by him, if only Pittalakos would get up (genitive absolute). Finally they persuade him to get up from the altar.

Section Thirteen: Neaira as married woman

This section continues the story of Neaira. As in Section 12 there are long exercises which practise the grammar which has been introduced. Once again you may decide to do the exercises when they occur, or to continue reading to the end of Section 13 and then go back to revise the grammar and do the relevant exercises.

13A

Page 162

1–4 The main clause (δῆλά ἐστι τὰ τεκμήρια 'There are clear proofs that …') is delayed until the end of the sentence. The subordinate clauses (ὅτι μὲν … δούλη ἦν Νέαιρα … καὶ ἀπέδρα … καὶ ὁ Φρυνίων … κατηγγύησε …) come first. These clauses are all subordinate to the main clause.

8 πρὶν Ἀθήναζε ἐλθεῖν πρίν + infinitive, *GE* pp. 272–273, #252: 'Before she came to Athens'. You will meet lots of examples of this in 13A and B.

8–9 ὥσπερ αὐτοῦ θυγάτηρ οὖσα 'as his own daughter'. Note the breathing: αὐτοῦ could have meant someone else's daughter αὐτοῦ or ἑαυτοῦ 'his own' belongs to the subject of the main verb.

10–11 καὶ δὴ ἴστε τὴν Φανώ … μαθοῦσαν Accusative and participle: 'You know that Phano had learned'.

14–16 Note the structure: 'Phrastor seeing (ὁρῶν) that (acc. + participle twice) …, and having found out (ἅμα δὲ πυθόμενος) that (acc. + participle) … was very angry (ὠργίσθη μάλιστα) … considering (ἡγούμενος) that he … (nominative + infinitives).'

17 πρὶν εἰδέναι 'Before he knew that …' Followed by accusative and participle construction.

18–20 εἰ … μὴ ἐξηπατήθη ὁ Φράστωρ καὶ Φανὼ γνησία ἦν, ἢ οὐκ ἂν ἐξέβαλεν αὐτὴν … ἢ ἀπέδωκεν … An unfulfilled condition in past time: ἄν + the aorist indicative. Note the negative in the 'if' clause is μή and in the main clause οὐ: 'if Phrastor had not been deceived and if Phano had been legitimate, either he would not have divorced her or he would have given back the dowry'.

21 ἐκπεσούσης δὲ Φανοῦς ἐκπίπτω is used as the passive of ἐκβάλλω. Note that this is a genitive absolute construction.

25–26 γνοὺς δὲ Στέφανος ὅτι ἐξελεγχθήσεται … καὶ ὅτι ἐξελεγχθεὶς κινδυνεύσει … διαλλάττεται … 'Stephanos, realising that he would be convicted, and

that, having been convicted, he would be in danger of … was reconciled
with …'

Page 163

28–29 ἀλλ' εἰ ἀστῆς θυγάτηρ ἦν Φανώ, οὐκ ἂν διηλλάχθη Στέφανος   What sort of
condition? Is there an ἄν? Are the verbs indicative or optative? What tense are
they? 'If Phano had been the daughter of a citizen, Stephanos would not have
been reconciled.' See *GE* p. 276, #254.

Translation for 13A

That Neaira was from the beginning a slave and a hetaira, and that she ran away
from Phrynion to Megara and that when she returned to Athens Phrynion
demanded securities from her before the polemarch on the grounds that she was
an alien, [of all this] there is clear evidence.

Now I want to demonstrate to you that Stephanos himself provides evidence
against Neaira that she is living with him as his wife although she is a
foreigner.

For Neaira had a daughter, whom she brought with her to the house of
Stephanos. And when they came to Athens they called the girl Phano. Formerly
she had been called Strybele, before she came to Athens. This girl was given in
marriage by Stephanos here, as if she had been his own daughter from a citizen
wife, to an Athenian man, Phrastor of the deme of Aigileia. And Stephanos gave
her a dowry of thirty minas. And furthermore you know that Phano, before she
lived with Phrastor, had learned her mother's character and extravagance.
Therefore when she went to Phrastor, who was a working man and reckoned his
income with precision, she did not know how to make herself pleasing to
Phrastor's ways.

Phrastor, seeing that she was neither well behaved nor willing to obey him, and
at the same time having found out clearly that Phano was not the daughter of
Stephanos but of Neaira, was very angry, thinking that he had been insulted and
tricked by Stephanos. For he had married Phano before he knew that she was the
daughter of Neaira. Therefore he divorced Phano, having lived with her for a
year; she was pregnant, and he did not give back the dowry. If Stephanos had not
deceived Phrastor and if Phano had been legitimate, either Phrastor would not
have divorced her or he would have given back the dowry.

When Phano had been divorced, Stephanos brought a suit against Phrastor, in
accordance with the law which requires a man who divorces his wife to give back
the dowry. But when Stephanos had brought this suit, Phrastor brought a charge
against Stephanos here in accordance with the law which does not allow anyone
to betroth the daughter of an alien to an Athenian man. Stephanos, realising that
he would be convicted of doing wrong and that having been convicted he would
risk meeting with the most severe penalties (for Phano was the daughter of an
alien woman), was reconciled with Phrastor and gave up his claim to the dowry
and withdrew the charge. And, before the case came to court, Phrastor also

withdrew his charge. But if Phano had been the daughter of a citizen woman, Stephanos would not have been reconciled.

13B

Page 164

3 ἐξεπέμφθη   What tense? It comes from ἐκπέμπω.

4 διετέθη   What tense? It comes from διατίθημι.

7 ὡς θεραπεύσουσαι καὶ ... ἐπιμελήσομεναι   ὡς + the future participle expresses purpose (*GE* p. 271, #251): 'They went to him *to look after him* and ...'

13–14 καὶ πρὶν ὑγιαίνειν ὑπέσχετο δὴ τοῦτο ποιήσειν ὁ Φράστωρ   'And before he got better, Phrastor promised that he would do this.' Note the future infinitive.

17–18 εἰ γὰρ ἄπαις ἀπέθανε Φράστωρ, οἱ οἰκεῖοι ἔλαβον ἂν τὰ αὐτοῦ   What sort of condition? Is there an ἄν? Are the verbs indicative or optative? What tense are they? 'For if Phrastor had died childless, his relatives would have taken his property.' See *GE* p. 276, #254.

Translation for 13B

I want to provide you with another piece of evidence from Phrastor and the members of his phratry and of his clan that this Neaira is an alien. For not long after Neaira's daughter was divorced, Phrastor fell ill and was in a very bad way and was in total need. Before he was ill there had been a long-standing difference with his relations, and anger and hatred. And Phrastor was childless. But in his state of need he was courted by Neaira and Phano. For they went to him, to look after him and to care for him enthusiastically (for Phrastor had no one who would look after him), and they brought remedies (things useful) for the illness and visited him. I am sure you know yourselves, jurors, how valuable is a woman in time of sickness when she is at the side of a man who is suffering.

Since they were doing this, Phrastor was persuaded, before he got better, to take back Phano's child and to make him his son. This was the child which Phano had borne when she had been sent away in a pregnant state by Phrastor. Before he got better, Phrastor promised that he would do this, making the natural and reasonable calculation that he was in a poor condition and did not expect to survive, but he wanted to take back Phano's child before he died (although he knew that he was not legitimate), since he did not want his relations to inherit his property, nor did he want to die without a child. For if Phrastor had died without a child, his relations would have got his property.

Grammar

Now make sure that you know the aorist infinitive passive (*GE* p. 270, #249) and the future participle passive (*GE* pp. 271–272, #250) and that you can recognise ὡς + the future participle used to express purpose (*GE* p. 271, #251) and πρίν + the infinitive = 'before' (*GE* pp. 272–273, #252).

EXERCISES FOR SECTION 13A–B

THE AORIST INFINITIVE PASSIVE

13A–B: 1

δοθῆναι, πεισθῆναι, ἐνεχθῆναι, λυθῆναι, τεθῆναι

FUTURE PARTICIPLES ACTIVE, MIDDLE, PASSIVE

13A–B: 2

λύσων -ουσα -ον	about to loose
λυσόμενος -η -ον	about to ransome
λυθήσομενος -η -ον	about to be loosed, ransomed
πείσων -ουσα -ον	about to persuade
πεισόμενος -η -ον	about to obey
πεισθησόμενος -η -ον	about to be persuaded
οἴσων -ουσα -ον	about to carry
οἰσόμενος -η -ον	about to carry off for oneself, win
οἰσθησόμενος/ἐνεχθησόμενος -η -ον	about to be carried
στήσων -ουσα -ον	about to set up
στησόμενος -η -ον	about to stand, set up for oneself
σταθησόμενος -η -ον	about to be set up
ληψόμενος -η -ον	about to take
ληψόμενος -η -ον	about to take for oneself, take hold of
ληφθησόμενος -η -ον	about to be taken

ὡς + FUTURE PARTICIPLE

13A–B: 3

1. ὡς ληψομένη αὐτήν
2. ὡς σώσοντας ἑαυτούς
3. ὡς πείσων αὐτήν
4. ὡς δώσοντες

πρίν + INFINITIVE

13A–B: 4

1. πρὶν π(ε)ίθεσθαι, πεισθῆναι
2. πρὶν τοὺς ἄνδρας ἀπιέναι, ἀπελθεῖν
3. πρὶν ἐσθίειν, φαγεῖν
4. πρὶν ἐκβάλλειν, ἐκβαλεῖν

REVISION EXERCISES FOR SECTION 13A–B

B/C – MORPHOLOGY AND SYNTAX

1.
ἐκβαλοῦντι	ἐκβάλλω	I throw out, divorce
ἐντευξομένη	ἐντυγχάνω	I meet
εἰσαχθησόμενος	εἰσάγω	I introduce, lead in
καταστήσοντι	καθίστημι	I establish, set up
παρέξοντες	παρέχω	I provide
ἐκδώσοντα	ἐκδίδωμι	I give in marriage
ἐρῶν	λέγω	I speak, tell
θησόντων	τίθημι	I place
ἀφαιρησόμενος	ἀφαιρέω	I take away
γνωσομένην	γιγνώσκω	I know
λήσουσαν	λανθάνω	I escape notice
ἐσόμενον	εἰμί	I am
ἀναγκασθησομένῳ	ἀναγκάζω	I compel
ἐπιδειξουσῶν	ἐπιδείκνυμι	I show, prove
πευσομένων	πυνθάνομαι	I find out
ἀποθανουμένη	ἀποθνῄσκω	I die
παραληψομένη	παραλαμβάνω	I receive from
ἐκπεσούμενοι	ἐκπίπτω	I fall out, I am thrown out, get divorced

2. Aorist passive infinitives

πεισθῆναι	πείθω
ἐκπεμφθῆναι	ἐκπέμπω
ἐξαπατηθῆναι	ἐξαπατάω
ἐξελεγχθῆναι	ἐξελέγχω
ὑβρισθῆναι	ὑβρίζω
ἐκβληθῆναι	ἐκβάλλω
διατεθῆναι	διατίθημι

Other infinitives

εἶναι	εἰμί
εἰδέναι	οἶδα
ἀποδιδόναι	ἀποδίδωμι
θεῖναι	τίθημι
δεικνύναι	δείκνυμι
ἀπολλύναι	ἀπόλλυμι
ἀποδοῦναι	ἀποδίδωμι
ἀφιστάναι	ἀφίστημι
τιθέναι	τίθημι

Exercise 3 is on the use of ὡς + future participle to express purpose, while Exercise 4 gives you practice in πρίν + infinitive = 'before'.

3. a. Those men came to the house of Stephanos to take away Neaira. ὡς
       ἄξοντες

    b. The women went off to Athens to live (spend time) in Stephanos' house
       and to work. ὡς διατρίψουσαι καὶ ἐργασόμεναι

    c. Therefore I am going to him to speak the truth and listen to lies. ὡς
       ἐρῶν... καὶ ἀκουσόμενος

    d. The man went into the lawcourt to defend himself and to be acquitted.
       ὡς ἀπολογησόμενος καὶ ἀπολυθησόμενος

4. a. Stephanos brought Phrastor to the lawcourt

     (i) πρὶν τὸν Φράστορα γράψασθαι γραφήν before Phrastor indicted him

    (ii) πρὶν τὸ τῆς Φανοῦς παιδίον γενέσθαι before Phano's child was born

   (iii) πρὶν τὸ παιδίον ἀναληφθῆναι ὑπὸ Φράστορος before the child was
         taken back by Phrastor

    (iv) πρὶν γνῶναι ὅτι ἐξελεγχθήσεται ἀδικῶν before he knew that he
         would be convicted of wrong-doing.

4. b. Phrastor withdrew the charge

     (i) πρὶν εἰσελθεῖν εἰς τὸ δικαστήριον before he came to court

    (ii) πρὶν ἐκπέμψαι τὴν Φανώ before he divorced Phano

   (iii) πρὶν ὑπισχνεῖσθαι ἀναλήψεσθαι τὸ παιδίον before he promised that
         he would take back the child

    (iv) πρὶν λεχθῆναι τούτους τοὺς λόγους ὑπὸ τῆς Νεαίρας before these
         words were spoken by Neaira.

13C

Page 165

1–2 ὅτι οὐκ ἂν ἔπραξε τοῦτο ὁ Φράστωρ, εἰ μὴ ἠσθένησε   ἄν + the aorist
    indicative expresses an unfulfilled condition in past time (*GE* p. 276, #254):
    'Phrastor would not have done that if he had not been ill.'

  2 ὡς ... τάχιστα 'as soon as ...'

4–5 ὅτι οὐχ ἑκὼν ἀνέλαβε τὸ παιδίον   οὐχ ἑκών 'not willingly': 'that he did not
    willingly take back the child'.

  5 ἀλλὰ βιασθεὶς διὰ τὸ νοσεῖν 'but forced by his illness'. Here the infinitive is
    used as a noun with the article. See *GE* p. 279, #257. This example is followed
    by three more: διὰ τὸ ἄπαις εἶναι καὶ τὸ θεραπεύειν αὐτὰς αὐτὸν καὶ τὸ τοὺς
    οἰκείους μισεῖν. Note that a whole accusative and infinitive phrase can be used
    in this way (*GE* p. 280, #258).

6–7 εἰ μὴ ἠσθένησε ... οὐκ ἂν ἀνέλαβε ...   What sort of condition? Is there an
    ἄν? Are the verbs indicative or optative? What tense are they?

Page 166

 10 εἰδότες   Can you recognise this participle? It comes from οἶδα.

10–13 The structure of the sentence is as follows: ἀλλὰ οἱ γεννῆται, εἰδότες ... καὶ
    ἀκούσαντες ... ἀποψηφίζονται τοῦ παιδὸς καὶ οὐκ ἐνέγραφον ... There is an

accusative + participle clause depending on εἰδότες and an accusative + participle + infinitive clause depending on ἀκούσαντες. 'But the clansmen, knowing that the woman was the daughter of Neaira, and having heard that Phrastor, having divorced her, had then taken back the child, because of his illness, voted against the boy and …'

13–14 Note that this is another unfulfilled condition.

14 λαχόντος οὖν τοῦ Φράστορος   Genitive absolute.

16–17 προκαλουμένων δ' αὐτὸν τῶν γεννητῶν   Another genitive absolute.

18 ἀλλ' εἰ ὁ παῖς …   What sort of condition? Is there an ἄν? What mood and tense are the verbs?

Translation for 13C

Now I shall prove to you by a great and clear piece of evidence that Phrastor would not have done this if he had not been ill. For as soon as Phrastor recovered from that illness, he took a citizen wife according to the laws, the legitimate daughter of Satyros of the deme of Melite, the sister of Diphilos. This is proof for you that he did not willingly take back the child, but was forced to do it because of his sickness and the fact that he was childless and because the women were looking after him and because he hated his relations. For if Phrastor had not been ill, he would not have taken back the child.

And furthermore, I want to show you another proof that this Neaira is an alien. For Phrastor, when he was ill, introduced Phano's son into the phratries and into the Brytidae, of whom Phrastor is a member. But the members of the clan, knowing that his wife was the daughter of Neaira, and having heard that Phrastor had divorced her and had then because of his illness taken back the child, voted against the child and did not register him in the clan. But if Phano had been the daughter of a citizen, the members of the clan would not have voted against the child, but would have registered him in the clan. Therefore when Phrastor brought a suit against them, the members of the clan challenged him to swear by the sacred mysteries that he truly believed the child to be his own son from a citizen wife legally married in accordance with the law. When the members of the clan challenged him, Phrastor abandoned the oath and went away before he could swear that his son was legitimate. But if his son had been legitimate and born from a citizen wife, he would have sworn.

REVISION EXERCISES FOR SECTION 13C

1. a. εἰ ἄπαις ἀπέθανε Φράστωρ, οἱ οἰκεῖοι ἂν ἔλαβον τὰ αὑτοῦ.
    If Phrastor had died childless, his relatives would have taken his possessions.

    b. εἰ ἀστῆς θυγάτηρ ἦν Φανώ, οὐκ ἂν ὠργίσθη Στέφανος.
    If Phano had been the daughter of a female citizen, Stephanos would not have been angry.

c. εἰ ᾔδει Φανὼ Νεαίρας οὖσαν θυγατέρα ὁ Φράστωρ, ἐξέβαλεν ἂν ὡς τάχιστα.

If Phrastor had known that Phano was the daughter of Neaira, he would have thrown her out (divorced her) as quickly as possible.

d. εἰ Φανὼ ξένης θυγάτηρ ἐκλήθη, Φράστωρ οὐκ ἂν ἐξηπατήθη.

If Phano had been called the daughter of a foreigner, Phrastor would not have been deceived.

e. εἰ μὴ ἔλαχε Στέφανος τὴν δίκην ταύτην, οὐκ ἂν ἐγράψατο Φράστωρ αὐτὸν γραφήν. If Stephanos had not brought this suit against him, Phrastor would not have brought this accusation against him.

N.B. Neither εἰμί nor οἶδα have an aorist, so the context will determine the translation.

13D

Page 167

3–4 ὁ μὲν γὰρ Στέφανος … 'For Stephanos bears witness against Neaira through his unwillingness (διὰ τὸ μὴ ἐθελῆσαι) to engage in litigation on behalf of her daughter about the dowry.'

5–9 Φράστωρ δὲ μαρτυρεῖ <u>ἐκβαλεῖν</u> … καὶ οὐκ <u>ἀποδοῦναι</u> … ἔπειτα δὲ αὐτὸς … <u>πεισθῆναι</u> διὰ τὴν ἀσθένειαν καὶ τὸ … οἰκείους <u>ἀναλαβεῖν</u> τὸ παιδίον καὶ … <u>ποιήσασθαι</u>, αὐτὸς δὲ <u>εἰσαγαγεῖν</u> … ἀλλ᾿ οὐκ <u>ὀμόσαι</u> … ὕστερον δὲ <u>γῆμαι</u> …   A string of infinitives depends on μαρτυρεῖ: 'Phrastor bears witness that he divorced … and <u>did not give back</u> the dowry, but then, <u>was persuaded</u> by … on account of his illness and because he was childless and because of his hostility to his relations, to <u>take back</u> the child and <u>make</u> him his son,… and that he himself <u>introduced</u> him to the clan, but he did not swear that … and that later he <u>married</u> a citizen woman …'

11–13 Look to see if there is an ἄν and note the mood and tense of the verbs.

Translation for 13D

Therefore I clearly demonstrate to you that the very members of Neaira's own family have furnished proof that she is an alien, both Stephanos here who has her now and is living with her and Phrastor who married her daughter. For Stephanos bears witness against Neaira because he was not willing to go to court on behalf of her daughter about her dowry, and Phrastor bears witness that he divorced the daughter of this Neaira and did not give back the dowry, and then was himself persuaded by Neaira and Phano, on account of his sickness and childlessness and his hatred of his relations, to take back the child and to make him his son, and he himself introduced the boy to the members of the clan, but did not swear that he was the son of a citizen woman, and that he later married a citizen wife according to the law. These actions are perfectly clear and form great proofs that they knew that this Neaira was an alien. For if Neaira had been a citizen, Phano would not have been sent away. For Phano would have been a citizen. And furthermore, if

Phano had been a citizen, the clan members would not have voted against her son. Because of the fact that Phrastor was not willing to swear an oath, and because the members of the clan voted against the boy, Stephanos is clearly committing an injustice towards the city and irreverence towards the gods.

EXERCISES FOR SECTION 13D

VERBS IN THE INFINITIVE USED AS NOUNS

13D: 1

1. διὰ τὸ φυγεῖν
2. μετὰ τὸ μέλλειν
3. ἀντὶ τοῦ παύσασθαι
4. τῷ μάχεσθαι
5. τοῦ φυλάξαι ἕνεκα

6. ἄνευ τοῦ μισεῖν
7. διὰ τὸ διανοεῖσθαι
8. τοῦ θορυβῆσαι ἕνεκα.
9. τῷ ἀπορεῖν
10. διὰ τὸ βοᾶν

REVISION EXERCISES FOR SECTION 13D

B/C – MORPHOLOGY AND SYNTAX

1. a. Illness is an evil. τὸ ἀσθενεῖν
   b. Phrastor took back the child on account of his illness and his hatred of his relations and his childlessness. διὰ τὸ νοσεῖν καὶ τὸ μισεῖν τοὺς οἰκείους καὶ τὸ ἄπαις εἶναι
   c. Stephanos was clearly doing wrong because he did not swear. διὰ τὸ μὴ ὀμόσαι
   d. The child clearly belongs to an alien woman, because the clansmen voted against him and did not register him in the clan. διὰ τὸ τοὺς γεννήτας ἀποψηφίσασθαι αὐτοῦ καὶ μὴ ἐγγράψαι εἰς τὸ γένος
   e. The clansmen were forced to vote against the child, because they knew that he was not legitimate. διὰ τὸ εἰδέναι
   f. Care is a good thing. τὸ θεραπεύειν
   g. And he made mention of these facts, that he was weak and that he was depressed and that he was being looked after by Neaira. τοῦ ἀσθενεῖν τε ἕνεκα καὶ εἰς ἀπορίαν καταστῆναι καὶ ὑπὸ τῆς Νεαίρας θεραπεύεσθαι
   h. Impiety is a great evil. τὸ ἀσεβεῖν
   i. I was compelled to go in by force (being forced). τῷ βιάζεσθαι

D – ENGLISH INTO GREEK

1. ὁ Στέφανος ἦλθε πρὸς τὸν Φράστορα ὡς ἐγγυήσων αὐτῷ τὴν Φανώ.
2. ὁ Φράστωρ ἔγημε τὴν Φανὼ πρὶν εἰδέναι αὐτὴν Νεαίρας θυγατέρα οὖσαν.
3. εἰ μὴ ἐθεράπευσε τὸν Φράστορα ἡ Φανώ, οὐκ ἂν ἀνέλαβεν ἐκεῖνος τὸ παιδίον.

4. Φράστωρ ἀνέλαβε τὸ τῆς Φανοῦς παιδίον διὰ τὸ νοσεῖν καὶ τὸ τὴν Φανὼ θεραπεύειν αὐτόν.

5. εἰ γνήσιος ἦν ὁ παῖς, Φράστωρ ἂν ὤμοσεν.

13E

In this section you will meet a new tense, the perfect active (I have -ed). If you want to find out about it before you meet it in reading, see *GE* pp. 282–283, #260–262. It is very easy to recognise.

Page 168

2 σκοπεῖτε τοίνυν   'Consider then', followed by two clauses, ὁποία … Νεαίρας and ὅπως … ἠδίκησαν: 'what sort of shamelessness …' and 'how they wronged the state'.

4 ἦν γάρ ποτε Θεογένης τις …   'There was a man called Theogenes.'

6 ὡς πάρεδρος γενησόμενος   ὡς + future participle expresses purpose.

9–10 οὐ γὰρ ᾔδει ὁ Θεογένης <u>ὅτου</u> θυγάτηρ ἐστὶ οὐδὲ <u>ὁποῖά</u> ἐστιν αὐτῆς τὰ ἔθη   'for Theogenes did not know <u>whose</u> daughter she was nor <u>what sort of</u> character she had' ('what sort were the characteristics of her').

11–12 καὶ εἶδεν ἃ οὐ προσῆκεν αὐτῇ ὁρᾶν, ξένῃ οὔσῃ   'and she saw what it was not fitting for her to see, being an alien'. Notice that ξένῃ οὔσῃ is dative agreeing with αὐτῇ.

11 καὶ εἰσῆλθεν <u>οἷ</u>   'and that she went in <u>to where</u>'. Cf. ποῖ 'where to?'

15–16 οὐ μόνον … ἀλλὰ καί …   'not only … but also …'

15–20 A series of examples of the perfect tense!

18 ἐκδούς   Can you recognise this? It comes from ἐκδίδωμι and agrees with the subject, Stephanos.

20 ὅτι δ' ἀληθῆ λέγω, αὗται αἱ πράξεις δηλώσουσιν   Note the rhetorical inversion of the clauses again: 'That I am speaking the truth, these actions will prove.'

Translation for 13E

Because of this, everyone knew that Phano was clearly an alien and not a citizen. Consider then what shamelessness Stephanos and Neaira showed and how they wronged the city. For they openly dared to allege that the daughter of Neaira was a citizen. There was once a certain Theogenes who was elected as basileus (King Archon), being well born but poor and inexperienced in affairs. Before Theogenes entered on his office, Stephanos gave him money so that he would become his assistant and share in his position. When Theogenes took up office, this Stephanos, becoming his assistant by giving him money, gave the daughter of Neaira to Theogenes as a wife and betrothed her as being his own daughter. For Theogenes did not know whose daughter she was nor what sort of habits she had. So greatly did this man despise you and the laws. And this woman made the secret sacrifices for you on behalf of the city, and saw what it was not fitting for her to see, being a foreigner. And she went into the place where no other Athenian goes except the wife of the basileus, and she was presented to Dionysos as his bride, and she performed on behalf of the city the ancestral rites to the gods which are numerous, sacred and secret.

I want to tell you in greater detail about these things. For you will be casting your vote not only on your own behalf and on behalf of the laws, but for respect towards the gods. I have shown you then that Stephanos has acted most irreverently. For he has made the laws invalid and has shown contempt for the gods, by giving the daughter of Neaira as a wife to Theogenes when he was holding the office of basileus. And then this woman has performed the rites and sacrifices on behalf of the city. That I am speaking the truth, these events will prove.

REVISION EXERCISES FOR SECTION 13E

B/C – MORPHOLOGY AND SYNTAX

1. τετ- τεθ- μεμ- γεγ- πεφ- πεπ- ἐπιδεδ- ἐπιδεδ- κεκ-
    τεθ- πεπ- ἐκβεβ- γεγ- ἐκπεπ- πεπ- βεβ- λελ- λελ-
    νεν- κεχ- πεφ- γεγ-

2. | | | |
    |---|---|---|
    | they have set free | λύω | λέλυκεν |
    | you have borne witness | μαρτυρέω | μεμαρτύρηκας |
    | he has conquered | νικάω | νενικήκασι(ν) |
    | we have honoured | τιμάω | τετίμηκα |
    | you (s.) have lived in | ἐπιδημέω | ἐπιδεδημήκατε |
    | I have written | γράφω | γεγράφαμεν |
    | you (pl.) have shouted | βοάω | βεβόηκας |
    | he has ordered | κελεύω | κεκελεύκασι(ν) |
    | we have done | πράττω | πέπραχα |
    | I have loved | φιλέω | πεφιλήκαμεν |
    | you (s.) have gone | χωρέω | κεχωρήκατε |
    | they have worried | φροντίζω | πεφρόντικεν |

13F

Here you will meet:
1. The aorist optative passive, which is easily recognised by -θ- and -είην (*GE* p. 285, #263).
2. The use of the optative in indirect speech (*GE* pp. 285–286, #264 (this is worth studying before you go on reading).
3. The future optatives (*GE* p. 287, #266). These are formed just as you would expect by adding the optative endings to the future indicative stems.

Page 170

2–3 γενομένων … ἱερῶν, ἀναβάντων … ἀρχόντων   Two genitive absolutes.

3–4 ἤρετο ἡ βουλή 'the council asked'. Followed by two indirect questions: τίς αὐτὰ ποιήσειε and πῶς πράξειαν οἱ ἄρχοντες.

5–7 The pattern continues.

7 ἐζημίου   This is a special use of the imperfect tense, 'proposed to punish', 'was inclined to punish'.

7–10 The structure of this sentence is: genitive absolute, genitive absolute, genitive absolute + ὅτι clause with two verbs in the optative (λάβοι, ἐάσειε) + infinitive, main verb (ἐδεῖτο) subject + participle + participle.

10 ἔλεγεν γὰρ ὅτι   'for he said that'. Note that the verbs in the ὅτι clause are all in the optative. This shows that they are part of what he said.

13–14 Here the construction changes to nom./acc. + infinitive. Greek does not repeat 'he said', but shows by the use of nom./acc. + infinitives that this is indirect speech. But the sentence starts with an infinitive which follows διὰ … τὸ: 'because of his inexperience in affairs and his innocence he had made Stephanos …'

17–19 The structure is: genitive absolute, ἡ βουλή (subject) ἅμα μὲν ἐλεήσασα … ἅμα δὲ ἡγουμένη + infinitive, ἐπέσχεν (main verb).

23 ἐξαπατηθέντι   'granted a pardon to him having been deceived', 'on the grounds that he had been deceived'.

Translation for 13F

Stephanos, then, married his daughter to Theogenes while he was holding the office of basileus, and this woman performed these holy rites. When these sacred rites had taken place, and the nine archons had gone up onto the Hill of Ares (Areopagos), the Council on the Areopagos inquired about the sacred rites, who had performed them and how the archons had acted. And immediately the Council started to ask who was this wife of Theogenes. And when it found out whose daughter Theogenes had as a wife, and what sort of things she had done, it showed concern about the rites and proposed to punish Theogenes. When arguments had taken place and the Council of the Areopagos was angry and punishing Theogenes on the grounds that he had taken such a wife and allowed her to perform the secret rites on behalf of the city, Theogenes began to beg them, imploring and entreating. For he said that he did not know she was the daughter of Neaira, but he had been deceived by Stephanos, and had himself accepted Phano as being his (Stephanos') legitimate daughter in accordance with the law. But on account of his inexperience in affairs and his naivety he had made Stephanos his assistant so that he could administer the office. He said that Stephanos appeared to be well disposed towards him; because of this he had allied himself to him by marriage before he found out clearly what sort of person he was. 'That I am not lying' he said 'I shall demonstrate to you by a great proof. I shall send the woman away from my house, since she is not the daughter of Stephanos but of Neaira.' Since Theogenes promised that he would do this and was entreating, the Council of the Areopagos, at once pitying him for his innocence and at the same time thinking that he had truly been deceived by Stephanos, held back. When Theogenes came down from the Areopagos, he immediately banished the woman, the daughter of Neaira, from his house, and removed Stephanos, who had deceived him, from the council board. When Phano had been sent away, the Areopagites ceased judging Theogenes and being angry with him, and pardoned him because he had been deceived.

EXERCISES FOR SECTION 13F

THE AORIST OPTATIVE PASSIVE

13F: 1

βληθείην, τιμηθείην, πεμφθείην, εὑρεθείην, δουλωθείην, διαφθαρείην, δοθείην, ληφθείην, τεθείην, κελευθείην, πεισθείην, ποιηθείην.

THE FUTURE OPTATIVE

13F: 2

I shall vote ψηφισοίμην   he will be guarded φυλαχθήσοιτο
you (pl.) will be saved σωθήσοισθε   they will be given δοθήσοιντο
you (pl.) will blame μέμψοισθε   we shall invite προσκαλοῖμεν
I shall run δραμοίμην   we shall carry οἰσοίμεθα

13F: 3

1. He answered that the king had died.   ἀποθάνοι
2. He said that the citizens would not be present.   παρέσοιντο
3. You (pl.) will see why they are angry.
4. You (pl.) knew where the enemy were assembling.   συνίοιεν
5. I know why he does not obey/ is not persuaded.
6. I knew why he would punish the slave.   κολάσοι

REVISION EXERCISES FOR SECTION 13F

B/C – MORPHOLOGY AND SYNTAX

1. a. The jurors asked what Stephanos had done, and what was the impiety of Neaira and how she had wronged the city. ὅ τι πράξειεν ὁποία εἴη ὅπως ἀδικήσειεν
    b. For Theogenes did not know whose daughter she was nor that she had worked with her body. ὅτου θυγάτηρ εἴη, ὅτι ἐργάζοιτο
    c. Theogenes said that he did not know what were Phano's habits and that he had been persuaded by Stephanos to do this. ὅτι οὐκ εἰδείη ὁποῖοι εἶεν, ὅτι πεισθείη
    d. The council was annoyed at the affair, that Phano had been given in marriage to Phrastor and that the sacred rites on behalf of the city had been performed by a foreigner. ὅτι Φανὼ ἐκδοθείη, ὡς τὰ ἱερὰ πραχθείη

   e. Didn't you hear that we went into the lawcourt and that those men were
      condemned and didn't you hear what was said in the prosecution? ὡς
      εἰσέλθοιμεν, ὡς καταδικασθεῖεν, ἅττα λεχθείη

2. a. Who did this?
      ἠρόμην ὅστις ταῦτα ποιήσειεν.
   b. How did the archons behave?
      ἠρόμην ὅπως πράξειαν οἱ ἄρχοντες.
   c. Who was Theogenes' wife?
      ἠρόμην ἥτις εἴη ἡ γυνὴ ἡ Θεογένους.
   d. What sort of woman was Phano?
      ἠρόμην ὁποία γυνὴ εἴη ἡ Φανώ.
   e. From where (for what cause) did Theogenes divorce his wife?
      ἠρόμην ὁπόθεν ἐκβάλοι τὴν γυναῖκα ὁ Θεογένης.

13G

Here you will meet the perfect middle and passive, the perfect infinitives and
participles and some important irregular perfects (*GE* pp. 291–295, #267–273).

Page 171

2 πεποιήκασι   What tense?

Page 172

4 καταπεφρονήκασιν   What tense?
5 μεμαρτυρήκασιν   What tense?
   καταπεφρονηκέναι   What is it? Perfect infinitive active. See *GE* pp. 292–293,
   #270. The infinitive shows that this is an indirect statement. 'For many people
   have borne witness that they have shown contempt for the city and for the gods.'
8 πεπολίτευμαι, γεγένημαι   These are perfect middle (*GE* pp. 291–292,
   #267–268).
   The rest of this section is full of various forms of the perfect active and middle.
   The perfect middle and passive are the same.
12–13 οἳ ἂν ἀποφαίνωσι   'whoever show': ἄν + subjunctive makes the relative
       clause 'indefinite'. You will meet this construction later in *GE* pp. 304–305,
       #282.
14 ἀλλ' εὖ ἴσμεν   'But we know very well that' is followed by a series of
    accusative + participle phrases; τὸν Στέφανον is the subject of all the
    participles.

Translation for 13G

STRYMODOROS   Oh what lawlessness! For Stephanos committed many disgraceful acts.
EUERGIDES   If indeed Apollodoros is speaking the truth, Stephanos and Neaira have done
            the most sacrilegious things. For they have shown contempt for the laws of the
            state *(lit.* on behalf of the state) and the gods.

STR.   It is probable, at least. For many people have borne witness that they have shown contempt for both the city and the gods. I wonder what Stephanos will ever say in his defence.

KOMIAS   Stephanos will say the sort of things which all defendants say in their defence, that 'I have been a good citizen' and 'I have been responsible for no disaster in the city.' For you know well that all the defendants claim that they have performed their state duties patriotically and that they have won many glorious victories in the games (contests) and that they have accomplished much good for the city.

EU.   Reasonably. For the dikasts have often acquitted those who have done wrong who can point out the virtues of their ancestors and their own good services. But we know well that Stephanos is not rich, nor has he been a trierarch, nor has he been appointed choregos, nor has he been a good citizen, nor has he done any good to the city.

13H

Page 172

3 κέχρηται   What tense? What verb? It comes from χράομαι, which takes the dative.

5 ἐξελεγχθήσεται   What tense? What verb? Try ἐξελέγχω.

7 εἴληφε   This is an irregular perfect from λαμβάνω. See list at *GE* p. 295, #272.

Page 173

8 Στέφανος αὐτὸς ὑφ' αὑτοῦ   'Stephanos himself has been condemned by himself.'

12 εἴρηται   Perfect passive from λέγω: see *GE* p. 295, #272.

15 πεφύκασι   'They have been born', i.e. 'they exist', 'they are born to make mistakes'. This shows clearly how close the perfect is to the present in meaning.

Translation for 13H

STRYMODOROS   What then? What will Stephanos say in his defence? Will he say that Neaira was a citizen and that he lives with her in accordance with the laws?

KOMIAS   But Apollodoros has employed the strongest evidence, proving that Neaira was a hetaira and became the slave of Nikarete, and was not born a citizen. So that it is clear that Stephanos will be convicted of lying, if he says such things.

STR.   What then? That he did not take Neaira as his wife but as a concubine in his house?

EUERGIDES   But Stephanos has brought evidence against himself. For the children, who were Neaira's, and who were introduced to the phratries by Stephanos, and the daughter, who was given in marriage to an Athenian man, these clearly prove that Neaira was living with Stephanos as his wife.

STR.   Yes, and it is clear that the truth has been spoken by Apollodoros. Therefore Neaira has been put in the most terrible danger on account of the things that have been done by Stephanos.

EU.   And Stephanos also is done for, as it seems to me; all men indeed are born to make mistakes.

131

Page 173

1–3   μεμαθήκατε   This is followed by two sets of accusative + participle phrases, followed by two sets of nominative + participle phrases.

  2   ἠσεβηκυῖαν   Acc. s. fem. of the perfect participle of ἀσεβέω. Note the form of the reduplication when the verb starts with a vowel, also ἠδικημένοι and ὑβρισμένοι.

3–4   ὁ Στέφανος ἄξιός ἐστιν ουκ ἐλάττω δοῦναι δίκην … ἀλλὰ καὶ πολλῷ μείζω 'Stephanos is worthy to pay no less penalty than …, but a much bigger one.'

Page 174

  8   πεφυκότας   Cf. p. 173, line 15 'those who have been born to …': 'those who by nature are more inclined to impiety rather than piety'.

Translation for 131

You have heard the evidence, judges, and you have learned in detail that Neaira is an alien and has shown a lack of reverence towards the gods, and that you yourselves have been greatly wronged and insulted. Before you pass judgment, know that this Stephanos deserves to pay no lesser penalty than this Neaira, but a much greater one for what he has done. For I have proved that he, by declaring himself to be an Athenian, has thus shown much contempt for the laws and you and has been irreverent to the gods. You must therefore take vengeance upon those who have been impious to the gods and you must punish those who have wronged the city and are disposed to sacrilege rather than to piety.

Grammar

Now make sure that you know both active and passive forms of the perfect indicative, and their participles and infinitives *(GE* pp. 291–294, #267–271), and make sure also that you look at the lists in *GE* pp. 294–295, #272–273, which show awkward cases where you cannot use an ordinary reduplication, and some irregular perfects. You will need to learn these by heart.

EXERCISES FOR SECTION 13G–I

PERFECT INDICATIVE MIDDLE AND PASSIVE

13G–I: 1

κεκώλυται	he has been prevented
τεθύμεθα	we have been sacrificed
γεγάμημαι	I have been married
τετιμημένοι εἰσίν	they have been honoured
δεδήλωσθε	you (pl.) have been shown

13G–I: 2

κεκωλῦσθαι, τεθύσθαι, γεγαμῆσθαι, τετιμῆσθαι, δεδηλῶσθαι

13G–I: 3

κεκωλυκότος	κεκωλυκυίας	κεκωλυκότος
κεκωλυκότες	κεκωλυκυῖαι	κεκωλυκότα
κεκωλυμένου	κεκωλυμένης	κεκωλυμένου
κεκωλυμένοι	κεκωλυμέναι	κεκωλυμένα
τεθυκότος	τεθυκυίας	τεθυκότος
τεθυκότες	τεθυκυῖαι	τεθυκότα
τεθυμένου	τεθυμένης	τεθυμένου
τεθυμένοι	τεθυμέναι	τεθυμένα
γεγαμηκότος	γεγαμηκυίας	γεγαμηκότος
γεγαμηκότες	γεγαμηκυῖαι	γεγαμηκότα
γεγαμημένου	γεγαμημένης	γεγαμημένου
γεγαμημένοι	γεγαμημέναι	γεγαμημένα
τετιμηκότος	τετιμηκυίας	τετιμηκότος
τετιμηκότες	τετιμηκυῖαι	τετιμηκότα
τετιμημένου	τετιμημένης	τετιμημένου
τετιμημένοι	τετιμημέναι	τετιμημένα
δεδηλωκότος	δεδηλωκυίας	δεδηλωκότος
δεδηλωκότες	δεδηλωκυῖαι	δεδηλωκότα
δεδηλωμένου	δεδηλωμένης	δεδηλωμένου
δεδηλωμένοι	δεδηλωμέναι	δεδηλωμένα

13G–I: 4

it has been announced, they are standing, he has gone, you (pl.) have hurled you (s.) have suffered, he has been wronged.

13G–I: 5

εἰρήκασι, πεπόνθαμεν, ἕστηκα, ἐζήτηκας, ἀφῄρηται, ἐστέρηται, ἠδίκημαι

REVISION EXERCISES FOR SECTION 13G–I

B/C – MORPHOLOGY AND SYNTAX

1. a. You have governed well. εὖ πεπολίτευσθε
    b. We have been greatly wronged by Stephanos. ἠδίκημαι
    c. These words have been spoken by Neaira. εἴρηται
    d. You have used clear proof, gentlemen. κέχρησαι
    e. I myself have been condemned by myself (*lit.* I have had witness borne against me by myself). καταμεμαρτυρήμεθα
    f. Those men have done these things. διαπέπρακται
    g. Phano's son has been introduced to the brotherhood by Stephanos. εἰσηγμένοι εἰσίν
    h. These men have been the cause of many evils in the city. γεγένηται
    i. You have been treated most violently, gentlemen, and you have been greatly wronged. ὕβρισαι ἠδίκησαι
    j. The prosecutor has accomplished this. εἰργασμένοι εἰσίν
2. a. οἶδα σε εὖ πεπολιτευμένον.
       φάσκω σε εὖ πεπολιτεῦσθαι.
    b. οἶδα ἡμᾶς ἠδικημένους μεγάλα ὑπὸ Στεφάνου.
       φάσκω ἡμᾶς ἠδικῆσθαι μεγάλα ὑπὸ Στεφάνου.
    c. οἶδα τούτους τοὺς λόγους ὑπὸ τῆς Νεαίρας εἰρημένους.
       φάσκω τούτους τοὺς λόγους ὑπὸ τῆς Νεαίρας εἰρῆσθαι.
    d. οἶδα ὑμᾶς τεκμηρίῳ φανερῷ κεχρημένους.
       φάσκω ὑμᾶς τεκμηρίῳ φανερῷ κεχρῆσθαι.
    e. οἶδα καταμεμαρτυρημένος αὐτὸς ὑπ' ἐμαυτοῦ.
       φάσκω καταμεμαρτυρῆσθαι αὐτὸς ὑπ' ἐμαυτοῦ.
    f. οἶδα ἐκείνους τοὺς ἄνδρας ταῦτα διαπεπραγμένους.
       φάσκω ἐκείνους τοὺς ἄνδρας ταῦτα διαπεπρᾶχθαι.
    g. οἶδα τὸν Φανοῦς παῖδα εἰσηγμένον ὑπὸ Στεφάνου εἰς τοὺς φράτερας.
       φάσκω τὸν Φανοῦς παῖδα εἰσῆχθαι ὑπὸ Στεφάνου εἰς τοὺς φράτερας.
    h. οἶδα τούτους αἰτίους γεγενημένους πολλῶν κακῶν ἐν τῇ πόλει.
       φάσκω τούτους αἰτίους γεγενῆσθαι πολλῶν κακῶν ἐν τῇ πόλει.
    i. οἶδα ὑμᾶς μεγάλα ὑβρισμένους καὶ ἠδικημένους.
       φάσκω ὑμᾶς μεγάλα ὑβρίσθαι καὶ ἠδικῆσθαι.
    j. οἶδα τοῦτο εἰργασμένον τὸν κατήγορον.
       φάσκω τοῦτο εἰργάσθαι τὸν κατήγορον.
3. a. Stephanos has never paid the penalty.
       ἴσμεν τὸν Στέφανον οὐδέποτε δίκην δεδωκότα.
       οὔ φαμεν τὸν Στέφανον δίκην ποτε δεδωκέναι.

    b. Phano is an alien by birth (has been born).

      εὖ οἶδα τὴν Φανὼ ξένην πεφυκυῖαν.

      φημὶ τὴν Φανὼ ξένην πεφυκέναι.

    c. Neaira has been irreverent towards the gods.

      ᾔδεισθα τὴν Νέαιραν ἠσεβηκυῖαν εἰς τοὺς θεούς.

      ἔφασκες τὴν Νέαιραν ἠσεβηκέναι εἰς τοὺς θεούς.

    d. You have been appointed jurors.

      ἴστε δικασταὶ καθεστηκότες.

      φατὲ δικασταὶ καθεστηκέναι.

    e. Stephanos has given Phano in marriage as his own daughter.

      οἶσθα τὸν Στέφανον ὡς τὴν αὑτοῦ θυγατέρα τὴν Φανὼ ἐκδεδωκότα.

      φῂς τὸν Στέφανον ὡς τὴν αὑτοῦ θυγατέρα τὴν Φανὼ ἐκδεδωκέναι.

D – ENGLISH INTO GREEK

1. Sentences

    1. ἐπιδέδειχα τὴν Φανὼ τεθυκυῖαν τὰ ἱερὰ ὑπὲρ τῆς πόλεως.

    2. ἡ βουλὴ ἤρετο ὁποίαν γυναῖκα ἔγημεν ὁ ἄρχων βασιλεύς.

    3. Θεογένης ἔφη ἐξαπατηθῆναι ὑπὸ τοῦ Στεφάνου.

    4. Στέφανος εὖ πεπολίτευται καὶ πολλὰ καὶ καλὰ πεποίηκεν.

    5. εὖ ἴσμεν πάντες ὅτι οὐδὲν καλὸν οὔτε εἴρηται οὔτε πεποίηται
       οὐδέποτε ὑπὸ τοῦ Στεφάνου.

2. Prose

τὴν οὖν Φανὼ τῆς Νεαίρας θυγατέρα οὖσαν ἐπιδεδειγμένην εὐθὺς ἐξέβαλεν
ὁ Φράστωρ. ἡ δὲ ἐκβεβλημένη ὀλίγον χρόνον ἔμεινεν, βουλομένη τὸν
Φράστορα τὸ παιδίον ἀναλαβεῖν. καὶ οὐ διὰ πολλοῦ ἠσθένησεν ὁ Φράστωρ.
καὶ διὰ τὴν ἔχθραν τὴν πρὸς τοὺς οἰκείους καὶ διὰ τὸ μὴ ἐθελῆσαι αὐτοὺς
λαβεῖν τὰ αὑτοῦ, ἀνέλαβε τὸ παιδίον πρὶν ἀναστῆναι, οὐ βουλόμενος ἄπαις
τελευτᾶν. ὁ γὰρ Φράστωρ οὐδέποτ’ ἂν ἀνέλαβε τὸ παιδίον, εἰ μὴ ἠσθένησε,
δῆλον ὅτι. ἀναστὰς γὰρ γυναῖκα γνησίαν κατὰ τοὺς νόμους ἔγημεν.

E – TEST EXERCISE 13

After this, Menekles began to take thought so that he might not be childless, but
that he might have a child who would look after him before he died, and who
would bury him when he had died and would carry out the customary tasks on
his behalf in the period after his death.

    Since, then, he found no other relation closer to him than us, he started to enter
into an agreement with us and he said 'Fate did not allow me to have children
with your sister. But, indeed I would have had children from this family, if I had
been able. Therefore I want to make one of you my son.' And when my brother
heard this, he praised his words and said that because Menekles was an old man
and alone he needed me to look after him. 'For', he said, 'I am always abroad, as
you know; but my brother here', meaning me, 'who is always at home, will look
after your affairs and mine. Make him your son.' And Menekles said that it was
a good idea (that he was speaking well) and so adopted me.

My opponent here wishes now to disinherit me and to render the dead man childless and nameless. Do not therefore, gentlemen of the jury, being persuaded by him, take away the name from me. Instead, since the matter has come to you and you have become responsible for it, help us and that man who is now in the house of Hades, and bearing in mind the law and the oath which you have sworn and the things that have been said about the matter, vote for justice in accordance with the laws.

Section Fourteen: Guarding a woman's purity

14A

Page 176

1 ἐάσετε Future of ἐάω.
2 ἥν This is accusative s. fem. of the relative pronoun: 'she *whom* ...'
3 ἥ What is this?
4 ἤ This has a smooth breathing, so it cannot be a relative pronoun. Try 'or'.
5 ἐλήλυθεν What tense? What verb? Learn it!
6 ψηφιεῖσθε This comes from ψηφίζομαι, whose future is ψηφιοῦμαι. Cf. νομίζω νομιέω.
8–9 πρίν is followed by two accusative and infinitive clauses 'before she did x and y, and before you did z'. Do not translate πρότερον, which prepares for πρίν.
10 ἐπειδὴ δὲ πέπυσθε καὶ ἴστε ... Notice the present force of the perfect 'since you *have* found out and you all know (now, at this moment)'.

Translation for 14A

Gentlemen of the jury, will you then allow this Neaira to insult the city so disgracefully and so contemptuously, [this woman] who was neither left a citizen by her parents nor was she made a citizen by the people? Will you allow her to act irreverently towards the gods with impunity, she who has openly prostituted herself throughout the whole of Greece? For where has she not worked with her body? Or where has she not gone for her day-to-day earnings? Now that Neaira is clearly known by all as the kind of woman she is, will you vote that she is a citizen? And if you vote in this way, what fine thing will you say that you have accomplished to those who ask you?

For [formerly] her crimes existed, and the city was indifferent (*lit.* to the crimes), before this woman was charged by me and brought to trial and before all of you found out who she was and what sort of impiety she had committed. But, since you have found out and since you all know, and since you are able to punish her, you yourselves will be acting impiously towards the gods if you do not punish this woman.

14B

You now meet the subjunctive (*GE* pp. 300–304, #274–281) and one of its commonest uses with ἄν. This makes a clause indefinite (*GE* pp. 304–305, #282), 'when he says', 'whenever he says'. Do not confuse this ἄν with ἄν + optative, which is potential and means 'could' or 'would' (*GE* #283) or ἄν + indicative in unfulfilled conditions.

Page 177

1   τί δὲ φήσειεν ἄν   ἄν + optative: 'What would each of you say ...'
2   ἐπειδὰν γάρ τις ἔρηται ὑμᾶς   ἄν + subjunctive 'when someone asks (if they actually *do* ask).'
3   ἐρήσεται   What tense is this? You may find it useful to look up the principal parts of ἐρωτάω in the irregular verb list on pp. 436–442, #389 of *GE*.
4   ὅτι   should probably be translated as 'because'.
4–6   Look carefully at all the tenses here.
6   διηγήσεσθε   What tense is this?
7   κατηγορήθη   What tense is this?
8–11   οὔκουν ἤδη αἱ σωφρονέσταται τῶν γυναικῶν and καὶ δὴ καὶ ταῖς ἀνοήτοις γυναιξί.   This gives the predicted reaction of thoughtful women and foolish women.

Note that ἀνόητος is a compound adjective and has only two terminations, i.e. m. and f. endings are identical. Cf. ἀτιμώρητος p. 176, l. 3.
9   ἐπειδὰν πύθωνται   'When they find out'. This is the indefinite construction expressed by ἄν + the subjunctive (*GE* pp. 304–305, #282).
11   ἄδειαν διδόναι ποιεῖν   'To grant licence to do.'
ὅ τι ἄν βούλωνται   Another indefinite clause: 'what(ever) they like'.

Translation for 14B

And what would each one of you say when you go back to the house to your wife or your daughter or your mother if you have voted (having voted) to acquit Neaira? For when (whenever) someone asks you 'Where were you?' and you say 'We were trying a case', that someone will immediately ask 'Whom were you trying?' and you will say 'Neaira' (of course) 'because, though an alien, she lived with a citizen against the law and because she married her daughter to Theogenes when he was basileus and she performed the sacred and secret rites on behalf of the city and was given as a bride to Dionysos.' (And you will go through the other things about the charge saying how well and carefully and accurately on each point she was prosecuted.) And they, hearing this, will ask 'What then did you do?' and you will say 'We acquitted her.' Will not the most self-controlled of women, when they find out, be angry with you because you thought it right that Neaira should equally with them have a share in the business of the city and in the sacred rites? And moreover, you will seem to be granting licence to foolish women to do what(ever) they like. For you will seem to be contemptuous and yourselves to be in agreement with Neaira's standards of behaviour.

14C

Page 178

6 ἐπειδὰν γάρ τις καλῶς λέγῃ   An indefinite clause: 'when anyone speaks well'.

9 ἐὰν γὰρ ἀποψηφισώμεθα Νεαίρας, ἐξέσται   'For if we acquit Neaira, it will be possible': see *GE* p. 198, #176. It is normal to express a future condition as an indefinite.

10–11 ἄν + subjunctive. More indefinite clauses.

12–13 Note the opposites ἄκυροι, κύριαι.

19–20 What sort of condition is expressed here by ἄν + imperfect indicative?

Translation for 14C

STRYMODOROS   But why are you silent, Euergides, and why do you neither praise nor criticise the arguments? For I am very pleased, now I have heard the speech which Apollodoros has made. What do you say about what he has said? Are you, too, pleased by his words?

EUERGIDES   I am certainly very pleased, Strymodoros, with the speech which Apollodoros made. For whenever anyone speaks well and truthfully, who does not enjoy listening?

STR.   What then? Must we condemn Neaira?

EU.   Of course. For if we acquit Neaira it will be permissible for prostitutes to live with whoever they like, and to declare that their children belong to whoever they happen to find [to father them].

STR.   Not only that, Euergides, but there is also the fact that the established laws will become powerless, and hetairas will have the power to do whatever they like. What do you say, Komias? Do you think the laws will become powerless?

KOMIAS   You are concerned with hetairas and the laws, but I am concerned with none of these things. My concern is with female citizens.

STR.   Your concern is with female citizens? How do you mean? Perhaps you are saying something important, but I don't understand.

KOM.   If you were a woman, Strymodorus, you would understand, and you would be concerned about female citizens. Consider, then, Strymodoros.

14D

This section is full of future conditions (ἐάν + subjunctive) and indefinite relative and adverbial clauses ('whoever', 'however', 'in whatever way', etc.) expressed by ἄν + the subjunctive.

Page 179

1 ἀπορηθῇ   Can you recognise this? It is 3rd s. of the aorist passive subjunctive of ἀπορέω.

καθεστήκη   Can you recognise this? It is 3rd s. of the perfect active subjunctive of καθίστημι. The perfect is used because 'he has been placed in a situation' = 'he is in a situation', -η indicates the subjunctive, as it does in ἀπορηθῇ.

5   ἐάν τις βούληται   'If someone wants': ἐάν + subjunctive.

6   εἰ καὶ πένητος ὄντος   'Even if he is a poor man', πένητος ὄντος is genitive in apposition to ἀστοῦ in the previous line.

σκοποῦσιν   ὅπως + future indicative: 'see to it that ...', 'take care that ...'

8   ἀποδῷ   3rd s. aorist active subjunctive of ἀποδίδωμι.

10   ἐὰν δὲ ἀπολυθῇ Νέαιρα   'If Neaira is set free', 'acquitted': ἀπολυθῇ is the 3rd s. of the aorist passive subjunctive of ἀπολύω.

21   διελήλυθε   3rd s. perfect indicative of διέρχομαι, 'has gone through the argument'.

Translation for 14D

KOMIAS   For now, even if a woman is in dire straits and her father has fallen into poverty and cannot give his daughter a dowry, the law provides a sufficient dowry.

STRYMODOROS   What do you mean?

KOM.   If someone wants to rear children that are citizens, he must marry the daughter of a citizen, even if that citizen is poor. In this way the lawmakers take care that the daughters of citizens will not be unmarried –

STR.   If nature grants a girl moderate beauty.

EUERGIDES   What then?

KOM.   If Neaira is acquitted (freed), it will be permissible for the Athenians to live with hetairas and have children however they please. But if the Athenians have children however they please, how will it be possible for us to distinguish between the citizen and the alien? And if we cannot distinguish between the citizen and the alien, it will not be necessary for Athenians to marry citizen women, but they will be able to marry whomsoever they like. Therefore, if Athenians marry whomsoever they like, who will marry the daughters of poor men, who do not have a dowry? The function of prostitutes will come completely to the daughters of citizens because they have no dowry and the reputation of free women will come to hetairas. For hetairas will be allowed to have children with whomever they like and to share in mysteries and sacred rites and honours in the city. This is why I am concerned about citizen women.

EU.   Apollodoros has delivered his speech well, but this matter has been expressed by Komias even better and more sincerely. But be quiet, friends, for Apollodoros is ending his speech.

14E

Page 180

3   ὁμοίως Νεαίρᾳ τῇ πόρνῃ   'in the same way as Neaira the prostitute'.

6   καὶ ὅταν μὲν τοῦ κατηγορεῖν γένησθε   'and whenever you are concerned with prosecution'.

8 ὅταν δὲ ἐπὶ τοῦ ἀπολογεῖσθαι ἦτε   'and whenever you are concerned with the defence'.

Translation for 14E

I want each one of you to know that you are casting your vote, one of you on behalf of his wife, another on behalf of his daughter, another of his mother, another of his city and its laws and its religion. Do not show respect for these women in the same way as for Neaira the prostitute. Look after them, gentlemen of the jury, look after them with much good discipline and care, and give them in marriage in accordance with the laws. But Neaira with her many disgraceful ways has had intercourse with many men many times each day. And when you are concerned with prosecution, listen to the laws themselves, the laws through which we live in the city, and by which you have sworn to give judgment. And when you are concerned with the defence, remember the condemnation of the laws and the proof of the things which have been said which you have heard. And when you look upon the face of Neaira, think only of this one thing, whether, being Neaira, she has done these things.

14F

There are many more examples of the use of ἄν + the subjunctive in this section.

Page 181

10 ὡς ἀπολογησόμενος   ὡς + the future participle expresses purpose.
σιγῴης ἄν ... προσέχοις ἄν   ἄν + optative = a polite request, 'would you be quiet and concentrate?'
11–12 ὅπως + the future indicative: 'Take care that you...'

Translation for 14F

EUERGIDES   Good. So great then is the prosecution which Apollodoros has delivered. But now we must hear the defence of Stephanos and when we have heard it we must cast our vote.

STRYMODOROS   But what shall I say when my children and my wife ask whether I condemned or acquitted her?

EU.   If Neaira is condemned, Strymodoros, you will say that you condemned her, and if she is acquitted, you will say that you acquitted her.

STR.   Of course. But, although I am eager to do it, I cannot remember the prosecution; for the prosecutor leads me round in a circle, like a sophist, and puts me in great perplexity.

KOMIAS   And the defendant too will drag you round in a circle, as it seems, Strymodoros.

STR.   How then will it be possible for me to judge the trial?

EU.   First listen and then decide (judge).

STR.   Good. But when we have cast our vote, what next?

KOM.   What next? When we have got up from our seats and cast our votes, we shall
       receive our three obols, Strymodoros. It is very pleasant when I go home with
       my three obols in my mouth, and all the household welcome me because of the
       three obols.

EU.   With reason! But stop chattering, Komias. For Stephanos is now standing up to
       make his defence. Would you please be quiet and pay attention. And as for you,
       Strymodoros, see that you remember the things said by Apollodoros and that
       you pay attention to everything which Stephanos may say.

EXERCISES FOR SECTION 14

THE SUBJUNCTIVE

14: 1

he made a mistake	ἁμάρτῃ
he was stopping	the imperfect subjunctive shares the expect of the present subj. παύῃ
he will persuade/you (s.) will obey	no future subjunctive
he fell out/was thrown out	ἐκπέσῃ
they had	σχῶσι(ν)

14: 2

I have married	γεγαμήκω
he will go	ἴῃ
they are	ὦσι(ν)
we have become	γεγενημένοι ὦμεν
they placed	θῶσι
we make/do (for ourselves)	ποιώμεθα
they see	ὁρῶσι(ν)
they knew	γνῶσι(ν)
they were giving	imperfect (pres. subj. is διδῶσιν; see above)
he carried	ἐνέγκῃ

14: 3

ἐὰν ὁρῶσιν/ἴδωσιν   ἐπειδὰν ἀκούω/ἀκούσω   ὅστις ἂν ἴῃ/ἔλθῃ,
ὅπου ἂν ᾖ   ἐπειδὰν ἀπίωσιν/ἀπέλθωσιν   ἐὰν δουλῶμεν/δουλώσωμεν,
ὅστις ἂν ὦσιν, ἐπειδὰν εἰδῶ.

REVISION EXERCISES FOR SECTION 14

B/C – MORPHOLOGY AND SYNTAX

1. a. Whatever evidence the witnesses give and whatever they say, we always
        judge carefully. μαρτυρῶσι λέγωσιν

b. When(ever) the prosecutor speaks and persuades us, we condemn. λέγῃ πείθῃ

c. When(ever) a citizen goes to law or the clansmen reject (vote against) a child born from an alien, the laws are preserved. ἀγωνίσηται ἀποψηφίσωνται

d. Whoever is not condemned but acquitted by the jurors, we regard as innocent. μὴ καταδικασθῇ ἀπολυθῇ

e. If an evil man loses his citizen's rights (is placed in loss of citizen's rights), all the citizens are pleased. καταστῇ

f. Whenever you want to say something terrible and you reveal the truth, your enemies will always take vengeance on you. βούλῃ δηλοῖς

g. Whatever fine you think just and inflict, that is the penalty that the man who has been condemned owes to the city. ἡγῆσθε τιμᾶτε

h. The law provides an adequate dowry to any woman whose father does not give a dowry. μὴ δῷ

i. If you concentrate your mind carefully on the prosecution and are eager, you will condemn (vote against) Neaira. πρόσσχητε προθυμῆσθε

j. When you enter the house and your wife meets you, see that you flatter her. εἰσίῃς ἐντύχῃ

D – ENGLISH INTO GREEK

1. Sentences
    1. ὅταν οἱ δικασταὶ οἴκαδε ἔλθωσιν, αἱ γυναῖκες ἀσπάζονται αὐτούς.
    2. ὅταν γυνή τις χρήματων λάβηται, χαλεπὴ γίγνεται.
    3. ἐὰν προσέχῃς τὸν νοῦν πρὸς τὴν ἀπολογίαν, ἀπολύσεις τὸν φεύγοντα.
    4. ἐπειδὰν οἱ κατήγοροι λέγωσιν, ἀεὶ τὰ αὐτὰ λέγουσιν.
    5. ἐὰν φιλῇ ὑπὸ τῶν θυγατέρων, δώσουσί σοι ὅ τι ἂν βούλῃ.

2. Prose

ἀπολογούμενος οὖν τί λέξει ὁ Στέφανος; φήσει, δῆλον ὅτι, εὖ πεπολιτεῦσθαι καὶ πολλά τε καὶ ἀγαθὰ διαπεπρᾶχθαι. καίτοι εὖ ἴσμεν πάντες ὅτι οὐδὲν οὔτε καλὸν οὔτε ἀγαθὸν διεπράχθη ὑπ' αὐτοῦ οὐδέποτε. ἢ τοιοῦτό τι πρᾶγμα ἀκηκόατέ ποτε; οὐ δῆτα. οὔτε γὰρ οὑτοσὶ οὔτε οἱ πρόγονοι πρὸς τὸ εὐσεβεῖν πεφύκασιν ἀλλὰ πρὸς τὸ ἀσεβεῖν.

Note that it is possible to translate this passage into Greek in a number of different ways. This is only one of them. You may, therefore, find that you have constructed a different version and are still perfectly correct.

E – TEST EXERCISE 14

I want to tell you how they frame the laws in Lokris (among the Lokrians). For there they think the citizens ought to observe the long-established laws and preserve tradition. So that, if someone wants to make a new law, he proposes it with his neck in a noose. And if the law seems to be good and useful, the proposer lives and gets away. But if it does not, he is killed when the noose is drawn tight. In fact they do not dare to propose new laws, but they observe the ancient laws strictly. In the course of many years, only one new law is said to have been passed. For there is a law established in Lokris that, if a man knocks out an eye, the one who knocked out the eye must offer his own eye to be knocked out in return. An enemy is said to have threatened his enemy, who happened to have one eye, that he would knock out this one eye. When this threat had been made, the one-eyed man was upset, and thinking that his life would be unliveable if he suffered this, he is said to have dared to put forward the following law: if anyone knocks out the eye of a one-eyed man, he will have to give both his eyes to be knocked out in return. For in this way they would both suffer the same injury. And the Lokrians are said to have passed this law alone in more than two hundred years.

Section Fifteen: Alkestis in Euripides' play

In this section you are introduced to the verse of Greek Tragedy in a touching scene from Euripides' *Alkestis* (produced in 438 BC). Consult *GE* p. 310, #286 for a list of tragic usages. Note (e) here contains the warning: 'Word order in verse can be far more flexible than in prose; again, utterances can be far more oblique and tightly packed with meaning.' While it is probably true that you will find an increase of difficulty in this section, the Greek should prove manageable. We have tried to keep the translation as literal as possible throughout.

15A

Page 184

1 ἴστω   The third person singular imperative of οἶδα *(GE #207)*. οἶδα is followed by a participle ('know that …', see *GE #247*). The vocabulary tells you that κατθανουμένη is the future participle of καταθνῄσκω.
εὐκλεής = 'a glorious [woman]'. It is easiest to translate it as an adverb, 'gloriously'.

3 πῶς δ' οὐκ …;   πῶς γὰρ οὔ; (literally 'for how not?' = 'of course') has appeared from Section 1 onwards.

4–5 Difficult. Consult the translation.

11 ἐκ … ἐλοῦσα   This splitting of a verb from its prepositional prefix is called 'tmesis' ('cutting'). It is quite common in verse authors, but it is not always easy to recognise whether the preposition is there in its own right or if it is a case of 'tmesis'.

13 Ἑστία   Hestia is the goddess of the hearth, crucial for the continued existence of the home.

15 πίτνω   This form of πίπτω is very common in poetry.

16 τἀμά   See *GE* p. 310, #286. This squashing together of two separate words (τὰ ἐμά) is called 'crasis'.

Translation for 15A

CHORUS   Let her know then [that she] is going to die gloriously and by far the best woman of those under the sun.

FEMALE SERVANT   Of course [she is] the best. Who will disagree? What should this outstanding woman be called (how should she be described)? How could anyone declare more [clearly] that she holds her husband in honour than by being willing to die for him? And the whole city knows these things; but you will wonder as you hear what she did in the house. For when she realised that the appointed day had come, she washed her white skin in waters from the river, and, having taken out from their cedar home (i.e. chest) clothes and decoration, she adorned herself becomingly, and standing before the Household Hearth, she prayed: 'Mistress – [I am addressing you] for I am going beneath the earth – appealing to you for the last time, I shall beg you to look after my orphaned children. And join a dear wife in marriage to the boy and a noble husband to the girl. And may the children not die – as I their mother am being destroyed – before their time, but may they happily complete a pleasant life in their father's land.'

15B

Page 186

1 δόμους   Poetic plural – the house is in fact singular, but this use of the plural, which is fairly common in poetry, adds a sense of grandeur.

3 Note the prefix ἀ- ('not weeping, not lamenting').

4 μεθίστη   Imperfect (*GE* #230–234).

5 κἄπειτα   Crasis (*GE* p. 310, #286).

6 'δάκρυσε   The first syllable (ε) is elided (struck off) after the vowel at the end of the previous word (prodelision). As you will remember, elision usually works the other way round, i.e. the vowel at the end of a word disappears.

8 ἐκ + gen.   Here means 'from the action of ...'
περί + gen.   Here means 'for the sake of ...'

11 κεκτήσεται   Future perfect. Have a look at this rare form at *GE* pp. 309–310, #284–285. You will see that it is middle or passive, has reduplication and uses future endings.

Translation for 15B

She approached all the altars which [are] throughout the house of Admetos and she garlanded them and addressed them in prayer, unweeping, without lamentation, and the coming disaster did not change the graceful nature of her complexion. Then rushing into her bedroom and [falling onto] her bed, then indeed she wept and said these things: 'O bed, where I lost my virgin maidenhood to this man for whose sake I die, farewell. For I do not hate you; you have destroyed me alone; for shrinking from betraying you and my husband, I die. Some other woman will have you for her own; she could not be more chaste, but perhaps [will be more] fortunate.'

15C

Page 187

5 πολλά   Neuter plural used as an adverb, meaning 'often'.

10 ἄλλοτ' ἄλλον   'at one time one, at another time another'.

12 κοὔτις   Crasis of καὶ οὔτις.

page 188

16 λελήσεται   Future perfect of λανθάνομαι (*GE* pp. 309–310, #284–285).

17 που   The enclitic που can mean 'I suppose'. Here it gives the answer 'I suppose he does' to the question the Chorus ask.

19 χεροῖν   This is a dual ending. You will have this explained to you in Section 17. Translate 'in both hands'.

22 χειρός   Literally 'of his hand'. Translate 'in his hands'.

Translation for 15C

FEMALE SERVANT   And embracing [the bed], she kissed it and bedewed all the bed with a flood [of tears] welling from her eyes. But when she had had enough of many tears, she went headlong, throwing herself from (*lit.* falling out of) the bed, and often going out of the bedroom she turned back and flung herself back again on the bed. Her children, clinging to their mother's robes, were weeping. She, taking them into her arms, embraced now one, now the other, as she was on the point of dying. All the servants were weeping throughout the house, pitying their mistress. She stretched out her right hand to each of them, and no one was so low-born that she did not speak to him – and was addressed by him in return. Such are the evils in the house of Admetos. And, if he had died (*lit.* having died), he would, to be sure, have perished, but escaping death he has so much grief – which he will never have forgotten.

CHORUS   Does Admetos grieve over these evils, if he must be deprived of a good woman?

F.S.   Yes, he weeps, holding his dear wife in his arms, and begs her not to forsake (*lit.* betray) him, seeking the impossible. For she is dying and wastes away through the disease. Exhausted, a pathetic weight in his arms, but nevertheless still breathing (although [just] a little), she wishes to look towards the rays of the sun – as [she] never [will] again – but now for the last time.

Tragic verse metre

Read *GE* pp. 311–313, #287–290 and try to scan the first four lines of section 14B. Then read aloud to yourself as much of 14B as you can, trying to bring out the iambic rhythm first of all. Then read it naturally.

Section Sixteen: Official justice – ships, state and individuals

In this section you will meet a number of different features of grammar and syntax that are clearly described in *GE* pp. 315–318, #291–294. Notice particularly μή + aorist subjunctive = 'don't ...' (*GE* #292), and φοβοῦμαι μή + subjunctive = 'I am afraid that something may happen' (*GE* #293).

Also there are verbal nouns ending in -τέος which express obligation ('must'), *GE* #294–295.

16A

Page 192

3 ἀθύμως ἔχοντι   Agrees with Ἀριστάρχῳ. ἔχω + adverb expresses the state that someone is in, e.g. καλῶς ἔχω 'I am well', κακῶς ἔχω 'I am in a bad way.'

10 τοὺς ἐξηγητάς   These were state officials who advised what to do in cases of murder. Apollodoros' next question shows two of the procedures which they might advise on.

13 ἐπεποιήκει   What tense? see *GE* p. 315, #291.
   ἠδικήκει   What tense?

17 διεξελθόντι δέ μοι ... οὐκ ἔφασαν ἐξεῖναι ...   Literally 'to me having related ... they said that it was not possible to ...'
   ἐπεπόνθη   What verb? What tense? Try πάσχω πείσομαι ἔπαθον πέπονθα.

Translation for 16A

Apollodoros is going straight towards Ilisos, walking along the road outside the wall, beneath the wall itself. When he is at the gate, there he meets Aristarchos the son of Ariston, who is very depressed. Apollodoros, seeing Aristarchos coming towards him, addresses him.

APOLLODOROS   Where are you going to and where have you come from, Aristarchos?

ARISTARCHOS   From the agora, Apollodoros, and I am going home.

AP.   But, my friend, you seem to me to be depressed. For you seem to be upset about something. Tell me then, for what purpose were you spending your time in the agora?

AR.   I went to the officials, Apollodoros.

AP.   What do you say? Did you go to them about purification, as it seems, or about burial?

AR.   Yes, my friend. I went for this reason (thus) being angry with a violent man, Theophemos by name, for what he had done. For this man had wronged me particularly, going into the farm and offering violence to my family and what is more killing an old woman who was a freedwoman. Taking this tragedy to heart and wanting to take revenge on this man, I went to the officials, but when I had told them what I had suffered and what Theophemos had done, they said that it was not possible to take revenge in the way I had in mind.

16B

Page 194

1 μὴ ἀπορήσῃς, μηδὲ ἀθυμήσῃς   μή + aorist subjunctive = 'Don't …' (GE pp. 315–316, #292).

2 ἀθυμητέον, προθυμητέον   See GE pp. 317–318, #294–295. Verb forms in -τέος mean 'must'.

5 διέξει   What tense? What person? This is the second person singular of διέξειμι.

6 φοβοῦμαι μὴ σ' ἀπολέσω   See GE p. 316, #293. Fears for the future in primary sequence can be expressed by μή + subjunctive. That is what we have here. Note that although this looks like a future indicative at first sight, it is in fact the aorist subjunctive. The future is ἀπολῶ, the first aorist indicative is ἀπώλεσα and its subjunctive is therefore ἀπολέσω.

15 βοηθήσω   What mood and tense is this? compare ἀπολέσω. ἵνα + subjunctive expresses purpose.

18 συμβουλεύσωμαι   What mood and tense after ἵνα?

19 χάριν γὰρ εἴσομαι   Have you remembered that εἴσομαι is the future of οἶδα?

Translation for 16B

APOLLODOROS   Don't despair, Aristarchos, and don't be despondent any longer. For you must not be upset by what has happened nor be despondent. One must not despair but take heart. We must consider this matter from the beginning. Therefore don't regard me without respect (do not hold me in dishonour), but take heart, concentrating in every way on this, how you will relate the affair to me as clearly as possible. Speak now, my friend, and do not conceal anything.

ARISTARCHOS   But I am afraid that I may finish you off in telling you. For it is not a short story.

AP.   Don't be afraid that this will happen. For I have time to spare (leisure). Tell me therefore, and don't hold back.

AR.   Then I must tell everything from the beginning, as it seems. And indeed, Apollodoros, it is fitting for you to hear it (the hearing is fitting for you), for you are a clever prosecutor and reasonably experienced in legal matters. What then?

Do you want to listen while we go for a walk or while we sit down? The path along the Ilisos is in every way suitable for us to speak and to listen as we go.

AP.   Why not? For it is not yet the stifling midday heat. I am very eager to listen, so
       that I can help you in your despair and despondency. So that, if in your walk
       you go all the way to Megara, I shall not stop accompanying you, so that I can
       learn what has happened. You speak, so that when I have heard I can take
       counsel with you.

AR.   Certainly. I shall be grateful to you, if you listen.

AP.   And indeed I shall be grateful to you if you speak.

AR.   The gratitude would be twofold. Listen, then.

EXERCISES FOR SECTION 16A–B

THE PLUPERFECT

16A–B: 1

ἐτετιμήκης	you (s.) had honoured
ἐτεθήκει	he had placed
ἐτεθνήκεμεν	we had died
ἐβεβλήκεσαν	they had thrown
ἐβεβήκη	I had gone
ἐπεφιλήμεθα	we had been loved
ἐδεδούλωντο	they had been enslaved
ἐκεκρατήκετε	you (pl.) had conquered, held power

μή + SUBJUNCTIVE

16A–B: 2

1. don't (s.) do this   μὴ τοῦτο ποίει
2. don't (pl.) run   μὴ δράμητε
3. don't (pl.) stay   μὴ μένετε
4. don't (s.) fall, die   μὴ πέσῃς
5. don't (pl.) say this   μὴ λέγετε ταῦτα

VERBS OF FEARING

16A–B: 3

1. they are afraid he came, arrived
    φοβοῦνται μὴ ἀφίκηται
2. we are afraid they fled
    φοβούμεθα μὴ φύγωσιν
3. he is afraid we stayed
    φοβεῖται μὴ μείνωμεν
4. you (pl.) are afraid he was enslaved
    φοβεῖσθε μὴ δουλωθῇ
5. I am afraid they did not fight
    φοβοῦμαι μὴ οὐ μάχωνται

REVISION EXERCISES FOR SECTION 16A–B

B/C – MORPHOLOGY AND SYNTAX

1. a. Prevent the man.   μὴ κωλύσητε τὸν ἄνδρα.
    b. Take revenge on your friends.   μὴ τιμωρήσησθε τοὺς φίλους.
    c. Despise the gods.   μὴ καταφρονήσῃς τῶν θεῶν.
    d. Cast your vote.   μὴ θῇ τὴν ψῆφον.
    e. Forget this matter.   μὴ ἐπιλάθησθε τούτου τοῦ πράγματος.
    f. Tell the argument of the defence. μὴ κατείπῃς τὸν τῆς ἀπολογίας λόγον.
    g. Remember all the arguments. μὴ μνημονεύσητε πάντας τοὺς λόγους.
    h. Take the young men.   μὴ παραλάβῃς τοὺς νεανίσκους.
    i. Hold back. Restrain yourself. μὴ ἐπίσχῃς.
    j. Be eager.   μὴ ἐπιθυμήσητε.
    k. Be despondent.   μὴ ἀθυμήσῃς.
2. a. We are afraid that, hearing this, the man may be disheartened.
    b. I am dreadfully despondent in case my friend may not do this.
    c. Take care (see that) you do not tell lies to the jurors about what happened.
    d. I am afraid that Demosthenes did not save the men.
3. a. We must consider these things in detail. ἡμᾶς/ἡμῖν ἀκριβῶς σκεπτέον
       περὶ ταῦτα.
    b. You must go home. σοί/σὲ ἰτέον οἴκαδε.
    c. They must help. βοηθητέον αὐτοὺς/αὐτοῖς.
    d. The man must endure the disaster. τῷ ἀνδρὶ/τὸν ἄνδρα οἰστέον τὴν
       συμφοράν.
    e. You must make war. ὑμᾶς/ὑμῖν πολεμητέον.
    f. It is necessary to send you home. οἴκαδε πεμπτέον σέ.

16C

Page 196

1 ὅθεν 'from where'; this is the relative form of the interrogative πόθεν 'from
   where?'.
   ἵνα μάθῃς 'so that you may learn'. ἵνα + subjunctive expresses purpose.
4–5 ἐξιούσης τῆς ἀρχῆς Genitive absolute, 'the office finishing (going out)'.
6 καίπερ δέον καίπερ + participle = although … δέον is the neuter singular of
   the participle of δεῖ, used impersonally 'although it being necessary …' (*GE*
   p. 320, #296).
7 ἦν τότε, ὅτε … 'There was at that time, when …' Note τότε and ὅτε.
10 ὡς τάχιστα See *GE* p. 321, #297. ὡς + superlative = 'as … as possible'.
13 ἐξῆν What verb does this come from? Imperfect of ἔξεστι.
   οὐκ ἐξόν Accusative absolute 'it not being possible …'
14 γράφει Χαιρέδημος Note the change to present tense for vividness.
14–15 ἵνα … προστάττωμεν καὶ ἀναγκάζωμεν Purpose clause.

15 ὃς ἂν μὴ ἀποδιδῷ   Indefinite clause: 'whoever does not return them'.

18 ἦν   Back to the past tense. Note that as the main verb is now in the past we are in historic (or secondary) sequence and so the verbs in the ἵνα clause which follows are in the optative mood, not in the subjunctive, as they were before, in primary sequence. See *GE* p. 286, #265.

19 δέον   Accusative absolute again. 'It being necessary …'

Translation for 16C

I want therefore to tell you the origin of the enmity towards Theophemos (from where it arose) so that you may learn what happened and know that he wronged not only me but also the people and the Boule (Council). For I happened to be holding the office of trierarch, and as trierarch I had to receive the equipment and the trireme from Theophemos; for you know very well that it is necessary for someone who has been a trierarch, when his term of office expires, to hand over the trireme and its equipment to the person who is going to become trierarch, so that he too can prepare the ship. But although it was obligatory for Theophemos to hand over the equipment, I received none of the equipment from him. And moreover, there was at that time, when I was about to become a trierarch, great danger to the city because of the rebellion of the allies, so that it was necessary for the trierarchs to send out a rescue operation of triremes quickly. But although it was necessary for us to send out the ships as quickly as possible, there was no supply of equipment for the ships in the dockyard. For those who owed it had not given back the equipment, among whom was Theophemos.

In addition to this, there was not in the Piraeus an unlimited supply of sailcloth, tow and rope, so that it was not possible to buy them. And since it was not possible to buy them, and the people who owed them had not given them back, Chairedemos proposes a resolution so that we who have been appointed as trierarchs may order and compel those who had been trierarchs (whoever had not given it back) to give back the equipment. And the resolution orders us to get the equipment in whatever way we can so that we may prepare the ships as quickly as possible and send out the rescue mission.

Therefore there was great necessity for me to get the equipment so that I could prepare the ship and, having prepared it, send it out as quickly as possible. Since it was necessary for me to do this, I went to Theophemos in order to get the equipment.

EXERCISES FOR SECTION 16C

THE ACCUSATIVE ABSOLUTE

16C: 1

1. ἐξὸν ἡμῖν ἀπιέναι
    it being possible for us to go away
    since we can go away

2. δέον ὑμᾶς θεραπεύειν τὰς γυναῖκας
it being necessary for you to look after the women
since you must look after the women

3. δόξαν/δοκοῦν μοι ποιῆσαι τοῦτο
it seeming best to do this
because I thought it best to do this

4. τοῖς παῖσιν ἐξὸν παίζειν
it being possible for the children to play
since the children are allowed to play

5. δέον τοὺς ἄνδρας ἐκδοῦναι τὰς θυγατέρας
it being necessary for the men to give their daughters in marriage
since the men/husbands must give their daughters in marriage

16C: 2

ὡς ἄριστος, βέλτιστος	the best possible
ὡς ἐλάχιστος	the least/smallest possible
ὡς σαφέστατος	the clearest possible
ὡς σωφρονέστατος	the most prudent possible
ὡς φοβερώτατος	the most frightening possible
ὡς ἀδικώτατος	the most unjust possible
ὡς μέγιστος	the biggest/greatest possible
ὡς κάκιστος, χείριστος	the worst possible

REVISION EXERCISES FOR SECTION 16C

B/C – MORPHOLOGY AND SYNTAX

1. a. It is necessary for the one who owes it to the city to give back the equipment to the one who is about to become trierarch. I went to Theophemos.
δέον τὸν ὀφείλοντα τῇ πόλει τὰ σκεύη παραδιδόναι τῷ τριηραρχήσοντι, ἐγὼ ὡς τὸν Θεόφημον προσῆλθον.

b. Then it is not possible for me to prepare the trireme. I went to the Council.
εἶτα οὐκ ἐξόν μοι τὴν τριήρη παρασκευάζειν, προσῆλθον πρὸς τὴν βουλήν.

c. It was necessary for us to prepare the ships as quickly as possible. Chairedemos proposes a resolution.
δέον ἡμᾶς παρασκευάζειν ὡς τάχιστα τὰς ναῦς, γράφει Χαιρέδημος ψήφισμα.

d. It was not possible to buy any of the things needed in the Piraeus. The trierarchs were not able to prepare the ships.
οὐκ ἐξὸν ἐν τῷ Πειραιεῖ οὐδὲν πρίασθαι ὧν ἔδει, οἱ τριήραρχοι οὐκ ἐδύναντο παρασκευάζειν τὰς ναῦς.

16D

You have already met the idea of sequence of tenses in clauses in indirect speech introduced by ὅτι. See *GE* p. 286, #265, where the verb in the subordinate clause is indicative in primary sequence and optative in secondary sequence.

In purpose clauses (and indefinite clauses and fears for the future) the sequence of tenses is: primary – subjunctive, secondary – optative. See *GE* p. 323, #299, and p. 325, #300.

Page 198

1 Note genitive absolute followed by accusative absolute followed by aorist participle agreeing with the subject of the verb.

2 ἐκέλευον αὐτὸν φράσαι 'ordered him to tell' (aorist infinitive).

3 ὁπόταν 'when(ever)'; ὁπότε + ἄν denotes an indefinite clause.

5 Note the use of the imperfect. The situation was continuing until the action in the next sentence.

6–7 ἠρόμην ... πότερον ... εἴη, ἀπεκρίνατο ... ὅτι ... εἴη Two clauses in indirect speech in secondary sequence with the verb in the subordinate clause in the optative.

10 ἦλθον ... ἵνα ἴδοιμι Purpose clause in secondary sequence: 'so that I might see him'.

Translation for 16D

But since Theophemos was not there and it was not possible for me to see him, going to Euergos, the brother of Theophemos, I asked for the equipment and told him to tell Theophemos. For there is a resolution of the Boule to get the equipment in whatever way we can, whenever the people who owe it do not return it. Therefore I made my request and delayed for some days so that Euergos might tell Theophemos, but Euergos did not give back the equipment, but kept abusing me. So, having taken as many witnesses as possible, I asked him whether the property was shared or not, and when I asked, Euergos answered that the property was not shared and that his brother lived separately.

Having found out, therefore, from somewhere else where Theophemos lived, and taking an official from the board of officials, I went to the house of Theophemos to see him.

EXERCISES FOR SECTION 16D

PURPOSE CLAUSES

16D: 1

1. The woman came *to take her*.
   ἵνα λάβοι αὐτήν

2. I saw the men fleeing *with the intention of saving themselves*.
   ὅπως σώσειαν αὐτούς

3. The man gave money to the woman *in order to persuade her*.
ἵνα πείσαι αὐτήν

4. Where shall we go *to give* the food to the poor?
ὅπως διδῶμεν

REVISION EXERCISE FOR SECTION 16D

D – ENGLISH INTO GREEK

1. μὴ ἀθυμήσῃς, ὦ βέλτιστε.
2. ἆρα φοβῇ μὴ αὖθις πάσχῃς τι ὑπὸ τούτων τῶν πονηρῶν;
3. καίπερ τὸν Θεόφημον δέον ἀποδοῦναι τὰ σκεύη, οὐ δύναμαι ἀναγκάζειν αὐτὸν ταῦτα ποιῆσαι.
4. πρόσειμι πρὸς τὴν βουλὴν ἵνα ψήφισμα γράφωσιν.
5. ἦλθον πρὸς τὴν φίλου τινὸς οἰκίαν ἵνα πυθοίμην ὅπου οἰκοίη ὁ Θεόφημος.

16E

Notice *GE* p. 325, #300 about indefinite clauses in primary and secondary sequence. Note that in primary sequence the indefinite clause has subjunctive + ἄν, in secondary sequence it has the optative without ἄν.

Page 199

1–2 Note the use of the imperfect, here and later in this section. Aristarchos was in the process of making his demands, and Theophemos kept refusing.

2 ὅπου ἂν νῦν γε τυγχάνῃ ὤν   Primary sequence.

3 ὅπου ὢν τυγχάνοι   Secondary sequence.

10 εἴ τινας ἴδοι   Indefinite clause in secondary sequence.
ἵνα μάρτυρές μοι εἶεν ...   Purpose clause in secondary sequence.

10–11 καλέσαντος δὲ τοῦ παιδὸς καὶ παρόντων μαρτύρων τῶν ὑπ' αὐτοῦ κληθέντων   Genitive absolutes.

11–13 ἐκέλευον ... ἢ ... ἢ ...   'I ordered him ... either to ... or to ...'

13 ληψοίμην   Notice the future optative, representing a future indicative in direct speech, the sequence being historic (secondary).

Translation for 16E

Having knocked at the door, I asked where he was, and the woman answered that 'he was not inside, wherever he now happened to be'. Finding that he was not inside, I told the woman who answered to go after him, wherever he happened to be. And when Theophemos arrived, after the woman had fetched him, I asked him for the register of the equipment and showed him the resolution of the Boule, which ordered me to get the equipment in whatever way I could. And indeed I was not the only one who acted in this way, but others of the trierarchs [did] too, whenever someone did not give back the equipment.

But when the resolution had been shown to him, and the register had been requested, Theophemos did not hand it over. Therefore, before I did anything else, I ordered my slave to summon the citizens from the road, if he could see any, so that they might be witnesses for me of what had been said. And when the boy had summoned them, and when the witnesses summoned by him were present, I began to request Theophemos again either himself to follow me to the Boule, if he said that he did not owe the equipment, or to return the equipment. If not, I said that I would take securities from him in accordance with the laws and the resolutions.

EXERCISE FOR SECTION 16E

INDEFINITES IN SECONDARY SEQUENCE

16E: 1

1. If he does not do this ...   εἰ μὴ ποιοίη τοῦτο...
2. When(ever) I see him ...   ὁπότε ἴδοιμι αὐτόν...
3. Who(ever) they order ...   ὅντινα κελεύοιεν...
4. When(ever) I learn ...   ἐπειδὴ μάθοιμι...
5. If you give me those things ...   εἴ μοι διδοίης ταῦτα...

REVISION EXERCISES FOR SECTION 16E

B/C – MORPHOLOGY AND SYNTAX

1. a. He wanted to collect the equipment so that he could prepare the trireme.
       βούλεται κομίζεσθαι τὰ σκεύη, ἵνα τὴν τριήρη παρασκευάζῃ.
    b. I am afraid that Euergos may not explain the matter to Theophemos.
       ἐφοβούμην μὴ Εὔεργος οὐ δείξειε τὸ πρᾶγμα τῷ Θεοφήμῳ.
    c. I was telling the slave to summon the citizens, so that they might be witnesses for me of what had been said.
       κελεύω τὸν παῖδα καλέσαι τοὺς πολίτας, ἵνα μάρτυρές μοι ὦσι τῶν λεχθέντων.
    d. They do not cease following so that they may learn what has happened.
       οὐκ ἐπαύοντο ἑπόμενοι, ἵνα τὰ γεγενημένα μάθοιεν.
2. a. (i) Whenever he came in, he used to see the woman sitting down.
       (ii) When he came in, he saw the woman sitting on the altar.
    b. (i) I asked the slave where his master was.
       (ii) I was asking the woman to fetch her master, wherever he was.
    c. (i) I had already found out that he happened to be married.
       (ii) The master ordered him to give back to the city whatever he happened to have.
    d. (i) The slave summoned all the citizens whom he could see from the road so that they could be witnesses.

      (ii) The slave was ordered to summon any citizens he saw from the road to be witnesses

  e. (i) It seemed to us that each word we spoke about Love should be as beautiful as possible.

      (ii) Lysander, having arrived in Aegina, gave back the city to the Aeginetans, having collected as many of them as he could.

16F

Page 200

2 ἑστηκυῖαν Perfect participle of ἵστημι: 'standing'.

5 ἐπεπύσμην What tense is this? It would have been a gross breach of good manners and of social conventions for a man to enter another's house without invitation if that house contained a wife. This convention is further illustrated in Section 17.

γεγαμηκὼς εἴη This is the perfect optative, made up of the perfect participle + the optative of εἰμί. See *GE* p. 328, #301.

8 πεπονθὼς ἦ This is the equivalent of the pluperfect indicative, made up of the perfect participle + the imperfect indicative of εἰμί: 'all I had suffered'.

9 ἐπεπόνθη This is the usual form of the pluperfect indicative.

10 ἁλῶναι See *GE* p. 329, #302 for the principal parts of ἁλίσκομαι, 'to be captured' or 'to be convicted'.

Translation for 16F

Since he was willing to do none of these things, although he was ordered by me, I started to lead away the woman who had been standing at the door, the one who had gone to fetch him, so that I might have a witness. And Theophemos took her away from me, and I let the woman go, but went into the house to get some security for the equipment. For the door happened to be open (to have been opened). And before going in, I had found out that he was not married. As I went in, Theophemos struck me on the mouth with his fist and I, having called those present to witness, defended myself.

Since, then, the securities were taken away by Theophemos, and I had been struck by him, I went to the Boule to show my bruises and to tell all that I had suffered while trying to fetch the equipment for the city. And the Boule, being annoyed at what I had suffered and seeing what state I had been reduced to by Theophemos, wanted him to be convicted and fined. Therefore I was ordered by the Boule to impeach him on the grounds that he was committing a crime and hindering the expedition. For the Boule considered that it was not I who had been insulted but itself and the people and the law. For indeed the Boule knew very well that once Theophemos was impeached he would be convicted and fined. Then when the judgment was passed in the Boule, and when the members of the Boule found out that the city had been offended and that I had been wronged, Theophemos was convicted and fined. And although it was possible for him to

be fined five hundred drachmas, I, although I had been wronged, was moderate
and reasonable and agreed to a fine of twenty-five drachmas.

EXERCISE FOR SECTION 16F

ἁλίσκομαι

16F: 1

1. ἔγνω	ἔβη	ἑάλω
2. βάντες	γνόντες	ἁλόντες
3. ἁλοίη	βαίη	γνοίη
4. βῆναι	γνῶναι	ἁλῶναι
5. γνῷ	βῇ	ἁλῷ

16G

Page 201

4 παυώμεθα   See *GE* p. 330, #303; 'let us cease'.
  ἕως   ἄν + subjunctive. See *GE* pp. 330–331, #304; 'until (ever) …'
4–6 παυώμεθα, καθιζώμεθα, ἕως ἄν … γένηται   Note the subjunctives.

Page 202

15 πῶς πρὸς σε διέκειτο ὁ Θεόφημος;   διακεῖμαι + adverb describes someone's
   attitude or state of mind. 'How was Theophemos disposed towards you? What
   was his attitude to you?'
   κακῶς   Answers πῶς in the previous sentence.
15–16 τεκμαιρομένῳ   Agrees with ἔμοιγε: 'it seems to me inferring …'

Translation for 16G

APOLLODOROS   You were indeed moderate and reasonable about the things which
   Theophemos had done, Aristarchos. But why don't we stop walking?
   For the heat is now stifling, and if I walk more, I shall find myself in a state
   of great distress. Let us stop then, until I can recover myself from my
   weakness.

ARISTARCHOS   We must certainly do this if you want. (This must be done if it seems
   good to you.) Let us stop therefore and sit in peace beside the Ilisos, until the
   heat becomes gentler.

AP.   Lead on then, and let us consider where we shall sit down.

AR.   Do you see that very tall plane tree?

AP.   Of course.

AR.   There is shade there and a slight breeze and grass to sit on, if we like. Let us go
   there then, so that we can sit and rest.

AP.   Would you lead on? By Hera, it is a beautiful spot. Now that we have got here,
   let us remain until I recover from my weakness.

But you, Aristarchos, as you were saying, won the impeachment case. What [happened] after that? How was Theophemos disposed to you? (What was his attitude to you?) Badly, as it seems to me judging from the evidence of your despondency. Why then do you not finish telling me the story, if nothing prevents you? Since it seems to me that I shall keep you here until you tell me everything.

AR.   But naturally nothing prevents me from going through the story, until everything has been told. Listen then, so that you may learn more clearly.

EXERCISES FOR SECTION 16G

'LET US…' (SUBJUNCTIVE)

16G: 1

1. ἀκούσωμεν
2. μὴ ἀπίωμεν
3. λαβώμεθα
4. στῶμεν
5. μὴ δῶμεν

ἕως ἄν *'UNTIL'*

16G: 2

1. ἕως ἂν ὁρῶμεν τοὺς ἄνδρας
   until (such time as) we see the men
2. ἕως ἂν ὑπισχνῆται ἀκούσεσθαι
   until (such time as) he promises to listen
3. ἕως ἂν διδῶσι τὰ χρήματα
   until (such time as) they give the money
4. ἕως ἂν παραλαμβάνητε τοὺς μάρτυρας
   until (such time as) you (pl.) hand over the witnesses
5. ἕως ἂν εὑρίσκω τὴν ναῦν
   until (such time as) I find the ship

16H

Page 202

1   ἐνενικήκη   Tense?
2–3   Notice the use of the participles in the narrative. They match the order of events: ἐνθυμούμενος … βουλόμενος … <u>ἔλαχε</u> … φάσκων … (the main verb is underlined).
6–8   More participles: παρασχόμενος … ὑποσχόμενος … <u>ἐξηπάτησε</u> …
9–10   Again: ζημιωθείς … προσελθὼν … <u>ἐκέλευον</u> …
11   ἀντὶ τοῦ καταδίκην ἀπολαβεῖν   Here ἀντί + genitive is followed by the infinitive used as a noun: 'instead of accepting the fine'.

Translation for 16H

I had in fact won the impeachment case, but this, as they say, was the start of the trouble. For Theophemos at once took the fine very much to heart and, wanting to be revenged, he brought a suit for assault against me, declaring that I had begun the blows at the door. I kept quiet, not fearing that the jurors would condemn me. For I least of all expected that I would be convicted, since I was innocent. But Theophemos, having produced lying witnesses, Euergos his brother and Mnesiboulos his cousin, and promising that he would hand over [for torture] the body of the woman who had been standing at the door (which he has not done), deceived the jurors, who were persuaded to cast their vote for Theophemos. When I had incurred a fine in this way, not many days later, going to Theophemos I asked him to accompany me to the bank to collect the fine. But Theophemos instead of collecting the fine went to my farm.

EXERCISE FOR SECTION 16H

SEQUENCE OF TENSES

16H: 1

1. φοβοῦνται μὴ αὐτοὺς ζημιώσῃ.
   They are afraid that he may punish them.
2. ἦα ἵνα εἰσαγγείλαιμι τὸν μάρτυρα.
   I went to summon the witness.
3. εἴ σοι πείθοιμι πείσοιο ἂν σύ.
   If I were to persuade you, you would persuade me.
4. ἐφοβεῖτο μή τις ἐκφύγοι.
   He was afraid that anyone might escape.
5. ἐὰν εἴπῃ, ἀκούω ἀκούσομαι
   If you speak, I listen, I will listen.

REVISION EXERCISES FOR SECTION 16F–H

D – ENGLISH INTO GREEK

1. Sentences
   1. τὸ ψήφισμα ἐκέλευσε τοὺς τριηράρχους κομίζεσθαι τὰ σκεύη ᾧ τρόπῳ ῥᾷστα δύναιντο.
   2. ὁπότε οἱ τριήραρχοι καταλάβοιέν τινα μὴ ἀποδιδόντα τὰ σκεύη, ἐπανῆλθον πρὸς τὴν βουλήν.
   3. παυώμεθα πορευόμενοι καὶ καθιζώμεθα.
   4. ἐνταῦθα μενοῦμεν ἕως ἂν ἐκ τῆς ἀσθενείας συλλέγωμεν ἡμᾶς αὐτούς.
   5. πρὶν οἰκάδε ἐπανιέναι, ἐκεῖ καθιζώμεθα ἕως ἂν ἠπιώτερον γένηται τὸ πνῖγος.

2. Prose

οὐκ ἐξὸν κομίζεσθαι τὰ σκεύη, καὶ τῆς πόλεως ἐν μεγάλῳ κινδύνῳ οὔσης, τὴν βουλὴν ἔδει πράττειν τι ἵνα τριήρων βοήθειαν ὡς τάχιστα παρασκευάζοιμεν. ἐγὼ μὲν οὖν προσελθὼν πρὸς τὴν τοῦ Θεοφήμου οἰκίαν, καὶ αὐτὸν οὐκ ἔνδον ὄντα καταλαβών, ἐφοβούμην μὴ τὰ σκεύη οὐκ ἀποδιδοίη. ὥστε ὁ μὲν Χαιρέδημος ψήφισμα ἔγραψεν, οἱ δὲ τριήραρχοι τῷ μὴ ἀποδιδόντι, εἴ τινα εὕροιεν, ἐδείκνυον τὸ ψήφισμα.

E – TEST EXERCISE 16

When this man arrived in Thasos, I collected as many of the citizens as I could as witnesses, and the marines, and I went to him in the agora in Thasos. I told him to take over the ship from me as my successor, and to pay me the expenses for the period which I had served as trierarch beyond my time. I wanted to calculate this with him in detail while witnesses of what had been spent were with me, so that, if he objected to anything, I could refute his objection at once. For I had written down all the expenses in detail. But when I made this challenge, Polykles answered that he could not care less what I said (that there was no concern to him of what I said).

Having found Polykles there and the trierarchs and their successors and some others of the citizens, I went in immediately in front of the general and began to speak with him [i.e. Polykles]. I asked him to take over my ship from me, and to pay me the expenses for the extra time that I had served. When I challenged him in this way, he said: 'Who could endure your madness and extravagance, you who alone of the trierarchs have your own private equipment and pay a great deal of money to the sailors? You have become a teacher of bad habits in the army, corrupting the sailors and the marines, when you ought to be doing the same as the other trierarchs.' When he said this, I answered him: 'As for the sailors and the marines, if you say they have been corrupted by me, take the trireme yourself and provide sailors and marines for yourself who will sail with you without receiving any money. Take the ship, for it is no longer my business to be trierarch.' When I said this, he answered that his joint-trierarch had not come to the ship: 'I will not therefore take over the ship on my own.'

Section Seventeen: Private justice – trouble down at the farm

This continues the story begun in Section 16. Much of the syntax introduced continues to illustrate the primary – subjunctive, secondary – optative pattern. An important item of grammar is the verb (ἀφ)ἵημι (*GE* pp. 336–339, #308). There will be more about this after 17A, before the exercise on it.

Page 205

1–2 ἕως τὰ χρήματα παρέχοιμι   See *GE* p. 336, #307. ἕως ('until') (ever) can introduce an indefinite clause with, in primary sequence, ἄν + subjunctive and, in secondary, optative without ἄν. See also *GE* p. 341, #309–310

Page 206

8 ᾖξαν   This comes from the verb ᾄσσω 'to dash' or 'to dart'. See vocabulary.
ἕως ἅλοιεν.   See *GE* p. 336, #307. An indefinite clause in secondary sequence.

10 ἐκβληθείσης δὲ τῆς θύρας   Genitive absolute. This is the aorist passive participle. Can you recognise the verb it comes from? If not, look up (ἐκ) βάλλω in the list of irregular verbs on *GE* pp. 436–442 #389.

10–11 εἰσελθόντες ἐπὶ τὴν γυναῖκά μου   Notice the disgraceful intrusion into the women's quarters. Compare this with Hagnophilos' punctilious attitude in 17B.

11–12 πάντα τὰ σκεύη, ὅσα ἔτι ὑπόλοιπά μοι ἦν   'all the furniture, as much as was still left to me'.

12 ἃ βούλοιντο   Indefinite clause in secondary sequence: 'whatever they wanted'.

15–16 Note the parts of ἀφίημι. ἐλευθέρα ἀφειμένη: perfect passive participle, 'having been released free', i.e 'having been freed' (*GE* p. 338, #308).

22 ἕως εἰσέλθοιεν   'until they came in'. Indefinite clause in secondary sequence.

Translation for 17A

Theophemos then did not allow me to pay him the money. For he did not wait until I produced the money, but going off, he took fifty soft-fleeced sheep of mine, which were being pastured by the shepherd. Before I knew what had happened, Theophemos had taken not only the sheep but also everything that was accompanying the herd, and the shepherd along with them and then also a boy servant, who was returning a bronze water jar that had been borrowed from a friend and was very valuable. When all these things had been taken, Theophemos and Euergos went into the farm (I farm near the racecourse, and I have lived there since I was a youth), and first of all they dashed at the household slaves. But when the household slaves did not wait to be caught but escaped first (anticipated them escaping), they went to the house and broke open the door that leads into the garden. And when the door had been broken down, they rushed in on my wife and children, and carried out all the furniture that was left to me in the house, and they went off, taking whatever they liked.

In addition to this, before they entered the house, my wife happened to be having breakfast with the children in the courtyard, and with her was my old nurse, elderly now, a kindly and loyal creature who was a freedwoman (for my father had freed her. When she was freed by my father, she had lived with her husband. But when her husband died, since she was an old woman and there was no one to look after her, she came back to me. It was obligatory for me to look after her, since she had been my nurse). While they were having breakfast in the courtyard, these men charged in and found them and seized the furniture. While the furniture was being seized by them, the rest of the women servants (for they were in the tower, where they lodge) when they heard the tumult and the shouting, did not wait until they came in, but closed the tower before they charged it.

Grammar

ἵημι (stem ἑ) behaves exactly like τίθημι (*stem* θε) but it looks more complicated because its stem starts with a vowel instead of a consonant. Compare some of the tenses:

	Present	Imperfect	Future	Aorist	Aorist pass.
Active	τίθημι	ἐτίθην	θήσω	ἔθηκα	ἐτέθην
	ἵημι	ἵην	ἥσω	ἧκα	εἵθην
Middle	τίθεμαι	ἐτιθέμην	θήσομαι	ἐθέμην	
	ἵεμαι	ἱέμην	ἥσομαι	εἵμην	
Participles	τιθείς		θήσων	θείς	τεθείς
	ἱείς		ἥσων	εἵς	ἑθείς

It is worth taking a great deal of trouble to learn ἀφίημι, and to avoid confusing it with both εἰμί and εἶμι.

NB. εἰμί and εἶμι do not have rough breathings and ἵημι does; thus in compounds the difference can be clearly seen, as for example in the infinitive ἀφιέναι, whereas parts of εἰμί and εἶμι will appear as (e.g.) ἀπεῖναι or ἀπιέναι.

When you have learned it, try the following exercise, 17A: 2. (You may prefer to leave this until you have finished reading the whole section.)

EXERCISES FOR SECTION 17A

ἕως *'until'*

17A: 1

1. μένομεν ἕως ἂν ἔλθῃ.
   We are staying until he comes.
2. ἐμάχοντο ἕως νικῷεν.
   They were fighting until they were victorious.
3. δραμεῖν βούλονται ἕως ἂν στῆναι μὴ οἷοί τ' ὦσιν.
   They are willing to run until they are unable to stand.
4. ἔδει σε εὔχεσθαι ἕως σωθείης.
   You (s.) ought to have prayed until you were saved.
5. βουλεύονται ἕως ἂν συγχωρήσωσιν.
   They are debating until such time as they agree.

(ἀφ)ἵημι *'RELEASE, LET GO, SHOOT'*

17A: 2

1.	ἔδωκε	he gave	ἀφῆκε	he let go
2.	θές	put!	ἄφες	let go!
3.	στήσουσιν	they will set up	ἀφήσουσιν	they will let go
4.	διδοίη		ἀφιείη	
5.	τιθέναι	to place	ἀφιέναι	to let go
6.	ἵσταται	he is rising it is being set up	ἀφίεται	he is being released
7.	δόντας	having given (m.acc.pl.)	ἀφέντας	having released
8.	θῆ	ἀφῆ		
9.	στήσασθαι	to set up (for oneself)	ἀφέσθαι	to release (for oneself)
10.	δώσεις	you (s.) will give	ἀφήσεις	you (s.) will let go
11.	ἔθεντο	they placed	ἀφεῖντο	they let go
12.	ἐστάθη	it was set up	ἀφείθη	he/it was released
13.	δεδώκασιν	they have given	ἀφείκασιν	they have released
14.	θείη	ἀφείη		
15.	ἱστάμενοι	setting up (for oneself) m.pl.	ἀφιέμενοι	letting go
16.	δοῦναι	to give/have given	ἀφεῖναι	to release/have released
17.	τεθήσεται	it will be placed	ἀφεθήσεται	he/it will be released
18.	σταθῆναι	to have been set up	ἀφεθῆναι	to have been released
19.	δοῦ	give!	ἀφοῦ	let go!
20.	θεῖσαι	having put (f.pl.)	ἀφεῖσαι	having released

EXERCISE FOR 17A

B/C – MORPHOLOGY AND SYNTAX

1. a. The slave girl has been set free by my father.
      (was set free (aor. pass.) / will be set free / is being set free / was being
      set free)
   b. My father released the slave girl.
      (is releasing / has released (perf. act.) / was releasing / will
      release)
   c. The slave girl, having been set free by my father, married a man who
      had also been released by his master (perfect passive participles).
      (having been set free / having been released (aor. pass. part, f./m.))
      (while being set free / while being released (present passive participles
      f./m.))
      (being about to be set free / being about to be released (future passive
      participles f./m.))
   d. The Athenians released the slaves who had fought in that sea-
      battle.
      (have released / are releasing / will release / were releasing)

17B

Page 207

2 τετιμημένα   Perfect passive participle from τιμάω, which here means 'valued'
or 'reckoned'.

2–5 The words in parenthesis explain how Aristarchos' wife knew the facts which
she is speaking about. She knew the sheep had been taken because a neighbour
had told her, and she knew that the money was at the bank because she had
heard it from Aristarchos.

Page 208

7 οὐ παύονται πρὶν ἂν λάβωσι   For πρίν meaning 'until' see *GE* p. 342, #311.
It follows the normal pattern for indefinite clauses, with subjunctive + ἄν in
primary, and optative without ἄν in secondary sequence.

9 εἰς τὸν κόλπον   The basic meaning of κόλπος is 'a curve'. Hence it can
mean 'breast', 'lap', 'the fold of a garment', 'a bay in the coastline'; cf. Latin
sinus.

10 ἀφείλοντο   What verb does this come from? Try ἀφαιρέω.

10–11 οὕτω διέθεσαν τὴν γραῦν ὥστε …   'They treated the old woman in such
a way that …'; διατίθημι + adverb is a common idiom. See *GE* pp. 342–343,
#313.

13–14 οὕτω πονηροὶ ἦσαν ὥστε …   'They were so wicked that …' οὕτως … ὥστε
…, 'so … that, as a result …' This expresses a result clause. See *GE*

pp. 345–346, #314–317. The use of indicative shows that the result actually happened.

19–21 Notice that Hagnophilos, in contrast with the unprincipled brothers, observes the conventions and will not enter Aristarchos' house while he is absent. παρόντος δὲ τοῦ κυρίου, εἰσῆλθεν ἄν   'If the master had been present he would have gone in.' This represents an unfulfilled condition in past time (ἄν + aorist indicative), but instead of the 'if' clause, there is a genitive absolute.

24–25 ἕως … εἶπεν   'until he told them'. Here ἕως is followed by the indicative because this is a definite time (not an indefinite time). See *GE* p. 341, #309.
ἐιή   The optative is used because this is indirect speech in secondary sequence.

Translation for 17B

So they did not get in there, but they carried out the furniture from the rest of the house. My wife told them not to do this, saying that the furniture was hers and was valued as part of her dowry, and said that 'You have the fifty sheep and the boy and the shepherd, which are equal in value to the fine.' (For one of the neighbours had knocked on the door and reported this.) 'And the money is waiting for you at the bank.' (For she had heard this from me.) 'Therefore do not take the rest of the furniture before my husband returns with the fine, particularly as you also have the value of the fine.'

Although my wife said this, they did not stop until they had taken very many things. But the nurse, when she saw them inside, took the cup which was lying beside her from which she had been drinking, and put it in the fold of her dress, so that they should not take it. But Theophemos and Euergos, his brother, seeing her, snatched it away and treated the old woman so badly that her arms and wrists were blood-stained when she was pinioned and dragged along by them. And she had scratches on her throat, and was being throttled by them and her chest was bruised. They were so shameless that they did not stop trying to strangle the old woman and beating her until she fell to the ground, and then they took the cup from the fold of her dress.

When the neighbours' servants heard the noise and the shouting, they saw my house was being plundered by them. Some of them called to the passers-by from their own roof-tops, and others, going into the other road, and seeing Hagnophilos passing, told him to stand by. And Hagnophilos came, summoned by Anthemion, who is my neighbour, but he did not enter my house (for the master of the house was not present; if the master had been present, he would have gone in), but, being in Anthemion's farm, he saw the furniture being carried out and Euergos and Theophemos coming out of my house. And they were going away not only taking my furniture, but also leading my son, as if he were a household slave, until Hermogenes, one of my neighbours, met them and said that he was my son.

EXERCISES FOR 17B

ἕως 'UNTIL, WHILE' and πρίν 'UNTIL'

17B: 1

1. until he fell, should fall   Used indefinitely, optative shows this must be in secondary sequence, therefore in the past.
2. until he fell   Used definitely, indicative shows it happened.
3. until such time as he falls   Indefinite in primary sequence.
4. before falling   πρίν + infinitive.
5. until such time as we fall   Indefinite in primary sequence.
   Nos. 3 and 5 might change in poetry by dropping the ἄν.

διατίθημι, διάκειμαι 'TREAT, BE TREATED'

17B: 2

1. διετίθετο / διέκειτο — he was treated
2. διατιθέμενοι / διακείμενοι — being treated (m.n.pl.)
3. διατιθεῖτο / διακέοιτο — optative
4. διατίθεσθε / διακεῖσθε — you (pl.) are being treated /be treated!
5. διατίθενται / διακεῖνται — they are being treated

NB. All the διατίθημι items have been treated as passive, but could equally well be middle.

REVISION EXERCISES FOR SECTION 17B

B/C – MORPHOLOGY AND SYNTAX

1. a. The slave girls stayed in the tower until the men went away.
   b. The woman asked Theophemos not to take the furniture until her husband returned.
   c. 'But do not ask this either', said the neighbour. 'For these men are violent and will not cease plundering the house until they have taken everything away.'
   d. I was in the Piraeus while my house was being robbed, and I did not go home until the things that had happened were reported to me there.
   e. Before I left my house, I had told my wife that the money was lying at the bank.
2. a. ἡ γραῦς κακῶς διέκειτο διὰ τὸ συγκοπῆναι.
   The old woman was in a bad way because she had been beaten up.

b. Θεόφημος καὶ Εὔεργος οὕτω διέθεσαν τὴν γραῦν ὥστε ὕφαιμοι
   ἐγένοντο οἱ βραχίονες.
   Theophemos and Euergides treated the old woman in such a way that
   her wrists were blood-stained.

c. ἡ γυνὴ εἶπε τῷ Θεοφήμῳ ὅτι τὸ ἀργύριον κεῖται ἐπὶ τῇ
   τραπέζῃ.
   The woman told Theophemos that the money was lying in the
   bank.

d. ἡ γραῦς ἐνέθηκεν εἰς τὸν κόλπον τὸ κυμβίον ὃ παρέκειτο αὐτῇ.
   The old woman put the cup, which was lying beside her, in the fold of
   her dress.

17C

Page 209

1 τὰ γεγενημένα   This is the neuter plural of the perfect participle of γίγνομαι,
   'the having happened things'.

3 τὰ ἐκπεφορημένα   Perfect passive participle.

3–4 τὴν γραῦν οὕτω διακειμένην ὥστε ...   See *GE* pp. 342–343, #313 for the
   relationship between διατίθημι and διακεῖμαι. See *GE* pp. 345–346, #314–317
   for the use of ὥστε + infinitive to express a result clause: 'in such a state that
   (as a result) she was in danger of her life'. Note that ὥστε + the indicative
   stresses that the result actually happened.

4–5 καὶ ἀκούων τῆς γυναικὸς τὰ γενόμενα   Remember that after ἀκούω
   the source of the sound (his wife) is in the genitive, and the thing heard
   (the happenings) are in the accusative. Cf. 'He heard the words of the
   woman.'

6–8 ἐκέλευον δ' αὐτὸν ... ἀπολαμβάνειν ... ἀκολουθεῖν ... θεραπεύειν ...
   εἰσάγειν ...   ἐκέλευον is followed by a series of infinitives, 'ordered him
   to ...'

8 ὃν βούλοιντο   Why is the optative mood used here? See *GE* p. 325, #300 for
   indefinite clauses in secondary sequence.

9 κακά με πολλὰ εἶπεν   Note that κακὰ λέγειν, like κακὰ ποιειν (53), takes a
   double accusative: 'to speak bad words [to] someone', 'to abuse someone'.

Page 210

11 μεθ' ἑτέρων ὁμοίων αὐτῷ   'with others like himself'. Note that αὐτῷ =
   ἑαυτῷ (the reflexive form) and so has a rough breathing.

15–16 This might be the moment to learn the numerals at *GE* pp. 346–347,
   #318. You will find useful resemblances to Latin and to mathematical terms
   (pentagon, hexagon, octagon, decimal, kilometre) as well as correspondence
   between the cardinal, ordinal and adverb forms. NB. also μύριοι and
   myriads.

17 τὰ ἡρπασμένα   What participle? What verb? Try ἁρπάζω.

17–18 οὐκ ἔφη ἀποδώσειν ...   'He said that he would not give back ...' Note the
position of οὐ. It is always placed before φημί (rather than before the infinitive),
meaning 'He refused ...' or 'He denied ...'

20 εἰσεληλυθότα   Can you recognise this? If not, look up the principal parts of
ἔρχομαι, GE pp.436–442, #389.

21 οὕτως ἐπλεονέκτει ... ὥστε ...   A result clause is introduced: 'was so
grasping that...'

22 ἐκτετεισμένης τῆς δίκης   Genitive absolute. You should be able to recognise
the participle from the context. If not, check ἐκτίνω in the vocabulary.

23 οἴχοιτο   Why is the optative used here? Because it is indirect speech in
secondary sequence.

Translation for 17C

Well then, when these events were reported to me in the Piraeus by neighbours,
I went to the country, but I was not now able to catch these men (for I did not
arrive until they had gone), but seeing all the things that had been carried off
from the house, and the old woman in such a state that she was in danger of her
life, and hearing from my wife what had happened, I was very angry and went
to Theophemos on the next day at dawn in the city, taking witnesses. I told him
first to accept the fine and to follow (me) to the bank, then to look after the old
woman whom they had beaten and to bring in whatever doctor they liked. While
I was saying this and earnestly entreating him, Theophemos got angry and
abused me vigorously (*lit.* said many bad things to me). But then Theophemos
came along with reluctance, causing delays and saying that he wanted to get
witnesses himself. But this Euergos immediately set out from the city with
others like himself to go to my farm. The remaining furniture, whatever had
been in the tower on the day before and did not happen to be outside, had been
carried down by me because of our need. Euergos, breaking open the door
(which they had broken open on the previous day as well), went off taking my
furniture.

Meanwhile I was paying the money to Theophemos, one thousand, three
hundred and thirteen drachmas and two obols, in the presence of many witnesses,
and I asked him to give back the sheep and the slaves and the furniture which had
been seized by him, but Theophemos refused to give them back to me (said he
would not give them back to me) .When he gave this answer, I made those present
witnesses of this reply, and I paid the fine. For I did not know that Euergos had
gone to my house on that day, but I paid the fine at once. But Theophemos was
so grasping that he took the fine and kept the sheep and the slaves and the furniture, and, the moment the fine had been paid, a messenger came to me, a stone-
mason who was working on the monument near by, saying that Euergos had gone
away again, after carrying off the rest of the furniture from the house.

Grammar

Don't forget to learn the numerals.

EXERCISE FOR SECTION 17C

RESULT CLAUSES

B/C – MORPHOLOGY AND SYNTAX

Note that ὥστε + infinitive has negative μή, while ὥστε + indicative states a matter of fact and therefore has negative οὐ.

1. a. Those men were so wicked that they (actually) beat the woman and took away the cup from her.

   ὥστε τύπτειν τὴν γυναῖκα καὶ ἀφελέσθαι ἀπ᾽ αὐτῆς τὸ κυμβίον.

   The men were wicked enough to beat the woman and take away the cup from her.

   b. Those men were so abominable that they were (actually) not ashamed to rush in to my wife.

   ὥστε μὴ αἰσχύνεσθαι εἰς τὴν γυναῖκα εἰσιόντες.

   Those men were so abominable as not to be ashamed at going in to my wife.

   c. They are doing everything so that they do not (as a result) pay the penalty.

   ὥστε μὴ δίκην διδόναι.

   They do everything so as not to pay the penalty.

   d. The fellow reached such a pitch of impiety that, coming into the shrine, he (actually) dragged a suppliant away from the altar.

   ὥστε εἰσελθὼν εἰς τὸ ἱερὸν ἱκέτην ἀφελκύσαι ἀπὸ τοῦ βωμοῦ.

   The fellow reached such a pitch of impiety as to come into the shrine and drag a suppliant away from the altar.

Note that *GE* pp. 345–346, #314–317 suggest that ὥστε + infinitive should be translated by 'so as to' and ὥστε + indicative by 'so that'. This may be useful for the exercise, and the distinction between the 'potential' and the 'actual' result is a valid one; but in practice it will often sound more natural to translate ὥστε + infinitive by 'so that', which is the commonest way to express result in English, just as ὥστε + infinitive is the commonest way to express result in Greek.

17D

Page 211

1 Note that ἔδει is past: 'What then was I to do?' or 'What ought I to have done?'

3–4 συνεκόπη   Can you recognise this? It is 3rd s. second aorist passive (i.e. no θ).

4–5 ἐβουλήθη, ἐδυνήθην   See *GE* p. 350, #324 for a list of deponent verbs which have their aorists in passive form.

6 ἕκτῃ οὔσῃ ἡμέρᾳ   Dative expressing a point of time: 'on the sixth day'.

   ὕστερον ἤ   'later than ...', 'after ...'

7–8 ἵνα εἰδείην 'so that I might know'. Purpose clause in secondary sequence.
ὅ τι ποιητέον 'what must be done'.

9 τό τε ὁρμηθῆναι αὐτούς … καὶ ἐλθεῖν τό is followed by two infinitives used as nouns with the subject in the accusative: 'the fact that they had charged … and that they had come …'
εἰς τοῦτο ἀσελγείας ἐλθεῖν ὥστε … 'to reach such a pitch of depravity that …' Literally 'to reach this [point] of depravity that …' See *GE* pp. 345–346, #317.

12 διὰ τὸ μὴ ἀφεῖναι Once again the infinitive is used as a noun: 'owing to the fact that she did not give up the cup', 'because she would not give up the cup'.

15 εὐλαβήθητι Aorist passive imperative. See *GE* p. 349, #321.
εὐλαβήθητι μή … 'take care lest …' The construction is the same as after a verb of fearing. See *GE* p. 316, #293 and p. 332, #305.

16 The case for prosecution could only be brought by a relation or the master of the deceased. The old woman was neither family nor slave. Therefore Aristarchos could not legally bring a case against Theophemos and Euergos for her murder. All he could do was to go through a ritual of purification to free himself and his household from the pollution of the death, and try to think up some other means of vengeance.

Translation for 17D

What should I have done, Apollodoros, and where should I have turned, since the furniture had been carried off, the old woman was in danger of her life, and the fine had been paid? But then, if nothing else, I ordered Theophemos to look after the old woman who had been beaten and to bring in whatever doctor he wished. But when Theophemos was not willing and I could not persuade him, I brought in a doctor whom I had used for many years. But yesterday, on the sixth day after they had charged into the house, my old nurse died. I was at once very angry, and I went early (as I have said) to the officers to find out what should be done about this, and I told them all that had happened, the fact that they had charged into the farm and reached such a pitch of depravity that they had not been ashamed to burst in on my wife and children, and to beat up the old woman for the sake of a cup, and to carry off the furniture. In addition to this I recalled the goodwill of the woman and that she had died because she would not give up the cup.

Having heard the story from me, the officers gave this advice: 'Since you yourself were not present, but your wife and children, and since other witnesses did not appear for you, take care that you do not make a public denunciation of anyone by name, and that you do not bring a suit for murder before the king archon. For the woman is not one of your family, nor is she a slave, from what you say. But having purified yourself on behalf of your household and yourself, bear the tragedy as easily as you can, and take vengeance in any other way you like.'

EXERCISES FOR SECTION 17D

MORE IMPERATIVES

17D: 1

1.	λυθήτω	let him/her be set free (s.)
2.	κολασθέντων	let them be punished
3.	λήφθητε	be taken (pl.)
4.	τιμήθητι	be honoured (s.)
5.	γράφητε	be written (pl.)

17D: 2

1. γνῶτε	3. στήτω	5. γνώτω
2. βῆθι	4. φαθί	

17E

This section introduces two new pieces of syntax, the deliberative subjunctive (*GE* p. 351, #325–327), and correlatives (*GE* pp. 351–352, #328). Otherwise it brings in as much as it can of the syntax that you have learned in Sections 16 and 17. Make sure that you have digested it and fully understand it all.

Page 212

1 ποιήσω, τράπωμαι, γένωμαι   All these are deliberative subjunctives. See *GE* p. 351, #325. 'What am I to do?', 'Where am I to turn?' etc.

2 χρῶμαι   χράομαι + dative means 'to use' or 'to treat someone'. Here 'I do not know what to do with myself' (*GE* p. 351, #327).

2–3 οὕτως ... ὥστε ... + infinitive indicates result.
ἄν + optative expresses potential: 'could' or 'would'.

3 οὐδ' ἄν ...   'Nor would I dare to lie even if I knew well that ...' Here you need to understand 'dare to lie' repeated from the previous line.

4–5 οὐ γὰρ οὕτω τούτους μισῶ ὡς ἐμαυτὸν φιλῶ   For the use of correlatives see *GE* pp. 351–352, #328. 'I do not hate them *in such a way as* I like myself.' 'I do not hate them *as* much *as* I like myself.'

5 τί δρῶμεν   Why is the subjunctive used here?

6 σκοπῶμεν   'Let us consider'.
μὴ φοβηθῇς μή ...   'Don't be afraid lest ...' μή + aorist subjunctive expresses the prohibition, and the second μή introduces the fear for the future with its verb in the subjunctive in primary sequence (optative in secondary): *GE* #292, and #293, or Reference Grammar 404.

7 δεινὸν ἂν εἴη   Note the ἄν. What effect does it have?

7–8 The desire to inflict vengeance on one's enemies was regarded as natural and proper by the majority of people in the ancient world. (Socrates was unusual in taking the opposite view that it is never right to do wrong, even in retaliation.)

In general, vengeance was just as much a matter of honour for the man in the street as for the Homeric hero. Thus a friend could be expected to give all possible help in making plans for revenge.

10 χάριν εἴσομαι   What tense of οἶδα is this?

11 ποιώμεθα, ἀναλάβωμεν   What mood and why?

12 οὐ κυνὶ πλανητέον   'It ought not to be wandered by a dog,' 'Not even a dog should be wandering about.' See *GE* p. 317, #294 for verbal nouns expressing obligation. The idea comes from the opening of Menander's *Misoumenos*.

12–13 ποίησον, ἀφικοῦ   What part of the verb is this? Revise aorist imperatives, if you are not sure: *GE* #198–199, and #206–207.

13 καὶ μὴ ἄλλως ποιήσῃς   Literally this means 'Don't do otherwise', but it is frequently used to beg someone to do what you suggest: e.g. the Greek for 'Do please come' would be 'Come and don't do otherwise.'
ἵνα βουλευσώμεθα   Why the subjunctive? It is the verb in a purpose clause in primary sequence. See *GE* #298–299 or Reference Grammar #399.

16 πρὶν ἂν συμβουλεύωμαι   For πρίν meaning 'until' see *GE* #311–312 and compare this with indefinite clauses in general. See *GE* Reference Grammar p. 457, #398.

16–17 ἐὰν θεὸς ἐθέλῃ   'If god is willing.' For future conditions see *GE* pp. 304–305. #282, and for conditions in general, Reference Grammar p. 460, #402.

Translation for 17E

ARISTARCHOS   So be it. You have the story. What am I to do? Where am I to turn? What will become of me? For I do not know what to do with myself. For surely I would not be so foolish as to dare to lie to the jurors, nor would I do so, even if I knew that I would convict my enemies of doing wrong. For I do not dislike them as much as I like myself. Consider then what we are to do.

APOLLODOROS   Let us consider together, my good friend, and do not be afraid that I won't share your enthusiasm. For indeed it would be a terrible thing for a good friend not to share his friends' desire to be revenged on their enemies. So it is necessary for me most of all to help you in your perplexity.

AR.   Indeed I shall be grateful to you, my excellent friend, for sharing my enthusiasm.

AP.   But let us do this later and resume our talk. For it is raining, and, by the Gods, not even a dog should be wandering about now. But you act thus for me. Come to my house tomorrow at dawn, please come (and don't do otherwise), so that we can take counsel about these very things.

AR.   I am delighted by what you say, Apollodoros, and I agree that I must do nothing before I have consulted with you. I will come to you tomorrow, if God wills it.

AP.   Let us do this. Let us be going, then.

REVISION EXERCISES FOR SECTION 17

D – ENGLISH INTO GREEK

1. Sentences
    1. αἱ θεράπαιναι οὐκ ἔμειναν ἕως ἄλοιεν.
    2. οὐκ ἐπαύσαντο ἐκφοροῦντες τὰ σκεύη ἐκ τῆς οἰκίας πρὶν πάντα ἁρπάσειεν (ἁρπάζοιεν).
    3. τὸν ἐμὸν υἱὸν ἦγον ἕως γείτων τις εἶπεν ὅτι υἱὸς οὐ δούλου ἀλλὰ πολίτου εἴη.
    4. ὠργίσθην ὅτι ὑβρισταὶ ὄντες οὕτω διέθεσαν τὴν τίτθην ὥστε περὶ ψυχῆς ἐκινδύνευεν.
    5. οὕτως ὠλιγώρουν ὥστε εἰσελθόντες εἰς τὴν οἰκίαν ἐκφορεῖν τὰ σκεύη.

2. Prose

There are a several alternative ways of translating the English into Greek. It is quite possible, for example, to use a subordinate clause instead of a participle, or to choose a different Greek word in some places.

ἡ δὲ ἐμὴ γυνὴ ὀργισθεῖσα, ‘μὴ τὰ σκεύη λάβητε’, ἔφη. ‘ἆρ’ οὐκ ἤδη πεντήκοντα ἔχετε πρόβατα; περιμένετε δή· οὐ γὰρ δεῖ ὑμᾶς ἀπελθεῖν πρὶν ἂν ἐπανέλθῃ ὁ ἐμὸς ἀνήρ.’ οἱ δὲ οὐκ ἀκούσαντες τῆς γυναικὸς ταῦτα λεγούσης, πάντα λαβόντες ἀπῆλθον. μετὰ δὲ ταῦτα, ἄγγελός τις προσελθὼν πρὸς τὸν Πειραιᾶ ἐπήγγειλεν ἐμοὶ τὰ γεγενημένα. ἐγὼ δέ, πάντ’ ἀκούσας, ἐκινδύνευσα οὕτως ὀργισθῆναι ὥστε τὸν Θεόφημον αὐτὸς παίειν. τῇ δὲ ὑστεραίᾳ, προσελθὼν πρὸς αὐτόν, ἐκέλευσα ἀκολουθεῖν ἐμοὶ ἐπὶ τὴν τράπεζαν ἵνα τὸ ἀργύριον τὸ ἐνταῦθα κείμενον συλλάβῃ.

TEST EXERCISE 17

SOCRATES   Let us talk then, my dear Phaedrus; certainly we have the time, it seems (lit. there is leisure, as it seems). And at the same time the cicadas seem to me to be watching us, singing and talking to one another. If they were to see us, like most people, at midday not talking but sleeping and being bewitched by them through idleness of thought, they would rightly laugh at us, regarding us as slaves who sleep like sheep round the spring. But if they see us talking and sailing uncharmed past them as if they were the Sirens, perhaps they would be pleased and grant us the gift which they have from the gods to give to men.

PHAEDRUS   What is the gift? Don't keep it a secret. For I really am unaware of it, as it seems.

SOC.   What am I to do? It is clear that I must tell you. For, although it is proper to call you a lover of music and literature, I am afraid that you may appear to be uncultured if you are ignorant of such matters. It is said that once upon a time cicadas were men, before the Muses existed. But when the Muses were born and song appeared, then some men of that time were so astounded and listened with such delight that while singing they neglected food and drink and did not notice that they were dying. And from these men the race of cicadas later sprang, receiving this gift from the Muses, that they should need no food, but that without food or drink they should sing until they died, and after that, going to the Muses, they should tell them which of men honoured the Muses. Therefore, for many reasons we must have some conversation and we must not sleep in the middle of the day.

PH.   We must indeed make conversation.

From now on you may find it increasingly useful to use the Reference Grammar.

# 352–388	has tables of nouns, adjectives, pronouns, verbs.
# 389	provides an essential list of irregular verbs and their principal parts
	(ultimately you should make it your goal to know all these by heart).
# 390–391	gives lists of prepositions and particles.
# 392–394	give uses of ὡς,(ὥς), participles and infinitives.
# 396–406	gives a summary of the main syntactical constructions.

Section Eighteen: How Zeus gave justice to men

This passage is reproduced unadapted from Plato, *Protagoras* 320c–323a. The style is not typical of Plato. It is likely that he is here imitating the style of the sophist Protagoras, into whose mouth he puts the speech, but the iambic rhythms also suggest that the myth may be based on a long established story which had been told often in verse, perhaps in tragedy. Whatever its origins, it is a fascinating passage which describes the creation of the world and the social necessity for man of possessing δίκη and αἰδώς (a sense of right and a moral awareness of others and their response to one's actions). The introduction to this section in *Reading Greek* is important.

18A

Page 216

1 The verb 'to be' is often used in the sense of 'to exist'.

2 χρόνος εἱρμαρμένος 'allotted' in the sense of 'allotted by destiny', 'fated'.
γῆς ἔνδον 'within the earth'.

3 τῶν = ἐκείνων. Here the article is used as a demonstrative pronoun. This is rare in Attic Greek, though normal in Homer.
ὅσα πυρὶ καὶ γῇ κεράννυται 'as many as are mixed with fire and earth'. This refers to air and water, the other two elements. (Some Greek philosophers believed that all things were composed of four elements, earth, air, fire and water.)

5–6 νεῖμαι, νείμαντος, νέμει, νέμων Note the repetitions, and also that the aorist stem of νέμω is νειμ-.

6 ἐπίσκεψαι Can you recognise this? What kind of imperative is it? (2nd s. aorist.)

6–9 Note the careful patterning of the phrases:
τοῖς μέν ... τοὺς δέ ..., τοὺς δέ ... τοῖς δέ ... (ABBA) followed by ἃ μὲν γὰρ <u>σμικρότητι</u> ἤμπισχε ... ἃ δὲ ηὖξε <u>μεγέθει</u> ...

10 καὶ τἆλλα = καὶ τὰ ἄλλα 'and he assigned the other qualities also ...'

Translation for 18A

There was once a time when gods existed but mortal creatures did not. When the appointed time came for these also to be born (time of birth), the gods formed them within the earth out of a mixture (having mixed) of earth and fire and of the

239

things that are compounded with fire and earth. And when they were ready to bring them to the light, they ordered Prometheus and Epimetheus to equip them and assign powers suitable to each one. Epimetheus asked Prometheus [to allow him] to do the distributing himself, 'And when I have done it', he said, 'you review it'. Having thus persuaded him, he began to distribute the powers. In his distribution, he gave some creatures strength without speed, but to the weaker he gave speed; some he armed with weapons, while for others, to whom he gave an unarmed nature, he devised some other power for their protection. To those on whom he bestowed smallness, he allotted winged flight or an underground dwelling; those whom he enlarged in size, he protected by that very quality; and he assigned the other qualities also, balancing everything in this way. He planned these things, taking care that no species should be destroyed.

18B

Page 218

1 ἀλληλοφθοριῶν   This is made up of two words: ἀλλήλους which means 'One another', and the root φθορ as in διαφθορά 'destruction'. Cf. διαφθείρω.
ὥρας   'hours' or 'seasons'.

2 στερεοῖς   'thick', 'solid'. Steroids thicken your physique, stereophonic sound is 'dense' or 'thick'.
δέρμασιν   Cf. 'dermatology', 'dermatitis', 'epidermis', 'pachyderm'.

3 Notice ἱκανοῖς μέν ... δυνατοῖς δέ ...   and understand a repeat of ἀμῦναι in the second phrase.
εἰς εὐνὰς ἰοῦσιν   'for them going to bed'. What part of the verb is ἰοῦσιν?

4 τὰ αὐτὰ ταῦτα   'these same things (i.e. skins)'. This is the subject of ὑπάρχοι. Remember that a n. pl. subject has a singular verb.

5 ἄλλοις ἄλλας   'different foods for different creatures'.

6–7 ἔστι δ᾽ οἷς ἔδωκεν ...   'and there were some to whom he gave ...' This use of ἔστι + relative pronoun is a fairly common idiom.

7, 8 ὀλιγο-γονία, πολυ-γονία   These should be guessable. The root γεν-, γον- stands for 'race', 'birth', 'family'. Herodotus (3.108) also points out that animals that are preyed on reproduce rapidly.

Translation for 18B

When he had provided enough means of escape for them from mutual slaughter, he contrived comfort against the seasons sent from Zeus, clothing them with thick hair or tough skins, sufficient to ward off the winter's cold and capable of withstanding also the summer's heat; and he planned that when they went to bed, the same skins should serve as individual and natural coverings for each one. And he shod them too, some with hooves and some with tough and bloodless skin. Next he provided different sorts of food for them; for some grass from the earth, for some fruit from the trees, and for some roots. And there were some to whom he gave the flesh of other animals for their food. These he made less fertile, while those on whom they fed, he made more fertile, thus conserving the species (providing safety for the race).

18C

Page 219

1 ἅτε + participle means 'since', 'in as much as'. See *GE* p. 356, #330.
καταναλώσας ἀναλίσκω (ἀναλωσ-) means 'I spend' or 'I expend'.

2 τὰ ἄλογα 'the speechless ones'. The power of speech is what distinguishes man from beasts, and so τὰ ἄλογα becomes the normal word for 'beasts'.

3 ἠπόρει ὅ τι χρήσαιτο This is a deliberative question in secondary sequence: 'What am I to use?' becomes 'He was in doubt what he was to use.' See *GE* p. 356, #329.
ἀποροῦντι δὲ αὐτῷ ἔρχεται Προμηθεύς 'to him being in doubt, Prometheus comes ...'

6–7 ἀπορίᾳ οὖν σχόμενος ... ἥντινα σωτηρίαν ... εὕροι See note on line 3 above.

8 τὴν ἔντεχνον σοφίαν ἔντεχνον is a compound adjective and has only two terminations; thus it does, in fact, agree with σοφίαν.
Hephaistos is the god of fire and the master-craftsman. Athene is the goddess of wisdom, and so both their attributes are reflected in the phrase. In addition, τέχνη covers both the skill of the craftsman and the creative genius of the artist, and so this phrase encompasses both meanings. It is difficult to find an adequate translation; possibly 'technical knowledge' would suit the context best here.

8–9 ἀμήχανον ... γενέσθαι 'for it was impossible for it (αὐτὴν = τὴν ἔντεχνον σοφίαν) to be possessed (κτητήν) by anyone (τῳ = τινί) or to be useful (χρησίμην) without fire'.

9–10 Notice the contrast between τὴν περὶ τὸν βίον σοφίαν and τὴν πολιτικήν. Man now has the skills to stay alive, but has not yet acquired social skills which enable him to live in a community.

10 ταύτῃ 'in this way'.

Page 220

13 ἐφιλοτεχνείτην This is a dual. See *GE* pp. 356–358, #331–332. The dual can be used in verbs, and in nouns and adjectives, when two people or things are the subject, usually when they are a pair, e.g. two hands, a chariot team or, as here, a couple. It is worth looking at the pattern of the duals, but it is not essential to learn them by heart. You will probably be able to recognise them when you meet them.

Translation for 18C

Now, since Epimetheus was not particularly brilliant, he did not notice that he had used up all the powers on the animals (he escaped his own notice having used up the powers). But the human race was still left over for him, without any attributes, and he did not know what to do. While he was still at a loss, Prometheus came to inspect the work (the distribution) and he saw that the other creatures were well provided with everything, but that man was naked, unshod, without a bed and without weapons; and already the appointed day had come on which man too had to emerge from the earth into the light. Prometheus, therefore, being at a loss to find any protection for man, stole from Hephaistos and Athene the gift of technical skill together with fire – for without fire it was impossible for anyone to possess or use this skill – and so he gave it to man. In this way man acquired skill to keep him alive, but he did not have political skill; for that was in the keeping of Zeus, and Prometheus no longer had permission to enter the acropolis, the house of Zeus – moreover, the sentinels of Zeus were terrible. And so he secretly entered the house shared by Athene and Hephaistos in which they practised their art, and stealing Hephaistos' art of working with fire and the other art of Athene, he gave them to man. As a result of this man had the means of life, but Prometheus, thanks to Epimetheus, so the story goes, had later on to stand trial for theft.

18D

Page 221

1 μοίρας   Here this simply means 'portion', but it can mean 'one's portion in life', hence 'destiny', 'doom'. It can also mean 'that which is rightly one's portion', hence 'one's due'. Μοῖρα (personified) is the goddess of fate. The μοῖρα referred to here is the skill of fire and the technical skill to use it, which were divine prerogatives.

2 θεοὺς ἐνόμισε   Here νομίζω means 'to acknowledge', not 'to think'.
As Xenophanes (fr. 6) points out, man imagines gods in his own image:
'But if cattle and horses and lions had hands or could draw and make works of art with their hands as men do, then horses would draw the images of their gods and make their bodies like horses, and cattle would make them like cattle, just like the body that each species possesses.'

5–11 This is a most ingenious explanation of the need for social skills. Men had to live in scattered groups because they had not the πολιτικὴ τέχνη to live peacefully and cooperatively in cities (or to organise an army). Whenever they tried, they had to give up and then in their small groups they once again fell prey to wild beasts.

5 κατ' ἀρχάς   This means 'in the beginning', 'at first'.
σποράδην   This is an adverb, cf. English 'sporadically'.

7 δημιουργική   A δημιουργός is a craftsman (from δῆμος and ἔργον).

9–10 ὅτ' οὖν ἀθροισθεῖεν   'whenever they gathered together'. The verb in the optative shows that this is an indefinite clause.

10 ἅτε οὐκ ἔχοντες   'since they did not have', ἅτε + participle expressing the cause.

10–11 ὥστε ... διεφθείροντο   The verb in the indicative, rather than the infinitive, shows that this is an actual result, something that actually took place.

Translation for 18D

Since man had a share in the portion of the gods, first of all, because of his divine kinship, he alone of living creatures believed in the gods and set to work to build altars and images of the gods; and secondly, he quickly discovered speech and names by his art, and invented houses and clothes and shoes and bedding and food from the earth. Thus provided for, men lived to begin with in scattered groups, and there were no cities. Therefore they were destroyed by the wild beasts, since they were in every way weaker than them, and the technical skill which was sufficient help to them in getting food was not adequate for fighting the beasts – for they did not yet have the political skill of which the art of war is a part. They did indeed seek to come together and to protect themselves by founding cities, but whenever they gathered in communities, they injured one another because they did not have political skills, with the result that they scattered again and were again devoured.

18E

Page 222

1 δείσας   This is in no way related to δεῖ, but is the aorist participle of δείδω, an irregular verb. See vocabulary.
Notice the position of πᾶν at the end of the clause, making it emphatic: 'lest it might be destroyed totally'.

2 αἰδῶ τε καὶ δίκην   Two immensely important words which have a wide range of meanings.
αἰδώς means 'shame', 'modesty', the capacity to feel ashamed if you act wrongly to others; hence, respect for others and their rights. It contains an element of fear – men behave well through fear of what others may think of them if they do not. E. R. Dodds in *The Greeks and the Irrational* discusses the nature of the 'shame culture', and it is everywhere apparent in Homer – the heroes must not 'lose face'.
δίκη is here more abstract, although, as you already know, it can range from abstract justice to a legal case or the penalty inflicted.
In this passage the two words express the two qualities which make community living possible: respect for others and a sense of justice and the rule of law, or private morality and public observance of the law.

2 ἵν' εἶεν ...   'so that they might be ...' A purpose clause in secondary sequence; the main verb πέμπει is a 'historic present'. That means the present is used instead of the past to make the story more dramatic, but the narrative is still about a past event and the verbs in the subordinate clauses still reflect a secondary sequence.

κόσμοι   κόσμος is another important and wide-ranging word. It means 'decoration' ('cosmetic'), 'order', and then 'the thing that is ordered', 'the universe' ('the cosmos') or the 'world' ('cosmopolitan'). Here the sense is 'order'.

δεσμοί   These are 'bonds' or 'fetters'. (Cf. δεσμωτήριον 'a prison'.)
Note once again the chiasmus (ABBA pattern) in πόλεων κόσμοι τε καὶ δεσμοὶ φιλίας, i.e. genitive, nominative – nominative, genitive.

3   ἐρωτᾷ   Continuing use of the historic present. You will see that δοίη is optative, and thus reflects secondary sequence.
τίνα οὖν τρόπον   'in what way'. The accusative is used adverbially.

4   νείμω   Can you recognise what mood this is, and why? It is not the future (νεμῶ), but it is the aorist subjunctive (aorist stem νειμ-), used in a deliberative question, 'Am I to assign these (qualities) in this way?' See *GE* p. 351, #325–326.

4   Be careful not to confuse εἷς with εἰς.

5   ἰδιώταις   Often ἰδιώτης means 'a private individual as opposed to one of a citizen group', but here it simply means 'individuals'. Notice how the meaning has deteriorated over the centuries into 'idiot'.

6   θῶ, νείμω   Do you recognise the deliberative subjunctives?

7   μετεχόντων   Can you recognise this? 'Let them all have a share …'

7–8   οὐ γὰρ ἂν γένοιντο πόλεις, εἰ ὀλίγοι αὐτῶν μετέχοιεν   The optative mood of the verbs and presence of ἄν will tell you what sort of a condition this is. See Reference Grammar #402, p. 460.

8–9   τὸν μὴ δυνάμενον … κτείνειν, ὡς νόσον πόλεως   This is the law they must enforce. The use of μή, rather than οὐ, makes the participle phrase indefinite: 'whoever is incapable of …' rather than 'the one who is not capable …' Here the difference in meaning is slight, but in some cases it can be significant. The brutal extermination of those without the right qualities underlines the importance which Zeus attaches to them.
κτείνειν   Poetic. The normal prose use would be ἀποκτείνειν.
οὕτω δή   Introduces the conclusion, the summing-up of the meaning of the myth, which illustrates the difference between specialist knowledge and expertise, and the basic human qualities which all should share.

9–10   οἵ τε ἄλλοι καὶ Ἀθηναῖοι   Literally this means 'both the others and the Athenians'. In effect it means 'the Athenians in particular'.

10   ὅταν μὲν … ᾖ λόγος   'whenever the argument is concerned with …'

12–13   ὅταν δὲ … ἴωσιν   A balancing and contrasting clause to the previous one.

14   προσῆκον   Accusative absolute. See *GE* p. 320, #296, or Reference Grammar #395.

15   αὕτη, ὦ Σώκρατες, τούτου αἰτία   Q.E.D. Protagoras rests his case.
He goes on to describe how Athenian education was aimed, from earliest childhood, at developing the potential for political skill.

Translation for 18E

Therefore Zeus, fearing that our whole race would be destroyed, sent Hermes to take to men the qualities of respect for others and a sense of justice so that there could be order in the cities and bonds of friendship uniting men. Hermes asked Zeus in what way he was to give justice and respect to men: 'Am I to distribute these gifts in the same way as the skills have been allocated? They have been distributed in this way: one man having the skill of a doctor is sufficient for many individuals (laymen), and the same is true of other experts. Am I then to give justice and respect to men in this way, or am I to assign them to all men?' 'To all men', said Zeus, 'and let all men have a share; for there could never be cities if only a few people shared in these qualities as in the other arts. And moreover lay it down as a law from me that if anyone is incapable of sharing in justice and respect he must be put to death as a plague to the city.'

Thus it is for these reasons, Socrates, that, whenever the debate is about skill in architecture or any other expertise, the Athenians, like other people, believe that only a few are capable of giving advice, and if anyone outside these few gives advice, they do not tolerate it, as you say – reasonably in my view – but whenever they seek advice on political wisdom, which must always follow the path of justice and moderation, they rightly listen to every man, since they think it is proper for every man to have a share in this virtue or there would not be any cities. That, Socrates, is the reason for this.

Section Nineteen: The story of Adrastos

This passage is reproduced unadapted from Herodotus, *Histories* 1.34–45. Herodotus writes in the Ionic dialect (see Introduction). You will find that you get used to this quite quickly, and the vocabularies will help you as well. However, before you start, you may want to look at *GE* pp. 359–360, #333–334 'The Dialect of Herodotus'.

It is very important to read both the introduction on pp. 225–226 of *RGT* and the beginning of the story, pp. 227–229, which is translated for you.

19A

Page 230

1 νέμεσις 'retribution'. This is not punishment for an evil act, but punishment for 'thinking more than mortal thoughts'. Perpetual happiness is the prerogative of the gods and not of man. Croesus commits an act of 'hubris' by exhibiting pride in his continuing happiness, and thus attracts the vengeance of the gods.

2 ἑωυτόν = ἑαυτόν.
ὀλβιώτατον Note the emphatic position.
οἱ 'to him'.

2–3 ἐπέστη ὄνειρος The dream is personified; it 'stood over him', or 'stood beside him'.

4 διέφθαρτο Literally this means that 'he had been destroyed', a brutal word for 'handicapped' (cf. 'written off'), but it shows Croesus' feeling that he had only one son, for all practical purposes.

5 ὦν = οὖν. Note this carefully. You will meet it frequently, and it is always easy to confuse it with ὤν 'being'. Apart from the accent, its position near the beginning of a sentence should help to distinguish it.

6 ἀπολέει Here the future of ἀπόλλυμι means something like 'will lose' rather than 'will destroy'. The form is uncontracted, as are many of the verbs.
μιν 'him'.

8 ἐωθότα δὲ στρατηγέειν μιν … Object of ἐξέπεμπε in the next line.
οὐδαμῇ 'nowhere'.

9–10 ἀκόντια δὲ καὶ δοράτια καὶ τὰ τοιαῦτα πάντα Objects of both ἐκκομίσας and συνένησε.

11 μή τί οἱ κρεμάμενον … 'lest anything having been hung over him might…'

Translation for 19A

After Solon had gone, great retribution from god, to make a reasonable guess, overtook Croesus, because he thought himself to be the happiest of all men. Straightaway a dream came to him when he was asleep which revealed to him the truth of the evils which were going to happen with regard to his son. Croesus had two sons, of whom one was disabled (for he was deaf and dumb), but the other was far superior to his contemporaries in every way; his name was Atys. And it was this Atys that the dream pointed out to Croesus that he would lose, struck by an iron spear-head. Then when he woke up and took counsel with himself, fearing the dream, he first brought a woman in marriage for the boy, and then, although he had been accustomed to command the Lydians in battle, Croesus no longer sent him out on this sort of venture anywhere, and he also removed javelins and spears and all such weapons as men use in war from the men's quarters and stacked them in the inner chambers, lest anything hanging over the boy might fall on him.

19B

Page 232

1 ἔχοντος ... τὸν γάμον   '(with) his (οἱ) son having his marriage in hand ...'
    ἀπικνέεται = ἀφικνεῖται.

1–2 συμφορῇ ἐχόμενος   Literally 'being held by disaster', perhaps 'gripped by disaster'.
    οὐ καθαρὸς χεῖρας   'not clean in respect of his hands'. This is an accusative of respect. See *GE* p. 360, #335.
    ἐών = ὤν 'being'.

3 καθαρσίου   The neuter of the adjective καθάρσιος, 'purificatory', is used here as a noun; it is the object of ἐπικυρῆσαι. Catharsis is the rite of purification which the perpetrator of a crime (whether voluntarily or involuntarily committed) must undergo before he can cease to be regarded as polluted and return to normal life and relationships.

5 ἐπυνθάνετο   The imperfect tense suggests that Croesus 'began the process of finding out' or 'wanted to find out'.

6 ὀκόθεν = ὁπόθεν; also in the next line κόθεν = πόθεν.

7 ἐπίστιος = ἐφέστιος. This means literally 'by the hearth'. A suppliant would sit by the hearth and was under the protection of Zeus Epistios. (Cf. 19F, line 10, p. 239.) Once he had been accepted into the house, the relationship of guest-friendship would be established. Thus ξένος can mean 'stranger', 'guest', 'host' and 'friend'.
    ἀμείβετο   There is no augment, but you can tell that the verb is past because of the ending.

9 ἐμεωυτοῦ = ἐμαυτοῦ.
    ἀέκων is the uncontracted form of ἄκων.

ἐξεληλαμένος   From ἐξ-ελαύνω ἐλάω ἤλασα ἐλήλακα ἐλήλαμαι ἠλάθην.
See list of irregular verbs, *GE* pp. 436–442, #389.

12 ἐν ἡμετέρου   'in [the house] of ours'. Cf. 'at the doctor's', 'at the dentist's'.

Translation for 19B

While his son was occupied with his wedding, there arrived in Sardis a man who
was beset by misfortune and whose hands were polluted (not pure), being a
Phrygian by birth, and related to the royal family. This man, coming to the house
of Croesus, begged him to cleanse him of his blood-guilt in accordance with the
laws of the country. And Croesus did cleanse him. The process of purification is
very similar in Lydia and in Greece (among the Lydians and among the Hellenes).
When Croesus had performed the customary rites, he started to ask who he was
and where he came from, saying these words: 'You, sir, who were my suppliant,
who are you and where in Phrygia do you come from? What man or woman did
you kill?' And he answered, 'O King, I am the son of Gordias, the son of Midas.
I am called Adrastos, and I am here because I killed my own brother by accident;
I have been driven out by my father and deprived of everything.' Croesus
answered him in these words; 'You are the son of men who are my friends and
you have come to friends, where you shall be in need of nothing while you remain
in my house. It will be best for you (you will profit most) if you bear this misfortune as lightly as possible.'

19C

Page 233

2 ὑὸς χρῆμα μέγα   Literally 'a great thing of a boar'. Cf Section 5A line 6, p.
54: 'τὸ χρῆμα τῶν νυκτῶν'.

3 διαφθείρεσκε   The ending in -έσκω is 'frequentative', and shows that the
action took place repeatedly. Cf. ποιέεσκον later in the same line. No augment
for either.

4 ἀπικόμενοι = ἀφικόμενοι.

Page 234

10 οἱ   'to him'.

11 τοῖσι ἰοῦσι   'to those going'. Dative plural of the participle.

Translation for 19C

So he took up residence in the house of Croesus, and at this same period, on the
Mysian Mount Olympus, a huge monster of a boar appeared. Making forays from
this mountain, this creature used to destroy the Mysians' crops, and the Mysians,
often setting out against it, did it no harm, but were harmed by it. Finally, coming
to Croesus, messengers from the Mysians spoke thus: 'O King, a huge monster
of a boar has appeared in our land, which is destroying our crops. Although we
are eager to destroy it, we cannot do so. Now therefore we ask you to send us your

son and a selected band of young men and hounds, so that we may rid our country of it.' They made these requests, but Croesus, remembering the words of the dream, spoke these words to them; 'Do not mention my son any more; for I would not send him to you; he is newly married and this is what concerns him now. However, I shall send selected bands of Lydians and the whole pack of hounds and I shall order those who go to be as eager as possible to join in ridding your land of this creature.' This was his answer.

19D

Page 234

2   οὐ φαμένου   See *GE* p. 361, #336 for the meaning of οὐ φημι. Cf. Latin *nego*.
σφι   'to them'.

3–4   τὰ κάλλιστα … ἡμῖν ἦν … φοιτέοντας εὐδοκιμέειν   Literally 'the most glorious and noble deeds were once formerly to us (mine), going to wars and to hunts to win fame', φοιτέοντας does not agree with ἡμῖν, because it is seen as part of an accusative and infinitive phrase which explains the first statement.

5   ἀποκληίσας ἔχεις   Herodotus often uses a past tense made up of ἔχω + aorist participle.

6   τέοισι ὄμμασι   τέοισι = τίσι: 'with what eyes?' How will he look to observers? What will people think of him? How will he appear in their eyes?

7   κοῖος = ποῖος.

7–8   Notice the crescendo of indignant questions.

8   μέθες   'Let me go.' This is the aorist imperative from μεθίημι.

11   ὄψις ὀνείρου … ἐπιστᾶσα   This echoes the ἐπέστη in Section 18A.
ὀλιγοχρόνιον   You will be able to guess this if you derive it from the two words you know.

12   πρός   'with regard to', 'in consideration of'.

13–14   εἴ κως …   'if in some way …'
διακλέψαι   'steal you (from death or Fate)'.

14   τυγχάνεις ἐών   Here the meaning is 'you really are' rather than 'you happen to be'.

15   διεφθαρμένον τὴν ἀκοήν   'destroyed in respect of his hearing', i.e. 'deaf'. τὴν ἀκοήν is an accusative of respect.

16   τοι = σοι.

17   τό is both the object of μανθάνεις and accusative of respect with λέληθέ σε 'there is something which you do not understand, and in respect of which the dream has escaped your notice (which you have failed to observe in the dream)'.

Page 236

19–21   εἰ μὲν γὰρ … εἶπε … , χρῆν …   This is an unfulfilled condition, but, as often, there is no ἄν used with χρῆν, for χρῆν was felt to be virtually potential on its own.

20 ὀδόντος Cf. 'odontology', 'orthodontist'. τοι = σοι.

ἢ ἄλλου τευ ὅ τι τούτῳ οἶκε 'or of anything else which seems like to this'.
τευ = τινός, οἶκε = ἔοικε.

23 ἔστι τῇ 'there is a way in which …', 'somehow'; Cf. ἔστι τις 'there is a sort
of person who …', 'someone'.

Translation for 19D

Although the Mysians were contented with this, the son of Croesus went to him,
having heard what the Mysians were asking. Since Croesus was refusing to
send his son to them, the young man spoke thus to him: 'Previously, Father, it
was most honourable and noble for me to go to war and to the hunt to win glory.
But now you have barred me from both these activities, although you have
noticed no cowardice or lack of spirit in me. Now to what eyes must I appear
as I walk to and from the agora? (What must people think of me?) What sort of
person shall I seem to the citizens, what sort of man to my new-wed wife? With
what sort of husband will she seem to be living? You must therefore either let
me go to the hunt, or persuade me by reason that these things are better for me
if done this way.' Croesus answered in these words: 'My son, it is not because
I have noticed any cowardice or any other disagreeable trait in you that I do
this, but because the apparition of a dream came to me in my sleep, and standing by me said that you would be short-lived, and that you would perish by an
iron spearhead. Because of this dream, I hastened this marriage of yours and I
do not send you on this undertaking, taking precautions to see if I can somehow
steal you [from death] for as long as I live (for the period of my life). For you
are in reality my only son; for the other one is deaf (disabled in respect of
hearing), and I do not consider that he exists, as far as I am concerned (for
me).'

    The young man answered with these words; 'I forgive your protectiveness for
me, Father, since you have had such a dream; but what you do not understand and
have failed to observe in respect of the dream, it is right that I should point out to
you. You say that the dream says that I will die by an iron spearhead; but what
sort of hands does a boar have, what sort of iron spearhead does it have that you
should fear? For if it had said to you that I would be killed by a boar's tusk, or
something else like this, then you ought to be doing what you are doing. But, as
it is, it is a weapon that is to kill me. Since therefore our fight is not against men,
let me go.' Croesus answered, 'My son, it is the case that you conquer me,
showing me your opinion about the dream. So, then, defeated by you, I change
my mind and let you go to the hunt.'

19E

Page 237

1 εἴπας This is the aorist participle formed from the first aorist εἶπα which is
the alternative to εἶπον.

3 ὑποδεξάμενος ἔχω Another example of this form of past tense. Cf. 19D line
5, ἀποκληίσας ἔχεις.

4 προποιήσαντος χρηστὰ ἐς σέ 'having done good things for you
previously'.

χρηστοῖσί με ἀμείβεσθαι 'to repay me with good things'.

5 What does ὁρμωμένου agree with?

6 ἐπὶ δηλήσι = ἐπὶ δηλήσει 'with a view to harm'.

φανέωσι Can you recognise this? φαίνω has a second aorist passive ἐφάνην.
This is the aorist subjunctive, in an uncontracted form. Here the aorist passive
form is used instead of the aorist middle.

7 ἀπολαμπρυνέαι For -έεαι, 2nd person sing. of future tense.

8 ἄλλως 'otherwise', 'in other circumstances'.

ἔγωγε ἂν οὐκ ἦια ἄν + the past tense of εἶμι ('I go') make this an unfulfilled
condition, ἦια = ἦα.

Page 238

9 οἰκός = ἐοικός 'likely' or 'fitting'.

10 πάρα = πάρεστι 'it is present'; τὸ βούλεσθαι = 'the will', 'the wish' – the
infinitive is used as a noun.

ἂν ἶσχον ἄν + the imperfect indicative continues the unfulfilled condition:
'I would be holding myself back.'

11–13 Notice the highly dramatic use of short phrases as the climax is reached: 'I am
ready to do this / your son / whom you order me to guard / unharmed / thanks
to his guardian / expect to return to you.'

Translation for 19E

Having said this, Croesus sent for the Phrygian Adrastos, and when he arrived he
spoke to him like this; 'Adrastos, I gave you purification when you had been
stricken by an unpleasant misfortune (for which I do not blame you), and I have
received you in my household, providing for all your expenses; now therefore,
because you owe it to me, who first did you a good turn, to return my generosity,
I ask you to be the guardian of my son when he sets out for the hunt, lest any evil
thieves appear to do you harm on the road. In addition, it is right for you to go
where you can distinguish yourself by your deeds; it is your birthright and besides
you have the strength.'

Adrastos answered: 'O King, under other circumstances I would not go to
such a contest; for it is not seemly for a man who has experienced such a
disaster to join his peers who are more fortunate, nor could I wish it, and for
many reasons I would restrain myself. But now, since you are eager, and it is
my duty to please you (for I owe it to you to return your generosity), I am
ready to do these things, and you can expect to see your son, whom you
command me to guard, return to you unharmed so far as depends on his guardian.'

19F

Page 239

2–5   Notice the succession of short clear phrases as the dramatic climax is reached. Notice also the formal description of Adrastos as 'the stranger, the one who had been cleansed of blood-guilt, called Adrastos'. This reminds us of Adrastos' history, Croesus' act and the bond of guest-friendship between them. Similarly, 'he struck the son of Croesus' reminds us of the full significance of the relationship with Croesus. The formal expression seems to give a ritual quality which emphasises the universal truth underlying the story and to make it more than the personal fate of individuals. This technique is used even more forcefully later in this passage. The brief plain phrases leading inexorably to the disaster are deeply moving.

2, 3   ἐζήτεον, ἐσηκόντιζον   Imperfect: 'they began to …'

5   ἁμαρτάνει, τυγχάνει   The present tense is used for dramatic effect.

5–6   The emphasis is on the fulfilment of the prophecy, and its effect on Croesus.

6   ἀγγελέων   Future participle expressing purpose. (You can tell it is future by the single λ and the -εω ending.)

8   συντεταραγμένος   A very strong word, ταράσσω means 'to throw into confusion', as with a defeated army, so 'overwhelmed', 'distraught', 'shattered'.

9–13   Croesus calls on Zeus in three capacities, καθάρσιος, ἐπίστιος and ἑταιρήιος, illustrating the tragic consequences of his observance of the proper duties in each case. Under the auspices of Zeus Katharsios he had purified the stranger, under the auspices of Zeus Epistios he had taken him into his house and under the auspices of Zeus Hetairesios he had befriended him and sent out as guardian of his son the man who proved to be his murderer. Once again the inevitable progress of predestined events is made clear.

10   πεπονθὼς εἴη   The perfect optative is used because this is in indirect speech in secondary sequence: 'bearing witness to the things which he had suffered'.

12   τὸν ξεῖνον φονέα τοῦ παιδός   The contrast is enhanced by the juxtaposition.

13   φύλακα … πολεμιώτατον   Here the antithesis is marked by placing the contrasting words at the beginning and the end of the clause.

13–14   The focus of attention moves from the Lydians ('there they were'), then to the corpse and then to the solitary figure of the killer, following behind. He is given no name and he dominates the coming passage.

Page 240

14–17   Again the short, clear phrases, and the succession of vivid impressions. The killer and the killed, the attitude of surrender, the plea for death with the brutal word ἐπικατασφάξαι thrown into prominence as the first word in its clause, and finally the quiet statement of utter despair.

15   ἐπικατασφάξαι   σφάζω means 'to kill with a sword', and is often associated with sacrificial slaughter.

17–21 The reaction of Croesus. Among mortals there can be pity, nobility and
       forgiveness, in contrast perhaps to the relentless force of destiny fulfilling the
       design of the gods. Cf. Euripides' *Hippolytus,* where the reconciliation of
       Theseus and his son contrasts with the unrelenting vengefulness of Aphrodite.

   20 εἶς = εἶ 'you are'.

21–25 The climax opens quietly. Κροῖσος μέν ... buries his son; then our attention
       moves to Ἄδρηστος δέ ... (Adrastos is now given his full formal name at this
       final moment of the story.) Next, ὁ φονεὺς μέν ... , φονεὺς δέ ... the repetition
       recalls the double tragedy. (Adrastos is the 'destroyer' of the man who purified
       him, in the sense that by killing his son he has destroyed his life.) Finally, when
       all is quiet and the mourners have gone from the tomb, 'realising that, of all the
       men whom he knew, he was βαρυσυμφορώτατος' (a most weighty and
       impressive word saved to the last to make it even more emphatic),
       ἐπικατασφάζει τῷ τύμβῳ ἑωυτόν. A dignified and moving end.

Translation for 19F

When he had answered Croesus with these words, they set off after this accompanied by the selected young men and the hounds. When they arrived at Mount
Olympus, they started to look for the boar, and having found it and surrounded
it they began to hurl javelins at it. And there the stranger, the one who had been
ritually cleansed of murder, the man called Adrastos, hurled his javelin at the
boar, missed the boar, but hit the son of Croesus. Then indeed he, being hit by a
spearhead, fulfilled the prophecy of the dream; and someone ran to tell Croesus
what had happened, and when he reached Sardis, he told him about the fight and
the fate of his son. But Croesus, overwhelmed by the death of his son, was even
more grieved because he himself had cleansed of murder the man who had
killed him. In his grief at this tragedy, he called in anger upon Zeus the Purifier,
bearing witness to the things that he had suffered at the hands of the stranger,
and he called upon him as the god of the hearth and the god of friendship,
naming this same god, calling upon him as the god of the hearth because having
received the stranger into his house he had unwittingly nurtured the murderer
of his son, and calling upon him as the god of friendship on the grounds that he
had sent him as a guardian for his son and found him to be a most deadly
enemy.

   After this, the Lydians came bearing the corpse, and the murderer followed
behind. And standing before the body, he offered himself to Croesus, and stretching out his hands, he begged him to slay him over the corpse, and, speaking of
his former disaster, and how in addition to it he had destroyed the man who had
cleansed him, he said that life was no longer liveable for him. But Croesus,
hearing this, pitied Adrastos, even though he was in such personal distress, and
spoke thus to him: 'Stranger, I have full justice from you, since you condemn
yourself to death. You are not the one who is responsible for this tragedy, except
in so far as you unintentionally did the deed, but it was some god, who prophesied
to me long ago the events that would come to pass.'

Croesus then buried his son as was fitting. But Adrastos, the son of Gordias the son of Midas, the one who had been the killer of his own brother, and the destroyer of the man who had cleansed him, when it was quiet and the crowd of people had gone from the tomb (when it was quiet of people about the tomb), regarding himself as the most accursed of all men whom he knew, killed himself upon the tomb.

Note

You may perhaps want to read through this whole section again, so that, without having to struggle quite so hard to understand the Greek, you can appreciate fully both the dramatic effect of the story and the varied artistry of Herodotus' narrative technique.

EXERCISE FOR SECTION 19

THE DIALECT OF HERODOTUS

(a) νεανίας, συμφορά

(b) πράττω, φυλάττω

(c) μόνος, ἕνεκα

(e) ἐγένου, καλούμενος, ἀπολεῖ, ποιοῦμεν

(f) Περσῶν

(g) ταύταις, χρηστοῖς

Section Twenty: Odysseus and Nausikaa

Here you have the whole of *Odyssey* 6, partly in Greek and partly in translation. Make sure you read the excellent Introduction, *RGT* pp. 243–244, and notice *GE* p. 362, #337 on some vital features of Homeric dialect and syntax, and *GE* pp. 362–364, #338–339 on Homeric hexameters and Greek metre. There is also the Reference Grammar pp. 378–382, #349–352 'Homeric dialect – the main features'.

Remember that this is poetry in the oral tradition. Oral poets did not commit a poem to memory verbatim, but they had in their minds a huge collection of formulaic phrases which fitted neatly into a hexameter line and they could use these to tell the story. Do you remember the rhapsode in Section 1H, with the 'wine-dark sea' (ἐπὶ οἴνοπα πόντον) and the 'black, hollow or swift ship'? These were 'formulas'. You will quickly come to recognise such phrases, and it is interesting to consider how Homer uses them.

20A

Page 246

1 ὥς   with an accent = οὕτως 'so', 'thus'.

ἔνθα   Odysseus is sleeping under an olive bush, having covered himself with leaves.

καθεῦδε = καθηῦδε. The absence of the augment is very common in Homer. See *GE* p. 362, #337(a).

πολύτλας δῖος Ὀδυσσεύς   A formulaic phrase; Odysseus is often referred to by this description, and it is entirely apt. πολύτλας: πολύ = 'much', -τλας is from τλάω 'I endure', thus 'much-enduring'.

3 βῆ = ἔβη. No augment.

ῥ' = ῥά. An abbreviated form of ἄρα: 'then'.

4ff. The passage in English gives the earlier history of the Phaeacian people, and then returns to where it started, with Athene making her way to Phaeacia. This is known as 'ring composition' and is a common feature in Homer.

page 247

20 ἀνέμου   Cf. 'anemometer' = 'wind-measurer', 'anemone' = 'wind-flower'.

21 στῆ = ἔστη; μιν = αὐτήν.

πρὸς ... ἔειπεν   'spoke to', 'addressed'. The preposition is 'cut off' from its verb. This is called 'tmesis' ('cutting'), *GE* p. 362, #337(j). Here the verb is used with two accusatives, 'addressed her a word'.

22 ναυσικλειτοῖο   Genitive ending (*GE* p. 362, #337(d). The Phaeacians were famed for their nautical skills.

23 οἱ = αὐτῇ (*GE* p. 280, #350); ἔην = ἦν.

κεχάριστο   This is the pluperfect of χαρίζομαι (not the perfect, as *GE* says in the vocabulary for 19A). You can see it is pluperfect because, although it has no augment, it ends in -στο, not -σται.

Page 248

24 γλαυκῶπις Ἀθήνη   Another formula. This is a standard epithet for Athene; it means either 'grey-eyed' or owl-faced', ὤψ = 'face' or 'eyes', γλαυκός = 'gleaming' or 'grey-green', ἡ γλαύξ is 'the owl', the bird of Athene, as seen on the Athenian silver drachma.

25 τί νύ σ' ὧδε ...   Literally 'How did your mother bear you thus lazy?', 'How did your mother come to have such a lazy daughter?'

26 τοι = σοι. This is the 'dative of the person concerned'. There is also a particle τοι which means 'in fact', 'look here'. It is usually the second word in the sentence, but only the context will help you to decide between them. Here it is almost certainly the pronoun: compare this example with 20B line 59, where μοι is equivalent to τοι in this line.

27 ἵνα + indicative means 'where', and does not express purpose.

καλά   Understand εἵματα from the previous line.

αὐτήν   Agrees with σε (understood).

28 τὰ δὲ τοῖσι   The article is normally used for 'them' or 'these' in Homer instead of αὐτόν and οὗτος, *GE* p. 362, #337(i)). 'And you must provide others for those who ...'

οἵ κέ σ' ἄγωνται   κε or κεν = ἄν. Therefore this is an indefinite clause, although in Homer an indefinite is very close to a future: 'those who will lead you'. See *GE* p. 362, #337(k).

29 τοι   Here this probably means 'in fact', and is not equivalent to σοι, another ethic dative 'as far as you are concerned'; but it could be either in the context.

ἀνθρώπους ἀναβαίνει   Understand another ἀνά before ἀνθρώπους: 'goes up among men'. In poetry the preposition is often left out if it is used as the prefix to the verb.

30 πότνια μήτηρ   πότνια is a stock epithet for goddesses and great ladies, and is frequently found with μήτηρ. It is often translated 'lady'.

31 ἴομεν = ἴωμεν. Present subjunctive, 'let us go'.

πλυνέουσαι   Future participle expressing purpose.

32 τοι = σοι. ἕπομαι takes the dative.

32–33 ὄφρα ...ἐντύνεαι   ὄφρα + subjunctive/optative expresses purpose.

33 τοι   Here probably the particle 'indeed'.

ἔσσεαι = ἔσει   'you will be'.

35 τοι = σοί. Possessive dative, 'where is the race to you yourself also', 'where is your race too', 'and they are your nation too'.

36 ἄγ' = ἄγε. 'Come on', followed by a command.

   ἐπότρυνον   Aorist imperative (*GE* pp. 189–190, #198–199).

37 ἡμιόνους   'mules' as in Section 8E.

   ἄμαξαν   'wagon' as in Section 6H.

   ἐφοπλίσαι   Aorist infinitive of ἐφοπλίζω.

38 ῥήγεα σιγαλόεντα   Cf. line 19 ἀκηδέα σιγαλόεντα.

39 πολὺ κάλλιον   Understand ἐστί.

40 ἀπὸ ... εἰσί   Tmesis again, 'are distant from'.

41 ὣς εἰποῦσα   'so speaking', ὥς with an accent = οὕτως 'so', 'thus'.

42 Οὔλυμπόνδε   The suffix -δε means 'towards', e.g. οἴκαδε.

43 ἔμμεναι = εἶναι   This is a common form of the infinitive in Homer. See *GE* p. 381, #351(iv).

47 διεπέφραδε   Aorist of διαφράζω. Cf. 'phrase'.

41–47 Ring composition again: (line 4) ἀπέβη γλαυκῶπις Ἀθήνη ... ἔνθ' ἀπέβη γλαυκῶπις (line 10). In between these repeated phrases there is a marvellous description of Olympus, the home of the gods. It was copied by Lucretius in *De rerum natura* 3. 18–22, and by Tennyson:

Where falls not hail, or rain, or any snow,

Nor ever wind blows loudly. (*Idylls of the King* 1.428–9)

Translation for 20A

So much-enduring, godlike Odysseus slept there, overcome by sleep and weariness; but Athene went to the people and the city of the Phaeacian men …

* * *

She, like a breath of wind, hurried to the bed of the girl, and stood above her head and addressed her a word, making herself like the daughter of Dymas, famous for ships, who was of the same age as her and was very dear to her heart. Likening herself to her, the grey-eyed Athene addressed her.

'Nausikaa, how has your mother borne such a lazy [daughter as] you? The shining clothes are lying uncared for by you (as far as you are concerned) – and your wedding is near, when you must wear fine [clothes] yourself and provide others for those who will escort you. For from these things indeed a good reputation spreads among men, and a father and lady mother rejoice. But let us go and do the washing as soon as dawn appears; and I will go with you as a helper, so that you may get ready very quickly, since you will not be a maiden much longer; for already the noblest of all the Phaeacian men throughout the people are courting you – you are of the same race as them. But come, ask your famous father before dawn to equip you with mules and a wagon to take the girdles, the robes and the shining covers. And it is much better for you yourself to go in this way than on foot; for the washing-places are far from the city.'

So speaking, the grey-eyed Athene went away to Olympus, where they say the safe seat of the gods is for ever; it is not shaken by winds, nor wet by showers, nor does snow come near, but a very clear sky spreads over it, cloudless, and a white radiance covers it; in it the blessed gods enjoy themselves all their days. There the grey-eyed one went, when she had spoken to the girl.

20B

Page 250

48 μιν   'her', explained by Ναυσικάαν εὔπεπλον in the next line.

50 βῆ δ' ἴμεναι   Literally 'she went to go', a very common idiom in Homer. It means 'she went', ἴμεναι is a form of infinitive. See *GE* p. 381, #351(iv).
ἵν' ἀγγείλειε   ἵνα + optative expresses purpose in secondary sequence.
τοκεῦσι   'to her parents', itemised in the next line, and then described more fully with ἡ μέν … in line 52, and τῷ δέ … in line 53.

52 σὺν ἀμφιπόλοισι γυναιξίν   Another formula which fits the second half of the hexameter.

53 ἠλάκατα στρωφῶσ' ἁλιπόρφυρα   'spinning the sea-purple wool', ἁλι- is from the word meaning 'salt' or 'sea'. 'Sea-purple' because purple, or crimson, dye came from the murex (a shell-fish). It was particularly valuable, hence 'royal purple', 'in the purple'. Nausikaa uses this same phrase (p. 265, line 308) when speaking to Odysseus.

53–54 τῷ δὲ … ξύμβλητο   'She met him …' ἐρχομένῳ agrees with τῷ.

53 θύραζε = θύρασδε.

54 βασιλῆας   'chieftains', 'nobles' (not 'kings'), as often in Homer.

55 ἵνα + indicative means 'where'.

56 μάλ' ἄγχι   'very close', 'right up close', as daughter to father.

57 πάππα φίλ'   This is informal: 'Daddy, dear'.
οὐκ ἂν δή μοι ἐφοπλίσσειας   A polite request: 'Wouldn't you provide me with …'

59 τά = ἅ 'which'.
μοι   Another ethic dative (dative of the person concerned). Cf. 19A line 19.

60 σοὶ αὐτῷ ἔοικε   This is followed by accusative + infinitive: 'it is right for you yourself to discuss plans (βουλὰς βουλεύειν) being among the foremost men (ἐόντα) having (ἔχοντα) clean clothes on your body'.

66 αἴδετο   'felt reticent about'. Nausikaa was modest about her marriage, not ashamed.
θαλερὸν γάμον   'fruitful marriage', almost certainly a stock epithet.

68 τευ = τινος.   See *GE* p. 380 #350.

71 τοί = οἱ 'they'. Note the accent. It cannot be τοι = σοι.

Translation for 20B

At once fair-throned dawn came and she woke fair-robed Nausikaa; at once she was amazed at the dream and she went through the palace to tell it to her parents, her dear father and mother. She found them indoors; she (her mother) was sitting by the hearth, with her servant women, spinning sea-purple wool; him she met going towards the door, on his way to his distinguished counsellors to a council to which the Phaeacian nobles called him.

She stood very close to him and addressed her dear father: 'Daddy dear, won't you get ready for me a high well-wheeled wagon, so that I may take the lovely clothes to the river to wash them? They are lying there, I know, dirty. And it is fitting for you yourself, when you are with your nobles, to discuss plans with clean clothes on your body. Five dear sons have been born to you in the palace; two are married and three are thriving bachelors; they all wish to go to the dance with newly washed clothes. All these things are a concern to my mind.'

So she spoke; for she was hesitant to mention fruitful marriage to her dear father; but he realised all and replied: 'I do not be grudge you mules, child, nor anything else. Go. The servants will equip for you a high well-wheeled wagon, fitted with a canopy.'

So saying, he ordered the servants and they obeyed.

20C

Page 252

110 ἔμελλε 'She was going to return home.' Almost 'It was time to go home.'

112 ἀλλ' ἐνόησε Note the accent on ἄλλο: 'planned something else'. ἀλλά (as in line 110) means 'but'.

113 ὡς + optative expresses purpose in secondary sequence.

114 οἱ = 'him' (dative), ἡγήσαιτο takes the dative and it is in the optative because it continues the purpose clause started in line 113.
πόλιν 'to the city'. The preposition is omitted.

115 σφαῖραν 'sphere'. Remember the sophist in Section 6F 'catching up the argument like a ball'.
βασίλεια Nominative and feminine.

117 ἐπὶ μακρόν Adverbial, = 'loudly'.
ἄϋσαν Three syllables; the breathing (ἀ) and the diaeresis (ϋ) show this.

Page 253

119 ὤ μοι ἐγώ Difficult to translate naturally. Perhaps 'Oh dear me!'

119–121 A most important consideration on arriving in a strange land. If the inhabitants are 'god-fearing', they will respect the laws of hospitality and look after the stranger kindly. Odysseus had the same thoughts before he met the Cyclops, but here he is more fortunate.

119 τέων = τίνων.

121 σφίν 'to them'. See *GE* p. 380, #350. It is a possessive dative.

123 νυμφάων This recalls the simile likening Nausikaa to Artemis and her nymphs on p. 173, lines 33–39.
ἔχουσι ἔχω often has the sense of 'have (as their home)', i.e. 'inhabit'.

126 πειρήσομαι ἠδὲ ἴδωμαι   These verbs are both subjunctives, 'let me ...'
ἠδέ 'and'. Cf. ἠμέν ... ἠδέ ... 'both ... and ...'

Translation for 20C

But when she was about to go back home again, after yoking the mules and folding the fine clothing, then again the grey-eyed goddess Athene planned something else, that Odysseus should wake up and see the beautiful girl who would lead him to the city of the Phaeacian men. The princess then threw a ball to a hand-maiden; it missed the handmaiden and fell into the deep eddy, and they shrieked loudly. Godlike Odysseus awoke, and, sitting up, considered in his heart and mind.

'Oh dear me, to the land of what people have I come this time? Are they violent, savage and not just, or are they hospitable and have a god-fearing mind? The female shriek of maidens surrounded me – of nymphs, who inhabit the steep peaks of mountains and sources of rivers and grassy meadows. Or am I now somewhere near men who speak with human voices? But come, let me try and see for myself.'

20D

Page 254

128 κλάσε = ἔκλασε. Aorist of κλάζω without the augment.
παχείη   Cf. 'pachyderm', a thick-skinned animal.
129 φύλλων   Goes with πτόρθον in the previous line, 'a leafy branch'.
φωτός   Be careful not to confuse φώς φωτός 'man' and τὸ φῶς (φάος) 'light'.
130 βῆ δ' ἴμεν   See note on 20B line 50 above.
130–134 Just as our attention was drawn to Nausikaa with a simile (Artemis and the nymphs), so at this point it is focused on Odysseus. The simile of the mountain lion, driven down from the hills by hunger to raid the village animals, is apt. Odysseus appears as savage and terrible as a lion to the girls; and he too is storm-tossed and driven by desperate necessity to come from the wild to seek help in a civilised community.
131 εἶσ' = εἶσι: 3rd s. of εἶμι, 'who goes'.
ὄσσε   A dual (GE #331–332). Note that the verb (δαίεται) is singular, as with a neuter plural subject, ἐν probably belongs to δαίεται and is cut off by tmesis. οἱ is a possessive dative, 'his eyes'.
132 ὀΐεσσιν   Four syllables. Cf. note on 20C line 117 ἄϋσαν.
133 ἑ = 'him', accusative. See GE p. 380, #350.
γαστήρ   Cf. 'gastric', 'gastritis' etc.
134 δόμον   Here referring to the 'pens' where the sheep and cattle were kept.
136 περ = καίπερ.
137 φάνη = ἐφάνη, the aorist of φαίνομαι.
138 ἄλλυδις ἄλλη   The whole phrase means 'in different directions' (as in GE); literally, 'a different one in a different direction'.

139 οἴη   The feminine of οἶος 'alone'. Do not confuse this with οἷος 'such as'.

141 σχομένη   Middle participle of ἔχω. Literally 'maintaining herself', so 'holding her ground'.

142 γούνων ... λαβών   Touching or clasping the knees was a sign of supplication.
εὐώπιδα κούρην   Another formulaic phrase. Cf. p. 252, line 113.

143 μειλιχίοισι   *GE* gives this as 'winning', 'soothing'. Its basic root is μέλι 'honey', and 'honeyed' would be equally appropriate here. 'Honeyed words' is a frequent formula; they are often employed by Odysseus, the arch-persuader.

144 δοίη   Aorist optative of δίδωμι. δείξειε is also an aorist optative. Both are in an indirect question in secondary sequence, 'to see if she would show him the city and give him clothes'.

145 κέρδιον   'more profitable', 'more advantageous'. This shows the shrewdly calculating mind of Odysseus, and is picked up by κερδαλέον ('subtle', 'crafty') in line 148.

147 μὴ ... χολώσαιτο   'lest she be angry'.

Translation for 20D

Speaking thus, godlike Odysseus emerged from the bushes; with his broad hand he broke a leafy branch from the thick-foliaged bush so that shielding (around) his body he could hide his male genitals. He went forward like a mountain-bred lion trusting in his strength, who goes on, though rained upon and blown upon, and his eyes burn; but he attacks the oxen or sheep, or goes after the wild deer; hunger orders him to go even into the densely-packed pens, to make trial of the sheep. So Odysseus was going to meet the maidens with beautiful hair, naked though he was; for need was upon him. He seemed terrible to them, disfigured with brine, and they ran in different directions along the jutting shores. Alcinous' daughter alone remained; for Athene put courage in her heart and removed the fear from her limbs. She stood and faced him, holding her ground; Odysseus debated whether to take her knees and beseech the beautiful girl or simply with honeyed words at a distance to beseech her to show him the city and give him clothing. It seemed to him, as he thought about it, to be better to beseech her with honeyed words from a distance, in case the girl should grow angry in her heart with him for taking her knees. At once he addressed to her a honeyed and cunning speech.

20E

Page 256

149 γουνοῦμαι   *GE* gives this as 'beseech'. It literally means 'I clasp your knees' – the very thing that Odysseus has not done!
θεός νύ τις ἦ βροτός ἐσσι;   'Are you a god or a mortal?' A splendid piece of flattery and also of reassurance, for no man is going to offend or rape a goddess.

150 θεός ... τοί   τοί is a plural relative pronoun, after a singular antecedent
θεός. The construction follows the sense: 'if you are one of the gods
who'.

151 Ἀρτέμιδι   This recalls the simile on p. 252, lines 102–109, where Nausikaa is
likened to Artemis. It is also particularly suitable, since Artemis is a virgin
goddess.

152 εἶδός τε μέγεθός τε φυήν τ'...   All these are accusatives of respect: 'I liken
you to Artemis in appearance, etc. ...'

153 εἰ δέ τίς ἐσσι βροτῶν ...   More flattery and reassurance as Odysseus develops
the second possibility, that she may be a mortal.

155–157 There are more constructions here that go with the sense rather than with
strict grammar. λευσσόντων 'agrees' with σφισι in line 155 'when they see ...',
and the feminine participle εἰσοιχνεῦσαν 'agrees' with the neuter noun
θάλος.

158–159 The climax and another reference to Nausikaa's marriage. This is a recurring
theme in the Phaeacia story, and both Nausikaa and her parents hope at some
time that Odysseus might perhaps remain and become her husband.

160–165 Note the transition from his admiration and awe at the beauty of Nausikaa to
his own story and the 'hint' to her (mentioned in the introduction), that
he has been a person of some importance: line164 πολὺς δέ μοι ἕσπετο
λαός.

162 Delos was sacred to Apollo. It was there that Leto gave birth to Apollo and
Artemis and in honour of this their father, Zeus, created the palm and the bay
tree.

162–163 Note the order in which the ideas are presented: 'in Delos once ... such a ... by
the altar of Apollo ... of a palm ... the young shoot springing up ... I saw',
τοῖον agrees with ἔρνος. The point of the comparison is the slender beauty of
the palm and the awe it induces in the beholder.

167 δόρυ   This refers to the palm, and brings us back in the 'ring-composition'
structure to the starting-point of the simile.

168–169 δείδια ... γούνων ἅψασθαι   Another example of ring composition. Cf.
γουνοῦμαι in line 8 at the start of the speech. Odysseus has, of course, also to
explain to Nausikaa why he is not clasping her knees in the attitude of formal
supplication.

Page 258

170–174 Now he speaks of his past sufferings and his foreboding for the future.

170 χθιζός   An adjective agreeing with the subject Odysseus. Literally
'yesterday's'. Translate 'yesterday'.
οἴνοπα πόντον   'the wine-dark sea', a formulaic phrase.

172 νήσου ἀπ' Ὠγυγίης   This was the island of Calypso where Odysseus was
detained for seven years.

173 ὄφρα ... πάθω   ὄφρα + subjunctive expresses purpose: 'so that I may suffer
some trouble (κακόν) here as well (καί)'.

173–174 οὐ γὰρ ὀΐω παύσεσθαι 'I do not think it will cease.' παύσεσθαι = future middle infinitive of παύω.

174 τελέουσι In form this could be present or future. The sense suggests future.

175 σε Governed by ἐς in the next line: 'I came to you first.'

178 δεῖξον Aorist imperative of δείκνυμι.

ῥάκος Very close to 'rag'. He means any old piece of material, whatever they wrapped the washing in.

ἀμφιβαλέσθαι An explanatory infinitive, 'a rag to put round me'.

180 δοῖεν Optative for a wish, 'may they give'.

181 ὀπάσειαν Another optative expressing a wish, 'may they grant'.

182 τοῦ Genitive of comparison, 'than this'. 'This' is explained in the next line, ἢ ὅθ' 'than when …'

183 ὁμοφρονέοντε, ἔχητον These are both duals; the subject is ἀνὴρ ἠδὲ γυνή.

Translation for 20E

'I beseech you by your knees, princess; are you a god or a mortal? If you are a god, such as inhabit the broad heaven, I liken you most closely to Artemis, daughter of great Zeus, in appearance, stature and beauty. If you are one of the mortals who live upon earth, thrice blessed are your father and lady mother, and thrice blessed are your brothers; for surely the heart within them always warms very much with pleasure through you when they see such young beauty entering the dance. But he in his heart is most blessed above [all] others who, after loading you with gifts, leads you home [as his wife].

'I have not seen with my eyes such a one, neither man nor woman; awe holds me as I look. In Delos once, near the altar of Apollo, I saw such a young shoot of a date-palm growing up; I had gone there, and a large company followed me, on that journey on which evil troubles were destined to befall me. In the same way as, when I saw it, I delighted in my heart for a long time, since no such shoot ever yet came up from the earth, so, lady, I look at you in awe, I am astonished and I am terribly afraid to touch your knees; but hard grief has come upon me.

'Yesterday, on the twentieth day, I escaped from the wine-dark sea; for so long the waves and swift storms carried me always from the island of Ogygia; now a god has cast me up here, so that I may suffer some evil here too; for I do not think it will stop, but the gods will accomplish even more before that. But, princess, have pity; after suffering many evils I have come to you first, and I do not know any other of the people who inhabit this city and land. Show me the city, give me a rag to put round myself, if you had any wrapping for the clothes when you came here.

'To you may the gods give all that you desire in your heart, a husband and a home, and may they grant beautiful harmony: for there is nothing greater and better than this, than when in harmony of mind a man and woman share a home;

they are a great grief to their enemies and a delight to their friends; they themselves are greatly respected.'

Page 260

186 λευκώλενος 'white-armed'. This is an epithet which is applied only to
women, and women who do not work in the fields and get sun-burned. It is
therefore complimentary. On Minoan frescos women are conventionally
coloured white and men terracotta. It is a compound adjective with only two
terminations, so that the -ος ending can be feminine.

187–189 Nausikaa means that since Odysseus is sensible and intelligent he must accept
whatever fate Zeus sends him.

189 ἐθέλησιν = ἐθέλη, 3rd s. pres. subj., 'just as he pleases'.

190 τετλάμεν Infinitive of τλάω. Odysseus is described in the first line of this
book as πολύτλας.

191–193 A complicated clause. The meaning, starting with the previous line, is 'So you
will lack neither clothing nor anything else which it is right for a poor suppliant
[to have] when he has met [someone to help him].' In grammatical detail:
'You will not lack (+ gen.) clothing or anything else which (ὧν is genitive by
relative attraction, see 218b) it is right (ἐπέοιχ᾽) for a poor suppliant (ἱκέτην
ταλαπείριον) not to lack (μὴ δεύεσθαι is understood from οὐ δευήσεαι in the
previous line) having met [someone].'

194 ἐρέω Future of λέγω.

197 *GE* tells you that ἐκ governs τοῦ and that ἔχεται ἐκ means here 'depend on',
hence, 'On him the power and might of the Phaeacians depend.'

198 ἦ ῥα A common formulaic phrase: ἦ = 'she spoke'. Cf. ἦ δ᾽ ὅς in sections 7D
and 7E (Plato, *Euthydemos*). ῥά = ἄρα.

199 στῆτέ μοι 'stop, please'. The μοι is rather like our colloquial phrase 'Will you
do this for me?'

200 φάσθ᾽ Here this is more like 'consider' than 'say'.
ἔμμεναι = εἶναι.

201 This is easy to mistranslate: – *not* 'this is not a mortal man', but 'there is not a
mortal man living who …' The accent on ἔσθ᾽ shows that it means 'exists'
rather than 'is'. διερός occurs in Homer only here and in *Od.* 9.43.

204–205 ἀπάνευθε, ἔσχατοι The Phaeacians live far away on the edge of the known
world, almost in a fairy-tale land, beyond the reach of pirates and enemies and
with their magic ships that need no helmsman to take them anywhere they wish
to go. Tradition has it that Phaeacia is the modern Corfu.

207 πρὸς Διός πρός here means 'under the protection of'. You first met these lines
in Section 4C p. 48, lines 31–32. Once again the religious requirement of
hospitality is emphasised.

210 λούσατε Note that this is active. Nausikaa tells her maids to wash Odysseus,
not to take him to a place where he can wash himself.

Translation for 20F

Then white-armed Nausikaa answered him in reply: 'Stranger, since you seem to be neither an evil nor a foolish man, Olympian Zeus himself apportions happiness to mankind, to good and bad, just as he pleases, to each; and so he has given you these things, and you must doubtless endure them. But now, since you have come to our city and land, you will not lack for clothing nor anything else which it is right for a poor suppliant [to have] when he has met [someone to help him]. I will show you the city and tell you the name of the people. The Phaeacians inhabit this city and land; I am the daughter of great-hearted Alcinous; on him the power and might of the Phaeacians depend.'

She spoke, and gave orders to her handmaidens with pretty hair: 'Stop, handmaidens; where are you fleeing after seeing a man? Surely you do not think this is one of the hostile men? That mortal man does not exist, nor will he ever be born, who would come to the land of Phaeacian men bringing slaughter; for we are very dear to the immortal gods. We live far away in the loud-roaring sea, the furthest [of peoples], nor does any other of mortals have dealings with us. But this is some poor wanderer who has arrived here, whom we must now look after; for all strangers and beggars are under the protection of Zeus, and a gift is small but welcome. But, handmaidens, give the stranger meat and drink, and wash him in the river, where there is shelter from the wind.'

20G

Page 261

211 ἔσταν = ἔστησαν 'they stopped'.
212 κάδ ... εἶσαν   Note κάδ = κατά; the root of ἕζω = ἕδος. They escorted Odysseus to a sheltered spot and sat him down there.
214 πάρ = παρά   Note the shortening of some prepositions to monosyllables – κάδ has just occurred and recurs in line 230; ἀνά can be treated in the same way.

Page 262

218–220 ὄφρ' ... ἀπολούσομαι ... χρίσομαι   ὄφρα + subjunctive expresses purpose. The two verbs look like futures, but are in fact aorist subjunctives.
219 ὤμοϊιν   Dual – he has two shoulders, although the ordinary plural is used in lines 225 and 235.
221 αἰδέομαι   It was normal practice in the world of Homer for girl-slaves to bath male visitors. Odysseus refuses their assistance because his body is in such a dreadful state after his hardships that he 'is ashamed to be naked among maidens with well-ordered hair'.
224 νίζετο   The verb takes two accusatives here, 'washed his body' and 'washed the brine', where we would have to say 'washed the brine from his body'.
226 ἀτρυγέτοιο   A regular epithet for the sea. It means 'unharvested' and so 'unharvestable' and so 'barren'.

228 ἔσσαθ'   First aorist middle of ἕννυμι: 'he put on'.

230 εἰσιδέειν   An explanatory infinitive, 'greater to look upon'.

231 ὑακινθίνῳ ἄνθει ὁμοίας   Presumably thick, clustering curls are like the wild hyacinth petals.

232–234 In this simile Athene enhances the appearance of Odysseus as a skilled craftsman puts the finishing touches to a work of art.

233 δέδαεν   Takes two objects, 'whom ... have taught all skill'. You may remember the passage from Plato in Section 18, where Athene and Hephaistos are the gods who are the masters of the craftsman's art.

235 τῷ   Indirect object, 'on him', with 'on his head and shoulders' in apposition.

238 μετηύδα   From μεταυδάω 'I speak to'.

244 αἲ γάρ = εἰ γάρ; εἰ γάρ + optative expresses a wish.
       πόσις   'husband'.

245 οἱ ἅδοι   'and that it might be pleasing to him ...' ἅδοι is the aorist optative of ἀνδάνω.

248 πόσιν   Here = 'drink'.

Once again the marriage theme. Nausikaa is to be disappointed. The last we hear of her is in Book 8, lines 457–468, where there is an underlying pathos when Odysseus speaks his last words to her the day before he leaves for Ithaca, never to see her again.

Then Nausicaa, with the gods' loveliness on her stood beside the pillar that supported the roof with its joinery, and gazed upon Odysseus with all her eyes and admired him, and spoke to him aloud and addressed him in winged words, saying:

'Goodbye, stranger, and think of me sometimes when you are back at home, how I was the first you owed your life to.' Then resourceful Odysseus spoke in turn and answered her: 'Nausicaa, daughter of great-hearted Alkinoos, even so may Zeus, high-thundering husband of Hera, grant me to reach my house and see my day of homecoming. So even when I am there I will pray to you as a goddess, all the days of my life. For, maiden, my life was your gift.'

Translation for 20G

So she spoke, and they stood and encouraged each other. They sat Odysseus down in shelter, as Nausikaa daughter of great-hearted Alcinous ordered; next to him they put a cloak and a tunic as clothing and gave him moist olive-oil in a golden oil-jar, and they told him to wash in the stream of the river.

Then indeed godlike Odysseus said to the handmaidens: 'Handmaidens, stand thus far off, so that I myself may wash the brine from my shoulders and anoint myself with olive-oil. For indeed ointment has been absent from my body for a long time. But I will not wash in front of you ; for I am ashamed to be naked coming among maidens with lovely hair.'

So he spoke, and they went far off and told the girl. But from the river godlike Odysseus washed from his body the brine which lay thick upon his back and broad shoulders. From his head he wiped the scum of the unharvested sea. But when he had washed all and richly anointed himself, and put on the clothes which the unmarried girl provided for him, then Athene, daughter of Zeus, made him taller and broader to look upon; down from his head she sent bushy hair, like the hyacinth flower. As when a skilled craftsman, whom Hephaistos and Pallas Athene have taught all skill, lays gold on silver and completes graceful work, so she poured on him grace, on his head and shoulders. Then going along the seashore, he sat far off, shining with beauty and grace; the maiden watched him admiringly. Then indeed she spoke to her beautiful-haired handmaidens.

'Listen to me, white-armed handmaidens, so that I may say something. Not against the will of all the gods who inhabit Olympus has this man come among the godlike Phaeacians. Earlier he seemed to me to be wretched, but now he is like the gods who inhabit the broad heaven. Would that such a man might be called my husband dwelling here, and that it might please him to remain here. But, handmaidens, give the stranger meat and drink.'

So she spoke, and they readily heard and obeyed her, and put beside Odysseus meat and drink. Then indeed much-enduring godlike Odysseus drank and ate greedily, because for a long time he had not tasted food.

Now read on in English to the end of Book 6.

In Book 7 Odysseus follows Nausikaa's advice and, with Athene's help, he goes to the palace and appeals to the Queen. He is welcomed and, after some debate, given hospitality. On the next day (Book 8) the Phaeacians hold games at which Odysseus establishes his prowess. In the evening there is a banquet, and after the banquet the singer Demodocus tells the story of the wooden horse at Troy. Odysseus is moved to tears, and Alcinous at last asks him who he is. Odysseus reveals his identity and starts to tell his story. In Books 9–12 he tells what has happened to him since he left Troy until the time he was washed up on the shore of the island of Calypso. In Book 13 he departs from Phaeacia and the story moves forward again to his return to Ithaca and all the problems which await him there.